W9-DAQ-721

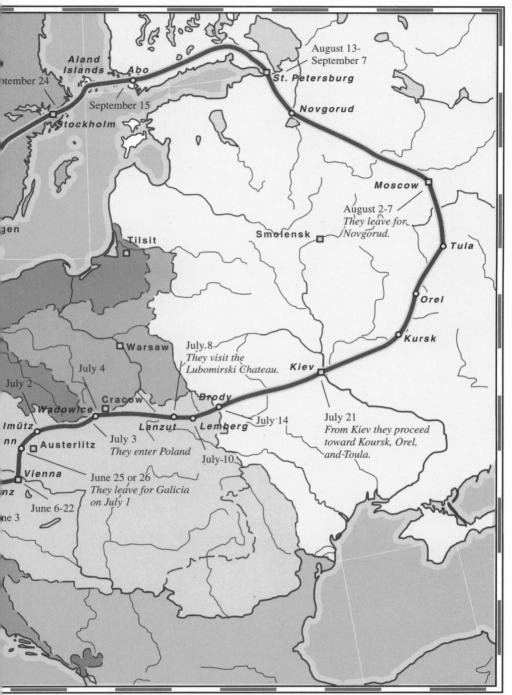

Aland
Islands
September 24
September 15
Abo

Stockholm

gen

Tilsit

Novgorud

St. Petersburg

August 13-
September 7

Moscow

August 2-7
*They leave for
Novgorud.*

Tula

Orel

Smolensk

Warsaw

July 8-
*They visit the
Lubomirski Chateau.*

Kursk

Kiev

July 4

July 2

Wadowice

Cracow

Brody

Lanzut

Lemberg

July 14

July 21
*From Kiev they proceed
toward Koursk, Orel,
and Toula.*

Imütz

nn

Austerlitz

July 3
They enter Poland

July 10

Vienna

nz

June 25 or 26
*They leave for Galicia
on July 1*

June 6-22

ne 3

Ten Years *of* Exile

Madame de Staël, 1803. Portrait by Rehberg.

(Collection château de Coppet)

Ten Years *of* Exile

Germaine de Staël

Translated by

Avriel H. Goldberger

NORTHERN ILLINOIS UNIVERSITY PRESS

DEKALB   2000

CABRINI COLLEGE LIBRARY
610 KING OF PRUSSIA ROAD
RADNOR, PA 19087

41176650

© 2000 by Avriel H. Goldberger

Published by the Northern Illinois University Press, DeKalb, Illinois   60115

Manufactured in the United States using acid-free paper

All Rights Reserved

Design by Julia Fauci

Library of Congress Cataloging-in-Publication Data

Staël, Madame de (Anne-Louise-Germaine), 1766–1817.

[Dix années d'exil. English]

Ten years of exile / Germaine de Staël; translated by Avriel H. Goldberger.

p.   cm.

Includes bibliographical references and index

ISBN 0-87580-255-9 (alk. paper)

1. Staël, Madame de (Anne-Louise-Germaine), 1766–1817—Exile. 2. France —History—Consulate and First Empire, 1799–1815. 3. Women authors, French—19th century Biography. 4. Women intellectuals—France Biography. I. Goldberger, Avriel H. II. Title. III. Title: 10 years of exile.

DC146.S7A25   2000

944.04'092—dc21

[B]   99-23994

CIP

Publication of this book was assisted by grants from the French Ministry of Culture and PRO HELVETIA, the Arts Council of Switzerland.

For my sister,

Ada Lerner,

with all my love

Contents

Acknowledgments

For the third time the Pro Helvetia Foundation has supported my translation of a book by Germaine de Staël, and I am deeply grateful. I am also pleased to thank the French Ministry of Culture for its own generous subvention. Thus Mme de Staël's two countries, France and Switzerland, have recognized her contribution to their cultures and to the world beyond their borders.

In *Ten Years of Exile,* an unfinished book, the author's experience is tightly interwoven with the events and people of the French Revolution, the Consulate, and the Empire. Consequently special problems of interpretation frequently arose; they were solved with the help of Simone Balayé, the prize-winning historian who has made Mme de Staël her life's work. We spent many hours together pouring over sentences, terms, and events, and out of her vast knowledge and her extensive personal library, she helped me find the explanations needed to convey the author's meaning. Further, she was kind enough to photocopy her draft biography of Mme de Staël for my use.

While the introduction to the American edition is based on the one she wrote for the French critical edition, we agreed that it needed adaptation for readers of English, and the result was a fruitful collaboration. Each time I needed a phrase, a sentence, a paragraph to make some important point clear, I had only to place a transatlantic call and the desired answer would quickly arrive in the mail, elegantly crafted and requiring the translator's closest attention to convey its beauty and precision. These are but a few examples of Simone Balayé's priceless generosity and affection as scholar and friend.

Edith Finch's close reading of the manuscript and her tactful, always perceptive remarks have once more proved invaluable as they sharpened my own reading of the texts—Mme de Staël's original and my translation. Her work with me crowns a cherished friendship of almost forty years standing.

Count Othenin d'Haussonville's enduring encouragement has been precious, his answers to my questions enlightening, and his help in finding pictures to illustrate the present volume invaluable.

I treasure Frank Bowman's continued support, erudition, wise counsel, and delicious humor. My thanks go to Patricia Schramm of the Swiss Consulate in New York, Denis Coigny of Pro Helvetia, Michel Delon, Jean Pierre Perchellet, Jacob Oppenheim, and David Kornacker. I warmly thank reference librarians Janet Wagner of Hofstra University and Ray Wile and Irina Zaionts of Great Neck.

Finally, I am grateful beyond words to my extraordinary family: Ellen and Josh Oppenheim, Ada Lerner, and my dear husband, Arnold Goldberger—"staëlwarts" all—who have been essential to my work on a book that I particulary cherish.

Introduction

SIMONE BALAYÉ AND AVRIEL GOLDBERGER

"Exile cut the roots that bound me to Paris
and I became European."

—*Germaine de Staël*[1]

Germaine de Staël was a major writer in an era that produced very few. She had a rare gift for political thought and action during a time of increasing authoritarianism and hostility to women of independent mind. Yet the family and social context into which she was born in 1766 nurtured these talents so richly displayed in *Ten Years of Exile,* her powerful attack on Napoleon's tyranny. In this militant book—at once autobiography, historical account, and polemic—she tells the dual story of Bonaparte's rise to power—first over France, then over Europe—and her personal experience of his unrelenting tyranny. It tells the story of a man who held absolute power over a woman who, having no other weapon than the spoken and written word, became one of his leading opponents.

An unflinching defender of all forms of liberty, Mme de Staël had always been a natural target for authoritarian governments. But the intermittent persecution that began in 1792 when the monarchy fell and continued under the post-Thermidorean Convention and the Directory is not the subject of her book. The "ten years" in the title speak of the exile imposed on her by First Consul Bonaparte in September 1803 and maintained implacably when he became Emperor; they stand as a major unifying element of a book centered on Napoleon. So often reiterated in the book's pages and in her letters, this period of time gradually takes on a hauntingly obsessional quality, a constant reminder of growing—and warranted—fears for herself and her children.

Napoleon barred Mme de Staël first from Paris, the city of her birth, then from France. When his hegemony in Europe was at its height, he confined her to a few square miles of Switzerland between her family home in Coppet on the shores of Lake Geneva and the city of Geneva. Aware of her plan to flee to England when she was hounded out of France in 1810, he ordered the channel ports closed to her. She despaired of ever returning to her native land or of reaching a free country. Following a lifetime pattern of writing when she could not act, she set out to compose *Ten Years of Exile* in the semi-confinement of Coppet. The story begins in 1797, focusing on Napoleon Bonaparte and the shifting political climate that two years later made possible his successful coup d'état of 18 Brumaire. This first section of the book breaks off in 1804—several months after Bonaparte crowned himself Emperor of France. The second begins in 1810 with the author's definitive exile at the age of forty-four; it gives us an intriguing sense of her life at Coppet and Geneva and of the intellectual and political activity of those who lived with her or came for long visits. Its crescendo is reached in the account of her extraordinary flight to England in 1812—with the manuscripts in her baggage—by way of Austria, Poland, and Russia, barely ahead of Napoleon's Grand Army. The text breaks off in mid-sentence as she describes crossing the Gulf of Finland on the way to Stockholm and freedom. Although she continued working on her book in Sweden and England, political action and another project intervened, followed by her untimely death.

Thus instead of filling in the period from 1804 to 1810 or carrying the tale of her flight to its conclusion in London, she decided to put *Ten Years* temporarily aside to write the story of her beloved father's political life. She had conceived this idea when Necker died in 1804 but no doubt quickly saw that she could not end her narrative of his life with his defeat and resignation; she had lived through too much, she had acted and reflected too much in the intervening years to stop on so melancholy a note. But in 1812, with the prospect of Napoleon's eventual defeat in view, her immediate project became *Considerations on the French Revolution,* her last book. Starting with the origins of the Revolution, it proceeds to the beginning of the Restoration, allowing her to examine the Revolution and its consequences, the Consulate and the Empire, the rise and fall of Napoleon, and the advent of the Bourbon's parliamentary monarchy. The book was to conclude with hoped-for triumph rather than defeat. Once it was completed, her plan was to turn again to *Ten Years of Exile.* As she wrote in *Considerations:*

I am reserving for another work, several pieces of which are already written, all the circumstances of my exile, and the journeys to the borders of Asia that resulted; but as I have virtually forbidden myself portraits of living men, I could not endow a personal story with the kind of interest it ought to have.[2]

In retrospect, Mme de Staël's whole intellectual life seems to lead ineluctably to these last two books, one a major work of political philosophy, the other a meditation on the storm-battered reality of her life, on grief more often than on joy, ironic, violent, and combative. Although in *Ten Years* she is not intellectually objective, her reporting of facts is remarkably accurate, and while anger clouds her view of Napoleon's achievements, her analysis of the lasting harm he did to Europe and to Europeans is persuasively graphic and lucid.

A brief examination of her family, her upbringing, and her young adulthood demonstrates her unusual gift and preparation for a politically engaged life. She was the daughter of a remarkable Swiss couple from Geneva who achieved fame and wealth in France during the last years of the Old Regime. Her father, Jacques Necker, came from a long line of Lutheran ministers. Ambitious for worldly success, he arrived in Paris in 1747 at the age of fifteen with no fortune but a genius for banking that led him to wealth and power. He was unique as well for his unbreachable integrity in the corrupt world of Louis XVI's monarchy. Twice he served as finance minister, although without the title; it could not be conferred in a Catholic France that had never rescinded the anti-Protestant laws promulgated under Louis XIV in 1698. Necker's economic reforms were intelligent and urgently needed, but they came too late to save the monarchy from collapse.[3]

Men and women of the aristocracy and the wealthy bourgeoisie married for position and money, but Necker had chosen love. His bride, Suzanne Curchod, as austerely Protestant as he, was a penniless governess when they met. Beautiful, charming, and cultivated, she adored her husband and served his career well, founding one of the last great pre-Revolutionary salons. It was frequented by important and famous people: Encyclopedists such as Diderot, Helvetius, and the naturalist Buffon; writers such as Bernardin de Saint-Pierre; intellectual women such as Mme Geoffrin and Mme du Deffand; French and foreign diplomats such as Thomas Jefferson; statesmen and royal courtiers. Guests in Mme Necker's salon could count on lively interchange on every shade of political thought and on every important preoccupation of Enlightenment thinking.

Anne Louise Germaine, the couple's only child, was born in Paris in

1766. The education her mother designed for her gifted daughter was radical at the time, particularly for a girl. Impressed by Jean-Jacques Rousseau's pedagogical theories for *male* children in his treatise *Emile* of 1762, she applied them to Germaine, whom she taught to think independently, to trust her conscience, to make her own moral judgments, and to be natural. The child also studied English and Latin and read extensively in French and English. She wrote analyses of every play she saw, every sermon she heard, and her mother reviewed each essay critically for style and content. At an early age, Germaine came into her mother's salon, at first to listen and learn, but soon to participate in discussions. Encouraged by Mme Necker's admiring guests, she quickly developed a passion for politics and an understanding of its mechanisms that never dimmed. She learned to be comfortable in social situations, conversing easily with men and women alike. In a word, her mother's program was perfect for a writer-to-be, but the child paid an exorbitant price: however hard she tried, she could never satisfy her mother's expectations for her,[4] and by the age of twelve this small pseudo-adult, unable to endure the mental and emotional pressure, fell ill. On the advice of Dr. Tronchin she was sent to spend the summer of 1778 in the country. She recovered but would always suffer from an "obsessive fear of solitude and emptiness"[5] and from the terror of abandonment. Albertine Necker de Saussure said of her cousin: "It seems that Mme de Staël has always been young and was never a child."[6] How much less painful a life Germaine de Staël would have led, had she not been given the illusion of a freedom denied to women in her time and place, and the tools to put her fine intelligence and sensitivity to creative use. And how much less productive!

From portraits and accounts of her, one senses that while Germaine was not beautiful according to the conventions of her day, she was attractive, even lovely, particularly when engaged in conversation that animated her whole being. Although her parents had married for love, they envisioned a son-in-law who could offer their child rank and position. That he must necessarily be Protestant as well severely limited the range of available choices. Germaine could have married William Pitt but was unwilling to leave Paris and her adored father for a man and a society that did not then attract her. Baron Eric-Magnus de Staël-Holstein, Sweden's ambassador to France, had a gift for accumulating debts, and he coveted the heiress to Necker's fortune, beautiful or not. His abilities and character were mediocre at best; he was seventeen years older than she and devoid of her intellectual interests. In the end, Germaine accepted a marriage of reason that would have the real advantage of introducing her into the world of the aristocracy and the royal courts of Europe. Ignorant of the sexual side of marriage and its importance, she could not know that the union making her a baroness would not fulfill her as a woman. She was too inexperienced to heed the warnings of her own reactions. Her journal entry of October 23, 1785, is instructive. The baron had come to visit his nineteen-year-old fiancée in the country.

> My father told him to dance with me for a moment and began to hum a tune with charm and gaiety. M. de Staël with his pretty face, his competence in the art of dancing, shaped his steps nicely, but his movements were devoid of grace; his eyes fixed on me were animated by neither mind nor heart. His hand taking mine seemed like cold marble.

Then her father decided to show the baron how a man should dance with the young lady he loves. Germaine describes Necker's grace and charm and says, most revealing of all:

> Were I to describe the pangs I felt in my heart at the moment, what a heartbreaking comparison it would make! I could not go on, I fled to a corner of the room and burst into tears![7]

The married couple gave each other freedom and led separate lives. Eric-Magnus quickly managed to spend a large part of his wife's fortune, and rumor has it that he preferred members of his own sex. For a time and to a degree, however, Germaine de Staël was sustained by the universal admiration accorded to her father and by the reputation she won for herself throughout Europe with her books. Before her, no woman had met such acclaim for works of philosophy, politics, and criticism side by side with novels that met instantaneous success.

Her origins, her friends, and her thinking all led her to embrace enthusiastically the ideas that came of age in 1789 and that were debated in her parents' home and in her own salon. She knew true happiness in the early years of the Revolution, eagerly welcoming the "lawyers' revolution" of 1789. She would always see this time as the most splendid of her life, when she lived exhilarated by her father's popularity and by her personal admiration for him. She loved politics but had one flaw, and it was fatal: she had been born female at a time when the political theater was closed to women, when they could maneuver only behind the scenes. Endemic misogyny and politically based hostility militated against her in her own lifetime and have continued to do so ever since, for a false legend—fostered in no small way by Emperor

Napoleon—has been constructed around her as a political meddler, egocentric and promiscuous. The legend was strengthened then and later by the enemies of Romanticism and by hatred of Germany, for she was instrumental in introducing the ideas of both into France through her books.

The events of August 10, 1792, and the September Massacres that followed ended many original hopes of the Revolution, and with them ended the glorious period in the life of Germaine de Staël. On August 10, revolutionaries looted the Tuileries—the royal palace in Paris—and invaded the Legislative Assembly to demand the end of the monarchy. As a result, Louis XVI was deposed and incarcerated with his family in the Temple, a prison that had been headquarters of the medieval Knights Templar. On August 30, with émigré French nobles in their ranks, the Prussians attacked Verdun, and the government declared that the country was in danger. On the second and third of September, out of misplaced fear and vengeance, the terrified mobs of Paris murdered thousands of suspects held in prisons.[8] As the government grew increasingly extremist under the impetus of the Jacobins, moderates and defenders of individual rights were increasingly judged counterrevolutionary, and all the more so if they were women.

Mme de Staël was only twenty-six when those fateful events brought to an end her activities on the Parisian scene, the only one she thought worthwhile. On September 2, having contrived to save friends from prison and execution, she barely escaped death herself on the Place de Grève, where mobs were killing anyone perceived as from the upper classes. She was on her way to take refuge with her parents in Switzerland, forced, temporarily at least, to abandon her hopes for the future and to become familiar with the pain and disappointment that were to become her constant companions. The first years of exile had begun. From then on she returned to Paris only at the price of endless difficulties—harassment by local officials, rejection by old friends, and the permanent threat of arbitrary decisions by officials great and small, the more easily made since France's successive governments never recognized her as French.[9]

Late in December of 1792, she left Coppet for England, where she spent the next five months with émigré friends in Surrey. These included Louis Count de Narbonne, a wealthy aristocrat of old lineage, her lover since the fall of 1788, and the father of her two sons.[10] She met the English novelist Frances Burney, whose father, much to his daughter's chagrin, forbade her to see her new friend. The émigré nobleman M. d'Arblay, whom Ms. Burney later married, was "generously concerned that Frances and other English people should do justice to Mme de Staël":

People have slandered her if they do not do justice to her distinguished qualities of heart and mind. . . . Our ways . . . have so little in common with those
of this Country . . . that in truth it would be not only unjust but barbaric to
draw from them bases for judgment—our marriages for example. All of them,
if you will, were but sacrifices to the conventions which have always made
women their victims.[11]

When Mme de Staël returned to France in May 1793, she found that its
rulers would not be indifferent to her, much less favorable. From then on,
every government kept her out of Paris for long periods. Mme de Staël's
opinions, in no way counterrevolutionary, posed no danger to successive
governments, but everything about her—the freedom of ideas and expression she demonstrated in 1789, her salon where she knew how to persuade
those who did not always share her thinking—led governments to fear her;
they feared her far more than they did other women, more than many men.
All she did was express ideas of liberty, tolerance, and justice, which the
French, especially those in charge of the government, who saw no personal
advantage in supporting such opinions, were not yet prepared to accept.

On September 18, 1794, at the age of twenty-eight, she met Benjamin
Constant, the second central man in her life, her father being the first. Constant went on to become a noted novelist, historian of religion, and political
figure. From the first, he shared her opinions and was eager to share her life.
He was intensely attracted to her and pressed his suit persistently, but for a
long time he was unsuccessful since she found him temperamentally difficult and at first physically uninteresting. Their relationship, rarely free of
storms, is reflected clearly if not always accurately in two of his novels,
Adolphe and *Cécile*. In any event, these two brilliant people were intellectual
equals, and their conversation consistently reached dazzling heights with
each setting off the other. In May 1795, they came to a "chaotic Paris" to
work together for "a viable republic based on the principles of 1789."[12] In
June 1797, Mme de Staël gave birth to her daughter, Albertine, whose father
was probably Constant, who always had a special affection for her. Although
the liaison between Constant and Mme de Staël was over by 1809, their
friendship and intellectual entente were deep and permanent, and he never
fully recovered from her death.

In December of 1797, in Paris, Mme de Staël met General Bonaparte,
victor in the Italian Campaigns and immensely popular. Along with many
others, she believed him to be marvelously different from the men of limited ability and vision then in control. Perhaps she soon began to find him

disquieting as well; at least that is what she would say when she looked back on this time. Anecdotes about her efforts to seduce him and about her bitterness at his refusal seem to have stemmed from the endemic misogyny of the times, if not of Napoleon himself. In all events, the story of the persecution that Napoleon would force her to endure is rooted in these few weeks when she met him frequently in the salons of Paris. Retrospectively, she would accord them decisive importance for the rest of her life and would begin *Ten Years of Exile* at this precise moment.

Of the many people who crossed Napoleon's path—from the humblest to those entrusted with the gravest responsibilities, the highest honors, and the greatest wealth—all were swept along in the epic of a legendary conqueror, a latter-day Alexander or Tamerlane. Like those earlier warriors, Napoleon carved out an immense and ephemeral empire and threw Europe into upheaval. After him, people neither acted nor thought as they had under the Old Regime or even under the Revolution that had engendered these new times. They either adored this almost unprecedented sovereign or they detested him; they also used him to their advantage. Then he disappeared, leaving a multifaceted and ineradicable legacy.

Like so many of her compatriots, Mme de Staël at first saw Napoleon as a savior of the republic. Until 1800, nurturing more illusions about Napoleon than she cared to admit in *Ten Years,* she had not imagined to what length Bonaparte's anger would go once he became the master. Yet at the start, his power had been more fragile than she acknowledged when she describes, not without sarcasm, Bonaparte's march to supreme power. But hope turned into disappointment, then hate, through her own persecution and through the spectacle of Europe enslaved. Intensely opposed to the Emperor, she allowed no excuses for his conduct in her book. She conceded him nothing, ignoring possible future benefits for the sake of emphasizing the evil he had done. She refused to give him credit for restoring order because, although she knew order to be necessary, she saw its implementation by Napoleon as the selfish work of a man who advanced the public good only for personal advantage. Ultimately, she could not accept the state of permanent war he imposed on France and Europe, his will to conquer, or his nonchalant use of European nations as pawns on a chessboard. The romantic hero gave way to the tyrant. Peace was lost to perpetual war and conquest. Liberty disappeared and would return only with the defeat of the conqueror and of France, which, for this moment, had become one and indivisible. As Mme de Staël's fight for liberty moved from the personal to the international plane, revolt born of long suffering led her to reassert her own liberty as a writer and to use her pen as a weapon in the name of liberty for individuals and for nations.

Exile sent Germaine de Staël to Coppet on the shores of Lake Geneva; the château chosen by her father for his retirement became her home. She loved and dreaded Coppet; she found it boring or exciting according to whether it was deserted or peopled with friends and acquaintances. She and the people close to her who met there worked seriously, together and separately, at their intellectual endeavors. They also thoroughly enjoyed themselves. They formed the nucleus of what is now known as the Coppet Group, which—to name only the regular habitués of Mme de Staël's salon—included Constant; Sismondi, remarkable economic theorist, historian, sociologist, and literary critic; Bonstetten, philosopher and administrator; and Schlegel, translator, literary critic, and philosopher. In a real sense her salon moved to wherever she happened to be and welcomed those who shared the Coppet spirit and interests. Stendhal called Coppet "the Estates General of European thought."[13] Important in the realms of literature and philosophy, the group was equally significant in the realm of politics as a European center of opposition to Napoleon. The Emperor was well aware of the group's role, and it is hardly surprising that he detested Mme de Staël and never relaxed her exile, given his fear that she could and would influence Paris against him.

In the relative solitude of Coppet, Mme de Staël devoted herself to reflection in a variety of areas with the same intensity she brought to everything she undertook. In 1793, in a vain attempt to prevent the execution of Marie Antoinette, she published *Reflections on the Trial of the Queen;* in 1794, the tale *Zulma;* in 1795, *Reflections on Peace* and the short stories illustrating her *Essay on Fiction.* In 1796, *The Influence of the Passions on the Happiness of Individuals and Nations* appeared. In 1798, she wrote but did not publish *Present Circumstances That Can End the Revolution.* Publication of the first major book of the new century took place in May 1800: *On Literature in Its Relationships with Social Institutions.* Each of these works shows the moderate Enlightenment thought that was inimical to both the radical Jacobin left and resurgent reactionary Catholicism. Her immensely popular novels, *Delphine* in 1802 and *Corinne* five years later, mark the next steps toward a fame for which their author would pay dearly.

Mme de Staël's growing influence became unendurable to Bonaparte. It was not long before the First Consul, already a misogynist, set himself against this overly intelligent woman whom he rapidly judged a nuisance. He never tried to conciliate her but rather called her all sorts of insulting names: "crazy," "crow," "hussy," and others still worse. For her part, it was not long before she attacked in return, portraying herself as a victim of his oppression, which in fact she was. By 1803 the impact of her writing was manifest, and her salon had become a force with which to be reckoned.[14] It was a meeting place for members of the government, including the First Consul's brothers Joseph and Lucien, as well as for foreign diplomats. Liberals came, as did ideologues and members of the Tribunate, including, of course, Benjamin Constant.

In 1800, Napoleon saw to it that *On Literature* was attacked in the press. Two years later he had a similar attack made on *Delphine,* for he had just made his peace with the Catholic Church by means of the Concordat, and the novel expressed views inimical to the Church of Rome: it makes the case for divorce, praises liberal Protestantism, and ends with the heroine's suicide. Furthermore, it strongly praises the political system of the country he always considered his archenemy: England. While a liberal government could tolerate Mme de Staël, she was inadmissible in a consular and imperial system. On February 10, 1803, refusing to tolerate her opposition any longer, Napoleon forbade the author of these books to reside in Paris. Seven months later, extending the interdict to a distance of "forty leagues"—160 kilometers—from the capital in any direction, he dug an invisible moat she would be unable to cross freely until the Restoration. But it was Paris that held most of her friends; it was Paris that offered the pleasures of society, art, and the political scene. Everywhere else she suffered from loneliness and intellectual boredom. Since she prized the splendor of her social standing, the surest way to punish her was to make these things inaccessible. Another way was to refuse reimbursement of the two million francs her father had lent Louis XVI's Royal Treasury to guarantee the purchase of wheat in a time of famine. Napoleon understood that he could reduce her to silence only through multiple constraints.

Paradoxically, by reducing her to exile, the Emperor raised her to a far more exalted position, for he inadvertently led her to travel to the Germanic countries and to Italy, and so "cut the roots that bound [her] to Paris." Now she, who felt so tied to Paris and to French society, was no longer confined exclusively to France or to any single country. Henceforth, her culture, her literary ideas, and her political thought would be bound up with the whole Western world.

As an exile, she could study worlds and cultures very different from the French civilization Napoleon sought to impose on the countries he conquered. Astonished and enchanted with her discoveries, she would write major works destined to open France to the new knowledge amassed by the very people the conqueror despised. For a long time she believed that her books would win her pardon. In her generosity, she could not understand that Napoleon never forgave and that, famous as she was, she was of little consequence to a man who thought nothing of crushing legitimate sovereigns and of redistributing kingdoms. This kind of blindness can be surprising in a person of such clear-sighted political judgment, but in what concerned her personally, she confused her wishes with reality.

As early as 1803, she began gathering the materials she needed for *On Germany,* her most famous book. It would introduce German philosophy, literature, and Romanticism into France and thus was central to the advancement of that nation's Romantic movement. On October 23 of that year, she left for Germany with Constant and Albertine, now six years old. Everywhere she went she took time to look closely at what each place offered: monuments, cathedrals, museums, and so forth. Everywhere she went she met the leading people of her day for prolonged discussion. She was, for example, cordially received at the court of Weimar, where she often met Schiller and Wieland. She frequently saw Goethe, who admired her work and had translated her *Essay on Fiction* into German. In Berlin she met August Schlegel, already a well-known writer in his own country, and persuaded him to come to Coppet as her children's tutor as well as her own instructor in German language and culture. He remained her friend and her aide until her death.

Her stay in Germany was suddenly interrupted by her father's death, which she never truly ceased to mourn. On December 11, 1804, in an effort to emerge from unremitting sadness, she left for Italy with Schlegel and her three children: Auguste, age fourteen; Albert, twelve; and Albertine, seven. It was a crucial experience. There she discovered a dazzling sun-filled universe and the world of the ruins of ancient Rome. She was enthusiastically welcomed wherever she went—in her own right and as the daughter of the great Jacques Necker. She met the poet Monti and renewed her friendship with scholar-diplomat Wilhelm von Humboldt. Her understanding of Roman Catholicism deepened when she met the prelates of the church. Returning to Coppet, she broke off her work on the book about Germany for two years to write her second novel, *Corinne or Italy.* This book marks a calmer period, even though Napoleon expressed displeasure at the absence of the French among the important characters in a novel deliberately set in 1794 before his conquests began. It was highly influential; women as varied as the American Margaret Fuller and the British Elizabeth Barrett Browning read *Corinne* as a justification of female genius and as a call to seek independence and fulfillment in Italy.[15]

In the summer of 1810, Mme de Staël brought to a successful conclusion the ambitious and seminal *On Germany*. But when the printing was three-quarters finished, the work was banned and condemned to be ground to pulp on orders from the Emperor himself. This was a hideous moment for Germaine de Staël. Years of work were virtually erased. But she was able to save one copy of the book, and Schlegel another, which he took to his brother in Vienna for safekeeping. On the heels of the attack on her treatise, she was ordered out of France, excluded from Napoleonic Europe, restricted to Geneva and Coppet, and unable to publish in any country dominated by the Emperor.

With imperial power at its zenith, Mme de Staël reached the nadir of despair, alone with her children and a few loyal friends, themselves threatened with exile. Baron de Barante, prefect of the Léman, was about to be dismissed; those in high places were displeased with the intractability of the Genevans and the prefect's alleged forbearance in dealing with them and with Mme de Staël. They replaced him with Capelle, a despicable opportunist who found that persecuting Mme de Staël was an excellent path to Napoleon's favor. He had the assistance of Savary, Duke de Rovigo, who had followed Fouché as Minister of Police in 1810 and had directed operations against *On Germany*. It was from Rovigo that Capelle took his instructions and to whom he wrote disgraceful letters about his prisoner.[16]

Sure of support and reward, Capelle proceeded to make Mme de Staël's closest friends his targets. In June of 1811, Schlegel was ordered to return to his own country. Mathieu de Montmorency, guardian of the writer's children, and her close friend Mme Récamier were likewise singled out. While both had opposed Napoleon for a long time, the orders of exile were pointedly served to them, one after the other, at Coppet itself; henceforth they were banned from Paris and confined to country estates far from the capital and the world of politics. Watching them leave, Mme de Staël wept bitterly. As Capelle delightedly reported to Rovigo: "I am told they are in mourning at Coppet; so much the better."[17] Coppet was becoming a prison. Finding herself shut away in those few square leagues, destined to the total exile she called "death in miniature, torture that wears down the soul with its endlessness," she understood that she was condemned to perpetual banishment and could expect even worse, even a real prison. Although terrified and desperate, she rejected suicide as a solution. When the German poet Heinrich von Kleist killed himself in 1811, she wrote *Reflections on Suicide,* a meditation concluding with the rejection of an act she herself had portrayed in both *Delphine* and her drama, *Sappho*.

It was then that she met her last and most unlikely love, John Rocca. At twenty-three, he was hardly older than her elder son, Auguste. He was handsome and a fine horseman; he was not intellectual. He had gone off to join Napoleon's hussars for the disastrous Spanish wars and came home gravely wounded and bereft of illusions about the Emperor. Then he met Mme de Staël in Geneva, where his patrician family lived and where she was spending the winter of 1810–1811. Rocca was immediately fascinated with this celebrated writer, who, at forty-four and well past the bloom of youth, did not reciprocate his interest. But he was dazzled by what he saw and heard in her presence and, falling wildly in love with her, almost literally stormed his way into her life. In 1811, he stood with Germaine de Staël before a Protestant minister and they secretly pledged to marry. Improbable as it sounds, but then so much in her life is both improbable and true, the union worked. Rocca gave himself to her unconditionally as no other man could or would and never left her side so long as she lived.

The months stretching from the fall of 1810 to the spring of 1812 may have been bleak, but they were also full of work. Since the Coppet spirit required everyone to write, Rocca too sat down and managed to compose an interesting memoir on his experience of the Spanish Campaign.[18] There were diversions as well. From time to time Mme de Staël's salon was transformed into a theater where she and her friends and family performed both classics, such as Racine's *Phèdre,* and short plays she wrote herself. The practice was typical of the time, but what she did with it was not. In contrast to her personal situation, her farces are hilarious. They testify to the delicious sense of humor often mentioned in her contemporaries' memoirs but not always evident in her writing. *Captain Kernadec,* written in 1810, is a satire on the military mentality, strewn with funny double entendres. In 1811, with the Napoleonic vice tightening steadily around her, came two more comedies, in particular the *Signora Fantastici,* both farcical social satire and paean to the creative imagination. These plays work on the stage; people still laugh and applaud on the rare occasions they are performed.[19]

In 1810, when she returned to Geneva in the aftershock of the blow struck against *On Germany,* her hatred of Napoleon had reached new heights, and she decided to attack the tyrant systematically by relating the story of the persecution meted out to her since 1800. Such are the origins of *Ten Years of Exile.* At the time she had no difficulty blending her own destiny with the European calamity. In the foreword to his 1821 edition of the book, Auguste de Staël reminds us of the climate in which she decided "to preserve the trace of her memories and thoughts. As she proceeded to describe her personal circumstances, she included the various reflections which, from the inception of Bonaparte's power, the state of France and the march of events had inspired in her." He evokes the risks she took in putting any word of this on paper: "If printing such a work would have been an act of unbelievable daring at the time, the sole fact of writing it required a great deal of courage and caution, particularly in my mother's position. She could not doubt that every step she took was under police surveillance."[20]

In absolute secrecy Mme de Staël began to plan her escape, consulting only with Schlegel. No one suspected her plans. She had already thought of going to England by way of Russia in 1809.[21] She had given serious thought to going to America in 1810 and had obtained passports. The stay in a friend's château in Chaumont, described in Part Two of her book, was indeed the first step toward the channel ports that were soon closed to her since the administration did not want her to stop in England, which was on her route. For her part, she was afraid of the ocean and long crossings; winter was coming, and the destruction of her book was crushing. Thus it came about that on October 6, 1810, instead of setting out for New York or Philadelphia, she left for Coppet from Fossé (where she had gone from Chaumont) and continued her attempt to arrange a move to America.

She also requested passports for Italy, which were refused.[22] The authorities dismissed her efforts as the whims of an overwrought woman. The fact is that everything she did was specifically calculated to fool them. It would be a grave mistake to think of Mme de Staël as muddle-headed. Emotional, certainly, and easily frightened as well, she was nonetheless familiar with the world of banking and finance, and she was expert at managing her considerable fortune as well as her widespread investments, including some in the United States. Yet she was not above dealing with the details of travel arrangements and household questions large and small.[23] Her decision to flee to England was made in June 1811, before Schlegel left. Genevan society, her closest friends, the authorities, the police—all of them misunderstood, as have scholars who studied the period; none of them thought her capable of masking her true intentions.

Putting the plan into effect, however, was delayed by a circumstance that could not be circumvented: she was expecting a child. Without the obstacle of pregnancy, the great journey would have begun before France declared war on Russia. But she was stuck fast to Coppet until Alphonse Rocca was born on April 7, 1812; furthermore, she was now forty-six and slow to recover.

Albert de Staël. Portrait by Firmin Massot.

(Collection château de Coppet)

Albertine de Staël, 1808. Drawing by Friedrich Tieck.
(Courtesy of Mme de Pange)

Auguste de Staël, 1808. Drawing by Friedrich Tieck.
(Courtesy of Mme de Pange)

(right) The Chateau de Coppet in 1846. Lithograph by J. Dériaz.
(Collection château de Coppet)

Benjamin Constant. Artist Unknown.
(Collection château de Coppet)

Baron G. de Schlegel.
Aritist Unknown.
(Collection château de Coppet)

Madame Récamier. Portrait by Eulalie Morin.

(Collection château de Coppet)

News of the birth filtered into Geneva and even Paris, thanks to the prefect's zeal, and this had at least the advantage of keeping her trackers off guard. Schlegel, unaware of the pregnancy, restlessly marked time in Berne, knowing only that the growth of Napoleon's hegemony in Europe rendered more problematic each day the escape he was planning with and for Mme de Staël.

The escape unfolded like a carefully crafted adventure novel.[24] On Saturday, May 23, 1812, a fan in her hand, Germaine de Staël climbed into a light carriage with her fifteen-year-old daughter, Albertine, her son Auguste, and John Rocca as if for an afternoon's outing.[25] Schlegel joined them in Berne. At this point, Auguste returned to Coppet. At the age of twenty-two he assumed responsibility for managing the family estate and did not rejoin his mother until 1813, when she was settled in Stockholm. Rocca went back to Geneva to put some of their affairs in order and to confuse the police; he would meet her in Innsbruck under dramatic circumstances. Eugène Uginet, her factotum at Coppet, had already left on May 22 and joined the group at their first halting place. On May 27, her younger son, Albert, set out with two servants and the baggage in the family travel coach, so much more conspicuous than the light carriage; but it was not until early June that Capelle realized what had happened.

And so the great journey began. It would take the travelers across the Austrian Empire, Bohemia, Moravia, Galicia, Russia via Kiev and Moscow to Saint Petersburg, then Sweden, and later England. Mme de Staël took with her the manuscript of what she had written of *Ten Years of Exile*. She also took *Reflections on Suicide,* which she published in Stockholm in 1813, and her copy of *On Germany,* published later that same year in London.

To compound the already present difficulties, Austrian and Russian passports were essential for passage through Europe, and Napoleon, now at war with Russia, would send the Grand Army across the Niemen in June of 1812. Thus Mme de Staël and her traveling companions—Albertine, Albert, Schlegel, Rocca, and the servants—were compelled to make an immense detour. To reach Saint Petersburg in the north they had to go by way of Kiev in the south and proceed to Moscow, which they left just a few weeks before the French armies entered. They crossed the border between Austria and Russia on July 14. Ironically, on this symbolic day, she recovered her liberty by moving from the midst of conquered, divided peoples—Austrians, Galicians, Poles—to enter the country of serfdom. Paradoxically, Russia was now the symbol of the independent world, and Mme de Staël had the privilege of seeing Russia rise up against the invader in an extraordinary burst of courageous patriotism. The experience inspired her to include in *Ten Years of Exile* a great many observations on a people brought to its highest possibilities.

As soon as she reached the safety of Sweden, Mme de Staël was anxious to proceed with the book she had carried across Europe in various drafts. But first she would describe her dramatic journey—the essence of Part Two of *Ten Years of Exile*—while it was still fresh in her mind. And so for the moment, she thought, she would drop her narrative in mid-July of 1804 and resume with the critical events of 1810. Although the version we have is a first draft, which would doubtless have been revised, her account of the great journey is an astonishing description of the countries she crossed. Even at this early, unfinished stage, it is brilliant and accurate in most of its details.[26] Travel books were available at the time, as well as histories of Russia, but none of her predecessors had her gift for synthesis, nor could they match the visual power of her writing.

With the tale of the great journey, a striking and genuinely enriching change emerged in the nature, proportions, and tone of the work, which now shifted its main focus from Napoleon to her fascination with the new world he had inadvertently allowed her to enter. Long accustomed to observe and analyze everything and everyone she encountered, it is logical that Mme de Staël wanted to describe the countries she crossed, the peoples she glimpsed. She rapidly sketched in the Tyrol, Austria, Bohemia, and Moravia, not finding them very different from what she already knew. In Poland, however, which officialdom obliged her to cross eight or ten kilometers south of Cracow, she noticed something unusual, something exotic. And the Russia she shrewdly observed was still more surprising to her, both for its physical and moral landscape and for its location at the far edge of Europe, on the borders of Asia. She discovered Kiev and Moscow and visited Saint Petersburg in something of the fashion of a privileged tourist—and all this during a war that, with its promise of horrors to come, exacerbated the traveler's sensations and her sensitivity to the images coming successively into view.

In Saint Petersburg she met German patriots, foreign diplomats (including John Quincy Adams), and the first Englishmen to be in Russia since the breakdown of the short-lived 1802 Treaty of Amiens between France and Britain.[27] On several occasions, she was received by Czar Alexander; they pursued serious political discussions in which she made the case for the Russo-Anglo-Swedish Alliance that was indeed to prove important for the defeat of Napoleon. She met the Empress and the Dowager Empress, and she frequented and observed high society; all of them, like their ruler, were radically different from the aristocracy she had known in Western Europe.

She could also assess the difficulties in the military situation despite the patriotic groundswell so helpful to the sovereign, for there was everything to be feared from Napoleon, with his "genius for evil," who had so many times triumphed on the field of battle.[28]

After a few crowded weeks in the Russian capital, she made her way to Stockholm where she placed herself under the protection of her friend Bernadotte, now Crown Prince of Sweden. Formerly a general of the French army, he had risen to the rank of marshal, but by this time he had openly joined the opposition to Napoleon. She informed him of her discussions with Czar Alexander, bringing him the information he needed to resolve on joining forces with Russia and England against France. In June 1813, she left for England, where she continued her struggle against Napoleon with all her powers as a propagandist. For example, she served as Bernadotte's agent in promoting to English political figures his candidacy for the French throne. Thus at last she could play the active political role that she had always wanted and that her whole life, her talent, and her important European connections had prepared her to assume.

Another example of how seriously statesmen regarded her views may be seen in her correspondence with Thomas Jefferson on the War of 1812. She first met Jefferson when he was his country's Minister to France, from 1784 to 1789, and frequented her mother's salon. In a letter sent to him from Stockholm on November 10, 1812, Mme de Staël wrote that, while she could not claim to know what had impelled his country to war with England, she would make the case for America to desist. She presented England as the sole remaining barrier to Napoleon, pointing out how, should that country's fight be lost, the United States would inevitably be vulnerable to the tyrant. She began her argument with this reminder:

> You saw the first days of the revolution in France, and I remember that in my father's home you told the men of extreme opinions that their demagogic principles would bring despotism to France. Your prediction has come to pass: Europe and the human species are bent under the will of one man who means to establish his universal monarchy. Already, Germany, Italy, Holland, Denmark etc. are French provinces.

In a long and carefully reasoned reply, dated May 10, 1813, Jefferson agreed that Napoleon was "the greatest of the destroyers of the human race." Nonetheless his hopes for Europe were placed on the mediation of Czar Alexander of Russia, for in Jefferson's view, the enemy America needed to defeat was the one whose "object [was] *the permanent domination of the ocean, and the monopoly of the trade of the world.*"[29]

In England, as she watched from afar the last battles of 1813 and 1814, she was torn between her longing for Napoleon's defeat and her dread of what defeat would mean for France. When she returned to Paris in May 1813, a month after the Emperor's abdication, she received old friends along with sovereigns, ministers, and generals. But the sight of her city occupied by enemy armies was bitterly painful: "cossacks in the rue Racine," soldiers in uniform at the opera. None of this is to be found in *Ten Years of Exile,* set aside in favor of international politics and the book that became *Considerations on the French Revolution.*[30]

The three years from 1814 to 1817 were as full as those that preceded them. Coppet again became an international center. As had always been true there, private intellectual work went on as usual. Mme de Staël wrote most of *Considerations.*[31] She had many projects in mind for later. One of these was a book on the kingdoms of the North. The volumes in her personal library and those she borrowed in Stockholm by historians and travelers in Russia and Sweden, as well as her own travel notebooks and passages in her "mementos," testify to her interest in writing important studies on these countries.[32] On October 19, 1812, she wrote to her friend Claude Hochet: "I am planning to write on the North just as I did on the South. I think this will be interesting as both Europe and Asia."[33] On May 12, 1813, she remarked in a letter to the Russian diplomat Ouvarov, whom she had met in Vienna in 1808: "I should like to speak with you about Russia which so struck me on my rapid journey; nothing that has been said, and especially written, on the subject gives any idea of it."[34]

In the meanwhile the Restoration government returned a large part of the monies the French government owed to Necker. The future of the family was now secure. Her daughter would have the dowry she needed to marry the man she loved and who loved her, the liberal and intelligent Victor, Duke de Broglie, whose own family had been impoverished by the Revolution. But saddened by the presence of foreign victors in Paris, by the new Bourbon monarchy, and worried about Rocca's fragile health,[35] Mme de Staël decided to set off for Italy a second time in September 1815, accompanied by Rocca, Schlegel, and Albertine.[36] Sismondi and Broglie met them in Pisa where the young people were married on February 20, 1816, in a Protestant-Catholic ceremony, virtually unprecedented at the time.[37] Moreover, even then, even in Italy, Germaine de Staël's political activity continued. The apparently innocuous essay on translation she was asked to write for a Milanese literary journal—sponsored, ironically enough, by the head of the Austrian government in northern Italy—was read by that country's Romantics as a call for their country's independence.[38]

Now, at last, Germaine de Staël felt free to fulfill the pledge made before the Protestant pastor in 1811: she and John Rocca married secretly on October 10 and left for Paris six days later. She began to make concrete plans for a long-dreamed-of trip to the Middle East. But four months later, on February 21, 1817, fate intervened, and she was paralyzed in a fall. At the age of fifty-two, surrounded by family and friends, she died in the château of Coppet on July 14, five years to the day after crossing the Russian border in 1812.

The better world Germaine de Staël struggled to create—and did so in microcosm at Coppet—seems no closer to realization today than when she wrote *Ten Years of Exile*. Since then, and indeed ever since the Exodus from Egypt, Pharaoh has risen up time and again in every part of the world to enslave the minds, souls, and bodies of peoples; like some cruel and malicious god, he imposes torture and death for the slightest questioning of his will. The astonishing people who protest at immense personal cost are symbolically the heirs of Mme de Staël: Aung San Suu Kyi, the Nobel Laureate in Burma; the "Refuseniks" under Stalin; the dissidents of Tiananmen Square; Martin Luther King and Rosa Parks; the women who tenaciously fought Ulster and IRA extremists to bring peace to Northern Ireland—all of them using only the weapons of peace. The violent and bloody twentieth century has brought Hitler and Stalin in Europe; Perón, the Generals, and Pinochet in Latin America; Mao, Pol Pot, and Burma's military junta in Asia; and Amin and Botha in Africa. The list goes on and on.[39] What is certain is that without those who at each appearance of Pharaoh have the difficult, steadfast courage to stand up as did Germaine de Staël and say an eloquent, resounding "No!" there would be little hope for the moral and political progress that she believed in and that we so desperately need.

EDITIONS OF *TEN YEARS OF EXILE* AND THE CHALLENGES OF EDITING

In her will, Mme de Staël left instructions for publication of *Considerations* as well as of her complete works and those of her father.[40] She did not mention *Ten Years of Exile*. But Auguste de Staël judged that, even unfinished, the text was marvelously alive, and he published it in Volume 15 of his mother's *Complete Works* in 1821. For the rest of the nineteenth century, readers assumed they had before them a book that was much as she had planned it. But although Auguste was a faithful son and despite his disclaimers, he made important changes to the book. Some were called for by the time and place in which he lived; others stemmed from a personal sense of how best to present a book that was incomplete and had only in part gone through the series of revisions that were Mme de Staël's normal practice. For eighty-three years this was the one available edition.

Auguste de Staël's duty was traced out for him: if he decided to publish *Ten Years*, he would need to remove and modify a great deal of material; otherwise he would need to wait until enough time had passed to make that material politically innocuous and to spare the feelings of people still alive who were likely to feel insulted. Deciding on the first solution, he wrote in his "Editor's Preface" that he had followed the plan laid out by his mother and had eliminated from Part One those passages already used in her book on the French Revolution, asserting he had not "ventured the slightest addition." No additions perhaps, but most certainly a great many subtractions!

Although he did not intervene so frequently in the politically less sensitive Part Two, he must not be believed when he writes that he presents his mother's text "without a single change"; nor is he to be believed when he writes that he even found it hard to make "slight corrections in style, so important did it seem . . . to preserve in this draft all the vivacity of its original character." His corrections are in fact no more satisfactory than his other modifications, for when you examine the language he substituted, you see that in the process of "correcting" he softened judgments, suppressed nuances, and altered meanings. As a result, all that was available to the public until the early twentieth century was a dimmed reflection of his mother's work.

In 1904, Paul Gautier published the second edition of *Ten Years of Exile*.[41] One of the rare specialists on Mme de Staël at the time, he realized the public's utter ignorance of *Ten Years* and decided to prepare a new edition based on the manuscripts rather than on the text Auguste de Staël had printed in 1821. Gautier meant to be faithful to the original and effected numerous desirable changes by restoring and rectifying some—but by no means all—of Auguste de Staël's omissions and "corrections." He retained and improved the system of division into chapters initiated by his predecessor and kept Auguste's prefaces and notes. Perhaps because he was pressed for time and the handwritten originals were difficult to read, Gautier interwove different manuscripts.

Furthermore, his notes are too sparse to help modern readers understand the book's multiple allusions to people, events, and issues. It is this useful but still seriously defective edition that was translated into English by Doris Beik and published by the Saturday Review Press in New York in 1972.

Only through the critical edition published by Simone Balayé and Mariella Bonifacio in 1996 have we been able to see what the author actually wrote and intended.[42] When they assumed the task of editing the manuscripts long buried in the archives at Coppet, they immediately understood that they would have to tread through a virtual minefield of problems as they traced the evolution of the text. They found that the manuscripts comprise two distinct "sets."

The *First Set* is made up of three manuscripts transcribed by several copyists, then corrected and numbered by Mme de Staël herself. One of these was transcribed into "decoded" language when the author reached Stockholm. The two that follow chronologically were drafted at Coppet while she was under police surveillance and were copied into "disguised" or coded language. Together, these constitute what Simone Balayé calls the *first version* and cover the years from 1797 to 1805. They were published for the first time in the critical edition of 1996. Since the main interest of these texts is to scholars, they have not been translated for the present book. On the other hand, because the so-called disguised and decoded texts place in sharp relief the threat hanging over Mme de Staël for so many years, a sample is given here in Appendix I.

The *Second Set,* far longer than the first, is the substance of the present volume.[43] Comprising two parts entirely in the author's hand, it is known as the *second version:* Part One, starting in 1797, as in the First Set, stops in 1804 and is a second draft. Part Two, from 1810 to 1812, is entirely new and in all likelihood a first draft. The differences between the first and second versions are so great that the first is not simply a variant, as Balayé discovered in examining them. But, since identical sentences or sentence fragments are reproduced in the second, Mme de Staël apparently had the First Set of manuscripts in front of her when she sat down to rethink and rewrite her text.

The Second Set is divided into seven copybooks and has two distinct sections. Part One (1797–1804) shows that Mme de Staël originally intended to continue with her trip to Italy as in the last disguised manuscript, for she wrote the words "Italian Journey," which she later crossed out, thus stopping on the threshold of the experience that yielded her major novel, *Corinne.* The contents of this new draft show a certain disorganization that is particularly marked in the first part because of cross-references, material the author moved from one copybook to another or crossed out in the course of her writing.

According to Auguste de Staël his mother deleted the passages she meant to use in *Considerations,* and therefore he omitted them from his edition of 1821. He may have been right, for the strong resemblance between the opening of *Ten Years* and *Considerations* suggests that the author might have done likewise had she lived to finish her book. They have, however, been retained in their original place in the present edition since they represent her initial conception of *Ten Years*.

Furthermore, many sheets are covered with interpolations and words written over other words that make them difficult to decipher. Since she was working rapidly, the author was sometimes mistaken on the chronological sequence of events, forgot to cross out repeated words, forgot to insert the nobiliary particle *de* or, as is often the case, added it (*de* Capelle, *de* Rocca). Names of people and places were often written as she heard them. Certain important passages would have been better located elsewhere in the text, for its organization, much revised already, clearly needed further modification, which Madame de Staël would not have failed to make.

Auguste de Staël tells us that when his mother reached Sweden, she set to work on a fair copy of her memoirs but broke off in the year 1804 to describe her flight across Europe while her memories were more sharply vivid than they would ever be again. We also have a second copy of Part One in her handwriting that goes from 1797, when she met Bonaparte, to 1804, after her father's death and General Moreau's trial; it comes to a stop one year earlier than the disguised manuscript, which extends to May 1805. There is no way of knowing when she drafted it—perhaps in Stockholm after she broke off Part Two in mid-sentence or even in London. All that we have for the period extending from the spring of 1804 to the summer of 1810 are numerous preparatory notes. What is certain is that she planned to turn again to *Ten Years* once she had completed *Considerations on the French Revolution*.

While a detailed comparison of the drafts of Part One is beyond the scope of this introduction, it should be understood that there are numerous and important differences in detail among them. These differences suggest progressive enrichment as the author rewrote and revised: changes in the order of presentation, adaptations, and the choice of events and anecdotes recorded. Notably, in the unpublished version, historical events are restricted to those that can serve as background to the author's personal trajectory. Here the recurrent and increasingly powerful theme of exile, present throughout the narrative, reaches its crescendo. It shows the arbitrary nature of power first as an event, next as a habit, and finally as the legislative norm. To make these points, Mme de Staël emphasized her personal life and her painful ordeals as an exile. In her last draft, however, she extensively developed the historical events that formed the basis of her own adventures, achieving a new equilibrium between the two aspects of her book.

Dating the various drafts was a major problem for the editors since it is hard to determine exactly when the First Set was written. In one place, Auguste suggests it was begun late in 1810, in another, the summer of 1811. At all events, a letter from Sismondi to Constant, dated September 6, 1811, shows that Mme de Staël was working on the book at that time. "Our friend," he wrote, "has just sealed a letter she was writing to you, and she forgot to tell you that she is fruitlessly searching her head for what she did during the year 1800–1801, that she has absolutely forgotten, and that she asks you to remind her."[44]

The first part of the unpublished manuscript begins with details from the time of her first encounters with Bonaparte in 1797 and rapidly skims the period 1798–1799, when Bonaparte was in Egypt. It returns to a meticulous narrative with the coup d'état of the eighteenth of Brumaire (November 10, 1799), a giant step in his ascent to absolute power. One of the two major themes found here, one that was planned from the very first draft, is the unhappiness of her exile. Several weeks before she left Coppet on May 23, 1812, she wrote to Claude Hochet: "I have been suffering for nine years and for the last two I have not been alive. It is a rather unusual condition and I am tempted to write a book called *On Exile* which, I believe, will be full of rather new observations on the human heart. I shall include myself as an episode."[45] She did not add that her personal story was coupled with a powerful political attack for fear that her friend might be tempted to mention it in Paris.

After discussing the inception of this draft in his preface, Auguste de Staël explains the genesis of the disguised manuscripts. His mother was faced at all times with unannounced police perquisitions. As she was the object of the prefect's unremitting surveillance, he tells us, "the greatest precautions were advisable." Thus "scarcely had she written a few pages than she had them transcribed by one of her closest friends [Fanny Randall], being careful to replace all names with those drawn from the history of the English Revolution. In this disguise, she carried the manuscript" with her as she fled across Europe in 1812.[46]

These details allow an approximate date for the initial draft of Part One. For reasons of character, the prefect could not have been the fair-minded

Barante, dismissed in November 1810. His successor, the mean-minded and ambitious Capelle, took office on February 11, 1811, and kept Mme de Staël under ever-tightening observation until she fled in May of 1812. As a result, until the end of the account of her Italian journey of 1805, she pretended to write various episodes from English history, using English names to hide the names of persons, places, and institutions. The only surviving disguised manuscripts begin in 1804, with the episode of the execution of Mary Stuart used to recount the murder of the Duke d'Enghien.

The beginning of this first version (1797 to early 1804 in Berlin) was doubtless transcribed in clear language in Stockholm under her personal direction, since the coded text would have been largely incomprehensible to the uninitiated copyist. The resulting decoded manuscript was quite possibly preceded by a second or even a third disguised manuscript in her own hand, lost or destroyed, perhaps, because they were no longer useful when she decided to redraft her work from the beginning. Was her goal a quick revision for immediate publication? Did she decide instead to do more and do it better? There is no way of knowing. What we do know for certain, however, is that these various stages are typical of her method of work; that is, for each complete work there are at least three manuscripts, sometimes four, as is true with *Corinne* and *On Germany*.

Part One with its various versions raises many thorny problems that do not arise in Part Two since we have only one manuscript. Entirely in Mme de Staël's handwriting, it covers the period from the summer of 1810 to her arrival in Stockholm two years later and constitutes a travel diary bearing the only subtitles in the book: *Crossing Austria, Journey through Russia, Leaving for Sweden*. Unless manuscripts have been lost or destroyed, it is a first draft. That she began it in Stockholm is proved by the words of her friend Brinkman, a former Swedish diplomat who saw her daily in Stockholm and read at least a few pages.[47] As her son tells us, she started with the destruction of *On Germany*, portrayed the persecution that intensified to the point she felt compelled to flee in the spring of 1812, and then broke off to tell the story of her escape and her flight across Europe.

Textual questions were not solved by the fair copy of the second version located in the collection of Geneva's Public and University Library. Called the Randall Copy, it poses its own questions. Who made it? Why? When? The writing is that of Fanny Randall, Madame de Staël's English friend and companion who lived with the Broglie family after her patron's death. Its pages show nothing to suggest that she did it at the author's request, but the traces it bears of Auguste de Staël's corrections lead us to suppose that it was done at *his* request to help him prepare his edition. It seems to be the first stage of his work. For while it contains Auguste's brief interpolated text explaining the gap between the book's two parts—translated here in Appendix I—it is clearly not the copy, now lost, used by the printer since it shows none of the far-reaching changes effected for the 1821 edition.

The need for extensive historical annotation in such a book is obvious. But Simone Balayé had another less apparent set of goals, the first of which was to determine whether Mme de Staël made factual errors. As a result we see that the author was well informed and rarely made mistakes in this domain. The editor's second goal was to measure any deformation of facts meant to heighten the author's charges against Napoleon: consequently we see in enlightening detail that Mme de Staël's interpretation of those facts lends itself to discussion and evaluation. Thus Balayé's annotation has, in the main, been retained to make it possible for readers to evaluate the author's vision of her world.

In sum, the drama of Mme de Staël's life and of the era in which she lived is echoed in the story of the writing and editing of *Ten Years of Exile*.

TRANSLATOR'S NOTE

As always my goal in translating is to come as close as possible to an author and work distant from my own time as well as social and geographical space. It is to retain the tone and flavor of a style developed at the close of the Age of Enlightenment with echoes of Classicism and traces of both the Romantic era to come and the modern world in the making. I work to carry the shades of meaning and feeling in the French across frontiers of language. Thus I have tried to avoid anachronisms of language and structure and to retain the flavor of Mme de Staël's world and her personal style. It follows logically that there is no anachronistic use of inclusive language here.

A number of intriguing problems arose in the translation process. As I worked, I always kept in mind that *Ten Years of Exile* is an unfinished book. Although Mme de Staël reviewed and revised Part One, she may have done so incompletely, and she did not review Part Two at all. I was careful not to smooth out any awkwardness of style encountered along the way, particularly in Part Two, and not to correct errors or contradictions.

Spelling is modernized here as in the Balayé-Bonifacio edition. However, like the French editors, I retain the author's spelling of Russian names of people and places, which represents nineteenth-century usage in Europe (for example, *Kiew* for *Kiev*). I have used modern English forms in the notes.

Since French punctuation is often different from American usage, I have introduced a number of changes to make the book more accessible.

I have followed the French editors in eliminating the division into brief chapters introduced by the author's son Auguste in his 1821 edition. Like Simone Balayé, I have placed Auguste de Staël's introductory texts in an appendix and his notes among her own explanatory notes precisely where he himself had situated them. Notes I have added are indicated as such by *[Trans.]*.

A few observations on language follow here. At one point Mme de Staël tells us that the word "comfort," which does not appear in French this early in the nineteenth century, would convey her meaning nicely but that it is an English word. Except for this single mention, she does not use it. I avoid the word as well to keep her from having to seemingly contradict herself, and I use words such as "well-being" even when comfort would seem more appropriate to my late-twentieth-century ear.

The dictionary translation of "ci-devant" is "former," a neutral word in English. But when the Revolutionaries abolished feudal rights and privileges (including titles) in 1789, the former nobles were pejoratively referred to as "ci-devants." Therefore the French word has been retained throughout. In Part Two, the author says that Russians rarely experience "l'amour sentimental." The obvious translation would seem to be "romantic love," but this was a relatively new expression at the time and was not used here by the author; therefore I decided to translate it literally as "sentimental love." For similar reasons, the word "sensibility" is selected over "sensitivity," which has connotations in contemporary English that are inappropriate here. As in *Corinne*, the untranslatable *"patrie"* is a problem since it is "country" with the added connotation of "land of the fathers." In the present book, the words "country," "native land," and "homeland" are the most usual renderings.

Chronology

THE LIFE AND TIMES OF GERMAINE DE STAËL

(*Ten Years of Exile* is autobiographical and political; it is not confessional. The chronology is thus limited to events, personal and historical, pertinent to the book).

1766.   April 22. Birth of Anne Louise Germaine Necker in Paris.

1767.   October 25. Birth of Benjamin Constant in Lausanne.

1769.   August 15. Birth of Napoleone Buonaparte in Corsica.

1776.   Jacques Necker is named Deputy Director of Finance.
        Germaine is in England with her parents from April 13 to early June.

1777.   June. Necker is named Director General of Finance. He resigns on May 19, 1781.

1783.   Summer. Mlle Necker goes to Switzerland with her parents. She rejects a proposed marriage to William Pitt.

1784.   May. Necker takes his family to Switzerland and buys the château at Coppet.
        —October 21–April 1785. The Necker family travels in the Midi.
        —October 30. Napoleon enters the Ecole Militaire in Paris.

1785.   June–August. It is decided that Mlle Necker will marry Baron de Staël, the Swedish Ambassador to France.

1786.   January 6. The royal family signs the marriage contract at Versailles. The wedding takes place in the chapel of the Swedish Embassy.
        —January 31. Mme de Staël is presented at the French court.
        —March 15. She sends the first of her letters with news of society and literature to Gustave III, King of Sweden.

—She writes her play *Sophie, or Secret Sentiments* and begins the *Letters on Jean-Jacques Rousseau.*

1787.   April 13. Necker is exiled by order of King Louis XVI; the order is revoked in June.
—On or about July 22, she gives birth to her first child, Gustavine, goddaughter to the King and Queen of Sweden.
—She writes the tragedy *Jane Gray*.

1788.   August 8. The Estates General are convened.
—August 26. Necker is called back to the Finance Ministry.
—Fall. Mme de Staël's liaison with Narbonne begins.
—Late that year. Publication of a limited edition of *Letters on the Works and Character of J.-J. Rousseau,* reprinted many times.

1789.   April 7 or 8. Death of Gustavine.
—May 4. Mme de Staël attends the solemn procession of the Estates General and its opening session on the 5th.
—June 17. The Third Estate proclaims itself the National Assembly.
—June 29. Tennis Court Oath: Locked out of their meeting hall, the deputies go to the Jeu de Paume and swear not to disband until they give the kingdom a constitution.
—The Assembly proclaims itself the Constituant Assembly.
—July 11. Dismissal and exile of Necker. He is soon recalled and Mme de Staël joins him for his triumphant return to Paris.
—July 14. Storming of the Bastille.
—July 17. The emigration of nobles begins.
—August 4. Feudal rights and privileges are abolished.
—August 26. Declaration of the Rights of Man and the Citizen.
—October 5–6. Mme de Staël witnesses the riots at Versailles and is in the palace when the rioters enter.

1790.   February 13. Religious orders are abolished.
—July 12. The Civil Constitution of the Clergy is adopted, leading to a break with the Vatican.
—July 14. She attends the Fête of the Federation.
—Birth in Paris of Mme de Staël's first son, Auguste.
—September 3. Necker resigns and leaves for Switzerland.
—October. She publishes *Sophie* and *Jane Gray*.

1791.   January 8–early May. She lives in Paris. Her salon is a meeting place for moderates. The Royalists are enraged.

—April 16. Her first known article is published, unsigned, in *The Independents*.

—June 20. The royal family flees and is caught the next day at Varennes.

—July 16. Austria's Emperor summons his fellow sovereigns to act in concert against France.

—December 6. Narbonne is named Minister of War, in part as a result of her efforts.

1792.   March. Narbonne is dismissed. Along with the Girondins, Mme de Staël contributes to the fall of the ministry.

—March 16. Assassination of Gustave III. One of the conspirators is Count Adolphe de Ribbing.

—April 20. The French Assembly declares war on Austria.

—July. Mme de Staël, Narbonne, and Malouet offer the King a plan for escape, which Queen Marie Antoinette refuses.

—August 10. Mme de Staël saves a number of friends arraigned for trial.

—August 13. The King and Queen are imprisoned in the Temple.

—August 30. The Prussians lay seige to Verdun.

—September 2–6. Massacres in the prisons of Paris.

—September 2. On the Place de Grève, as she leaves Paris for Switzerland, Mme de Staël barely escapes the mobs killing anyone seen as upper class.

—September 20. The Prussians are defeated at Valmy.

—September 21. Day one of the Year I. Royalty is abolished. The First Republic is proclaimed. The National Convention is established to rule France.

—November 20. Birth of Mme de Staël's second son, Albert.

—The end of December. After a stay at Coppet, she leaves for England.

1793.   January 17. King Louis's death is voted. He is executed on the 21st.

—January. Britain, Holland, Spain, Sardinia, and the Kingdom of Naples form the First Coalition to wage war on France. It lasts until 1795.

—January 20–May 25. Mme de Staël lives in England: sometimes in London, sometimes at Juniper Hall in Surrey with émigré friends, Narbonne, Talleyrand, Mathieu de Montmorency. She works on *The Influence of the Passions*.

—March 3. The Royalist counter-revolution starts in the Vendée (Brittany).

—March 25. England and Russia form an alliance against France.

—April 6. The Committee of Public Safety is formed.

—May 31. The Reign of Terror begins.

—June 18–September, approximately. Mme de Staël stays at Coppet, meets the exiled Swedish regicide Ribbing.

—Mid-August. She rents Trachsel Haus, an inn near Nyon, to hide French émigré friends and Ribbing.

—Early September. She publishes *Reflections on the Trial of the Queen*.

—October 16. Trial and execution of Marie Antoinette.

—October 24–31. The Revolution turns on its own: the Girondins are arrested, tried, executed. Six months later the Dantonists meet this fate.

1794. April 6. She publishes a short story, *Zulma*.

—Mid-May to the end of August. She lives in a château near Lausanne, and arranges to get several endangered friends out of France.

—May 15. Her mother dies.

—July 27–28. With the arrest and execution of Robespierre and Saint-Just, the Thermidorean reaction against the Terror sets in.

—The Treaty of London initiates a blockade of French seaports.

—September 18. Mme de Staël meets Benjamin Constant.

—At the year's end: First edition of *Reflections on Peace Addressed to M. Pitt and to the French*, printed in Switzerland by her friend, François de Pange.

1795. February. Publication of *Reflections on Peace* in Paris.

—Beginning of May. Publication of *Selected Miscellaneous Pieces* (three short stories and the *Essay on Fiction*).

—May 26. Mme de Staël and Constant come to Paris. She re-opens her salon, a gathering place for politically active moderates.

—June 3. She publishes a profession of republican faith.

—June 26. Failed invasion by émigré army landing in Brittany.

—Late July. *Reflections on Internal Peace* is printed.

—August 18. At a session of the Convention, a deputy accuses her of conspiracy. She prudently leaves Paris early in September.

—August 22. Promulgation of Constitution of the Year III.

—October 6–7. Mme de Staël decides not to offer *Reflections on Internal Peace* for sale.

—October 15. The Committee of Public Safety orders her out of France.

—October 21. Elections for the Council of the Five Hundred and the Council of the Ancients under the new constitution.

—October 31. Election for the Directory, which replaces the Convention.

—About October 20 to November. She is in France, outside of Paris.

—December 20. She leaves for Switzerland where she will spend 1796.

—December 31. Armistice between France and Austria on the Rhine.

—Winter at Coppet and Lausanne. She completes *On the Influence of the Passions.*

1796.   March 2. General Bonaparte is named to lead the Army of Italy.

—April 10. The victorious Italian Campaign begins.

—April 22. The Directory decrees Mme de Staël's arrest if she returns to France, as she learns by chance on May 17.

—May 31. France invades Germany.

—Early October. She publishes *On the Influence of the Passions.*

—November 17. Bonaparte is victorious at Arcola.

—December 18 or 19. Without authorization, she leaves Coppet for France with Constant.

1797.   January 12. Bonaparte is victorious at Rivoli.

—March 5. The French occupy Berne.

—April 7. Armistice between Bonaparte and Austria.

—April 18. Preliminary to peace with Austria, Belgium is ceded to France.

—End of May. Mme de Staël returns to Paris.

—June 8. She gives birth to her daughter, Albertine.

—Constant, Mme de Staël, and other moderates found the Constitutional Club.

—July 16. Talleyrand, whom she brought back from America, is named Foreign Minister.

—September 4 (Fructidor 18). Republican Directors stage coup against the Royalists. Mme de Staël and Constant accept it as saving the Republic but condemn the repression that follows. She saves several endangered friends and leaves Paris for a time.

—October 27. The Treaty of Campo Formio (France and Austria).

—December 6. Paris. Mme de Staël meets Bonaparte, newly returned from his conquest of Italy. She sees him occasionally in society and tries to dissuade him from invading Switzerland.

—At the end of 1797, England is France's last undefeated enemy.

1798.   Around January 7 or 8. Mme de Staël leaves Paris for Coppet.

—January 27. The French Army invades the Swiss canton of Vaud.

—February 20. The French arrest Pope Pius VI and send him to France.

—At an undetermined period of 1798, she writes but will not publish *The Present Circumstances Which Can End the Revolution.*

—April 15. The French Army takes Geneva. It is annexed to France on June 13.

—May 19. Bonaparte sails for Egypt from Toulon.

—June 11. Bonaparte takes Malta.

—July 2. Bonaparte takes Alexandria.

—July 21. Bonaparte wins at the pyramids and enters Cairo on the 24th.

—August 1. Admiral Nelson destroys the French fleet at Aboukir.

—August 19. France signs Alliance with the Helvetic Republic.

—September 9. Turkey declares war on France.

—Late October. Mme de Staël returns to Coppet; Constant leaves there for Paris early in February. She begins her treatise *On Literature.*

1799.   March 1. The Second Coalition (Britain, Austria, and Russia), which lasts until 1802, goes to war with France.

—April 16. Bonaparte defeats the Turks.

—June 18. In a coup d'état, the Councils remove the Directors' power. Jacobin offensive to regain power.

—October 9. Returning from Egypt, Bonaparte lands at St. Raphael.

—November 9 (Year VII). After four months at Coppet, Mme de Staël arrives in Paris on the night of the coup d'état of 18 Brumaire. The Directory is abolished. Bonaparte, Sieyès, and Ducos are appointed Consuls.

—December 12. Constitution of the Year VIII. Beginning of the Consulate with Bonaparte as First Consul.

—December 24. Constant is named to the Tribunate by Sieyès.

1800.   January 5. Constant's maiden speech in the Tribunate, which arouses Bonaparte's anger at him and Mme de Staël.
—March 19. Bonaparte accuses her unjustly of leaving her husband in poverty. She is obliged to clear her name.
—April 25–26. She publishes *On Literature in Its Relations with Institutions.* Violent attacks on the book in the press, at Bonaparte's direction.
—May 17 or 18. She leaves Paris for Coppet and stays until the fall. There she begins her first major novel, *Delphine,* learns German, and prepares the second edition of *On Literature* (published about mid-November).
—December 24. Failed Royalist attempt to assassinate Bonaparte.

1801.   Mme de Staël returns to Coppet and meets Sismondi, who becomes a faithful friend.
—February 9. Treaty of Lunéville between France and Austria.
—March 23. Czar Paul I is murdered. He is succeeded by his son, Alexander I.
—September 10. Bonaparte ratifies the Concordat with the Vatican.
—December–May 1802. Mme de Staël resides in Paris, obtains a legal separation from M. de Staël, and returns to Coppet until the following November.

1802.   January 17. Twenty members of the Tribunate, including Constant, are excluded.
—February. Bonaparte sends an expeditionary force to depose Toussaint l'Ouverture in Haiti, and reestablish slavery which had been abolished by the Revolution. He drops plans for a colonial empire in America.
—March 25. Treaty of Amiens between France and Britain.
—The night of May 8. Mme de Staël sets off to take her ailing husband to Coppet; he dies en route.
—August 2. Bonaparte is proclaimed First Consul for Life.
—July–August. Encouraged by Mme de Staël, Camille Jordan publishes *The True Meaning of the National Vote on the Consulate for Life.* Necker publishes his *Last Views on Politics and Finance.*
—Mid-December. She publishes *Delphine.* The three books infuriate the First Consul who judges her responsible for them.

1803.   February 10. He forbids her to stay in Paris.
—May 3. The French offer to sell the Louisiana Territory to the

United States is approved by President Thomas Jefferson.

—Spring. War with England resumes. After May 23 the English in France face arrest. Several of Mme de Staël's friends suffer this fate.

—September 16. She settles not far from Paris.

—October 3. The First Consul orders her out of France. She is informed on October 15.

—October 23. She leaves for Germany accompanied by Constant.

—October 26–November 8. Metz. Here she learns a great deal about Germany from Charles de Villiers and decides to write *Letters on Germany*.

—December 14–February 29. Weimar. She is cordially received at court, and often sees Goethe, Schiller, Wieland.

1804.   March 1. She leaves Weimar for Leipzig, and Constant leaves for Geneva.

—March 18–April 19. Berlin.

—March 21. On Bonaparte's orders, the Duke d'Enghien is kidnapped, given a sham trial, and executed.

—March 24. The new Civil Code is promulgated.

—Mme de Staël is presented at court in Berlin, frequents the city's salons, and persuades August Wilhelm Schlegel to become her children's tutor.

—April 9. Necker dies.

—April 18. She leaves Berlin thinking her father is only ill. Constant meets her in Weimar on April 22 to tell her the news and lend his support.

—May 8. Bonaparte is proclaimed Emperor Napoleon I.

—May 19. Mme de Staël reaches Coppet. She still refuses to marry Constant.

—End of September–mid-November. Coppet. She publishes the *Manuscripts of M. Necker*, preceded by her essay: *On M. Necker's Character and Private Life*. At her insistence, her friend Bonstetten publishes his *Visit to the Scene of the Last Six Books of the Aeneid* and Sismondi begins his seminal *History of the Italian Republics*.

—December 2. Napoleon crowns himself Emperor at Notre Dame.

—December 11. She leaves Lyons for Italy with Schlegel. Sismondi joins them on the way.

—December 29–January 13, 1805. Milan. Mme de Staël meets the poet Vincenzo Monti.

1805.   February 3 or 4–March 9: Rome and Naples.
—March 13–May 11. Again she settles in Rome; she frequents society, renews her friendship with diplomat-scholar Wilhelm von Humboldt.
—May 11–June 4. Florence and Venice.
—May 26. Milan. Napoleon crowns himself King of Italy.
—June 4. She returns to Milan. Leaves for Coppet on the 15th.
—June 28–November 8. Coppet. Summer: the brilliant international period begins. She again refuses to marry Constant. She begins her most influential novel, *Corinne or Italy.*
—August 9. Britain, Russia, and Austria form the Third Coalition to fight Napoleon's armies. It lasts until the French victory at Austerlitz, December 2.
—August 21. Chateaubriand comes to Coppet.
—October 21. Nelson wins at Trafalgar, crippling the French navy. England now dominates the seas.
—November 9. Mme de Staël writes a play, *Hagar in the Desert.* From December 30 to March 31, 1806, she stages plays at home at Coppet and in Geneva.

1806.   January 23. Death of William Pitt, Germaine Necker's suitor and Napoleon's strong enemy.
—April 1. Joseph Bonaparte becomes King of Naples.
—April 26 or 27. Mme de Staël arrives in France, receives a few friends but is bored with provincial life.
—October 30. Constant begins the novel *Adolphe.*
—End of November–April 20 1807. She lives near Meulan and finishes *Corinne.*
—December 28. Constant reads *Adolphe* to her and she is furious.

1807.   Early in the year, Napoleon is annoyed to learn that she is close to Paris.
—After a few clandestine days in Paris, she leaves for Coppet.
—April 30 or May 1. *Corinne* is published, meeting immediate and immense success.
—June 25. Napoleon and Czar Alexander confer on a raft in the Niemen River.
—July 7–9. The result is the Treaty of Tilsit (France, Russia, and Prussia).
—A brilliant summer at Coppet. Mme de Staël stages plays.

—Fall. She writes a play, *Geneviève de Brabant*. Schlegel publishes his *Comparison between Euripede's Phèdre and Racine's*, which is attacked in the press as anti-French.

—December 4. Mme de Staël leaves for Vienna. Arrives on the 28th.

—December 30. Napoleon grants Auguste de Staël an audience but refuses to modify his stand.

1808.   A brilliant winter in Viennese society. She sees the Prince de Ligne often and works on an anthology of his writings.

—March 31. Schlegel begins his *Course on Dramatic Literature*, which becomes a major Romantic document.

—May 28 and June 4. Twice she meets Friedrich von Gentz, a militant opponent of Napoleon, thus increasing the Emperor's vengeance. She proceeds to Dresden, Weimar, and Munich.

—June 5. Constant secretly marries Charlotte de Hardenberg.

—June 6. Napoleon proclaims his brother Joseph King of Spain.

—About July 5, Mme de Staël is back at Coppet. She begins *On Germany*.

1809.   Early February. Publication of *Letters and Thoughts of the Prince de Ligne* meets with great success.

—May 9. Charlotte de Hardenberg meets with Mme de Staël to tell her that she and Constant are married. She agrees to keep it a secret, and Mme de Staël takes Constant off to Coppet; he stays five months.

—May 13. Napoleon enters Vienna.

—June 11. Pope Pius VII excommunicates Napoleon.

—July 5–6. French victory at Wagram. The Pope is arrested.

—Mme de Staël spends the winter at Coppet.

1810.   —April. Mme de Staël moves to the château de Chaumont on the Loire. Many friends, including Constant, visit her there. The printing of *On Germany* begins.

—August 18. She leaves Chaumont for the château de Fossé.

—August 21. Bernadotte becomes Crown Prince of Sweden.

—September 23. She finishes correcting the proofs of *On Germany*.

—September 24. At Napoleon's command, Police Minister Rovigo orders that she be made to leave France within forty-eight hours and to have the manuscripts and proofs of her book turned over to him.

—October 6. She leaves for Coppet. Her book is pounded into pulp on the 14th and 15th.

—Early November. She settles in Geneva for the winter, and meets John Rocca.

1811.   February 27. Capelle replaces Barante as Prefect of Léman. Official malevolence intensifies, and at Schlegel's urging, she considers escape.

—She begins *Ten Years of Exile,* writes the play *Sappho* and the essay *Reflections on Suicide,* gathers material for an epic on *Richard the Lionhearted.*

—May. Before a Protestant pastor, Mme de Staël and John Rocca make a pledge of marriage.

—August. Visit to Valsainte with Montmorency. When they return to Coppet, Montmorency receives an order exiling him from Paris.

—September. Mme Récamier comes to Coppet. She too is immediately exiled.

1812.   April 7. Coppet: Louis-Alphonse Rocca, son of Mme de Staël and John Rocca, is born in secret.

—May 23. She escapes from Coppet and leaves for England by way of Vienna, Saint Petersburg, and Stockholm. (See itinerary below for details.)

—June 24. Napoleon leads the Grand Army across the Niemen to invade Russia.

—July 14. Mme de Staël crosses the Russian frontier at Brody.

—September 14. Napoleon enters Moscow, which Mme de Staël had left on August 7 for Saint Petersburg.

—September 24–June 1813. Stockholm: She resumes work on *Ten Years of Exile* and begins *Considerations on the French Revolution.*

—October 19. Napoleon evacuates Moscow and the retreat begins.

—December 5. He leaves the Grand Army and reaches Paris on the 18th.

1813.   January. Mme de Staël publishes *Reflections on Suicide.*

—May 4. Napoleon defeats Russia and Prussia at Lützen. In the next five months his armies win three battles and the Allies win eight.

—June 18. With Auguste, who has joined them in Stockholm, she and Albertine leave for London.

—July 12. Albert de Staël, now a Swedish Army officer, is killed in a duel.

—*On Germany* is published in French in London. In 1813 and 1814, she edits or re-edits several other works.

—She plays an increasingly important role in the fight against Napoleon.

—October 7. Wellington invades France.

1814.   March 31. The Allies enter Paris.

—April 6. Napoleon abdicates.

—May 12. Mme de Staël returns to Paris, where she receives sovereigns, ministers, and generals. When Bernadotte's candidacy fails, she reluctantly rallies to the Bourbons.

1815.   February 26. Napoleon escapes from Elba and three days later lands near Cannes with a small army.

—March 10. At the news, Mme de Staël leaves Paris for Coppet. She criticizes Constant's support of Napoleon but approves of the Additional Act, promulgated on April 20, which he drafted. (It guaranteed freedom of religion and the press, and broadened the electorate.)

—March 20. Napoleon enters Paris.

—June 18. Napoleon is defeated at Waterloo, abdicates on the 22nd, and will be sent to exile on Saint Helena.

—July 7. The Allies re-enter Paris.

—September. The Royal Treasury reimburses the two million francs her father had lent France in the last days of the Old Regime. Albertine is engaged to Victor, Duke de Broglie. They all leave for Italy with Schlegel and Rocca.

1816.   January. In Milan she publishes *The Spirit of Translations*. She spends the winter in Pisa, caring for Rocca who is gravely ill.

—Albertine de Staël marries Victor de Broglie.

—October 10. Mme de Staël secretly marries Rocca. Plans a trip to the Middle East.

—October 16. They leave for Paris.

1817.   January. Constant begins a great journalistic career at the *Mercure de France*.

—February 21. Mme de Staël falls and is paralyzed.

—July 14. She dies and is buried at Coppet. When her will is opened, steps are taken to recognize Alphonse Rocca officially. The family will watch over him as one of their own.

1818.   January 30. John Rocca dies. Auguste de Staël publishes *Considerations on the French Revolution.*

1821.   May 5. Napoleon dies on Saint Helena.
—Auguste publishes *Ten Years of Exile* and the *Complete Works.*

1827.   Death of Auguste de Staël

1838.   Death of Albertine de Broglie.

CHRONOLOGY OF THE GREAT JOURNEY OF 1812

(The route is marked on the map provided in this volume.)

May 23.   Mme de Staël leaves Coppet with her daughter, her agent Uginet, and his wife, who will be with her throughout the journey. Her son Auguste will go with them as far as Berne. (Then he returns to Coppet to manage the family affairs.) Rocca will rejoin them at Salzburg, and her son Albert will leave on the 27th and meet them in Vienna.

May 25.   They arrive at Zurich with Schlegel who has joined the group.

May 28.   They enter Bavaria by way of Bregenz.

May 30.   They leave Innsbruck for Munich, which they reach on the 31st.

June 2.   Salzburg.

June 3.   Linz.

June 6.   They arrive in Vienna. Steps taken to get Russian passports.

June 22.   Mme de Staël leaves with her children and Rocca, leaving Schlegel and Uginet to continue their efforts to get passports.

June 24–25.   The Grand Army crosses the Niemen.

June 25 or 26.   They arrive in Brünn (Brno).

July 1.	Mme de Staël leaves for Galicia with her daughter and son. Rocca, forced by the police to go by way of Silesia, rejoins them only at Brody.
July 2.	Olmütz (Olomouc).
July 3.	They enter Poland.
July 4.	Wadowice.
July 8.	They arrive at the Lubomirski's château in Lańcut.
July 10.	Lemberg (Leopol).
July 14.	Mme de Staël enters Russian territory at Brody.
July 21.	The travelers pass through Kiev and leave from there for Koursk, Orel, and Toula.
August 2.	They arrive in Moscow. They visit the city.
August 7.	They leave for Novgorod.
August 13.	They reach Saint Petersburg. Mme de Staël devotes herself to political and social activity; she begins to explore the city and its environs.
August 17.	She is presented to Emperor Alexander, Empress Elizabeth, and the Dowager Empress the day the Battle of Smolensk begins. The French take the city the next day.
September 7.	She leaves Saint Petersburg for Sweden with her family.
September 15.	In Åbo (Turku), they hear that Napoleon has won the Battle of Borodino.
September 24.	After crossing Finland and the Gulf of Bothnia, they land in Stockholm; when they arrive, they hear that Moscow has fallen.

Ten Years *of* Exile

Part One

1797–1804

It is not to draw public attention to myself that I have set out to relate the circumstances of ten years of exile. The misfortunes I have endured, however bitter, count for so little amid the public disasters we confront that it would be shameful to speak of oneself if the events that concern us were not connected to the great cause of endangered humanity. Emperor Napoleon, whose character is fully revealed in everything he does, has persecuted me with meticulous care and inflexible asperity at an ever-increasing pace. And through my relations with him, I came to know what he was long before Europe had found the key to the enigma and, failing to guess what it meant, let herself be devoured by the sphinx.

People raised in France in the years before the Revolution are necessarily more attached to liberty than those whose childhood was spent under the bloody reign of the Terror. The war in America, the progress of enlightenment, the always admirable example of England's government had disposed minds to regard representation on a national scale as necessary to the constitution of any monarchy or republic. And I think I may state that in my generation, the one that came of age with France's Revolution, there are very few young men or women who, at the time, were not filled with the hope the Estates General led France to envisage. My father, bound by loyalty to the King of France, whose minister he was, nonetheless nurtured in his soul the political principles he believed as favorable to the enduring power of a virtuous monarch as to the happiness of an enlightened nation.

It is not to excuse my enthusiasm for liberty that I explain the private circumstances that inevitably made it even dearer to me; I believe one should take pride in that enthusiasm rather than make excuses for it; my intention was rather to make known at the outset that Emperor Napoleon's chief complaint against me is the love and respect for true liberty that have always been deeply my own. These feelings were handed down to me as a legacy from the moment I could reflect on the noble thoughts they derive from, and on the fine deeds they inspire. The cruel scenes that dishonored the French Revolution could not damage the cult of liberty, it seems to me, since they were simply acts of popular tyranny.[1] At most, one might be discouraged for France, but if this country's misfortune was the inability to take possession of the noblest of treasures, that is no reason to proscribe it from the earth. When the sun disappears from the horizon of northern countries, their inhabitants do not curse its rays for still shining on other countries more favored by the sky.

I have no intention of going into the events preceding Bonaparte's arrival on the scene. If I write my father's life as I have planned,[2] I shall tell what I saw in those first days of the Revolution whose influence changed the fate of the world. I mean to recount here only the part of that vast picture concerning me. But as I glance at the whole picture from so limited a perspective, I feel sure that I myself will often disappear into the background as I tell my own story.

When General Bonaparte won renown through the Italian Campaigns, I felt the strongest enthusiasm for him. Republican institutions were losing all dignity in France through the means employed to maintain them.[3] One felt a kind of remorse for the most honorable opinions when the words that designated them were found in the most absurd and cruel decrees. It was disturbing to both mind and soul when, in the name of liberty, bloodthirsty men made victims of the worthiest citizens. The new institutions could still rightfully claim the interest of thinking people, but those responsible for making the institutions work completely degraded their essence. On the other hand, those who rightly opposed the revolutionaries gave no credit to the principles on which national representation is based. It was impossible to be wholly for any party—either with the persecutors or even with the persecuted—and man's finest faculty, admiration, did not know where to turn. Military glory readily inspires that sentiment.[4] Bonaparte's proclamations from Italy were designed to inspire confidence in him. They were governed by a tone of noble moderation that stood in contrast to the revolutionary harshness of France's civilian leaders. In those days, the warrior spoke like a judge, while the judges used the language of military violence. Bonaparte had not carried out the barbaric laws against the émigrés. He was said to be passionately in love with his wife, whose character is so gentle and kind. In a word, no one was ever so mistaken about a man as I was about Bonaparte, for I thought him generous and sensitive.

That belief had so filled me with admiration that, when I first saw him, emotion almost kept me from speaking to him or answering him.[5] He'd just come from Italy, renowned for the most brilliant, the most difficult military triumphs he had yet achieved. Far from enjoying supreme power at the time, he was even threatened with persecution. The homage I paid him had a disinterested and genuine quality that he has since been unable to earn or to obtain. From the very first moment, he inspired the deepest sense of fear that any human being has ever made me feel. I had seen ferocious men and estimable men. Bonaparte's effect on me had nothing in common with my reactions to them. I quickly realized that his character could not be defined by the words we customarily use. He was neither good nor violent, neither cruel nor mild in the way of humankind, rather he was a creature unlike any other, unable to feel or inspire sympathy in anyone. And it is precisely because he is not like a creature of our species that he inspires everyone with a sort of dread that in weak souls changes to submission. He hates no more than he loves, since for him there is only himself, and men act on his soul only as facts or as objects, never as his fellows. His strength lies in an imperturbable egoism that neither pity, nor charm, nor religion, nor morality can for an instant divert from its course. It may be said that he is the world's great celibate.[6] No one of his nature exists. If he is first in the art of the calculated act, he is last in the sphere of feelings. He is a clever chess player whose opponent, the human race, he proposes to checkmate.

The antipathy I felt for him heightened each time that I saw him. In vain my past admiration struggled against my present reaction, in vain I was struck by the superior mind Bonaparte revealed each time he spoke on a serious subject: I felt something like a sharp, cold sword in his soul that would chill even as it wounded. I sensed in his mind an irony for everything good and beautiful that his own glory did not escape, for he dared to scorn the nation whose suffrage he wanted, and no spark of enthusiasm—even for his own triumphs—mixed with his need to astonish others. Emperor Napoleon is as much a system as an individual, and in the following account it will be seen that his life has demonstrated all the effects of godlessness on the human heart.

I met Bonaparte in the interval between his return from Italy and his departure for Egypt. His face was less unpleasant then than it is now—he was thin and pale at least, and one could think that his own ambition was devouring him, whereas for the last few years he has seemed to fatten on the unhappiness he causes. But his bearing has always been common, his gaiety vulgar, his courtesy awkward when shown at all, his manner coarse and rough, particularly with women.[7] You might have thought that Providence, to punish the French for misusing their splendid qualities, was subjecting the nation most remarkable for its grace and sense of chivalry to the man most alien to that charm and that quality. During Bonaparte's stay in Paris in the winter of 1797–1798, before he went to Egypt, I met him several times in various circles and the discomfort he had made me feel was not dispelled. One day, at a party,[8] I found myself beside him by chance without realizing it, and I drew back, although at the time he was as civil to me as he judged appropriate to his situation. I drew back in an instinctive terror that I was unaware of but that was all the more justified.

In society he would tell stories from his military career with a pungent turn of phrase that, at times, was even a bit reminiscent of the gift Italians show. But overall, his manners were stiff but not shy, unpolished but not good-natured. He was already possessed of a grand vocation for the role of prince, and the questions he addressed to those presented to him resembled the ones circulating in all courts where the master thinks he does you honor, not by what he says, but simply by talking to you at all, and he surely asked trivial questions out of calculated arrogance.

One day I dined with him at M. de Talleyrand's. He took a seat beside me at table and I found myself between him and Abbé Sieyès.[9] A curious position, particularly if the future had been revealed to me. I examined General Bonaparte's countenance closely. But each time he caught my observant gaze, he skillfully cleared his eyes of expression and his whole face became impassive, except for a vague smile set on his lips as a precaution to divert notice from any genuine signs of his thinking. Throughout dinner Abbé Sieyès conversed as a man of superior mind. General Bonaparte was constantly on his guard. He asked this one if he was married, that one if he was off to the country, continually repeating "Citizen Garat," "Citizen Talleyrand," with an almost ridiculous affectation, for in society people hardly kept up that usage.[10]

Abbé Sieyès spoke of my father with heartfelt respect. He called him a man who combined to the highest degree the calculation of a great financier and the splendid imagination of a poet. The praise was flattering because it was precise and accurate. Bonaparte, too, said a few kind words about my father, but as a man interested only in people he can make use of. In general, he wanted to be charming in those days, but one would have thought he was the prophet Balaam in reverse, cursing when he meant to bless; and his ascendancy over other men came rather from the effect of his sharpness of temper than from the care he thought he was taking to flatter them. Also, a sorry fact was already contributing to his power over other men: their conviction that nothing could move him but their potential usefulness to him. What matters to him is neither eloquence, nor wit, nor charm, nor affection. For him, individuals are revenue or expenditure; their moral qualities have no effect on his soul, and I believe that there has never ever been a head of government in France who has said so many offensive things to those around him.

He gave signs of this behavior while still a general. After dinner he approached a woman well known in France for her beauty, her wit, and her ardent opinions. He stopped right in front of her like a German prince.

"Madame," he said, "I don't like women meddling in politics."

"You are right, General," she answered, "but in a country where women's heads are cut off, they naturally want to know why."[11]

He made no answer to that retort because it was witty. I have thought ever since that if those around him had managed to resist what he said with trenchant replies, he would have spoken to them with greater tact. But for that matter, he degraded them in so many other respects that they could well endure one affront more. Since that time, people have quoted many of the rough and humiliating remarks he allowed himself with men and especially with women, telling this one that she was old, asking that one if she was good, and other sweet nothings of the sort. This behavior is deliberate, like everything with respect to men. He has rightly judged that every individual who tolerates a flagrant insult is dominated by the person to whom that advantage has been allowed, and consequently, Bonaparte sets out to assume that position with respect to others. He takes calculated risks on the baseness of human nature, and it must be admitted that up to now his investments have not suffered. There is something less voluntary in his relations with women, but his feeling for them is completely opposite to the one they ordinarily inspire; he does not like these beings who are not so readily subject to the fear or the hope at his disposal; there is something disinterested in their existence that displeases him. In some respects they are like the clerical orders that answer to heaven alone. We might have seen Napoleon try to banish women from the earth if he had not needed their children for soldiers. It is so true that he regards them mainly in this light that several times he has been heard to repeat coarsely to young women: "Make soldiers for me," as if the lion deep in his lair asked ewes to give birth to little ones for him to devour.

As General Bonaparte did not find me at home when he came by to visit, I went to see him at his wife's apartments. He invited me into his study and I tried to speak on behalf of Switzerland, then under threat of invasion by French troops. I was unaware that he had incited the invasion himself to find in Berne's modest treasury the funds for a distant expedition,[12] and I was persuaded that if I portrayed Switzerland's happiness for Bonaparte, I might be useful to the country where my father had taken refuge. The call for the independence of the Vaud region, which did not enjoy the privileges of the sovereign cantons, was an attempt to arouse Switzerland, and a great stir was made over a few acts of the Berne government, which had abused its power less in a hundred years than French troops would do in a single week.

General Bonaparte responded to my portrayal of the Vaud's prosperity by saying that it was subject to the canton of Berne, that it had no political rights, and that men could no longer exist without those rights. I tempered this republican ardor as best I could by pointing out that the inhabitants of the Vaud were perfectly free and enjoyed full civil rights, that if they were refused the possibility of joining in the government, this advantage was of little value in a state where the exercise of political authority brought neither money nor prerogatives and could only be considered a sacrifice to the nation.

"Pride and imagination," he went on, "make us hold dear the right to participate in governing our country, and it is unjust to exclude any group whatever of its citizens."

I admitted to General Bonaparte that theoretically he was right, and I could have used the language that has so displeased him since that time— ideology, liberal ideas, and so forth—to make my point. But confining myself to the simple truth, I contrasted the abstract good he lauded with the real evils that would fall upon the most upright country on the Continent.

That conversation ended with my reply, and he began to tell me about his plans for retirement, his weariness with life. In fact I got a better idea of how pleasing he could be when he assumed a certain affability, the most dangerous of all his ruses. He has made much use of it since then, and has often been seen telling the most perfidious lies with the guilelessness of the head of a family describing his business to his children. Even though he had seemed pleasanter to me in our conversation, each time I saw him afterward I felt more constrained in his presence. He knows how to torture good and bad people alike, and events have proved that the stifling air he brings to bear on everything around him has been one of the primary causes of his ascendancy over the French. It was precisely because he was a foreigner that he won such power over them. A French temperament could not have dominated the French nation. Richelieu, who spent half his life in Italy, had studied the politics and adroitness of the Italians. For Mazarin they were an inborn talent. Catherine de Medicis was long able to retain the wretched power of tearing France apart, and it may be said that of the kings who have exercised the most despotic authority, most had foreign blood in their veins through their mothers.[13] This French nation, endowed with such brilliant qualities, apparently did not receive from heaven the necessary dignity and firmness to be governed only by laws enacted with her consent.

I attended the solemn reception the directors accorded General Bonaparte in the Luxembourg. There was no room large enough for the ceremony inside the palace itself; therefore the courtyard was spread with sand, and over two thousand personages attended this presentation, out-of-doors, in the month of December. The directors were dressed in Roman togas. General Bonaparte arrived in a very simple uniform, followed by his aides-de-camp, who were a foot taller than he but already stood at the respectful distance they have so carefully maintained ever since.

General Bonaparte looked to the right and to the left at the multitude planted even on the rooftops to watch him pass by. His face expressed a sort of casual curiosity about all those human shapes he planned to bring into subjection as soon as he had the power to do so. It was easy to see as well that the supremacy of the five men who made up the Directory seemed ridiculous to him at the very least, and that he was reciting his speech before them with a studied nonchalance. That speech, however, contained notable remarks, among them one foretelling the era of representative government in Europe. But for Bonaparte, opinions were already nothing but means to an end. His Republican proclamations had not prevented his ceding an ancient republic, Venice, to Austria.[14] He'd given very wise advice to Genoa on protecting itself from demagogy,[15] and he was fomenting the overthrow of Switzerland under the pretext that several of its governments were aristocratic. He is a man who actually believes that nothing but self-interest counts for anyone, and who considers that everything said about morality and sincerity in this world is like the complimentary closing of a letter that obliges no one to obey those whose humble servant he calls himself. M. de Talleyrand replied with a very flattering speech in which he spoke to him of his taste for reading Ossian.[16] He was in fact said to like the poet, but I still do not believe that either the heart's reveries or the clouds can be enough for such a man.

Toward the end of the year 1797, the time of General Bonaparte's welcome to Paris, people were talking only about the invasion of England.

One of the most prominent deputies had said that if it were not under-taken, the French government would be the laughingstock of Europe. In one of the fêtes for the Directory on the Champ de Mars,[17] French troops were portrayed attacking and taking an English ship. I remarked that the French had only taken these ships on land. The Directory forgave my little joke, for it must be said in all fairness that it was rather open-minded de-spite the revolutionary principles that led it astray. It takes a tyrant, and an irascible tyrant like Napoleon, to punish the slightest word as though it were a crime. Thus Caracalla, writes Gibbon, had a woman's head cut off for "an unseasonable witticism."

General Bonaparte was named to lead the invasion of England by the di-rectors. He proceeded to the coast of France and, recognizing the impossi-bility of the invasion,[18] returned with several different projects in mind. His strong preference at the time was the resumption of war with Austria. With this in mind, he had the Directory instruct General Bernadotte, then ambas-sador to Vienna, to arrange a break between France and Austria, either be-cause he wanted to give himself the honors of peace and war by turn, or be-cause he wanted to harm General Bernadotte in whom he sensed the rival who would one day fly the flag of generous sentiments against the banner of crime. In his uncertainty, Bonaparte went every evening to the home of Barras, where I sometimes met him, and he sought to assume a familiar or dignified bearing in turn, but failed to get the right tone for either, since he could only be natural in tyranny.[19]

One day, alone with Barras and seated beside him, he spoke about his in-fluence over the peoples of Italy.

"They wanted to make me Duke of Milan or King of Italy," he said, "but I'm not thinking anything of the sort."

"You're right," Barras answered, "for tomorrow, if the Directory wanted you led to the Temple, there wouldn't be four people against it."

At those words, Bonaparte sprang from his chair to the fireplace, and the next day informed the Directory that he'd decided on the Egyptian cam-paign.[20] Popular feeling in fact remained too strong in France to allow reac-tion in the opposite direction. The Directory still held influence over minds; people thought it powerful, and in France when people hold this view, it becomes reality.

A few months earlier, Bonaparte had sent General Augereau of the Army of Italy to lend support on the fatal day when the Directory crushed na-tional representation,[21] and paradoxically, he found a way to appear as the hope of the party of upright men at the very time he was helping to drive them out of the Legislative Body. But people already sensed that he did nothing without calculation, and the Royalist party preferred calculating men to genuine Republicans who were men with a firm doctrine.

One evening before Bonaparte arrived, I met General Augereau at Barras's home. He was considered a patriotic general—that is, opposed to the return of the Old Regime—for he'd hardly reflected on political ideas and saw the sword as the only answer in all matters.

"Is it true, as rumor has it," I asked, "that General Bonaparte is thinking of having himself made king?"

"Good God, no!" he replied. "That young man is too well-bred for such a thing."

I laughed heartily at his response, which in fact characterized the times we lived in particularly well. Such abuse had been heaped on royalty that good people in the patriotic party truly believed it dishonest to think that way. People at all capable of reflection easily discerned Bonaparte's ambitious plans already. For that reason above all he did well to leave for Egypt, since those plans could not be realized at the time, and excited suspicions that might have committed the Directory to undermine his reputation. He maintained that reputation in the Orient. The fighting at the Pyramids, in the deserts of Arabia—all those names from antiquity—kept the imagination alert to Bonaparte's fate.

I returned to Coppet in the early days of January 1798 to be with my father when the French were considering the invasion of Switzerland. He was on the list of émigrés, and there was still a decree imposing the death sentence on any émigré found in territory occupied by French troops. My father, however, insisted on remaining in his refuge, close to my mother's ashes; so we found ourselves, he and I, completely alone with our servants and my young children in the vast château at Coppet. The French officers on the Vaud side, headed by General Suchet, were on good terms with my father by natural impulse and by order of the Directory. The moment the French entered Switzerland, Geneva lost her independence, and the government of France began by destroying a city which owed to that independence all her historical brilliance.[22] The soldiers of the French Republic entered the country of William Tell bearing their abstract liberty and their concrete tyranny even into the mountains where simple men preserved—and preserve—intact the treasure of their virtues and their laws.

A curious destiny for the Revolution in France! Throughout continental Europe it has destroyed the very principles of liberty on which it claimed to be founded. So it is that every unbridled enterprise must perish, that every enterprise in which man does not invoke God in any way will inevitably redound upon him, and that he who recognizes no barrier will never reach his goal.

Throughout Switzerland there was talk of the resistance that the canton of Berne and the democratic cantons planned to offer the French troops. For the first time I made vows to heaven against the French, and I no longer knew on what altars I might dedicate the most religious of all earthly sentiments, love for one's native land. The small cantons sent their contingents to Berne; those devout soldiers knelt in front of the church when they came to the public square. They had no fear of the approaching French because, they said, "there are four hundred of us, and if that isn't enough, we're ready to send as many more to the aid of our country." Who would not be moved by that great confidence in such slender means? Ah, the days of the three hundred Spartans were over![23] Numbers were all-powerful, and the greater the numbers, the less public opinion counts, for men become sheep the moment they become so numerous that they are forced to give unlimited authority to a handful of leaders.[24]

On the day of the first battle between the Swiss and the French, although Coppet was thirty leagues from Berne, we heard the cannon fire resounding from afar, echoing from the mountains in the silence of the night. To discern the deadly noise more clearly, we hardly dared breathe, and though all the probabilities favored the French, the beauty of nature and the goodness of the inhabitants surrounding us gave hope for a liberating miracle. That anticipation was not rewarded. The Swiss were defeated in a pitched battle. The magistrate, M. de Steiger, old and blind, had himself led close to a battery of cannons in the hope of dying.

The French directed their efforts against the small cantons. But they defended themselves for a long time in the mountains, and it was never possible to bring the small cantons into subjection to the Republic one and indivisible—the pretext for tyranny in those days, as freedom of the seas is its pretext now.[25] Those poor inhabitants of primitive Switzerland wanted nothing to do with the hypocritical gift sent to them by cannon fire. Women and children joined in the resistance. Priests were massacred in their sanctuaries.[26] But since in that confined space there was a strong national will, it was enough to arrest the progress of the French and oblige them to come to terms with the only men certain of never being vanquished: those of unswerving resolve.

What mixed sentiments we felt, my father and I, during those days of such painful anxiety! The least of the evils threatening us was the loss of our entire fortune. A large part of our income came from feudal rights,[27] and confiscation threatened any man entered in whatever way on the list of émigrés. My father decided to ask the Directory to strike his name from that list. His request was drawn up with the force of logic and the dignity of character that, I venture to say, distinguish everything he has written. He pointed out that he had been born a foreigner, that the state he came from had named him its minister to Paris, that chosen three times by Louis XVI to direct his finances, he had left France for his native country only when a formal decree of the Constituent Assembly authorized him to do so. His case was so clear that the moment I delivered my father's memorandum to the Directory on my return to Paris, his name was struck from the list by unanimous vote. Barras, Treilhard, and Merlin, directors at the time, contributed effectively to the successful outcome.[28] But people had not come to believe, as they do today, that there is no law but Emperor Napoleon's decrees. But even these decrees mean nothing if circumstances make it desirable to violate them. At times, several Councillors of State have in fact tried to oppose the Emperor with his own decisions in contentious or administrative matters, and he was as angry at his own past wishes as at those of another.

At this juncture, I shall relate what happened in 1798 with respect to my father's funds, that is, the two million he entrusted to the Public Treasury, and no slightest part of which we have been able to obtain to this day.[29] As Minister of Finance, my father was entirely free to carry off his own fortune from the Royal Treasury when he left his position; he did not want to withdraw it, however, in that time of crisis. He was the one minister, from the beginning of the French monarchy on, who for seven years constantly refused the hundred thousand écus due to the Minister of Finance. No man was more justified in reclaiming at least what belonged to him, when he had not only served the state without salary, but devoted his capital to the display required by the office of France's Prime Minister. Short supplies threatened Paris with the cruelest famine. Messrs Hope of Amsterdam[30] would send wheat to France only on my father's personal guarantee. My father renewed that guarantee, and it locked up his two million at the very moment a *lettre de cachet* exiled him from France. Never has money called to mind a greater number of honorable circumstances than that two million, and for twenty years, under France's various governments, finance administrators have without fail termed these funds the most sacred of debts. The Directory recognized it as such, but at first offered to pay my father in national assets, which meant that he might receive properties belonging to émigrés, and my father did not want those at any price. He agreed rather to defer full payment of what was owed him until peace came. We shall see by what follows how Emperor Napoleon judged it proper to elude every form of justice respecting this debt. The fatal day of 1797,[31] when the Directory admitted soldiers within the precincts of the Legislative Body, suppressed all moderation in the application of France's civil law. The power of public opinion disappeared entirely in the face of military force, and what good faith there had been in the Republican party gave way to the calculations of ambition. People sensed that the vault was about to come crashing down, and each one sought shelter for himself.

War broke out anew; it did not go well at first. In 1799, the Russians won great victories in Italy. A revolution inside the Directory, as in a harem, brought in new men to replace those introduced by another faction.[32] Only one among them deserves mention: Sieyès. The others were there only to obey the men who had made them directors. Sieyès is a man of superior mind, and he has transcendent views on every subject; but his character is an impenetrable barrier to any benefits that might be drawn from his mind. Two serious flaws, a quick temper and fear, keep him from acting upon weak men and subject him to the strong. The moment he is not understood he gets angry, disgusted; and far from blaming himself, he blames others, a serious fault in political matters; it is not enough to be right, you must persuade the people you need that you are right. You must know how to adapt to the faculties of the mediocre people you are addressing. Virtue resides in intentions but is to be judged only by success. A certain degree of superiority is not understood by the multitude, but one degree further yields the secret of all the ways to make yourself heard. Fear, a natural result of the sedentary life Sieyès led until he was forty, posed yet another obstacle to his talent for conducting political affairs: it gave him impulses to despotism and timid resolve in turn, a deadly combination for the conduct of affairs.

Sieyès, even as he detested military government, sought a general's support, imagining quite wrongly that he could use it as a tool. From the start of the Revolution, Sieyès had plans for a constitution to which he attached great importance. He was convinced that he would find a general to back him in his attempt to establish it. Moreau, whose character is as moral as his genius is military, had neither talent nor taste for political factions.[33] Pichegru had lost the confidence of liberty's friends by embracing the Royalist party. Heading the Republican army, General Bernadotte, through superiority of mind and impassioned determination of soul, should have won Sieyès's confidence. But Sieyès could not hope to bring such a man under subjection.

And so the State floated at random without a hand firm enough to save it. During that crisis the Jacobins tried to assert their authority. The allied coalition boasted of its victories over the French armies. Bonaparte's two brothers, Joseph and Lucien, both deputies in the Council of Five Hundred and both highly intelligent, although to different degrees, wrote to their brother that the state of affairs in France was such that, were he present, he could hope to win the greatest influence.[34]

General Bonaparte was then in Egypt, calling himself General Bonaparte, Member of the Institute, to seduce French Republicans, and beginning his proclamations with a profession of Moslem faith to fool the Arabs. One day, he received newspapers and letters from France and shut himself in to read them. Emerging from his study, he told those he trusted that he needed to return to France.[35]

But in the interval between the dates of the news he received and his arrival, the face of matters in France had changed completely. Public opinion rejected the Jacobin bid.[36] Such a scourge can subjugate only a nation that has never known its like. To see it twice in the same country is completely impossible. The French armies came back to life as foreigners approached their territory. Massena successfully defended Switzerland. Moreau maintained the French position in Italy. The English raiding party in Holland was forced back to sea. Finally, General Bernadotte, whose conduct has since proved his administrative skills equal to his military genius, managed to reorganize the army in the space of two months as Minister of War; that very benefit offended the weak directors whose minister he was, and they deprived themselves of their one support by sending him away.[37] In the long run, such a man could truly show who he was only by holding the highest rank.

And so, when General Bonaparte landed in Fréjus,[38] his help was no longer needed, and men were better able to resist him. All danger was past, but it was recent, and both foreigners and the French themselves confused events that took place at very close intervals. At the time it was thought that Bonaparte had saved the ship of state, although he'd taken command only when it was afloat once more. Along with his staff, he disregarded the law enacted to protect Europe through quarantine of those arriving from the Levant.[39] Had the Directory then been at the height of its power, it would have had General Bonaparte arrested for such a violation and for leaving his army.

When he left for Egypt, Director Reubell had said on one occasion that they must accept Bonaparte's resignation if offered, because the Republic would never lack for a successful general to head its armies.[40] And however Reubell acted, we must give credit to a remark that so honors the French nation, for what would be the quality of a nation of twenty-four million inhabitants if it needed a man who deemed, not the law, but his own will as supreme?

In any event, France was so ill-governed when Napoleon arrived that she looked to anyone at all to be her master. And so this Caesar, far from having Pompey to fight, met as his Cato and Crassus a poor wretch of a local journalist, Gohier, a drunken soldier, General Moulin. Bonaparte himself has said that he found the crown of France lying on the ground and picked it up. Never has a more apt expression been used, since for six months before he arrived they had been offering power to anyone willing to take it. Therefore we must add to Bonaparte's good luck and subtract from his reputation the circumstances that made him France's leader.

I was with my father at Coppet when I learned that, on his way from Egypt, General Bonaparte had passed through Lyons, where he was greeted wildly.[41] The news made a painful impression that could lead me to believe in the instinctive sense of the future—the second sight the Scots speak of that may be nothing more than the illumination of feeling, independent of rational thought.[42] There should have been every reason to rejoice in Bonaparte's arrival. I enjoyed his brothers' company greatly. Most of the people who would be around him were more or less of my world. But I sensed the tyranny in Bonaparte's character, a tyranny that was to be proportionate to the events of every kind that had preceded it.

I left to spend the winter in Paris and had the uncommon luck to arrive on the eighteenth of Brumaire, the ninth of November, the day Bonaparte's political career began.[43] As I was changing horses a few leagues from Paris, I was told that Director Barras, accompanied by gendarmes, had just passed by on his way back to his estate at Grosbois.[44] The postilions were telling the news of the day, and this way of hearing it increased its power over the imagination. This was the first time since the Revolution that I had heard a proper name on every tongue. Until then, they would say the Constituent Assembly did such and such, the King, the people, the Convention. Now there was talk only about the man who would take the place of them all and reduce the human race to anonymity, either by seizing a great deal of fame for himself, or by keeping everyone else on earth from acquiring any.

The very evening I reached Paris, I learned that General Bonaparte had spent the five weeks since his return preparing people's minds for the revolution that had just broken out. Each party in turn had offered itself to him, and to each he had given reason for hope. He told the Jacobins he would protect them from the return of the monarchy. He let the Monarchists believe he would restore the Bourbons. Sieyès was told that the constitution he'd been dreaming of since the Revolution began would finally see the light of day. He had charmed the public not attached to a party with hopes of repose, order, and above all, peace. One day in a salon he was told of a woman in society whose papers had been seized under orders from the Directory.[45] He protested the absurd atrocity of tormenting women—he who, for no reason, has condemned so many of them to endless exile. He talked interminably of the need to restore peace, he who has brought the world ever-recurring war. There was, in fact, something indefinably mawkish and hypocritical in his manner that was like the tiger's velvet paw. It was natural for the nation to fall into the trap.

The Constitution, good or bad but still in place, had been destroyed two years earlier when armed force was called in to support it.[46] Futile attempts to institute liberty had led to no reasonable outcome in a nation that scorns justice as foolishness, and deems immorality proof of a profound mind. Bonaparte had no man to conquer on the way to power. He had only one to fear: General Bernadotte. But the Directory, more jealous still of its defenders than of its adversaries if that is possible, had refused to call for his help. General Bonaparte shrewdly confided to him the secret of the revolution he planned, requesting his word of honor, as a brother-in-arms, not to betray him. General Bernadotte, who alone preserved the spirit of chivalry in an age when everything seemed to exclude it, replied that, as a private person, he would not reveal this secret entrusted to his honor, but that should the government name him commander of any military unit whatever, he would fight the man who attempted to overthrow the existing order of things. The Directory drew up the order recalling General Bernadotte to the Ministry of War. But Bonaparte's good fortune carried the day. He frightened Barras, who resigned rather than sign Bernadotte's nomination, and perhaps destiny reserved this commanding adversary for a time when the human race had earned its mercy through suffering.[47]

Lucien and Joseph gave their brother powerful support. They presented him to each party as a conquest they must make lest the other seize hold of it. They frightened the philosopher Sieyès with the revolutionary Barras, Barras with Bonaparte's popularity in the armies. His military glory was in fact the nation's glory and, in the absence of any personal consideration or any well-grounded institution, only the fame won by force stood out amid the fatal equality that derived from the complete ruin of all rather than the well-balanced strength of each. The revolution was brought on through an article of the Constitution allowing the Council of Ancients to move the Legislative Body to a city other than Paris;[48] and on that occasion I observed that, for every institution to which France's Revolution gave birth, there was the desire to legitimize the means of the change, as if revolutions could be bound by theory. Things human subsist as long as men respect them. When this respect is gone, everything serves as a pretext or motive to overturn them, and once decrees become nothing more than paper barriers, public opinion becomes indifferent to them and they no longer guide such movements. The Council of Ancients ordered the Legislative Body, that is, itself, and the Council of Five Hundred to remove to Saint Cloud on the next day, 19 Brumaire.[49]

On the evening of the eighteenth, when I reached Paris, the whole city was feverishly awaiting the great day that was to come, and without a doubt the majority hoped that General Bonaparte would have the upper hand. My own feelings, I admit, were more mixed than any I had yet felt during the Revolution. Once the battle was joined, if Bonaparte were driven off, the Jacobins would immediately be strong enough to compel all my friends, and myself foremost, to run from France. But I felt, as if the events that followed had been revealed to me, that the most fearful and, at the same time, the most degrading tyranny was about to weigh on France.

One of my friends was present at the Assembly of the Five Hundred at Saint Cloud.[50] He sent me couriers hourly. Once, he sent word that he thought the Jacobins would win. I sent for money and had my carriage prepared to set off again, taking with me what I held most dear. An hour later, the same friend sent word that General Bonaparte had the upper hand, that armed force had dispersed the nation's representatives, and I wept, not for liberty—it never existed in France—but for hope of it, which had been enough to exalt the soul for over ten years; and from that moment I have felt a difficulty in breathing that in the years since, I think, has become the illness of all Europe.

There have been various ways of talking about how the revolution of 18 Brumaire came about. But most important to understand clearly is what characterizes the man on whom the human race still depends. He meant to speak enthusiastically at the Council of Ancients. But first of all, he does not know how to express himself nobly, and it is only in ordinary language that his caustic and trenchant wit can be shown to advantage. Moreover, he has no enthusiasm for any subject. His egotism is composed more of scorn for others than of attachment to anything whatever. He is truly superior, then, in disdain and insult alone. To win votes at the bar of the Ancients, he told them, among other things: "I am the god of war and fortune. Follow me." But even in his arrogance there was no grandeur. He used pompous words in place of those he would have liked to speak: "You're scoundrels and I'll have you shot if you don't obey me." Such would have been the genuine expression of his soul. The rest was only the means advised in turn by daring or hypocrisy, never by truth.

Looking very grave, he walked slowly into the Council of Five Hundred, followed by two tall grenadiers whose height protected his slight stature. When he appeared in the hall, the deputies known as Jacobins broke into indescribable shouting. His brother Lucien, who was presiding at the time, rang the bell to restore order, but to no effect. Screams of "traitor" and "usurper" were heard everywhere, and one of the deputies, a compatriot of General Bonaparte's, the Corsican Aréna, came up to him and shook him by the collar of his uniform. People thought he had a dagger to kill him. It was nothing of the kind. A punch was all the tragedy there was.[51] Nonetheless, at that blow Bonaparte went pale with fright, his head sank to his shoulder, and to the two grenadiers at his side, he said: "Get me out of here." The grenadiers realized his anxiety and lifted him bodily from the midst of the deputies surrounding him. They carried him outside, and once there he recovered his presence of mind, mounted his horse, and prompted the troops to do his bidding. But in this situation, as in many others, one could see that he becomes confused when things go wrong. He recovers his faculties through reflection but emotion cuts them off. There are men, on the other hand, made greater by emotion. They are the ones who, above all, have strength of soul.

As his two grenadiers carried Bonaparte from the hall of the Five Hundred, the deputies opposed to him vehemently demanded that he be declared outlawed; it was then that his brother, Lucien, President of the Assembly, did him remarkable service by refusing, in the face of all threats, to put that decree to a vote.[52] Had he consented, the decree would have passed, and no one can know how the soldiers would have reacted. For ten years they had consistently abandoned those generals declared outlawed. The decisions of men and women of the people are most often determined by habit and, besides, resemblances between words have greater influence over them than differences between things.

General Bonaparte sent his soldiers to lead Lucien from the hall and, once he was safe, ordered his troops into the Orangerie where the deputies had gathered, and to force them out by marching forward so they had no room left to stand. The grenadiers advanced from one end of the hall to the other in squared-off battalions as if it were empty. Pushed against the wall, the deputies in their senatorial togas[53] were forced to flee through the window into the gardens of Saint Cloud. Elected representatives of the people had already been outlawed in France, but this was the first time since the Revolution that civil status had been made ridiculous in the presence of military status; and Bonaparte, wanting power founded on the debasement of legislative assemblies as well as of individuals, was pleased with his ability to deprive national representation of all respect with his very first steps.

The dreadful specter of the Terror was—and has not ceased to be—the sorcery Bonaparte has used to oppress France, and not just since that time but in the very epoch when he seized power. There was no reason to fear the return of Jacobinism.[54] That unbelievable hallucination could exist only when its effects were unknown. Nature does not twice produce such a scourge. To inflame minds to this degree of excess requires the fermentation of new ideas; it requires absolute ignorance of the consequences of those ideas and an undefined hope for the advantage they might bring to the individual and to the people as a whole. But how could one imagine a nation rushing headlong into the claws of the very monster that has torn it apart? Besides, the clergy's holdings that had formed the basis of the assignats no longer existed. Enthusiasm for the Revolution, good or bad, had at least weakened. Nothing begins anew among men at an interval too short for the human race to renew itself, and political experience serves for several generations at least. These truths, simple but indisputable in my eyes, excused my sorrow over 18 Brumaire. For had it been a question of seeing Jacobinism reestablished in France, or supporting Bonaparte unaware that his reign was to cost the human species ten million men, I would have acted like France, which did not like him but preferred him.

Never have more opportune and fortunate circumstances favored the one who wanted to take the reins of power. No man had acquired or retained a commanding reputation. A licentiously free press had spoiled most reputations, and moreover, the French, who showed great intelligence during the Revolution, have displayed so little character that they can easily be discredited in each other's eyes merely by bringing out variations in their behavior and political opinions.

All parties welcomed Bonaparte. Each idealized him as its hope. The Royalists expected him to return the Bourbons. The Jacobins wanted him to maintain them in their positions. A few days after 18 Brumaire one of them told me: "The principles of the Revolution must be abandoned, but power must stay in the hands of the men who made It." "Precisely the opposite seems preferable to me," I replied sharply, indignant as I was at the apostate selfishness that Bonaparte sought to excite in every possible way.[55] But, you will say, in France's state of anarchy at the time, wasn't a powerful hand needed to restore order? No doubt, but people were so dispirited that nothing was easier than governing France. A terror-stricken Europe asked only tranquillity. It took no more than a Machiavellian gift to bring new misfortune to bear on this weary land. But the simplest good sense was enough to make it happy, and a Wellington's[56] conscience was worth a hundred times more for the glory and prosperity of France than the diabolical genius who found in human degradation the fulcrum Archimides sought to lift the world.

Genuine Republicans were the one party to be sincerely saddened by 18 Brumaire. But they were few in number either because it requires daring hope to imagine a republic in France, or because any sort of opinion is a rarity now, since people have so often bowed to circumstance.

Since I have never been able to think of any political interest apart from the love of liberty, I was grieved more each day by 18 Brumaire; I learned each day some new trait of arrogance or guile in the man gradually taking hold of power.[57] I reasoned as best I could to fight the feeling that dominated me, but it kept rising up despite my efforts. I saw tyranny stealing upon us, sometimes stealthy as a wolf, sometimes with its head held high; but it seemed to me that from one hour to the next our oppression increased and that all moral life would soon be in chains.

Fifty deputies, chosen from the two councils, were charged with discussing the constitution to be given to France,[58] and some of the same men who had jumped out of the window when faced with Bonaparte's bayonets dealt as seriously with the abstract questions of a new constitution as if those questions still mattered. General Bonaparte lent himself willingly to those discussions, for he knew that the French like voicing their opinions even more than having them accepted. He let men accustomed to the tribune dissipate their energy in words, but when theory brought them too close to practice, he put an end to their difficulties by threatening to take no further part in their work, that is, to end it by force. Bonaparte himself is very fond of talking. His form of political dissimulation is not silence but a whirlwind of contradictory pronouncements that lead others to believe, in turn, the most contradictory things. He rather enjoyed the quibbles of a committee discussion on setting a particular order, as for the composition of a book, since it was not a matter of dealing tactfully with the higher orders of society, of maintaining privileges, of respecting laws or even customs. The Revolution had swept away everything in Bonaparte's path, and he had nothing to fight but discursive reasoning—a kind of weapon that was child's play in his hands since, when he chose, he opposed it with a kind of vehement gibberish that seemed quite lucid in light of the bayonets with which he could back it up.

Every evening I heard about each of those sessions that might have been entertaining if the fate of humanity had not been at stake. The courtier's servile turn of mind began to emerge in these men who had shown such revolutionary ruthlessness, and everything suggested that self-interest was the true Proteus who could at will take the most diverse shapes.

It was assumed that Sieyès would present the complete draft of the Constitution, which in the course of the Revolution was often spoken of as the Ark of the Covenant that would bring all parties together; but by a curious anomaly, he did not have one word on the subject in writing. Everything was in his head as if he had wanted to speak as an oracle, and the irascibility of his nature when he is not immediately understood added further to the difficulty of expressing his ideas. One day a well-intentioned young man asked the meaning of a passage in one of his pamphlets. "Read it again," he answered, irritably turning away.

General Bonaparte rapidly seized on what he needed from Sieyès's system, that is, to eliminate election of deputies by the nation. Sieyès had conceived of eligibility lists from which the Senate could select the people's representatives under the name of tribunes and legislators. Undoubtedly Sieyès had not devised that institution to establish tyranny in France. He had set up counterweights that might perhaps offset it, but Bonaparte, dismissing the counterweights, took hold of the critical words: no elections. Sieyès's metaphysics served to cloak or rather befog the actual power Bonaparte meant to obtain. Sieyès had said: no elections. Thus it was that the philosopher himself, and not the soldier, doomed the one right through which public opinion can make its way into a government.[59] These are the fresh waters that vitalize it, whereas permanent bodies are like ponds whose stagnant waves can more easily be corrupted. In a monarchy, and perhaps even in a republic, a hereditary body is necessary—wise men appointed for life, a whole conservative aristocracy; but the part of the government that authorizes taxes must issue directly from the nation.

Once General Bonaparte had ensured that he would have to deal only with paid men named by other paid men, he was sure of his power. For him, the noble name of tribune meant allowances for five years, and the grand title of senator, sinecures for life; and he quickly understood that one group would want to acquire what the other wished to retain. There was no one left within the State to whom the nation had granted any right whatever.[60] The circuitous method of awarding nominations to the Senate only made Bonaparte more certain of his influence. All these bodies issuing from the same power were nothing but the hypocrisy of despotism under different guises. General Bonaparte had his will echoed to him in different tones by the wise voice of the Senate, by the shouts of the Tribune produced on demand, by the silent balloting of the Legislative Body, and this three-part choir appeared to represent the nation, although the same master was its only coryphaeus. When the task was completed, he made a gift of land to Sieyès so that the philosopher would lose all popularity by exposing his sensitivity to the pleasures of wealth.[61]

He was remarkably shrewd in choosing the two consuls granted him to veil his despotic unity. One of them, Cambacérès,[62] had learned submission in the national Convention. A profoundly learned jurist, he had drafted the arbitrary decrees of the factionists as methodically as if he had been setting up the most just and carefully considered code of law. He told me one day in conversation: "In the Convention, when they proposed setting up the Revolutionary Tribunal, I saw right away the disasters that would come of it, and yet the decree was passed unanimously." And he was then a deputy in the Convention and contributed his vote to that very unanimity; but in the innocence of his fear, he did not even notice that fact, and I do not think he imagined it possible to resist force. Bonaparte saw him immediately as his paper colleague and real instrument. All he has looked for and has not stopped looking for in men is talent, it is never character.

They say he decided on the other acolyte, Lebrun, for a dedication he had printed under the Old Regime, and for his tractability in serving Chancellor Maupeou.[63] Observing him closely, Bonaparte saw a great deal of intelligence, a great deal of learning, integrity in domestic relationships, but such respect for circumstances that he was certain of bending him to the most powerful of them all: his own will. Cambacérès acted as his interpreter to the revolutionaries, Lebrun to the Royalists, and both of them, like Talleyrand and Fouché, whom I shall discuss shortly, translated the same text—Bonaparte's usurpation—in two different languages: Lebrun advised the Royalists to regain the institutions without the persons, and Cambacérès told the Republicans to retain the persons without the institutions.

Thus Bonaparte's political army consisted solely of defectors from both parties; on the one hand, they sacrificed their obligations to the old Bourbon family, and on the other hand, their love of liberty. In any case, no form of independent thinking would be displayed under his rule, for he could be king of self-interests but never of opinions. And by virtue of position as well as character, he smothered at once all that was knightly in royalty and in the Republic by debasing both nobles and citizens. When his position was constitutionally established, a great man pronounced on this order of things one of those sentences that echoes across the centuries: "It is a monarchy," said Mr. Pitt, "that lacks only legitimacy and limits." He might have added that only a monarchy with limits was truly legitimate.[64]

Bonaparte chose to live in the Tuileries, a choice of residence that was a political salvo. There, people had seen the King of France; there, the customs of royalty were still present to all eyes, and the walls had only to be left to themselves, so to speak, for everything to fall into place once more. I went to stand at a window in the château to watch Bonaparte enter the Tuileries in the first days of the last year of the century. He was still far from the magnificence he has elaborated since that time,[65] but already, the zeal of those around him to become courtisans first and then slaves revealed what they had perceived in Bonaparte's soul. When his carriage entered the courtyard, his valets opened the door and threw down the folding steps with a violence suggesting that even physical objects were insolent when they slowed their master's pace for an instant. As for him, he looked at no one, thanked no one, as if afraid he might be thought responsive to homage and grandeur. As he walked up the stairs amid the crowd making haste to follow him, his eyes turned neither to any object nor to any person in particular. His countenance expressed something vague and indifferent that hid what he was feeling, but that let others see what he always likes to show: cool composure toward fate and contempt for the human race.

Pamphlets were passed around saying that Bonaparte did not wish to be either Monk, or Cromwell, or even Caesar because, they went on, these were outworn roles, as if the events of the world could be thought of as tragic dénouements that must not be copied from their predecessors. But the important thing was not really to persuade but rather to suggest a sentence to those wanting to be fooled—a sentence they could repeat to all and sundry. For some time Machiavelli's doctrine has made such progress in France that all of French vanity is focused on political skill. You can let the whole nation into the comedy, so to speak; it will pride itself on being privy to the secret. When Bonaparte was negotiating with the Pope, a wig-maker said: "Me, I don't believe in anything, but *there has to be religion for the people.*" Each individual enjoys believing he is party to the deception practiced on all.

Bonaparte addressed mutually contradictory language to all the parties, who then reported it to one another, and far from being displeased by this stratagem, they praised its finesse; and well-contented with having seen through it, they took diplomatic pleasure in pretending to be taken in. No doubt the stratagem succeeded only because it safeguarded interests even as it trifled with opinions. When Bonaparte negotiated with the leaders of the Vendée, he hinted that he might one day restore the House of Bourbon. But meanwhile, he immediately awarded great concrete and personal benefits to the priest, Bernier, who had made use of Catholic and Royalist fanaticism without ever having truly shared in it.[66] You saw this Vendean priest installed in the waiting room of Police Minister Fouché, as if he were there only to discredit religion, were it to depend on its clergy. Thus the First Consul went about undoing another reputation daily, debasing proper names one by one, so that no person existed in and of himself, and so that his favor was needed all the more for the loss of public respect.

He carried the same system into his way of restoring wealth or taking it away. Half of France's former landowners were still on the list of émigrés when Bonaparte was named First Consul; on the other hand, owners of property confiscated during the Revolution, a no less powerful class at the time, feared the return of those whose property they had bought. It never occurred to Bonaparte, who always made his way between two opposing interests, to resolve them through justice, that is, through a law that reconciled former rights with new interests in an orderly manner. To one person he restored his property, another he refused. A decree on forests and another on national credit put almost everyone's wealth into his hands. Sometimes he restored the father's property to the son, the elder son's to the younger, according to his satisfaction with one or the other, and this arbitrary, unlimited action increased his power daily by making each person's existence dependent on one man's will. In every country, Turkey included, we meet with a religion, privileged groups, or at least one lowly class in peaceful possession of what fate has allotted it. But France's appalling Revolution, having torn everything down and put nothing in its place, did not strike only those who came close to power or wanted to acquire it as in despotic countries: the most unknown of men were placed on the list of émigrés. The poorest like the wealthiest, the least known like the most famous, women, children, old people, priests, conscripts had something to ask of the new government and that something was life, for it was not a matter of telling oneself: "I will forgo a despot's favor." You had to resolve never to see your native land again, not to recover the slightest part of what you once owned if you incurred the disfavor of the government that had reserved for itself the right to decide the fate, one by one, of almost every inhabitant of

France. This situation excuses the nation to a large extent, it seems to me; but it makes us aware of the unprecedented injustice of those magistrates who, to retain their positions, handed over to the First Consul the destiny of all their fellow citizens. I deeply pity those from whom misfortune wrenches an act of weakness. How can one know for certain that some greater degree of punishment might not have overcome the resistance one glories in? But ignominy for the sake of obtaining a position, ignominy for wealth gained at the expense of mankind and the liberty of one's country: from these no man can recover in the eyes of men.

This Tribunate, whose very name was an ongoing joke, never thought popular rights could be abandoned fast enough. It forbade itself initiative, it refused petitions. In sum, just as we had seen French nobles throw all their privileges, one after the other, at the feet of public opinion on the night of August 4, 1789, these alleged representatives of a nation that had not appointed them, threw themselves to the opposite extreme with equal violence, calling "Jacobin," like "aristocrat" in former times, anyone who took it into his head to demand any institution or any barrier to limit the authority of a single man.

The multitude of newspapers published in France was suddenly reduced to fourteen by a simple decree of the Council of State.[67] At that moment the appalling power of publications was established, with all of them repeating the same thing every day, and tolerating no shadow of contradiction of any sort. The discovery of printing was held to be liberty's safeguard because, until then, it had never been seen at the service of tyrannical authority. But just as regular troops have been far less favorable to European independence than militias, so the discovery of printing would be regrettable if it resulted in the tyranny of the press, and if the army of journalists was recruited and paid by the government. Before the discovery of printing, at least, people communicated by word of mouth, and individuals formed their opinions according to facts. But when all men's natural curiosity for the news is taxed with lies, when no event is recounted without an accompanying sophistry, when tyranny, by nature silent, becomes talkative to mislead the mind even as it withers the soul, the nation is depraved to its very depths and the most perverse doctrine is placed within reach of everyone.

The First Consul himself dictated, and still dictates, articles for the official newspaper, *The Monitor*.[68] His rather limited education should not allow him to write in French or any other language himself. But even though he does not know either spelling or grammar, he has a style. One senses the brutal fist, if it may be put that way, behind his every word. He loses patience with what he says as if the very attempt to persuade others showed too much regard for them. He enjoys insults, vulgar insults, even when, in his army bulletins, he ought to maintain the dignity of omnipotence. His former relations with the Jacobins have left him with a certain tone, something of a man of the people. It may be said that he is the Revolution incarnate, but the Revolution at once violent and corrupt, and assuredly not the one desired and conceived by the foremost classes of society. Roederer,[69] a highly intelligent man who certainly thinks precisely the opposite of what he has been saying for the past twelve years, lauded Bonaparte's gift for journalism and assures him that he sets a rather high value on it. Bonaparte feels that in France you must kill with irony those you mean to ruin in some other manner, and he handles this weapon somewhat clumsily, it is true, but always so as to inflict a great deal of harm. For when response is forbidden, every blow strikes home.

No man can act with great effect except in the trend of his century, and if you examine the story of all those who have changed the face of the world you will see that, for the most part, they have merely seized for their own advantage the trend of minds already in place. The bad philosophy of the end of the eighteenth century derided all cults of the soul. Bonaparte put this philosophy into practice. Bonaparte knows that force, as long as it is unrelenting, can never be ridiculous. And so he uses mockery against everything that resists power: public opinion, talent, religion, morality. "Your conscience is a dumb beast," he told M. de Broglie, bishop of Flanders, who resisted his wishes. "Don't you know that if God reigns in heaven, I am the one who commands on earth?" His whole doctrine amounts to saying: "Shame to the vanquished!"[70] which is worse than misfortune, and I believe that he would scorn himself were fortune to abandon him.

The only human creatures he does not really understand well are those who cling sincerely to some opinion, whatever the consequences. You would think he sniffs men out to make them his instruments or his prey. Bonaparte considers such men either simpleminded or merchants who overcharge, that is to say, who want to be bought for too dear a price.

It got back to him that I had spoken in my circles against this ever-growing oppression whose progress I foresaw as clearly as if the future had been revealed to me. Joseph Bonaparte, whose wit and conversation I enjoyed, came to see me and said: "My brother is complaining about you. 'Why,' he repeated to me yesterday, 'why doesn't Madame de Staël go along with my government? What does she want? Payment of her father's funds? I'll arrange it. Residence in Paris for him? I'll allow it. Come now, what does she want?'" "Good Lord," I answered, "the question is not what I want, but what I think." I do not know if my reply was reported to him, but I am quite certain at least that had he heard it, he would have attached no meaning to it, for he does not believe in the sincerity of anyone's opinions; he considers any kind of morality a formula as inconsequential as the complimentary closing of a letter. And just as it does not follow that a person can require anything of you after your assurance that you are his humble servant, Bonaparte thinks that when someone says he loves liberty, believes in God, prefers his conscience to self-interest, he is a man who conforms to convention and follows accepted practice to explain his ambitious pretensions or selfish schemes. Thus, as we shall see, Bonaparte has never been mistaken in this world except on honorable people, either as individuals or, above all, as nations.

A number of tribunes wanted to establish something like the English opposition in their assembly, and to take the Constitution seriously, as if the rights it assured were real and the alleged division of the State's institutions was not a simple matter of etiquette, of distinction among the Consul's various waiting rooms in which officials with different functions might be seated according to their status. I admit I was delighted to see those tribunes with no wish to emulate the Councillors of State in obedience to the Consul. Above all, I believed that those tribunes who had previously let themselves be carried too far in their love for the Republic owed it to themselves to remain faithful to their opinion when it became weakest and most threatened.[71] One of the tribunes, a friend of liberty endowed with one of the most remarkable minds nature has dealt to any man, M. Benjamin Constant, consulted me on a speech he proposed making to call attention to the dawning tyranny. I encouraged him with all the strength of my conscience.[72] Nevertheless, knowing he was thought to be my close friend, I could not help but fear what might happen to me in consequence. I was vulnerable through my taste for society. Long ago Montaigne said: "I am French through Paris."[73] If such was his thought three hundred years ago, what would it be with so many witty people gathered in the same city since then, and so many accustomed to using their wit for the pleasure of conversation? The specter of boredom has pursued me all my life; it is through that terror that I might have been capable of bowing to tyranny, had this weakness not yielded to the example of my father, to his blood running in my veins. Be that as it may, Bonaparte was quite familiar with my weakness as well as everyone else's, for he is perfectly aware of the bad side of everyone, since that is what brings them under his subjection. To the threat of power and the hope of wealth he holds out, he ties the tendency to boredom, and that too terrifies the French. In the long run, residence forty leagues from the capital, in contrast to all the advantages combined in the world's most agreeable city, weakens most exiles, accustomed from childhood to the charm of society.

The night before Benjamin Constant was to deliver his speech, gathered in my home were Lucien Bonaparte, M. de Talleyrand, Roederer, Regnaud, Ségur,[74] and several others whose conversation possesses, to varying degrees, the ever-renewed interest inspired by forceful ideas and graceful expression. Except for Lucien, each of them had been worn down by the Directory's proscription and was prepared to serve the new government, asking in return only a substantial reward for devotion to its power. M. Benjamin Constant came to me and said quietly: "Look at your drawing room filled with people you enjoy; if I speak, it will be deserted tomorrow; do think it over." "One must act on one's convictions," I told him. Exaltation inspired that reply, but I admit, had I known then what I was to suffer from that day on, I would not have had the strength to refuse Benjamin Constant's offer to forgo his speech and avoid compromising me. Today, Bonaparte's disfavor means nothing with respect to public opinion; he can have you put to death, but he cannot undermine your reputation. Then, however, the nation was not aware of his tyrannical intentions and, as each person hoped to win the return of a brother or friend, restitution of a fortune, whoever dared resist him was crushed with the name of Jacobin, and society withdrew from you along with the government's favor, an unbearable situation, especially for a woman, and whose cuts and stabs no one can know without having experienced it.

The day the signal for opposition in the Tribunate was given by one of my friends,[75] I was to have a number of people in my home whose company I enjoyed a great deal but who were partial to the new government. I received ten notes of excuse at five o'clock. I withstood the first and second well enough, but when those notes followed one after the other I began to feel uneasy. In vain I appealed to my conscience, which had counseled me to forgo all the pleasures of society dependent on Bonaparte's favor, but so many respectable people blamed me that I was unable to rely firmly enough on my own way of looking at things.

Bonaparte had done nothing precisely culpable as yet; many people insisted that he would protect France from great woes. In fact, if just then he had sent me word that he would be reconciled with me, I would have been overjoyed if anything. But he is never willing to make peace with anyone

without exacting something contemptible in exchange, and to impel accep-
tance he usually puts on so terrifying a display of rage that one gives in to
him completely. I do not mean that Bonaparte does not truly fly into a rage;
what is not calculated in him is hate, and hate is normally expressed as
anger. But calculation is so much stronger in this man, that he never goes
beyond what is expedient for him to show according to the circumstances
and the people concerned. One day a friend of mine saw him fly into a violent rage at a *commissaire des guerres*[76] who had not done his duty; he had
scarcely left, trembling all over, than Bonaparte turned to his aides-de-camp
and said, laughing: "I hope I've given him a good scare." A minute earlier,
you might have thought he had lost control of himself.

But his system of verbal terrorism has a clear basis: it sometimes spares
him the need to act; although he occasionally carries out his threats, he
rarely needs to go so far; his bursts of anger suffice. Besides, he degrades
those who displease him more effectively with words than with real punishments. He makes such vulgar and disdainful remarks about them, and
has so many courtiers to repeat them, that his conversation is as much to
be feared as his police. And that is what he desires, for prison could create
interest in the unfortunate people condemned to it while the bitter gibes
of omnipotence ruin a man in public opinion before it is useful to strike
him down completely.

The day after Bonaparte's anger at me exploded, he publicly scolded his
older brother, Joseph Bonaparte, for coming to my home. Joseph felt obliged
not to set foot there for three months, and his example gave the signal for
three-fourths of the people I knew to do likewise. According to those who
had been proscribed on 18 Fructidor, I was wrong to recommend M. de
Talleyrand to Barras as Minister of Foreign Affairs, and now they spent their
lives at the home of the same M. de Talleyrand they accused me of serving.
Those who behaved badly toward me were careful not to say they were giving in to their fear of displeasing the First Consul. But each day they invented a new pretext to do me harm, exerting all the energy of their political opinions against a defenseless, persecuted woman, prostrating themselves
at the feet of all the most dreaded Jacobins the moment the First Consul
brought them back to life with the baptism of his favor.

The Minister of Police, Fouché, summoned me to say that the First Consul suspected me of inciting my friend who had spoken in the Tribunate. I
replied what was surely true—that this friend was a man whose mind was
too superior for anyone to blame his opinions on a woman and, furthermore, that the speech in question contained absolutely nothing but reflec-

tions on the independence all deliberative assemblies must enjoy, and that there was not one word in it which could have offended the First Consul personally. He acknowledged as much. I added a few more words on the respect owed to freedom of opinion in a legislative body, but it was easy to see that he had little interest in these general observations; he knew perfectly well already that under the authority of the man he meant to serve, principles would not matter, and he accommodated himself accordingly. But since he is a man of transcendent intelligence in matters of revolution, he had already made it his practice to do the least possible harm given the admitted goal. His previous conduct could in no way herald morality, and he often spoke of virtue as an old wives' tale. Nonetheless, a remarkable sagacity led him to choose good as a reasonable alternative, and at times his enlightenment moved him to chance upon what conscience would have inspired in others. He recommended my going to the country and assured me that within a short while all would be calm again.[77] I obeyed. But when I returned, things were a long way from calm.

I had done M. de Talleyrand favors of the greatest importance, and what is worth more than any favor is the complete sincerity of my friendship for him. For ten years he had spent much of his life in my home. I had him brought back from America, I had urged Barras to save him from his creditors by appointing him minister, and I had in my possession several of his letters assuring me that he owed me more than life itself.[78] He was the first to show by his conduct that to please the First Consul, one was obliged to avoid me; and afraid of being taken for my friend because of our former social relations, he spoke about me to the First Consul in a way that made a profound impression. He did me the honor and the wrong of portraying me to Bonaparte as a woman with an all-powerful mind and repeated endlessly that I was an irresistible person—he, over whom I had no influence other than what the simplest friendship should have given. Since that time, I have not seen M. de Talleyrand.

He is a man eminently suited to conducting the affairs of this world, and I am astonished that he has lost favor with the Emperor, for I have always recognized his rare skill in the art of grasping the character of individuals he means to captivate. He speaks very little, making it easier for him to weigh his words. Since he has acquired knowledge through conversation alone, he has no taste for discussion that might betray his want of a sound education. He does not compensate with eloquence, because there is no eloquence without some impulse of the soul, and he is self-possessed to the degree that he could not be candid now even if he wished. But all that he says has piquancy and grace. It is strange that a man who can measure his words so carefully does not know how to write. It would seem that the earliest studies in childhood or natural inspiration are necessary to shape one's ideas in writing. For M. de Talleyrand, though certainly possessed of a remarkable mind, is not prepared to draft two pages on his own; and yet those who write his books, his speeches, and his dispatches, require the guidance of his taste and judgment.[79] Wealth and power are necessary to him not only to satisfy his tastes, but also to show his wit in its true light: that is, according to circumstances he drops a few bitter or flattering words among people who eagerly retrieve them and then serve them up, as he wills, for placing his return shots. He takes greater pains with powerful men he wants to captivate, but I do not know whether he shows himself as much to his advantage in this situation as in his natural indolence. Under the Directory I saw him do the impossible to assume a cordial look and show decided opinions; he was unable to inspire confidence in anyone, and among men of the people and their party[80] he did not have the look of a great lord in disguise but rather of an awkward parvenu trying to look sympathetic to the Republican cause. He was somewhat more in his element in Bonaparte's court, and the revolutionary general learned from him the great names, aristocratic customs, the Old Regime so that he might bring it all back to life and, if possible, lend a sense of age to his dynasty from its earliest days. As long as skill was required to negotiate with the European powers, M. de Talleyrand was the most useful of men to Bonaparte. An impassive face, impenetrable discretion, insolence combined with impressive courtesy—everything was well calculated to subdue those who, in this respect, already met him more than halfway. M. de Talleyrand's illustrious birth and his noble manners persuaded ambassadors that they were negotiating with a regular government, and thus clothed, the revolutionary spirit retained all of its formidable power under the most civilized manners. This circumspection has no longer been necessary since force has done it all, but Bonaparte was then still extending his claws with a certain gentleness.

I have paused a while to portray M. de Talleyrand because he surely contributed strongly to giving Bonaparte the idea of restoring decorations, titles, everything that gave him treasures of vanity to distribute. And so he flattered himself that in acquainting Bonaparte with all the nuances of pride in the old nobility, he would gain influence; but he did not know his man if he imagined that this was a way to hold him. Vanity was one more vice Bonaparte was quite prepared to make use of, while reserving the right, should it suit him, to break the man whose advice he had followed.

While M. de Talleyrand conducted foreign affairs, Fouché, at the Ministry of Police, was in charge of the revolutionary side of Bonaparte's government. And whereas devout Christian kings have been known to take two confessors to examine their consciences more closely, Bonaparte had taken on two ministers, one from the Old Regime and the other from the new, whose mission was to put at his disposal the Machiavellian devices of these two opposing systems. Bonaparte followed much the same system for all his appointments, taking people from left and right, so to speak: here an aristocrat, there a Jacobin. The intermediate party, that is, the friends of liberty, enjoyed his favor less than all the others because it was composed of the small number of men in France with opinions of their own. He preferred by far to deal with those who were tied to Royalist interests or discredited by their Jacobin violence as revolutionaries. He would even have liked to appoint Barère Councillor of State, but was dissuaded by the shudders of his colleagues;[81] he would have liked to give this ringing proof of his ability to regenerate everything as well as to upset everything. But for now he confined himself to commissioning the man to set up a newspaper, *The Mémorial*. Its purpose was to attack England as immoral, and the man who had put his words at the service of the executioner, who had been called the Anacreon of crime,[82] dared place his soiled hand on the Ark of the Lord,[83] and Bonaparte was not afraid that the nation itself might stand in defense of his enemy against such an adversary as Barère.

Bonaparte's government is characterized by a profound disdain for the intellectual treasures of human nature: virtue, dignity of soul, religion, enthusiasm; in his eyes, these are the eternal enemies of the Continent, to use his favorite expression. He would like to reduce man to force and guile, and to designate all the rest by the name of stupidity or madness. The English irritate him mainly because they have found the way to be successful with integrity, something Napoleon would have people consider impossible. This shining point in the world clouded his vision from the very beginning of his reign. Consequently, he decided to make an apparently conciliatory gesture to entwine England in his politics. He wrote directly to the King of England and, following English usage, it was the minister, Lord Grenville, who replied. Among the arguments offered in refusal of the proposed peace was that the First Consul's power depended on his life, and it was impossible to base a treaty on an ephemeral existence. These words were extremely insulting to the First Consul, and the man charged with refuting Lord Grenville's response in the *Moniteur* wrote, as one of his arguments: "With respect to the life and death of Bonaparte, these matters, my Lord, are beyond your reach." This was not the only attempt to frighten us with the eternity of Bonaparte's life on earth. Indeed, if it were one of the conditions of his pact with the devil, the human race would do well to cease propagating itself and leave him alone in the world just as he is alone in his own eyes.

The most exaggerated adulation was lavished on Bonaparte from the beginning of his reign; amid this immoderate concert, the Institute took upon itself to tell the First Consul he lacked one form of courage—that of enduring praise. In allowing this mendacious flattery, Bonaparte had not even the merit of loving glory.[84] It is power that he wants, and in the light of this system he prefers servile praise to genuine praise, because the first shows that he is the master, and the second would give proof of independence in those who paid him homage. Whatever he may say, he loves force too well to be concerned with posterity on which it can have no effect. He believes, and rightly so, that posterity will be concerned with him, but there is something too ideal in reputation after death for such a man to sacrifice to it any pleasures of ambition during his lifetime.

I do not even believe that Bonaparte had formulated the plan for a universal monarchy when he came to power, but I do believe what he himself declared to one of my friends shortly after 18 Brumaire: "Something new must be done every three months to capture the imagination of the French nation; whoever does not move in step with it is lost." He systematically infringed on the liberty of France and the independence of Europe every day, but what he did depended on circumstances. He circumvented the obstacle when it was too strong; he stopped short when the opposing wind blew too hard. This man, so impatient within himself, has the gift of standing motionless when necessary; he gets it from the Italians who know how to control themselves to win the object of their passion just as if they had chosen that object deliberately. He has subjugated Europe by his skillful alternation of guile and force. Besides, Europe is a big word. What was it really composed of then? A few ministers, none of whom were more intelligent than many men picked at random in the nation they governed.

Toward the spring of 1800 I published my work on literature,[85] and its success fully restored me to favor in society; my salon was peopled once more and I rediscovered the pleasure of conversatio; and conversation in Paris, I admit, has always been the most stimulating of all for me. There was not a word about Bonaparte in my book on literature, and the most liberal sentiments were, I believe, expressed vigorously. But at the time, Bonaparte was still far from able to shackle the freedom of the press as he can now. The government exercised censorship on newspapers but not on books, a distinction that might have been defensible had that censorship been used with moderation; for newspapers exert influence over the people, whereas books, for the most part, are read only by the educated and can enlighten opinion but not inflame it. In the Senate, as a mockery, I think, a commission on the freedom of the press had been created along with another on individual freedom; and even now their membership is renewed every three months.[86] Titular bishoprics and sinecures in England provide more to do than these committees, unless one sees them as vestals charged with burning funerary lamps beside tombs.

Since my work on the literature of the North and the South, I have published *Delphine, Corinne,* and finally my book on Germany, which was suppressed just as it was about to appear. But even though this last piece of writing won me bitter persecution, literature still seems to me no less a source of enjoyment and regard, even for a woman. I attribute what I have suffered in life to the circumstances that, from the moment I entered society, associated me with the interests of liberty upheld by my father and my friends, but the form of talent that made me known as a writer has always brought me more pleasure than pain. It is easy to bear criticism of your works when you have some nobility of soul and love great thoughts for themselves even more than for the success they may win. Besides, in the long run, the public is always quite fair, it seems to me; self-respect must adopt the habit of extending credit to praise, for with time one is always repaid as one deserves. In a word, even if one must suffer injustice for a long time, I cannot conceive of a better shelter from it than meditation on philosophy and the emotion prompted by eloquence. These faculties put at our disposal a whole world of discoveries and feelings where we always breathe freely.

Bonaparte had presented the prospect of peace to France as the hope that was to bind people to his government, and he was surely resolved on perpetual war interspersed with those moments of peace that have always increased his power even more than winning battles. His military gifts necessarily contributed to his glory, and the uneasiness natural to his character is such that, independent of his need to dominate, he cannot submit to a tranquil life, that is, to having only thirty million men to govern and make happy. Symptoms of that restlessness can be noticed in his every gesture, in his habitual manner: while his face remains imperturbably cold, he constantly takes tobacco or swallows mints. The armchair he uses in Council has to be changed every three months because he unconsciously hacks at it with a penknife. His habitual self-control makes his face immobile, but the inner agitation of his nerves is revealed unwittingly by these physical idiosyncrasies, which must not be overlooked when you want to know a man's character thoroughly.

In Germany, General Moreau had won great victories over the

Austrians;[87] thus he quite wrongly lent Bonaparte the support of his talent and regard for his character. How he was rewarded will be seen by what followed, but the military mind, even in the midst of the Revolution, was still distinct from the citizen's mind, and all the maxims of passive obedience found under royalty still served the revolutionary governments.

In the spring of 1800, Bonaparte himself left for the Italian campaign known mainly for the Battle of Marengo. He passed through Geneva, and since he expressed the wish to see him, my father paid a call, more to be helpful to me than for any other reason.[88] Bonaparte received him nicely, and spoke of his immediate projects in the confidential way that is in his character or, rather, in his calculations for that is always how his character must be described. He never says anything except what he intends, but he has discovered that spoken dissimulation is far more clever than silent dissimulation, not to mention that by allowing himself to mix the false with the true he assumes a pleasing air of good fellowship. He flatters by seeming to speak in confidence and puts into the heads of those he talks with the sentences it suits him to have repeated. My father did not at all have the same reaction to him as I.[89] He was not awed by his presence and found nothing transcendent in his conversation. I have tried to understand the difference between our two judgments, and I think that it comes mainly from the genuine and simple dignity of my father's manners that set him above all those he spoke with, and the fact that since Bonaparte's type of superiority comes more from skill at evildoing than from elevation of thought, his words probably do not suggest what distinguishes him; he could not and would not explain his own Machiavellian instinct.

What cannot be denied is his shrewdness in taking credit for M. de Melas's error in advancing on Nice. The old Austrian general refused to believe in the boldness of sending troops across the Saint Bernard Pass and made none of the preparations needed for resistance;[90] a military unit of moderate size would have sufficed, they say, to destroy the French Army in the mountain gorges that Bonaparte had it traverse. But on this occasion, as on several others, these verses of J.-B. Rousseau can be applied to Bonaparte's military successes:

> The inexperience unmanageable
> Of Paul Emile's good friend
> Made for all the success of Hannibal,[91]

meaning, in other words, that his opponents' errors have always been the source of Bonaparte's triumphs. I know that there is no disputing success, and that the force that wins it is always the sufficient force. However, if the reverses Bonaparte has sustained since then lead us to examine his true intellectual power, it may be found that he has never met an obstacle requiring the opposition of a man of genius.

My father made no mention to Bonaparte of his two million left in the Public Treasury; the only interest he wished to show was for me, and among other things, he said that just as Bonaparte took pleasure in surrounding himself with illustrious names, he must also like noted talents as ornaments for his power. Bonaparte replied amiably and so my father ensured my staying in France, at least for a while. That was the last time his protective hand was raised over my life; since then he has not been witness to the cruel persecution that would have disturbed him more than it does me.

Bonaparte proceeded to Lausanne to prepare the expedition of Mount Saint Bernard.[92] French troops were constantly seen crossing the peaceful countryside of Switzerland, whose inhabitants ought to be concerned only with the wonderful nature all around them. I arrived, as usual, to spend the summer with my father, at about the time the French Army was crossing the Alps. During the fine summer days and evenings on the shore of the lake, I was almost ashamed of worrying so much over worldly matters in the presence of that serene sky and those limpid waters, but I could not overcome my inner disquiet. I wanted Bonaparte beaten because it was the only way to put an end to his tyranny, but I did not yet dare admit that desire and the prefect of Léman, M. d'Eymar, a former deputy to the Constituent Assembly, recalling the days when we both fondly hoped for liberty, sent me couriers hourly to inform me of the French progress in Italy. It would have been difficult to explain to this man, otherwise so interesting, how France's best interests now required her to meet reverses, and I greeted the so-called good news he sent me with a constraint that was against my nature. But then, for ten years, have we not constantly had to hear of the victories of a man whose every success has been at the expense of all, and has one of his triumphs ever yielded happiness for unfortunate France?

The Battle of Marengo was lost for two hours, and it was the carelessness of General Melas, too confident of success, and General Desaix's boldness, that gave victory to the French Army.[93] While the battle seemed lost, Bonaparte rode slowly before his troops on horseback, pensive, his head lowered, more courageous in the face of danger than of misfortune, attempting nothing but waiting for luck. He has behaved this way several times and things have turned out well for him. I still believe that, had there been a man of both character and integrity among his opponents, Bonaparte would have stopped before that obstacle. His great talent is for terrifying the weak and making use of immoral men. Wherever he meets honesty, it is as if his guile is thrown off balance, like the devil's incantations at the sign of the cross.

The armistice that followed the Battle of Marengo, based on the surrender of all its positions in northern Italy, was very disadvantageous to Austria.[94] Bonaparte could have obtained nothing more even by extending his victories. But it was as if the continental powers did themselves honor by surrendering what would have been far better to let him take. As for Napoleon, they eagerly sanctioned his injustices, legitimized his conquests, whereas even though they could not vanquish him, they should at least not have supported him. That was surely the least that might have been asked of Europe's former cabinets, but they understood nothing about such a new situation, and Bonaparte dizzied them with so many threats and promises at once that they thought to gain by giving, and rejoiced in the word *peace* as if it had retained its meaning from the past. The illuminations, the bowing, the dinners, and the cannon shots to celebrate that peace were absolutely the same as in the past; but far from healing wounds, it introduced into the government signing it an infallible agent of death. Bonaparte never kills a State at one blow, but leaves the axe in the tree that it struck and the tree wastes away until renewed blows finish it off.

The sovereigns whom the Emperor found on thrones were the most typical aspect of his luck. Paul I, above all, did him incalculable services;[95] he was seized with the enthusiasm for Bonaparte that his father had felt for Frederick II, and he abandoned Austria while it was still attempting to fight. Bonaparte persuaded him that all Europe would be at peace for centuries to come if the two great empires of the East and the West were in agreement, and Paul II, who had a knightly turn of mind, let himself fall into the trap of those lies. For Bonaparte it was a stroke of luck to meet a crowned head so easy to inflame and who combined violence and weakness; and so he was acutely grieved by his death,[96] for no man was more useful for him to deceive.

Lucien, Minister of the Interior, knowing his brother's plans perfectly, published a pamphlet entitled *Monk, Cromwell, and Bonaparte,* in which he proved that neither the first role nor the second fit the present circumstances, and that grander ideas were required—a change of dynasty, a new Charlemagne. The publication was premature; it had a negative effect and Fouché used it to ruin Lucien. He told Bonaparte that the secret had been revealed too soon, and told the Republican party that Bonaparte disavowed his brother. In fact, he sent him to Spain as ambassador.[97]

Bonaparte's system was to advance month by month, step by step, in his career of power; he would have rumors spread to test public opinion on decisions he wanted to make. He usually took care to have what he planned exaggerated so that the thing itself, when it happened, would mitigate the fears circulating among the public. This time Lucien's impulsiveness had carried him too far, and Bonaparte judged that, to all appearances, he needed to sacrifice him for a while.

I returned to Paris around the month of November 1800. Peace was not yet made, although, by his victories, Moreau made it more and more necessary. Has he not come to regret the laurels of Stockach and Hohenlinden,[98] since they have been made into a crown of thorns, since France has been no less a slave than the Europe she defeated by his efforts? Moreau saw only France in the First Consul's order, but it was incumbent on such a man to judge the government that employed him and, in that kind of situation, to decide for himself where the true interests of his country lay. Nonetheless, it must be acknowledged that at the time of Moreau's most brilliant victories—that is in the fall of 1800—few people could yet discern Bonaparte's plans. What was clear from a distance was the improvement of finances and the order restored in several branches of the administration. Napoleon was obliged to follow the path *of the nation's good* to reach its misfortune; he had to enhance the *nation's* strength before he used it for personal ambition. It was strange the way he spoke about the Revolution to which he owed his existence. Sometimes he would say that the terrorists alone, meaning Robespierre's followers, showed character in the Revolution, but he always found fault with its original authors,[99] for with him, principles of liberty provoked much the effect of water on men struck with rabies.[100] One day he went to Ermenonville to visit Rousseau's tomb: "Still," he told the owner of the place, "this was the man who put us in the state we're in today!" It must be acknowledged, however, that Bonaparte had no reason to complain of this state of things; but he liked to seem scornful of his situation, and so to mark on every occasion his antipathy to those who, throughout time, have hated despotism.

One evening as I was conversing with friends, we heard a loud noise, but since we thought it was some sort of practice in firing canons, we went on with our conversation. Not many hours later we learned that on his way to the Opéra the First Consul had barely missed being killed by an exploding trail of gunpowder directed at him. Since he had escaped, everyone showed quickened interest in him; philosophers proposed restoring cruel torture for the authors of the attack.[101] He could see on all sides, at last, a nation holding out its neck for the yoke. That same evening at home, he calmly discussed what would have happened had he been killed.[102] Some said that Moreau would have replaced him. Bonaparte maintained that it would have been General Bernadotte: "Like Antony," he said, "he would have presented Caesar's bloody robe to the stricken people."[103] I do not know whether he really thought that France would have called General Bernadotte to lead her then. But what is certain, at least, is that he said it only to excite jealousy against General Bernadotte. If the infernal machine had been devised by the Jacobin party, the First Consul could have redoubled his tyranny from that moment on; public opinion would have supported him. But since the Royalist party had designed the plot, Bonaparte could not extract much advantage from it; he endeavored rather to smother than to use it, because he wanted the nation to see as the enemy only enemies of order, but not those of another order, that is, of the Old Regime.

Strangely enough, with a Senatus Consultum, Bonaparte used the occasion of a Royalist plot to have one hundred thirty Jacobins deported to the island of Madagascar—or perhaps to the bottom of the sea, for they have never been heard of since.[104] That list was made in the most arbitrary way; names were put on and taken off according to the recommendations of the Councillors of State who proposed it and the senators who sanctioned it. When you complained of the way the list was drawn up, decent people said that it was composed of very guilty men. That may be; but law, not fact, frames the legality of acts. When we allow one hundred thirty citizens to be arbitrarily deported, nothing will prevent highly respectable people from being treated in the same way, as we have seen since. Public opinion will defend them, you'll say. Opinion! What is it without the authority of the law? What is it without independent agencies? Public opinion was for the Duke d'Enghien, for Moreau, for Pichegru; was it able to save them? There will be neither liberty, nor dignity, nor security in a country where people are concerned with proper names when the issue is an injustice. Every man is innocent before a legally constituted tribunal has condemned him and, were a man to be the guiltiest of all, once he is put beyond the reach of the law, his fate should make decent people tremble like the others. But just as in England's House of Commons, when a member of the opposition leaves, he asks a member on the minister's side to withdraw likewise, and thus maintain intact the strength of the two parties, so Bonaparte never struck the Royalists or the Jacobins without dividing the number of blows equally between the two groups. This is the only form of distributive justice from which he has almost never deviated. Thus he made friends of all whose hatreds he served. It will be seen later that he has always counted on hatred to strengthen his government, for he knows that it is less inconstant in nature than love. After a revolution, partisan spirit is so bitter that a new leader can capture it by serving its vengeance even more than its interests; each man abandons, if he must, the person who thinks like him, provided that he who thinks otherwise is pursued.

The Treaty of Lunéville with Austria was proclaimed;[105] by that first treaty Austria lost only the Venetian Republic which it had received from Belgium in compensation, and this former Queen of the Adriatic, proud and powerful for so long, passed again from one master to another. Respect for history is unknown to that man, for he thinks of the world only as contemporaneous with himself.

My winter in Paris went by quietly. I never visited the First Consul; I never saw M. de Talleyrand. I knew that Bonaparte did not like me, but he had not yet reached the degree of tyranny that we have seen develop since. Foreigners treated me with the greatest honor; the diplomatic corps spent its life in my home and this European atmosphere was my safeguard.

M. de Lucchesini,[106] freshly arrived from Prussia, thought there was still question of a republic and was advancing what he had picked up of philosophical principles in his relations with Frederick II; he was warned that he mistook the lay of the land and told that he should turn instead to what he knew best of the courtier's spirit. He quickly obeyed, for he is a man of singularly pliant character; it is too bad that such distinguished faculties belong to so bent a soul. He finishes the sentence you begin or begins the one he thinks you are going to finish, and it is only by leading the conversation to the events of the previous century, to the literature of the Ancients—in a word to subjects unrelated to present-day people and things—that you can discover his superiority of mind. The habit of flattering power denatures all of nature's gifts in the human mind.

M. de Cobenzl, the Austrian ambassador, was an entirely different type of courtier, but no less eager to please power. M. de Lucchesini was educated as a man of letters. All M. de Cobenzl knew of literature were the French comedies in which he had played the roles of Crispin or Chrysale. It is known that at the court of Catherine the Second, he received dispatches one day disguised as an old woman; the courier was reluctant to recognize his ambassador in that costume.[107] M. de Cobenzl was a singularly banal human being; he would say the same sentence to everyone he met in a salon; he spoke to all with a sort of cordiality void of feelings and ideas. His manners were perfect, his conversation rather well-fashioned for society, but to send such a man to negotiate with the revolutionary strength and ruthlessness surrounding Bonaparte, made a spectacle worthy of pity. Duroc[108] complained of M. de Cobenzl's familiarity; he found it unbecoming for one of the first lords of the Austrian monarchy to shake hands with him freely and easily. These newcomers to the field of courtesy did not believe that a relaxed manner was in good taste; in fact, had they relaxed, they would have made terrible mistakes, and arrogant stiffness was still their best resource in the new role they wanted to play.

M. de Cobenzl had negotiated the Peace of Lunéville with Joseph Bonaparte. The latter was better at getting results, either because of his position or because of the natural subtlety of his mind. He invited M. de Cobenzl to his charming home in Mortfontaine,[109] and I happened to be there with him. Joseph thoroughly enjoyed the occupations of country life and he gladly and easily walked for eight hours on end in his garden. M. de Cobenzl tried to follow him, more winded than the Duke de Mayenne had been when Henri IV was pleased to make him walk in spite of his stoutness. The poor man sang the praises of fishing among the rustic pleasures, because it allowed one to sit; he spoke with forced animation of the innocent pleasure of catching a few little fish on a line. Paul I had mistreated him outrageously when he was ambassador to Petersburg. We were playing backgammon, he and I, in the drawing room at Mortfontaine, when one of my friends came to tell us of Paul I's sudden death. M. de Cobenzl then uttered the most official-sounding lamentations ever. "Although I may have reason to complain of him," he said, "I will always acknowledge the excellent qualities of that Prince, and I cannot keep from regretting his loss." He was rightly delighted as a man and as an Austrian, but in his words there was a thoroughly annoying courtier's grief. It is to be hoped that with time the world will be rid of the courtier's mind, the most insipid of all; but I will say nothing more on the subject for now.

Bonaparte was quite alarmed by the death of Paul I, and they say that at the news he let slip the first "Oh, my God!" ever heard from him. He could well be tranquil, however, for the French were then more prepared to suffer tyranny than the Russians. I visited General Berthier[110] one day when the

First Consul was to be there, and as I knew he spoke unfavorably about me, it entered my head that he might address me with one of the vulgarities he often liked to utter even to the women paying him court, and before I went to the party I jotted down the various proud and biting replies I might offer depending on what he said to me. I did not want to be caught off guard if he took the liberty of offending me, for that would have shown lack of character even more than of wit; and since no one can promise not to be troubled in the presence of such a man, I prepared in advance to face him bravely. Fortunately, it was unnecessary; he asked me the most ordinary question in the world. The same thing happened to those of his opponents he thought able to answer him; he never attacks in any area unless he feels by far the strongest. During supper Bonaparte stood behind Mme Bonaparte's chair, swaying from one foot to the other like the Bourbons. I pointed out to my neighbor this vocation for royalty already so evident.[111] The fact is, since princes give long audiences without sitting, a number of them have taken on the unpleasant habit of swaying. Bonaparte has always shown a certain discomposure that lends awkwardness to his compliments but in no way tempers his insults.

The Tribunate carried on its opposition—that is, some twenty members out of eighty[112] tried to speak out against the measures of every kind preparing the tyranny to come. An important issue arose, the one that gave the government the fatal power of creating special tribunals to judge those accused of treason, as if delivering a man up to those tribunals did not mean judging in advance the matter at hand: that is, whether he is a criminal, and his crime treason, and as if, of all offenses, political offenses were not those requiring the greatest caution and independence in the way they are considered, since the government is normally the opposing party in such cases. In Robespierre's day, people were in earnest when they said: "Judicial forms are pointless; the innocent don't need them, and the guilty don't deserve them," as if judicial forms were not established specifically to determine whether a man was innocent or guilty.[113] Since then, we have seen what it means when these military commissioners judge treason; and the death of the Duke d'Enghien alerted everyone to the horror inevitably inspired by the hypocritical power that cloaks murder as law.

The opposition in the Tribunate, weak as it was, still displeased the First Consul; not that it presented him with an obstacle, but that it fostered the nation's habit of thinking, which was inadmissable to him at any price. He had an outlandish argument against the opposition placed, with others, in the newspapers. Nothing is simpler than opposition in England, it ran, since there the King is the enemy of the people; but in a country where the executive power is itself chosen by the people, to fight the representative of the people is to oppose the nation. How many sentences of the sort have Napoleon's writers not let loose on the public in the last ten years! In England, a simple peasant would laugh at that kind of sophism; in France, all people want is a sentence to give their self-interest the appearance of firm belief.

Bonaparte went on choosing men from all parties to fill the various posts.[114] The primary condition of eligibility was devotion to his power. Their earlier lives counted for nothing either positive or negative; you might have thought that the political birth of each man dated from the eighteenth of Brumaire. Very few proved immune to desire for a position; a great many had been ruined, and the interests of their wives and children, or their nephews if they had no children, or their cousins if they had no nephews, compelled them, they said, to desire government jobs. The great strength of heads of state in France is the Frenchman's prodigious taste for holding positions; vanity makes them even more desirable than need for money. The French are particularly pleased by whatever distinguishes one man from another. There is no nation less suited to equality; they proclaimed it so as to take the place of the Ancients, who were their superiors. They wanted to modify inequality, but not to resign themselves to the one possible political code worthy of admiration, the one that makes all men equal before the law. Bonaparte received thousands of requests for every position, from the lowest to the highest. If he had not by nature held the human race in profound contempt, he would have acquired that sentiment as he skimmed through the requests signed by so many names illustrious by their ancestry or celebrated for revolutionary deeds that contrasted with the new duties they coveted.

Those who would excuse Bonaparte's conduct strongly emphasize the wrongs committed by the French nation. France undoubtedly has the unfortunate defect of showing more vanity than pride in all matters, and of setting far more value on the slightest successes than on the noblest sacrifices. But where is the nation that a government cannot deprave? The world is so arranged that, in the ordinary course of life, the advantages of vice and of virtue carry almost equal weight, and it is for conscience to tip the balance. But when the weights on the scale are suddenly increased on the side of vice by both the seduction of eight hundred million francs and the fear of eight hundred thousand bayonets, the majority of men are no match for the lures and terror surrounding them. Compare the English in the times of Henry VIII, Cromwell, and Charles the Second with the English since they have become possessed of their admirable liberty, and you will see that they do not differ as much in these different eras as our French of today from our French of the past and, if God wills, of the future.

In the winter of 1801, the government sent the Legislative Body a mass of decrees on internal administration that were, in the main, quite reasonable; a great many absurdities perpetrated by the revolutionary regime needed mending. Besides, it cost the First Consul nothing but the exaggerated statements on his good works that reverberated in the news sheets: roads, canals, charitable organizations, etc. Bonaparte, personally, has no taste for giving. When money is a means, he is lavish with it; when it serves generosity or justice alone, he economizes. The moment something can be useful to his plans, such as decrees for raising troops, he signs drafts on the National Treasury. Ecus and conscripts are equally unimportant to him, but he never does what he would call useless—that is, a good deed with no political yield. Nothing, then, tries one's patience more than praise accorded the benevolence of a man who draws from the National Treasury what it suits him to give, and who does not curtail the slightest luxury required by his schemes or his vanity. In general, and it is impossible to repeat this too often, there is no virtue without sacrifice; all that one does for oneself, whatever its dimensions, must never earn us the admiration of others.

The winter of 1801 in Paris was quite pleasant, thanks to Fouché's willingness to grant the various requests I addressed to him for the return of émigrés; thus, in the midst of my disfavor, he gave me the pleasure of being useful. For that, I retain a certain gratitude toward him.[115] It must be admitted that there is always a measure of coquetry in everything women do, and most of their virtues are tinged with the desire to please and to be surrounded by friends who cling to them more intimately for the services received from them. It is from this sole point of view that they must be pardoned for enjoying credit for what they do; but one must know how to give up even the pleasures of helpfulness for the sake of dignity. For one may do everything for others except debase one's character. Our own conscience is God's treasure; we are not permitted to spend it for anyone.

Bonaparte still bore some expenses of the Institute he had been proud of in Egypt, but among men of letters and scholars there was a small philosophical opposition, unfortunately of a deplorable kind, as its total thrust was against reestablishing religion.[116] By a lamentable peculiarity, the enlightened men in France wanted to console themselves for the slavery of this world by seeking to destroy the hope of another. This singular incongruity would not have been found either in the Greek religion or the reformed religion. But the Catholic clergy had enemies that its courage and misfortunes had in no way disarmed as yet, and perhaps it is difficult indeed to reconcile the authority of the Pope and of priests subject to the Pope with the system of a state's liberty. Whatever the case may be, the Institute did not show for religion, apart from its ministers, the deep respect inseparable from great power of soul and genius, and Bonaparte could take a stand against men far worthier than himself on the basis of sentiments far worthier than these men.

He did not even trouble, however, to show a little genuine hypocrisy. Faithful to the system of overt deception, that is, of offering lies as pretexts to those who asked nothing more than to make use of them, he assured the priests that Catholicism was the one truly orthodox religion, and on the same day, speaking with Cabanis, an eighteenth-century philosopher, he said: "I want to reestablish religion as you do vaccination—inoculate it to destroy it." This is a remarkable sentence. He pronounced several of the sort that deserve to be collected as a kind of revelation of the principle of evil; besides, it is impossible to repeat a single word of his that shows grace or true greatness. Even his flatterers have been unable to contrive anything of the kind for him; when he means to be good, he is common; when he means to be dignified, he is bombastic. His natural manner being scorn and arrogance, he is awkward and constrained in any other; and this nation so accustomed to shine in the eyes of Europe for its mind and spirit, and above all for the chivalry of both, has for its sole representative a man without a spark of resemblance to that image.

Under the reign of Louis XIV there was flattery, no doubt, but the nation reaped, if you will, the fruit of what it gave; for this King invested his pride in the great men who made his reign illustrious. Bonaparte wants instruments alone; no genius would please him in any area; a great poet, even writing on no subject that might hurt him, would offend merely by diverting attention from him. Dare I say that he disliked hearing people repeat that Mme Récamier[117] was the most beautiful woman in Paris and that I was the most practiced at conversation? He wants no one of the first rank, man nor even woman, in any domain. His wish is that the French nation be anonymous, that—from the jumble of people forced to march under his banners, obey his orders, or live and die in oblivion—nothing stands out but the letters that make up his name. He wants to be a man, or something more than a man, at the head of an anthill called Germans, Italians, and French, but soon to be designated as no more than Bonaparte's subjects. One day an astronomer, Méchain, wrote to the Minister of the Interior saying that he had discovered a new planet and asked permission to present it to the First Consul. He had grasped the truth of the moment, for if Bonaparte could manage it, the stars themselves would shine in the heavens only on condition of belonging to his court.

The First Consul ordered Spain to make war on Portugal that year, and the poor King of that illustrious country condemned his army to an expedition as servile as it was unjust. He marched against a neighbor who wished him no ill, against a power allied to England, which has since proved so true a friend to Spain, all to obey the man preparing to despoil him of his whole existence.[118] Since then we have seen these same Spaniards energetically give the signal for the resurrection of the world, we are learning to understand what nations are, and whether they are to be refused a legal way to express their opinions and to influence their destiny.

Toward the spring of 1801, the First Consul was struck with the idea of making a king—a king from the house of Bourbon.[119] He gave Tuscany to this king, designating it by the erudite name of Etruria, thus beginning the great masquerade of Europe. That poor Infant of Spain was summoned to Paris to show the French a prince of the old dynasty humiliated before the First Consul—humiliated by his gifts when persecution would never have succeeded. With this royal lamb, Bonaparte tried his hand at making a king wait in his anteroom. He allowed applause at the theater when this verse was recited:

I who have made kings and have not wished to be one,[120]

while planning to be more than a king when the opportunity arose. Every day brought some new tale of blunders committed by that poor King of Etruria. He was taken to the Museum and to the Natural History Room[121] where several of his questions on fish and quadrupeds, questions that a well-brought-up child would no longer ask at the age of twelve, were quoted as witty remarks. In the evening he was taken to visit the Minister of the Interior, where opera dancers came to mingle with the new ladies,[122] and despite his piety, the little King preferred dancing with them, and the next day, by way of thanks, he sent them good and beautiful books for their instruction. This passage from revolutionary usage to monarchical usage was a singular moment for France; the absurdities of both harmonized to perfection and, since on the one hand there was no independence and on the other no dignity, they were able, each in turn and in his own way, to group themselves around the motley power that used simultaneously the means of force of both regimes.

That year, July 14, the anniversary of the Revolution, was celebrated for the last time,[123] and a pompous proclamation from the three consuls recalled all the benefits stemming from that day. There was not one of them, however, that the First Consul did not plan to abolish. He would greatly increase taxes, reestablish a multitude of bastilles,[124] exile and imprison as Louis XIV in times past never could have ventured with his *lettres de cachet*. But for this man, today's truth was always tomorrow's lie. Of all collections, the strangest is that of his proclamations. It is a compendium of the most contradictory statements that can possibly be made, and were chaos charged with indoctrinating the world, it would doubtless foist on humanity this eulogy of peace and war, of enlightenment and prejudice, of liberty and despotism—praise and invective for all governments, all religions.

A witty man has said that Bonaparte had hell in his heart and chaos in his head; the former is true perhaps, but as for the latter, it should be noted that the gibberish of his language serves the clarity of his goal. He wants to sow confusion in everyone's thoughts so that nothing remains clear but the varied self-interests he felt sure he would seize and control.

It was also around this time that he sent General Leclerc to Santo Domingo,[125] calling him *"our brother-in-law"* in his decree. That first royal "we," associating the French with his family's property, was acutely repugnant to me. He compelled his pretty sister to go to Santo Domingo with her husband, and there her health was undermined. A singular act of despotism on the part of a man who moreover was unaccustomed to great strictness of principle around him! But he makes use of morality only to foist it on others to thwart or dazzle them. I have learned from persons who have known him intimately that in early youth he liked to make his sisters get up when they were sick and to keep his sisters-in-law far from their husbands; in this way he made his authority felt by small afflictions until such time as fate raised him to the rank of scourge of the human race.

Peace was subsequently concluded with the leader of the Negroes, Toussaint-Louverture. He was very much a criminal, but Bonaparte nonetheless signed terms with him. In defiance of those terms, Toussaint was brought to a French prison where he met a miserable death. Perhaps Bonaparte does not even remember that crime because he was reproached with it less than with others. His conscience has no memory, for he is perhaps the only man to whom remorse might conceivably be unknown. In his eyes, good and evil are successful or unsuccessful schemes. I do not believe he takes any other component of human nature seriously.

At a mint in Petersburg,[126] I was struck by the violence of machines driven by a single will; those hammers, those anvils seem like people, or rather voracious animals, and if you tried to resist their force, it would annihilate you. However, all that apparent fury is calculated, and those springs operate by the movement of a single arm. In my mind's eye, this is the image of Bonaparte's tyranny; he causes the death of thousands of men just as these wheels strike coins, and his agents, for the most part, are as insensitive as this wood and this iron that fulfill their function without relying on themselves for guidance. The invisible momentum of these machines comes from a will at once diabolical and mathematical that transforms moral life into a servile tool. Finally, to complete the comparison, it would be enough to damage the driveshaft for the whole thing to come to a stop once more.

As was my happy custom, I went to spend the summer with my father.[127] He was indignant at the course of events, and as he had loved true liberty all his life as much as he had hated popular anarchy, he felt called to write against the tyranny of one man after he had fought so long against the demagogy of all. My father loved glory and, despite the sobriety of his character, no risk was displeasing to him when it was necessary to expose one's self to merit public respect:

> Romans, I love glory and on that score cannot be still,
> For human labors it is the finest payment.[128]

The proverb saying that the voice of the people is the voice of God points, in fact, to the kind of marvelous effect produced on the soul by this universal acclaim, whose power would fade, perhaps, if we knew one by one those who grant us their approval. I was well aware of the dangers I would face through a work by my father that displeased the First Consul, but I could not bring myself to stifle this swan song, which was to resonate once more on the tomb of French liberty. And so I encouraged my father to work and we put off until the following year the question of whether he would publish what he was writing.[129]

At the news of the peace preliminaries signed between England and France, Bonaparte's success reached its apex.[130] When I learned that England had recognized him, it seemed to me that I had been wrong to hate his power, but it was not long before circumstances relieved me of that scruple. The most remarkable condition of the preliminaries was total withdrawal from Egypt.[131] Thus that whole expedition had no purpose other than to promote talk about Bonaparte. You can see that in all matters he loves not glory but power. With respect to power, he is like a fanatic who sacrifices everything to his primary goal, and for that reason, his conduct is impossible to predict, for he turns toward circumstance like a compass to the north, and nothing in him is fixed except the will to reign, by whatever means.

Many have claimed that, jealous of Kléber's power, Bonaparte had him[132] assassinated in Egypt, and persons worthy of belief have told me that discussion on the subject had provoked the duel where General Destaing was killed by General Reynier. I find it hard to believe that Bonaparte had the means to arm a Turk against the life of a French general while he himself was so far from the scene of the attack. Several articles and pamphlets beyond the reach of his power accuse him of the crime; nonetheless, it seems to me that nothing must be said against Bonaparte that is not proved. If a single error of the kind were found among the purest truths, their brilliance would be tarnished. This man must not be fought with any of his own arms. He must be defeated only because man has a conscience and the universe has a God. If it is doubtful that Kléber's death is his doing, there is no doubt that he had the sick men at Saint Jean d'Acre poisoned.[133] He sent for Doctor Desgenettes to propose he give them opium and, on Desgenette's refusal, dared call weak-minded a man who showed more courage in that situation than it takes to be a Bonaparte. A vile lackey carried out Napoleon's wishes, and all the sick were poisoned. I have often wondered at the reason for that atrocious and unmotivated deed, for he could have abandoned those poor unfortunates to their fate without assuming the odium of their death. But he did not want the news sheets able to say that wounded soldiers in Bonaparte's army had fallen into the hands of the Turks, and, with neither anger nor pity, he thought it more fitting to kill them than to let them live or die naturally.

I delayed my return to Paris to avoid the Festival of Peace.[134] I do not know a more painful sensation than public rejoicing when the soul recoils. One develops a certain scorn of the common people, gaping as they celebrate the yoke being prepared for them: those ungainly victims dancing in front of the palace of the man who will sacrifice them, the First Consul, called the Father of the Nation that he was about to devour. That whole mixture of stupidity on the one hand and guile on the other, the insipid hypocrisy of courtiers throwing a veil over the arrogance of the master, filled me with a disgust I could not bear. Feelings had to be kept in check, and one was liable to meet with official merriment that was easier to avoid at other times. Among the placards made up for this festival of peace was one saying that Napoleon shared sovereignty with Jupiter; several years later, it was with Pluto. But for now, Bonaparte was proclaiming peace as the world's foremost need. Every day he signed a new treaty that ra[m]bled the care Polyphemus took to count the sheep as he admitted [to] his cave. A single treaty, the one with the Algerian Regency[135] began: "[The] First Consul and the Algerian Regency, recognizing that war between the two states is not natural, are agreed that . . . etc." Those two governments did in fact owe one another fraternity.

The United States of America also made peace with France,[136] sending as plenipotentiary a man who did not know one word of French, apparently unaware that the most perfect command of the language was hardly sufficient to discern the truth in a government so adept at concealing it. When M. de Livingston[137] was presented, the First Consul, with the help of an interpreter, complimented him on the purity of American morals, and he added: "The Old World is very corrupt." Then, turning to M. de Talleyrand, he twice repeated: "Do tell him I'm saying the Old World is very corrupt; you know something about that, don't you?" It was one of the mildest remarks he has addressed in public to this courtier with better taste than his fellows, and who would have liked to maintain some dignity of manner while sacrificing dignity of soul to ambition.

Meanwhile, in the shadow of the Republic, the institutions of monarchy moved forward. A personal honor guard was formed; the crown diamonds were used to ornament the First Consul's sword; and in his dress, as in the political situation of the day, a mixture of the old and new regimes was seen. He had outfits made all of gold, straight hair, short legs and a large head, as well as something hard to describe that was awkward and arrogant, scornful and diffident that seemed to combine all the parvenu's lack of charm with all the tyrant's boldness.

His smile has been praised as agreeable; for my part, I believe it would have been supremely unpleasant in another person, for starting from gravity and ending there, it was more like a metal spring than a natural reaction, and the expression of his eyes and lips never matched. But since he reassured those around him with his smile, the relief it inspired was taken for charm. I recall a member of the Institute, a Councillor of State, telling me seriously that the First Consul's fingernails were perfectly formed; he apparently meant to speak of his claws. Another time, General Sébastiani[138] burst out with: "Bonaparte's hands are charming." "Ah," answered a young lord from the old French nobility, who was not yet chamberlain at the time: "For pity's sake, General, let's not talk politics today." This same General Sébastiani, speaking fondly of his relative, the First Consul, said: "He often shows a childlike sweetness." He did in fact enjoy innocent games at home. He has

s generals; and even in Munich, at home with the
.ria, who were not cheered by his gaiety, I think.
in the Spanish style, like Charles, Elector of Baden,
rial crown, and began to dance an old French
His apparel contrasted with his demeanor; that
:aped to the aid of the most graceless dance steps in
; was more unpleasant than the pretense of serenity
and ev.... , .   in who was depriving the entire world of them both.
For some time Bonaparte was rather afraid of jokes; he often repeated bitterly: "The French are a nation of scoffers." But he said later that power was
never ridiculous and, since he does not in fact conceive of power as separate
from terror, he is right; but authority based on public opinion would have a
great deal to fear from all that rightly lent itself to mockery.

Liberty's friends in the Tribunate kept up the fight against the ever-
growing authority of the First Consul. But public opinion gave them no
support at the time. Most of the opposition tribunes deserved the highest
regard in every respect, but three or four of those sitting in their ranks had
been guilty of the excesses of the Revolution,[139] and the government was
very careful to cast on all the discredit of a few. Nonetheless, in the long
run, men joined together in a public meeting are always galvanized with
nobility of soul, and such as it was, this Tribunate would have prevented
tyranny had it been allowed to remain in existence. Already, a majority had
nominated Daunou for the Senate, a man not at all to the First Consul's
taste: he was an honest, enlightened, and moral Republican, but certainly
not a man to be feared. For the First Consul this was sufficient grounds to
eliminate the Tribunate, that is, to dislodge its twenty most energetic men,
one by one, by the Senate's choice, and then replace them with twenty others, loyal to the government.[140] Every year the same process would be repeated on one-fourth of the remaining eighty members. Thus they were
taught a lesson on what they must do to retain their positions, that is, their
yearly income of fifteen thousand livres. The First Consul wanted to maintain this mutilated assembly a while longer to serve for two or three years as
a mask of popular approval for acts of tyranny. But, I ask, how would the
English react to a proposal by a Council of State that the House of Lords select twenty members of the opposition in the House of Commons for ex-
pulsion? The House of Lords, however, is as independent as the French Senate is servile. A good many of my friends stood among the proscribed
tribunes, but my opinion in this respect is independent of my attachment.
Still, I may have felt stronger irritation at the injustice directed at persons

close to me, and I am afraid I ventured a few sarcastic remarks on the hypocritical art of interpreting even the unfortunate Constitution in which every attempt had been made to preclude even a breath of liberty.

For such is the force of public opinion in every country that the moment any sort of legal procedure allows, it will make itself heard. The Civil Code submitted to the Tribunate would one day be given as law to almost all of Europe. It is said that the Code has good things in it, for in fact Napoleon does not much care how one inherits or marries so long as he can get hold of everyone's wealth and send the husbands off to the army. Politics: there is his domain; everyday justice is a housekeeping detail he has left for the Councillors of State to discuss as they will. Nevertheless, from time to time he has set forth his views to the Council on the Civil Code to the great admiration of those who admire him.[141] Certainly, I do not deny the mental prowess of a man who has shaken the world, whatever the instrument used for the purpose, but I hold that whenever his personal advantage is not involved, his insights are wholly unremarkable.

That year, 1802, the First Consul's every step gave clearer proof of his boundless ambition. While negotiations for peace with England went on at Amiens, he convened the Cisalpine Council in Lyons—that is, the deputies of all Lombardy and the adjacent states, which had resolved themselves into a republic under the Directory and now asked what new structure they were to assume.[142] Since we were not yet accustomed to the idea that the unity of the French Republic might be transformed into the unity of one man, no one imagined that he meant to unite in himself the Consulate of France and the presidency of Italy. The position was expected to go to Count de Melzi, a man whose conversation was the wittiest one could possibly encounter and who was, furthermore, highly regarded in many respects. Suddenly rumor spread that Bonaparte was having himself named; at this news, minds came perceptibly to life for a moment. It was said that by the Constitution, whoever accepted posts in a foreign country lost his citizenship; but did he claim to be a Frenchman, the Corsican who meant to use the great nation only to oppress Europe, and Europe only to oppress the great nation more effectively? Bonaparte stole the naming of the president from all those Italians who, only a few hours before going to vote, learned that they must choose him. They were told to join to Bonaparte's name that of M. de Melzi as vice president. They were assured that they would be governed only by the man who would always be among them, and that the other wanted only an honorary title. He also said in his emphatic way: "Cisalpins, I will retain nothing but high-minded thought of your affairs." As for "high-minded thought," it meant absolute power. The following day, serious work continued on a constitution,[143] as if it could exist side by side with that iron fist. The nation was divided into three classes: the *possidenti,* the *dotti,* and the *commercianti:*[144] property owners to impress them, men of letters to silence them, and merchants to close all doors to them. But after all, those sonorous Italian words lend themselves to imposture even better than French.

Bonaparte had changed the name Cisalpine Republic to Italian Republic, and thus threatened Europe with his future conquests in the rest of Italy. Nothing was less pacific than such a step; however, Europe and even England were so anxious for peace, that it did not halt the signing of the Treaty of Amiens! I was at the home of the English minister, M. Jackson,[145] when he received the terms of that peace. He read them to all his dinner guests, and I cannot find words for my astonishment at each article. England gave up all her conquests; she gave up Malta, of which General Desaix had said that if no one had been in the fortress to open the doors, they'd never have gotten in.[146] To a power she had consistently beaten at sea, she surrendered everything without indemnification. What a curious effect of the passion for peace that had all Europe in its grip! And the man who had obtained such advantages as if by miracle did not even have the patience to exploit them for a few years and put the French navy in condition to test itself against England's! Virtually the day after the Treaty of Amiens was signed, Napoleon joined Piedmont to France by a Senatus Consultum,[147] and for the year the Treaty of Amiens was in force, not a day passed without new proclamations that led to its breaking. The motive behind this policy is easily fathomed. Bonaparte meant to numb the French, first with unexpected peace, then with wars that made him necessary. He believed that in every domain a storm was likely to favor usurpation. Instructed to laud the comforts of peace in the spring of 1802, the news sheets now said: "We are approaching the time when politics will not matter." In fact, if Bonaparte had so wished at the time, he could easily have given twenty years of peace to a frightened and ruined Europe.

Bonaparte made his way to the Senate,[148] and the senators were convinced that he had come to sit among them as a Consul of the Republic. Consequently, ten of the eldest came to welcome him at the foot of the stairs. But Bonaparte arrived surrounded by his guards. On his return to the Tuileries, he expressed contempt for those vacuous enough to think that such a man as he would act as an elected official. It is not only as a soldier that he scorns the civil state, it is above all as a despot that he is truly horrified by everything resembling laws.

At this same time, he took his biggest step toward the throne: the Concordat with the Pope.[149] He has professed an absolute lack of religion several times in front of a great many people. I do not know the truth of the matter. Superstition surely has a hold on him, for no man escapes some form of supernatural belief. But, to me, he seems more inclined to think himself a god than to raise his eyes to The One who created him to punish us, and Who will destroy him to absolve us. On one occasion he wrote to M. de Ségur, who thought he had lost his son: "Monsieur and Grand Master of Ceremonies, your son has returned to the Great Spirit,"[150] and he used the expression two or three times, no doubt to astonish with its strange novelty. Clearly he judged religion as no more than a political tool, but it would be interesting to observe what occurs within that kind of soul when he is alone, when he reflects on destiny, and when reverses have condemned him to look inward. He faces death bravely when he must; there is courage in his calculations but not in his blood, and I wish one could know the portion of his thoughts that have no immediate bearing on the affairs of the world. Even so, does he have any wherein the violence of his interests in this life absorb him completely? Be that as it may, he meant the Concordat to serve him as the pretext for presenting the people with the dress rehearsal of his future coronation.

The church of Notre Dame was chosen for the ceremony of reinstalling the clergy, and for the occasion, he named to ascend the pulpit the very Archbishop who had preached the sermon at Louis XVI's coronation in Rheims. The Archbishop, M. de Boisgelin, arrived from England where he had been an émigré for ten years.[151] Although he was a man of most distinguished mind, like a number of his fellows he hastened to issue pastoral letters exhorting to war with England, with the power that had showered him with kindness in his time of misfortune. They called it love of one's country. For in France there are, unfortunately, expressions for everything, and people do not have the decency to keep silent at least when they sacrifice conscience to self-interest. The First Consul had selected the Archbishop of Aix only because the man demeaned himself more than another would have done in serving at this new coronation after he had been chosen by Louis XVI for the sermon at his. The solemnity of that memory stood in contrast to the present conduct of M. de Boisgelin. He was seventy years old with a feeble voice that made almost inaudible the nicely phrased compliments he addressed to the First Consul in the church. His age and health did not presage a long life and, in fact, just three years later he was no longer alive. Still, he sacrificed his past reputation to the glimmer of prestige that came along to light his pale face before he died. At the same time, an Archbishop of Paris at the age of one hundred was the true model of an old courtier-priest.[152] It was an effort for him to hold himself erect under the weight of a century. He did not miss a single meeting with consuls, ministers, or prefects and, subsequently, with so many other employees at the court that he died from an excess of bowing and scraping. It was under such auspices, however, that religion was reestablished.

Bonaparte made his way to Notre Dame with all the pomp of royalty. Back in his Tuileries palace, he remarked to a few generals: "Well then, wasn't everything like old times today?" "Yes," replied General Bernadotte, "except for two million men who died for liberty and are no longer here."[153] An admirable response, and one that Napoleon endured like so many of the general's other acts of independence. He was thus miraculously spared despite the dangers he faced for his opinions and his courage. It was at this same time that I had the honor of seeing him frequently. The moment was decisive and this citizen-general wanted his companions-in-arms, defenders of those first days of the Revolution when love of liberty was sincere, to join with him and put a stop to Bonaparte's growing tyranny.

To mark these various peace treaties, the city of Paris wanted to raise a statue to Bonaparte, but since he required something more substantial than such futile honors, he exhausted his whole store of modesty in refusing and surreptitiously had the Senate informed that he preferred more concrete offerings. He was elected for ten years. In a speech, the Senate proposed ten additional years. That did not suit him. His mealymouthed reply was that life or even death would be sweet if his last sight were a happy France. But he added that the people must be consulted on whether they wanted what the Senate was proposing, and it happened, as if by accident, that the Council of State proposed the Consulate for Life rather than renewal for ten years, for which Napoleon had thanked the Senate.

Since the death of Louis XVI, nothing more shamefully deceptive has been seen in France than these speeches and popular votes. The authorities named by the government settle the matter of the public will as they do the receipts and expenses of their departments, and as a rule, the nation in no way shares the view it is made to express. This time, it was much worse. Voting registers were opened, and all those who had not written "no" were counted as voting "yes." Population lists were used as voter rolls, and the small number of men brave enough to put down their names as against the Consulate for Life was insignificant compared to the millions of men who, by not voting, were put down as approving it. The true "yes" votes were far more numerous than the "no" votes because all candidates for office—and in France they are many—wanted to show their goodwill. One man, General LaFayette, who has never swerved from the path of morality and liberty, went to inscribe his opposition in the register. He had already refused every post of senator or ambassador offered by the First Consul, and since then he has lived in the country, doing nothing to uphold his views except give them the support of his noble example.[154]

Memory lingers of a pamphlet written by a highly gifted man in which, though voting in favor of the Consulate for Life, he spoke out strongly against the title "Emperor of the Gauls," which rumor was spreading among the public.[155] Changing the beautiful name of France to Gaul sickened those men and women who remained truly French. Once, writing to the Helvetic government, Bonaparte called himself the highest officer of the Gauls, but this was a passing fancy, of little importance to him. He had the rumor spread that he meant to declare himself Emperor, although the issue being voted on was the Consulate for Life. When he actually ascended the throne he again used terror to make people judge the issue feared yesterday a lesser evil than the one that might threaten them tomorrow. It is a clever enough tactic with the common run of men, but it would have been thwarted by opposing everything, and capitulating on nothing, to a man who never flinches in the arena of power.

Gathering around General Bernadotte was a faction of generals and senators who wanted to know from him whether there were not some measures to take against the rapidly approaching usurpation. He proposed various plans, all based on some legal form since he considered all other means contrary to his principles. But, at a minimum, that legal form required deliberation by several members of the Senate, and not one of them dared endorse such an act. Throughout these highly dangerous negotiations, I saw General Bernadotte and his friends frequently; that was more than enough to ruin me had their plans been discovered. Bonaparte was already saying that people always left my home less attached to him than when they arrived. In a word, he was preparing to see me alone as guilty among all those who were far more so than I, but who were far more important for him to treat with consideration.[156]

I left in the midst of all this. The dreadful state of M. de Staël's health obliged me to go with him to a spa.[157] He died from another apoplectic seizure on the way, and I reached my father's home in a painful state of exhaustion and anxiety. Letters from Paris informed me that, after I left, he[158] had spoken sharply against my social ties to General Bernadotte, and everything suggested his determination to punish me. But he stopped short at the idea of striking at General Bernadotte, either because he needed his military talent too much, or family ties restrained him, or this general's popularity with the French Army was greater than that of all the others, or finally, because a certain charm in Bernadotte's manner makes it difficult even for Bonaparte to be fully his enemy.

Word came from Paris that the First Consul had indulged in strong comments against me. But what shocked him even more than the opinions he supposed I held was the number of foreigners who had come to see me. The son of the Stadtholder, the Prince of Orange,[159] had paid me the honor of dining in my home, and was reproached for it. The existence of a woman people visit for her wit and her literary reputation is nothing much, but this nothing much did not depend on him, and that was sufficient for his wanting to crush it.

When I saw my father again, the manuscript of his book *Last Views on Politics and Finance* had just been sent to the printer. However, when I told him the details of my uncertain situation with respect to the First Consul, he offered to withdraw it. I could not bring myself to agree. The work was truly beautiful. To me, it seemed perfectly noble to speak against the absolute power of a single person after fifteen years of fighting the people's party;[160] and I felt that, above all else, I wanted this last ray of glory for the sunset of my father's life. But never could a moment have been more dangerous for publishing such a work. It contained praise for the First Consul, permissible then since he had not yet crossed the Rubicon of crime,[161] but it called attention to the plan for a monarchy of apostates such as we have seen come into being since that time; and the very moment this prophetic work appeared, the Senate published the body of laws that would accompany the proclamation of the Consulate for Life.[162]

During the Revolution they always had key phrases to put in the mouths of fools for everything they wanted to do. "Organic laws" is one of them. What it means is less than clear, but some people were assured that they signified the Republic's completion, while others were promised, more accurately, that they meant its destruction. In this appendix to the Constitution, the new oath required of the First Consul for Life held that he would never make war except to defend the Republic. What did the French Army on the banks of the Moskva have to say about that?

Not content with decrees that placed supreme authority securely in the hands of Bonaparte; not content with enslavement of the press on the one hand and, on the other, the endless newspaper sophistry that every morning stuffed with lies the minds of those who read and of those who do not read—that is, who are incapable of reflecting on a book, and amuse themselves with serials; not content, I say, with all these precautions for muddling the public's common sense, they took up education—that is, the means of preparing the next generation for servitude—as if the example furnished by their fathers were not enough for the purpose. The Revolution, which produced scarcely any durable institutions, had nonetheless founded a Polytechnic School; from this institution have come most of the strong and independent men on whom France can still found her hopes. A Councillor of State delegated to review it asserted that in the future there would be only wise minds, that is to say in the language of the day, men able to submit to force and to conform in all things to calculations of self-interest.[163]

It was very difficult to win the First Consul's permission to teach Latin, but Greek was strictly banned.[164] Indeed, what use can it be in a state whose leader wants only workers and soldiers? Even so, he is annoyed by the need for workers to keep alive the men he will send to their death. All public education has assumed a military quality; a drumroll signals the time for declensions and corporals preside over instruction in literature. Bonaparte has been compared to Charlemagne, when in fact they might be contrasted, as the latter was far ahead of his century and the former is behind. It is perhaps a way for them to meet. Bonaparte spoke more truthfully about himself when, chatting with his intimates, he was distressed that, unlike Tamerlane, he did not command unreasoning peoples.[165] He must agree that since then the unfortunate French have mended their ways, retaining their distinctive intelligence without the liberty of thought and speech they once enjoyed even under their most despotic kings. Further, even if Bonaparte had been more liberal in his concept of public education, conscription to the degree he established it in France was quite sufficient to discourage parents from giving, and young men from receiving any kind of education. Such is the structure of his despotism that, come what may, it can only hold a legacy of misfortune and dark shadows for the generations of the future.

That year, on August 15, the First Consul's birthday was celebrated for the first time; and that anniversary took the place of all others. Among the host of speeches that filled the paper columns of the *Moniteur,* a prefect from the French coast facing England was seen to tell Bonaparte that God had rested once He created him. In a word, with each day, servility further undermined the foundations of human dignity. Uniforms were given to all employees from bailiffs to consuls; members of the Institute wore embroidered olive branches on theirs; and while in England even officers wear uniforms only within their regiments, in France the lowliest clerk had a slim thread of gold or silver to distinguish him from mere citizens. All these means of vanity gathered in the hands of a single man prepared the way for despotism under the name of monarchy, for the Republic had already ceased to exist, and enlightened men were restricted to wishing for a limited monarchy. But that was even less compatible with Bonaparte's character than the rule of factions, for he would rather have run the risk of being oppressed than give up the chance of being the oppressor.

In this same year of 1802, the affair of the German possessionary princes began; they were to be granted indemnification at the Congress of Rastatt.[166] The whole matter was dealt with in Paris to the great advantage, it was said, of the ministers entrusted with it. In any event, the plundering of all Europe by diplomacy began there and would stop only at its borders. We saw all the greatest lords of feudal Germany bring to Paris the obsequious ceremonies that pleased the First Consul more than the still offhand manner of the French, and ask the return of what belonged to them with a servility that should almost cost any rights to their possessions, so strong is the impression they give of totally discounting the authority of justice.

At the time, England, a nation preeminent for its pride, was not entirely free of a curiosity bordering on homage about the First Consul as a person. The governing party judged the man for what he was. The opposition party should have hated tyranny all the more for its supposedly greater enthusiasm for liberty; but the opposition party and Fox himself, whose talents and generosity cannot be recalled without admiration and emotion,[167] mistakenly treated Bonaparte with great indulgence and so prolonged the error of those who still wanted to confuse with France's Revolution the most stubborn enemy of the first principles of that Revolution.

Early in the winter of 1802 to 1803, when I read in the papers that Paris was bringing together so many of England's illustrious men and so many of France's witty men, I admit that my wish to be among them was strong. I make no secret that, for me, Paris has always seemed the most agreeable of places to live. I was born there, I spent my childhood and early youth there; as for the generation that knew my father, the friends who went through the perils of the Revolution with me, I can only see them there. The love of one's country, that took hold of the strongest souls, grips the soul still more vigorously when the inclinations of the mind blend with the affections of the heart and the habits of imagination. French conversation is found in Paris alone, and from earliest childhood, conversation has been my greatest pleasure. Fear of being cut off from sojourn there was so painful that reason proved ineffectual against it. I was in the full intensity of life when the need for vivid pleasures is precisely what leads most rapidly to despair, as it makes very difficult the resignation without which the vicissitudes of human existence are unbearable.

No ban on giving me passports for Paris had reached the prefect of Geneva, but I knew that the First Consul had said within his immediate circle that I would do better not to return. And on subjects of this nature he was already in the habit of dictating his wishes in conversation, so that people would relieve him of acting by anticipating his orders. Had he used this way of saying that so-and-so should hang himself, I think he would strongly disapprove if, in the light of the intimation, the obedient subject did not have the rope bought and the gallows erected. Another symptom of Bonaparte's antipathy was the way French newspapers treated my novel *Delphine,* which came out at the time; taking it on themselves to proclaim immoral a work my father had approved of, those courtier-censors condemned it. There could be found in the book the youthful fire and ardent will to happiness that ten years—and ten years of suffering—have taught me to direct otherwise. But my critics, insensitive by nature to this kind of injustice, quite simply obeyed the same voice that had ordered them to rip the father's work to shreds before attacking the daughter's. For it got back to us from all sides that the true reason for the Emperor's wrath was my father's last book, in which the entire scaffolding of the monarchy was mapped out in advance.[168]

My father was disturbed over the role he might have played in the First Consul's ill-tempered view of my return to Paris, and he wrote to Consul Lebrun, whom he had known through business, protesting that I had absolutely nothing to do with the publication of his book. Once again he spoke of the First Consul in the noblest, most flattering way and, in conclusion, confided that the thought of being the cause of my exile was the greatest sorrow that could afflict him in his old age. He considered Paris the only suitable place for bringing up my very young children,[169] for my relationships of a lifetime and, even more particularly, for my sort of mind. While my father was writing this letter he continually came into my room, adjoining his, to consult me on every sentence, and I do not believe that, in the course of a long career, he ever wanted anything more intensely than a favorable reply.

I believe that Bonaparte is the only man, or rather the only human being, capable of reading, unmoved, this letter from an old man not long since so brilliant a Prime Minister of France,[170] and who asked only one favor: that a great injustice not be done his daughter and that daughter's children. But

the more impressive the circumstances surrounding my father, the stronger
the First Consul thought he appeared by trampling them underfoot. It is always through scorn that Bonaparte has sought to convey the notion of his
grandeur. He did not know that magnanimity lies in respecting virtue without power, just as it is pride that leads us to defy power without virtue.

One morning my father came into my room, a letter in his hand. He was
very distressed, and in his eyes I saw tears he was trying to hold back.
"Here," he said, handing me Consul Lebrun's reply, obviously dictated by
Bonaparte. "They mean to lessen your affection for me by presenting me as
the cause of your unhappiness." Indeed, I defy anyone to compose a letter
more diabolically skillful than the one Consul Lebrun had been forced to
write. Everything that could hurt my father concerning his career as statesman and great writer, everything that could portray him as a father who had
sacrificed his children to his pride was pieced together with the bland civil-
ity and the hypocritical mildness used by the Emperor's representatives in
the attempt to reconcile the forms of the Old Regime with the revolutionary brutality of the new despotism.[171]

What troubled me most cruelly as I read the letter was that I had brought
it upon my father, and I hope I managed to persuade him that it added still
more to the affection he inspired in me. But I could not hide what weighed
only too heavily on my soul: regret at being kept away from Paris. To begin
with, all men, even those not endowed by nature with vivid imagination,
want what is forbidden. An unjust interdict disgusts every person with some
self-respect in his soul. Ultimately, attachment to the places where we have
spent our childhood, to the friends who have gone through the first years of
life with us—this love of one's country is so inherent in human nature that
warriors most hardened to all forms of suffering are at times invincibly
struck with homesickness. It does not follow that because Paris has great
charm one should love it less than a Lapp loves Lapland.[172] It affects me as
my country independently of the pleasure it brings me as a place of residence. The dynamic quality in minds and in exterior objects; the ease of social interchange between people and ideas; a certain interest in all that one
breathes in the air, like perfumes in Italy; a host of people who have conversation, and whose faculties are, as they say, ready money: all of this is an
agreeable distraction from the burden of life, and it is an effort to live elsewhere when one has grown used to life there!

My father shared my taste for Paris, and during her lifetime my mother
felt it strongly too. I was extremely sad at being separated from my friends
and unable to give my children the feeling for the arts that is hard to come

by in the country. Since in Lebrun's letter there was nothing stated against my return, only pointed insinuations, I devised a hundred schemes to return and test whether the First Consul, still careful of opinion at the time, would want to face the stir my exile would arouse. My father, ever ready to assume blame for his role in damaging my future, thought of going to Paris himself and speaking to the First Consul in my favor. I confess that my first reaction was to agree. I had such an idea of the influence my father's presence would necessarily exert that, to me, it seemed impossible to resist: his age, the beauty of his expression, such nobility of soul together with such subtlety of mind would subjugate even Bonaparte, I thought, and at first I did not refuse the proof of devotion my father willingly offered me. I did not yet know the degree of the First Consul's anger at his book. But fortunately for me, I saw on reflection that these very qualities in my father would have only further prodded the First Consul to humiliate the one who possessed them, and he would surely have found the means of doing so at least in appearance, for in France power has many willing allies; and if the spirit of opposition has often been seen to develop in this country, it is because governmental weakness has offered it easy victories. It cannot be repeated too often: what the French love in all matters is success; and in this country, power can easily contrive to make misfortune seem ridiculous. In the end, thank heaven, I awoke from the illusions I had indulged in and firmly refused the generous sacrifice my father wanted to make for me. When he saw that I was determined not to accept, I understood how great the cost would have been for him. Fifteen months later, I lost my father,[173] and had he gone through with the trip he was considering, I would have ascribed his illness to that trip and the poison of remorse would have envenomed my wound still more.

It was also in the winter of 1802 to 1803 that Switzerland took up arms against the unitary constitution they meant to give her.[174] How curious the French revolutionaries' obsession with forcing on every country the same political organization as in France! Doubtless there are principles common to all countries—all those guaranteeing the civil and political rights of free nations. But what does it matter whether a nation be a limited monarchy like England, a federal republic like the United States, or the thirteen cantons of Switzerland? And must Europe be reduced to a single idea, like the Roman people to one head, to make possible ordering and changing everything in a single day?

The First Consul certainly attaches no importance to this or that form of constitution, nor to any conceivable constitution; what was important to him was making the best possible use of Switzerland for his own benefit, and in that respect he acted carefully. He had himself named mediator for Switzerland and chose, among the various drafts offered him, a constitution that reconciled the old ways with the new exigencies rather well; he got more men out of Switzerland than he could have done had he oppressed the country immediately.[175] He summoned to Paris ten Swiss delegates named by the two parties, aristocratic and democratic, and on January 29, 1803, he met with them for seven hours.[176] He emphasized the need for restoring the democratic cantons as they were, spuriously inveighing against the cruelty of depriving shepherds tucked away in the mountains of their sole diversion—public affairs—and telling those closest to him what was foremost in his mind: his reasons for distrusting the aristocratic cantons instead. He strongly emphasized the importance of Switzerland to France. He spoke in short sentences that were probably supposed to seem full of depth and resemble oracles. Priestly power can always pronounce oracles, but their effect must be ascribed to the power of bayonets and not to that of thought. His own words are recorded in the minutes of the talks:

> I declare that, since I have been at the head of the government of France, not one major power has taken an interest in Switzerland. It is I who won recognition of the Helvetic Republic at Lunéville; Austria was not interested. At Amiens, I tried again; England refused, but England has nothing to do with Switzerland. Had she expressed the fear that I wanted to have myself declared *landamman,*[177] that is what I would have become. England was said to take an interest in the last uprising. If her cabinet had taken an official step in this regard, if there had been one word on the subject in the London news sheet, *I would have called you together."*

What incredible language! Thus the existence of a people, who for five centuries have ensured their independence in the middle of Europe by the most heroic efforts, could be wiped out in a fit of temper, and nothing was simpler than provoking it by chance in a person who, independent of all the rest, acts on whim.

In that same conversation, Bonaparte added that he found it unpleasant to draw up a constitution because it exposed him to being hissed, which he did not want. That expression bears the stamp of the falsely affable vulgarity he often likes to display. Roederer[178] wrote the Act of Mediation at his dictation, and this all happened while his troops were occupying Switzerland. Since then he has withdrawn them, and this country, it must be admitted, has been treated better than the rest of Europe by the Emperor, although politically and militarily, it is entirely under his yoke; thus it will remain calm amid the general rebellion. The peoples of Europe were inclined to a degree of patience such that it took Bonaparte to wear it down.

During this time, as the breach of the Treaty of Amiens drew near,[179] Bonaparte was preparing his finances to support the war he favored most: the war with England. He established a bank[180] and put finances in order, but always while making war, with himself as the center of everything, never peace and France. He paid no outstanding debts to those who could not be useful to him in the future, unconvinced that justice is independent of circumstances and that, nonetheless, it is the foundation for everything. This absence of justice also explains his having no credit; it is the only domain so intractable that despotism cannot use it at will. Lacking credit, he required contributions, for in no country are normal revenues adequate for the extraordinary expenditures of war. Thus, plundering foreign countries became a necessary part of the structure of Bonaparte's finances, and since everything was tied to the lifetime of his government, he needed resources as temporary as his own life.

The remaining days of peace saw the completion of the Civil Code, so well known since then as the Napoleonic Code. It is the only abstraction Bonaparte seemed to value, certain as he was of escaping his own legislation through military commissions and in a thousand other ways. He rather enjoyed ruling foreign nations according to the pattern he'd had fashioned in the Council of State. It was a way of *denationalizing* them, to use an expression of the day; and just as he insisted that Italians and Germans speak French, so he enjoyed changing the laws of every people. At times someone took the risk of citing the decrees he himself had issued, but he seemed as impatient with his own resolve of yesterday as with that of anyone else, and more than once he said: "Well, that law was dictated by the best interest of the people, and it is also the best interest of the people that inspires the opposite for us now." The revolutionaries of the Reign of Terror did well to call their government the Committee of Public Safety: there is no expression so broad and potentially so open to all possible arbitrary acts.

English newspapers attacked the First Consul with some bitterness; England was too enlightened not to see where all of that man's actions were leading. Nothing annoyed him so much as freedom of the press. Since tyranny is in fact established even more by guile than by force, publicity has to be the greatest fear of a despotic usurper. My father often told me that a free newspaper published in France would do Bonaparte more harm than an army of a hundred thousand men. Those who constantly talk of military measures forget that in many respects these depend on public opinion, and that although the army reasons more slowly than the rest of the nation, it nonetheless comes to understand in the long run. Each time a translation of English papers was brought to Bonaparte, he stormed at the English ambassador, who answered with as much composure as accuracy that the King of Great Britain himself was not protected from the sarcasm of journalists, and that the Constitution did not allow them to be attacked in this regard. Bonaparte, so slight of stature, circled around the tall and handsome Lord Whitworth[181] as he did around the principles of English liberty, able neither to attain nor to tolerate them. However, a case was brought against Peltier for articles in his paper directed against the First Consul. Peltier had the honor of being defended by M. Mackintosh, whose plea to the court on this occasion was the most eloquent we have read in modern times. I shall explain later under what circumstances it came into my hands.

Bonaparte sent his troops into Hanover; he expanded his conquests in Italy; his troops occupied Switzerland and Holland. He loudly demanded that, according to the Treaty of Amiens, the English must evacuate the island of Malta, which would leave them without a port on the Mediterranean.[182] The Treaty of Amiens was a serious mistake. Even after this treaty, there were assuredly more pretexts than needed to start the war again, but England's proclamation was unworthy of the cause she wished to defend; she asked that Switzerland and Holland be evacuated, and Italy returned to her along with Hanover. The most splendid social war waged since the Christian era began with a diplomatic discussion, as if an ordinary matter had been in question. The English are too scornful of speaking to Europe; it is enough for them to be eloquent among themselves. Nonetheless they must also be concerned with the opinion of the Continent whose influence is great. Bonaparte sent a memorandum to all the archbishops and bishops of France, after the manner of kings, to ask their prayers for the success of his armies. Cursed be those who did his bidding! That same Archbishop of Aix, become Archbishop of Tours, who had nothing left to lose, said in his pastoral letter that people must rally to a paternal, wise, firm, and legitimate government.[183]

One of my friends went to see the elderly Portalis,[184] Minister of Religions at the time. Finding him in the middle of an almost immoderate fit of joy, my friend asked: "Have you read the Archbishop of Tours' pastoral letter? It seems to me he's done justice to the First Consul's qualities." "Pooh! Pooh!" he answered. "As if we care about praise! But he said the right word: 'legitimate,' do you see? The man who crowned Louis XVI calls us legitimate. That's all we needed!" How strange that those who are sure of their right to oppress nations are particularly uneasy when they are not in line of succession to the throne. They admit their tyranny far more readily than their usurpation.

Each time Lord Whitworth went to the Tuileries shortly before war was declared, Bonaparte made the most unwarranted remarks possible against his government, and his furious gesticulations as he spoke were as absurd as they were disgraceful. Lord Whitworth naturally put one foot forward to keep him at a distance, and he was surrounded by a good many Englishmen of commanding height and appearance. Bonaparte was astonished at the futility of his outbursts, ordinarily so frightening to others; the sea and, still more certainly, the pride of independence set up a barrier between those senseless rages and true rationality. Why did Bonaparte so often indulge in those harangues against the diplomatic envoys of foreign powers at his court? "Because," you will tell me, "he cannot control himself, and your analysis of his character is wrong?" No, he believes, and rightly so, that his words are terrifying in the extreme. Until its nations awoke, Europe had scarcely any courage but military, and the bravest of men on the battlefield were totally irresolute of mind, and nothing so troubles weak characters as a certain violence of discourse that is far more terrifying than actual events. But these methods had no effect on the English, and it was utterly pointless to use them against Englishmen. But as I have said several times, and it cannot be repeated too often, Bonaparte does not understand men who are led by their opinions and not by self-interest, and just as the sign of the cross, they say, nullifies the devil's power, so does a scrupulous sentiment in others cloud the intelligence of his mind.

I was in Geneva, living by preference and circumstance in the company of English people, when news arrived that war had been declared. Rumor also spread that English travelers would be imprisoned. Since nothing of the kind had been seen in the civil law of any nation, I did not believe a word of it, and my confidence narrowly missed harming several of my friends; they did escape, however.[185] But men most foreign to politics—Lord Beverley, father of eleven children, returning from Italy with his wife and daughters, a hundred other people with French passports, scientific groups on their way to universities to obtain information or to southern regions to recover their health, and traveling under the safeguard of the accepted law of all nations—were arrested and have been languishing in provincial villages for ten years, leading the most miserable lives imaginable. This scandalous act served no purpose; barely two thousand Englishmen, mostly unconnected to the military, fell victim to the tyrant who capriciously inflicted suffering on a few poor individuals in a burst of temper at the all-powerful nation to which they belonged.

It was in the summer of 1803 that the farce of the great invasion began.[186] Flatboats were ordered from one end of France to the other; some were built in the forests along the main roads. The French, in all things zealously imitative, cut board after board, spoke one grandiloquent sentence after another. In Picardy they erected an arch of triumph for Bonaparte on which was inscribed: "The Road to London." Others wrote: "To Bonaparte the Great: We beg you to allow us aboard the vessel that takes you *to England,* and with you the fortunes and vengeance of the French people." This vessel, which Bonaparte was to command, had time to rot in port. Others put as slogans on their flags in the harbor: "A good wind and thirty-six hours." In sum, all of France resonated with boasts, while he alone knew the secret truth.

Bonaparte cannot endure freedom of the press, but he does like to make use of an enslaved press. He gets newspapers to speak in a thousand different ways. He knows the importance of public opinion and acts on it tirelessly and without pause, an example that ought to be followed elsewhere. It is also true that words are nowhere more contagious than in France. In this country, the riffraff of the salons delights in repeating sentences read in newspapers and embroidering a given story, each in his own way. One of those journalists, a literate corporal of Napoleon's, lamented the fate of liberty in England, compromised by the increase in troops forced on them by the fear of invasion. It must be acknowledged that this concern on the part of a French journalist for English liberty implied a charity wherein one loves his neighbor far more than himself. Bonaparte initiated military conscription which, used excessively, has turned all Europe into an armed camp ever since. He excited public spirit with his parades, his visits to ports, and to the boatyard in Antwerp with Mme Bonaparte. He did all that can be done when men cannot be stirred either by truth, or religion, or patriotism; that is, he used all possible means to commit them to the interests of one man in the hope that each would share in their leader's winnings. From that time on, Europe also began to follow the selfish politics that were its undoing. Prussia calmly watched the invasion of the electorate of Hanover, imagining it would one day be hers.[187] Russia let the French dictate laws for Hamburg and other Baltic ports. Poor Spain—since then the first to sound the alarm for liberty in Europe—was led by a more than stupid King, Carlos IV, and signed the treaty of offensive and defensive alliance with France.[188] In short, Bonaparte well understood that it would be easy for him to divide and conquer a Europe in which, far from making common cause against the great Leviathan that meant to overrun them all, each country sought to hand over its neighbor and take advantage of the spoils. To this day, the three great powers—Austria, Prussia, and Russia—have never joined forces and in their successive wars have constantly and in turn stood apart, as if it were important for each to have a tête-à-tête with the French Army.[189]

Toward the fall of 1803, I thought that Bonaparte had forgotten me. People wrote from Paris that he was totally engrossed in his English expedition, and that he planned to leave for the coast and board ship himself to lead the invasion. I did not have much faith in the project, but I let myself believe that he would accept my living twelve leagues from Paris, with the very small number of friends who would come that distance to see a person in disfavor. I also thought that as I was known well enough for my exile to be talked about in Europe, the First Consul would avoid that scandal. I had reckoned according to my desires, but I did not know the nature of the man who was to dominate Europe. Far from wanting to spare what was distinguished in any domain, he wanted to make a pedestal for his statue out of all those who rose in the world, either by trampling them underfoot or by making them serve his ends.

I came to a house in the countryside ten leagues from Paris with the idea of spending the winter in this retreat as long as the tyranny lasted. I could see my friends and occasionally go to the theater and the Museum.[190] That is all I wished of a stay in Paris given the environment of distrust and spying that was beginning to take hold, and I confess that I do not see what disadvantage there could be for the Emperor in leaving me in this voluntary exile.[191] I had been there quietly for a month when a woman, like so many who seek recognition at the expense of another woman better known than they, went and told the First Consul that the roads were covered with people coming to visit me. Surely, nothing was less true. The exiles people went to see were those who, in the eighteenth century, had almost as much power as the kings who sent them away; for power can be resisted when it is not tyrannical, and it can only be tyrannical when submission is universal. In any event, Bonaparte seized the pretext or motive given him to exile me, and one of my friends warned me that a gendarme would come within a few days to notify me that I must leave.[192] One has no idea, at least in countries where individuals are routinely protected against injustice, of the state one is thrown into by sudden news of certain arbitrary acts. Besides, I am by nature easily shaken; my imagination more readily conceives pain than hope, and although experience has often shown me that new circumstances dispelled grief, it always seems to me, when it comes, that nothing will ever release me from it. What is easy, in fact, is to be unhappy, especially when one aspires to the privileged lot in life.

I withdrew at once to the home of a truly good and intelligent woman to whom, I must say, I was recommended by a man occupying an important position in the government. I will not forget his courage in offering me a refuge, but were his intentions equally good today, he could not act the same way except at the cost of his very existence.[193] As tyranny is allowed to advance, it grows before one's eyes like a phantom, but takes hold with a firmer hand. And so I came to the country estate of a person I scarcely knew, amid a society entirely foreign to me, and bearing in my heart a searing grief that I did not wish to show. At night, alone with a faithful woman in my service for a number of years,[194] we listened at the window for a gendarme on horseback, and by day I tried to be pleasant and hide my situation. From that estate I wrote Joseph Bonaparte a letter expressing all my sadness, truthfully I think. The sole object of my ambition was a retreat twelve leagues from Paris, and I sensed with despair that once I was exiled, it would be for a long time and perhaps forever. Joseph and his brother Lucien generously did all they could to save me, and we shall see that they were not alone.

Mme Récamier, a woman celebrated for her face, whose beauty in itself expresses her character, sent word that I was invited to stay at her country home at Saint-Brice, two leagues from Paris. I was wrong to accept, but I did not then know that I could harm a person so foreign to politics; I thought her safe from everything, despite the generosity of her character. The most agreeable society gathered in her home, and there, for the last time, I enjoyed all that I was about to leave. It was during those stormy days that I received M. Mackintosh's brief for the defense.[195] There I read those pages portraying a Jacobin who, in the Revolution, had been the scourge of children, old people, and women, now bent under the rod of the Corsican who had despoiled him of the slightest share of the liberty on whose behalf he claimed to be armed. This bit of the finest eloquence moved me to the depths of my soul; without knowing it, superior writers can sometimes comfort the unfortunate of all countries and of all times. France was becoming so profoundly silent around me that this voice, which suddenly spoke to my soul, seemed to come down from heaven: it came from a country that was free.

After a week with Mme Récamier without hearing a word on my exile, I persuaded myself that Bonaparte had abandoned the idea. There is nothing more usual than to set your mind at ease on any sort of danger when you see none of its symptoms around you. I felt so far from any plan or any hostile act, even against that man, that it seemed impossible to me that he would not leave me in peace, and after a few days I returned to my country house convinced that, content to frighten me, he was deferring his decision against me. It was in fact quite enough not to change my opinion, not to force me to disavow it, but to repress forever the remains of the republican habits that had led me to speak too frankly the year before.

I was at the table with three of my friends in a room looking onto the main road and the entrance gate; it was the end of September. At four o'clock a man on horseback, dressed in gray, stopped and rang at the gate; I was sure of my fate. He asked for me; I received him in the garden. As I moved toward him, I was struck by the perfume of the flowers and the beauty of the sun. The sensations that come to us from social situations are so different from those of nature! He told me that he was head of the Gendarmerie at Versailles, but had been ordered not to wear his uniform for fear of frightening me. He showed me a letter signed by the Emperor,[196] ordering that I be forty leagues from Paris within twenty-four hours, and that I be treated, however, with all the respect due a woman whose name was well known. He added that, as a foreigner, I was subject to the police; this respect for the individual liberty of the French did not last very long, and soon after me, French men and French women were exiled without any kind of trial.[197] I answered the gendarme that to leave in twenty-four hours was suitable for conscripts but not for a woman and children, and therefore I suggested to the officer that he leave with me for Paris where I needed to spend three days to make the necessary arrangements for my departure. And so I climbed into my coach with my children and the officer, who had been chosen as the best educated of the gendarmes. He did indeed compliment me on my writing. "You see where being an intelligent woman leads," I told him. "Advise the members of your family against it, if you have the opportunity." I was trying to raise my spirits with pride, but I felt the claw in my heart.

I stopped for a few moments at Mme Récamier's where I met General Junot[198] who, from devotion to Mme Récamier, promised to speak with the First Consul the following morning. He did so, in fact, with the greatest warmth. One would think that a man whose rare military qualities made him so necessary to Bonaparte's power could influence him to spare a woman; but Bonaparte's generals, while they win innumerable favors from him for themselves, truly have no influence. When they ask for money or position, Bonaparte finds it quite acceptable; they are in line with the goal of his power since they become dependent on him. But if, as happens rarely, they wanted to defend the unfortunate or oppose some injustice, Bonaparte would quickly make clear that they are no more than appendages charged with maintaining slavery and submitting to it themselves.

I came to a newly rented house in Paris[199] where I had not lived yet. I had chosen it carefully to have the exposure I preferred, and imagination showed me already settled in the drawing room with several friends whose conversation, in my view, is first among the pleasures human life can offer. I entered the house, certain only of leaving it, and I spent the nights wandering through those rooms where I mourned even more happiness than I had hoped to find there. My gendarme came by every morning, as in the tale of Bluebeard, to ask if I did not want to leave the next day, and each time I could not resist asking for yet another day. My friends came to dinner every day, and sometimes we were merry, as if to drain the cup of sorrow; and we put on as pleasant a face as possible for one another as we were about to part for so long. They would tell me that the man who came daily to summon me to leave reminded them of those days of the Terror when gendarmes came to ask for their victims.

You will be astonished, perhaps, that I compare exile to death, but Bolingbroke himself argues which of the two penalties is the more cruel. Cicero, who managed to brave proscription, could not endure exile. One comes upon more men who are courageous in the face of the scaffold than of the loss of their native land. In all codes of law, perpetual banishment is considered punishment for a capital crime, and in France the whim of one man nonchalantly inflicts what conscientious judges only reluctantly impose on criminals.

Exile, in its various degrees—running from banishment from Paris or France to reclusion in a château—has been Emperor Napoleon's most successful means of terrorizing polite company in France into submission. Life in this country, where society's pleasures are so elegant and varied, is so highly prized by its inhabitants that they find it more painful to be deprived of their country than do the peoples of every other land. The Emperor, well aware of this French predilection, is still more arbitrary in this domain than any other. Prison and death excite a kind of interest and shudders that pave the way to resistance. Thus despotism must use those means sparingly. Blood is an expenditure even for one who considers it in this light alone, and every expenditure requires caution. But exile, to all appearances, is so calm and moderate a step that it is to the despot's advantage to inspire as much fear—and less stir—with this punishment as with more spectacular punishments. I think it is easy to show, however, that of all the powers reserved to a sovereign, exile is perhaps the most dangerous by virtue of the easy solution it offers him, and the most fatal by its inevitable effects. Public opinion in countries like France, where people have not acquired the habit of respecting the citizen's liberty, is weak in the defense of exiles. To take an interest in them is to run the risk of banishment oneself, and in nations long under arbitrary rule, we forget that our neighbor's misfortune threatens our home too, and that far from standing aloof to escape tyranny, we must join together to resist it.

Since exile strikes at the tastes and habits of each person, it is possible to hold up to ridicule the suffering it must cause, for just as all faces lend themselves to caricature, so each individual existence is touched with absurdity if one wants to examine it with no trace of affection or enthusiasm. But what results from these jokes at once barbaric and frivolous? He who makes them to gratify power is struck in turn, for infamy, however ingenious, cannot forever evade the anger of a man for whom the existence of a human creature is an annoyance the moment he no longer sees him as a docile tool. Yet the decree of exile, treated as if inconsequential, means that this one dies far from the family that would have restored him to life; that one cannot be at the bedside of his dying parents; another is separated from children and spouse; yet another, through absence, loses the affections that were his happiness; another, forced to abandon his fortune, is ruined; the faculties of another fade when he is deserted and forgotten. The wish to return means the loss of dignity or, if you persist, the loss of life's sweet pleasures. All are tormented in their most cherished inclinations. Exile acts on imagination and constantly presents itself as an obstacle to all desires, all plans, all hopes.

Special circumstances offered me a refuge and resources of wealth in Switzerland, my parents' native land. In this respect, I was less to be pitied than another, and yet I have suffered cruelly. I will not be useless to the world, then, when I point out all that must lead to never allowing a sovereign the right of arbitrary exile. No deputy will express his thought freely, no writer will dare express himself any longer if he can be banished when his candor displeases. No man will dare speak sincerely if it can cost the happiness of his whole family. A woman, above all, meant to support and reward enthusiasm, will strive to smother her generous feelings if they must result either in her being taken from the objects of her affection, or in seeing her loved ones sacrifice their lives to follow her into exile.

On the eve of the last day granted to me, Joseph Bonaparte made one more attempt on my behalf; and his wife, a person of the most perfect sweetness and simplicity, was kind enough to come to my home and invite me to spend a few days with her at her estate in Mortfontaine.[200] I accepted gratefully, for of course I was moved by the goodness of Joseph, who received me in his home when his brother was persecuting me. I spent three days at Mortfontaine, and in spite of the perfect cordiality of the master and mistress of the house, my situation was painful. I saw only men in the government, I breathed only the air of the authority that was visibly my enemy, and the simplest laws of courtesy and gratitude forbade my showing what I felt. With me I had only my elder son,[201] still too much a child for me to discuss such subjects with him. I spent hours contemplating the garden at Mortfontaine, one of the most beautiful to be seen in France, and whose owner, untroubled at the time, seemed enviable to me. Since then he has been exiled on thrones where I am sure that he misses his beautiful refuge.

I hesitated over the decision I would make when I left: would I return to my father or go on to Germany? My father would have welcomed his poor storm-tossed bird with a kindness beyond describing, but I feared the dejection of returning, ordered back to a country I was accused of finding somewhat monotonous. I also wished to recover, through the warm reception promised me in Germany, from the outrage done me by the First Consul; and I wanted to contrast the kind welcome of the ancient dynasties with the impertinence of the one preparing to subjugate France. Unfortunately for me, the impulse of pride won out; I would have seen my father again had I returned to Geneva.

I begged Joseph to find out from his brother whether I could go to Germany; for as things stood, the protection of the French ambassador—or at the very least the certainty that he would not claim me as French outside the country when I was outlawed as a foreigner within—was quite necessary. Joseph left for Saint Cloud. I was obliged to await his reply at an inn two leagues from Paris,[202] not daring to go back to my home in the city.

A day went by without news. Since I did not want to attract attention by staying in the same hostelry any longer, I circled the walls of Paris to find another, also two leagues off but on another road. That wandering life a few steps away from friends and home caused a grief I cannot remember without out a shudder. I can picture the room, the window where I spent the whole day watching for the messenger, a thousand painful details that misfortune drags in its wake, the excessive generosity of a few friends, the veiled calculations of a few others; everything threw my soul into a turmoil so cruel that I could wish it as an enemy only on the despot who brought it about. The letter that still offered hope came at last. Joseph sent me excellent letters of introduction for Berlin and bade me farewell nobly and gently.

And so I had to leave. The same highly intelligent friend who had been expelled from the Tribunate, Benjamin Constant, came with me, but since he too was very fond of life in Paris, I suffered from his sacrifice. Each of the horses' hoofbeats was painful, and when the postilions boasted of their speed, I could only sigh over the dismal favor they did me. I rode forty leagues in this state, unable to regain my composure. At last we stopped at Châlons; M. Benjamin Constant rekindled his wit and, with his astonishing conversation, momentarily lifted the weight that was crushing me. We continued the next day as far as Metz, where I wanted to stop and wait for news from my father. I spent two weeks there and met one of the most amiable and intelligent men that France and Germany together can produce: M. Charles de Villers.[203] His company was delightful, but it renewed my longing for that first among pleasures, a conversation where the most perfect harmony prevails in all one feels and all one says.

My father was indignant at the treatment I was subjected to in Paris; he pictured his family outlawed and leaving the country he had served so well as if they were criminals. He himself advised me to spend the winter in Germany and not to come back to him until spring. Alas! Alas! I looked forward to bringing him the harvest of new ideas I had gathered in my journey. For several years he had been saying that he clung to life only through my stories and letters. He was so keen and perceptive of mind that the pleasure of talking with him stimulated thought. I observed so that I could recount things to him, I listened so that I could repeat things to him. Ever since I lost him, I see and feel only half as well as when my aim was to please him by depicting my impressions for him.

When we reached Frankfort my daughter, then five years old, fell dangerously ill. I knew no one in the city; the language was foreign to me, not even the doctor caring for my child spoke French.[204] Oh, how my father shared my pain! What letters he wrote to me! How many doctors' opinions copied out in his own hand he sent me from Geneva! No one has ever carried the harmony of sensibility and reason further; no one was ever so strongly moved as he by the afflictions of his friends, always actively helping them, always careful in choosing the means to do so—admirable in sum. The needs of my own heart prompt these words, for what does even posterity's voice matter to him now?

I went on to Weimar where I took courage once more when, despite the difficulties of language, I saw immense intellectual treasures outside of France. I learned to read German, I listened to men who expressed themselves very well in French—Goethe and Wieland. I understood the soul and the genius of Schiller despite his difficulty in expressing himself in French. I thoroughly enjoyed the company of the Duke and Duchess of Weimar, and the three months I spent there studying German literature provided my mind with all the activity it needs if it is not to devour me alive.[205]

I left for Berlin, and there I met the delightfully charming Queen, destined since then to so many misfortunes.[206] The King welcomed me kindly, and I can say that in the six weeks I spent in that city I did not hear one individual speak other than praise for the government's justice. I think it always desirable for a country to have constitutional procedures that guarantee, through the enduring will of the nation, the advantages it enjoys from the virtues of a good king. Prussia, under the rule of its present sovereign, possessed all these advantages, but the public spirit developed since then through misfortune did not yet exist there. The military regime had kept public opinion from becoming a force, and the absence of a constitution allowing each individual to make a name for himself according to his merit had left the state deprived of talented men capable of its defense. The favor of kings, arbitrary by nature, cannot suffice for developing competition among men; circumstances relevant purely within courts can keep an able man from taking the helm and can give it to a mediocre man. Routine is also particularly dominant in a country where royal power is unopposed; a king's very sense of justice leads him to set up barriers for himself by retaining each man in his position, and it was virtually unprecedented in Prussia for a man to be removed from his civil or military service by reason of incompetence. What an advantage the French Army must have enjoyed, almost entirely composed of men who emerged from the earth like Cadmus's soldiers, formed by the French Revolution as were the Argonauts by the teeth of the dreadful dragon![207] What an advantage it must have enjoyed over those former commanders of Prussian posts or armies to whom nothing new was known! A conscientious king who does not, like England, have the blessing—and I use the word deliberately—of a parliament, makes a routine of everything for fear of overusing his own will; and given the times, all the old practices must be set aside to pursue strength of character and mind everywhere. Meanwhile, Berlin was one of the most fortunate countries on earth, and one of the most enlightened.

French writers had done Europe great good through the spirit of moderation and the taste for literature inspired in most sovereigns by their writing. The respect accorded the French mind by the friends of enlightenment was one cause of the errors destructive of Germany for such a long time.[208] Many people saw the Corsican's armies as propagators of the ideas of Montesquieu, of Rousseau, and sometimes even of Voltaire, whereas if there remained any trace of the opinions of those great men in Bonaparte's instruments of power, it was to break free of what they called prejudices and not to establish a single principle of regeneration. But during the spring of 1804 in Berlin and northern Germany, there were still many former partisans of the French Revolution who were not yet aware that Bonaparte was a far more bitter enemy of the first principles of that Revolution than the old European aristocracy.

At that time, I had the honor of meeting Prince Louis-Ferdinand, a man so consumed by his warrior's ardor that he could not survive the first reverses met by his native land.[209] He was full of warmth and enthusiasm but, for want of glory, he pursued too avidly all that can make life exciting. What he found most offensive in Bonaparte was his way of slandering all those he feared and, as a precaution, keeping those who served him under his control, denigrating them even in public opinion. The Prince often told me: "I give him leave to kill, but when it comes to moral assassination, I am disgusted." And indeed, picture for yourself the state we found ourselves in, when that great vilifier was master of all the presses of the European Continent and could write, as he often did, of the bravest men that they were cowards, and of the purest women that they were contemptible, without there being any way to contradict or to punish such statements.

Rumor of the grand conspiracy of Moreau, Pichegru, and Georges[210] began to circulate in Berlin. Among the principal leaders of the Republican and Royalist parties, there was surely a strong desire to overthrow the First Consul's authority, and to oppose the still more tyrannical authority he proposed to establish by having himself declared Emperor. But this conspiracy, which served as pretext for all of Bonaparte's crimes, was first provoked by Bonaparte himself, because he meant to use it with a diabolical skill whose every element it is important to discern.

He sent to England an exiled Jacobin who could get permission for return to France only through services to the First Consul. This man, by the name of Méhée, appeared like Sion [sic] in the city of Troy, saying he was persecuted by the Greeks.[211] He saw a few émigrés who had neither the vices nor the wit to fathom a certain kind of deceit. Consequently, it was easy for him to trap an old bishop, a former officer—in short, fragments of a regular government under which the very notion of factions was unknown. Then he wrote a witty pamphlet mocking everyone who had believed him and who, in fact, should have made up for the shrewdness they lacked by firmness of principles, that is, by never placing the slightest trust in a man guilty of evil acts. We have all erred in our way of seeing things; but from the moment a person proves treacherous or cruel, the Good Lord can forgive, but to Him alone is it given to read deeply enough into the human heart to know whether it has changed. Man must forever keep his distance from the man who has lost his respect. This disguised agent of Bonaparte claimed that there were stong elements of revolt in France. He went and found an English minister, Mr. Drake, whom he was clever enough to fool as well. A citizen of Great Britain was necessarily foreign to that web of guile interwoven with threads of Jacobinism and tyranny.

Georges and Pichegru, who sided entirely with the Bourbons, came secretly to France and agreed to act in concert with Moreau who wanted to overthrow the First Consul but not to derogate from the right of the French nation to choose the form of government that suited it best.[212] Pichegru wanted to meet with General Bernadotte, but—dissatisfied with the conduct of the venture, and wanting above all a guarantee for constitutional liberty in France—he refused. In their discussions, Moreau—a man of highly moral character, undeniable military gifts, and a very fair and enlightened mind—compromised himself by criticizing the First Consul too openly before he was sure of bringing him down. It is a failing quite natural in a generous soul to express his opinion injudiciously, but General Moreau so drew the First Consul's attention that such conduct was bound to destroy him. The First Consul needed a pretext to arrest a man who had won so many battles, and the pretext was found in his words for want of deeds. You wonder why the First Consul incited a conspiracy against himself when the consequences might have been so deadly. He felt sure of stopping it in time, but his need of a pretext for changing the form of the government was absolute.

The forms of the Republic were still in place; people were called "citizens" as if the most dreadful inequality—the kind that frees some from the yoke of the law while others are subject to arbitrary action—did not permeate all of France. Days were still numbered according to the Republican calendar;[213] the country took pride in being at peace with all of Continental Europe. Reports were made to the Legislative Body, as is still the case, on the building of roads and canals, on the construction of bridges and fountains—the type of services that cost nothing to a head of government who means to levy unlimited contributions from his country and from all of Europe. Ultimately, there was no apparent reason for changing an order of things people seemed to find so comfortable. Thus a plot implicating the English and the Bourbons was needed to stir the revolutionary elements of the nation once again, and to move them to establish an ultra-monarchial power under the pretext of preventing the return of the Old Regime. The key to the plot, which seems so complicated, was actually simple: make the revolutionaries fear for their own interests and then propose ensuring those interests by one last surrender of principle. Thus was it done.

Bonaparte's game would have been dangerous if the enemies he had encouraged by circuitous paths had been capable of assassinating him. They could have done so, but the England that Bonaparte challenged a hundred times with the most atrocious outrages constantly refused to cause the death of the man who was the keystone of hell, and the most difficult circumstances could not make them deviate from strict Christian principles in this respect. Georges said as much and proved it during his interrogation, and since that time the First Consul has had several opportunities to be convinced. England behaves with chivalry in all matters and does not think that national interest authorizes violations of morality that private interests would not permit.

Pichegru had quite simply become a Royalist just as he had been a Republican: his opinions had been turned around.[214] His character was superior to his mind, but neither was made to sway other men. Georges had more spirit, but he was not destined for the rank of leader either by education or by nature. When the plot was known in Paris, Moreau was arrested;[215] the borders were closed; it was announced that anyone giving refuge to Pichegru or Georges would be put to death, and all Jacobin measures were reinstituted to defend the life of one man.[216] Not only is he too important in his own eyes to show any indulgence where he himself is concerned; it was also a calculated plan to strike fear into peoples' minds, to remind them of the days of the Terror, that is, to inspire if possible the need to throw themselves into his arms to escape the disorder he himself fomented with all of his measures. Pichegru's hiding place was found and Georges was arrested in a tilbury, for no longer able to stay in any one house, he drove around the city day and night to escape pursuit by the police. The agent who took Georges was rewarded with the Legion of Honor. It seems to me that the French military should have wished a totally different reward for him.

The *Moniteur* was filled with statements congratulating the First Consul on the dangers he had escaped; the continual repetition of the same sentences in all corners of France offers an acquiescence in servitude unparalleled in any people. In leafing through the *Moniteur* you can find, according to the period, essays on liberty, on despotism, on philosophy, on religion, in which the departments and the fine cities of France do their utmost to say the same things in different terms. And you are astonished that men as intelligent as the French are content with successful wording and feel no desire for ideas of their own; you would think that competition of words was enough for them. Those hymns, dictated however with their accompanying exclamation points, proclaimed that all was calm in France and that the small number of agents from perfidious England had been caught. True, it did amuse a general, even though in his right mind, to say that the English had flung bales of cotton from the Levant onto the Normandy coast to give France the plague. But those solemnly ludicrous fabrications were simply deemed flattery addressed to General Bonaparte and, with the leaders of the conspiracy in the government's power along with its agents, there was reason to believe that calm was restored in France, but such was not the First Consul's intention.

I was living on the Quai de la Sprée in Berlin, and my rooms were on the ground floor. One morning at eight o'clock, I was awakened and told that Prince Louis-Ferdinand was under my window on horseback and asked me to come speak with him.[217] Very surprised by this visit so early in the morning, I hurriedly rose to greet him. He was a singularly graceful horseman and his emotion added to the nobility of his form.

"Do you know," he said, "that the Duke d'Enghien was kidnapped on the Duke of Baden's lands, turned over to a military tribunal and shot twenty-four hours after he reached Paris?"[218]

"That's insane!" I answered, "Don't you see, France's enemies spread that rumor?"

Indeed, I admit that however strong my hatred for that man, it did not extend to believing such a crime was possible.

"Since you doubt what I say," answered Prince Louis, "I am going to send you the *Moniteur* and you will read it there." With these words he left, his expression foretelling vengeance or death.

A quarter of an hour later, I held in my hands the *Moniteur* dated March 16 or Pluviôse 26,[219] which included a judgment pronounced by the military tribunal sitting in Vincennes, presided over by General Hulin—a man of the lowest origins—and composed of other individuals of his sort.[220] They began with a declaration that seemed a mockery: none of them was obliged to recuse himself since none was related to the accused. Yes indeed, those who behaved with that remarkable cowardice were not related to the Condés; but how shamelessly ironic was such a statement against the one they termed "the man commonly known as Louis d'Enghien!"[221] Thus have some Frenchmen designated the grandson of the heroes who were their country's glory! Even if one abandoned all the antiquated ideas of noble birth that would necessarily return with the monarchial way of life, even if one forgot that the Condés are Bourbons, could one so profane the memory of the Battles of Lens and Rocroi?[222] This Bonaparte, who has won his share of battles, does not even know how to respect them. For him, there is neither past nor future. His domineering and contemptuous soul has no wish to recognize anything as sacred to public opinion; he admits of respect only for the power currently in force. Prince Louis wrote to me, opening his note with these words: "The man commonly known as Louis of Prussia sends to ask Mme de Staël . . ." He felt the insult to the royal blood from which he came, to the memory of heroes among whose number he longed to stand. After that hideous deed, how could any king in Europe communicate with such a man? Out of necessity, you will say! There is a holy place in the soul where its influence must never gain entry; if this were not so, what would virtue mean on this earth? A generous diversion, suited only to the untroubled leisure of private life.

On the eve of the so-called judgment of the Duke d'Enghien, General Savary—on whose head are the three greatest crimes of Bonaparte's reign: the murder of the Duke d'Enghien, that of Pichegru, and the kidnapping of Spain's royal family—sent for a gardener and ordered him to dig a hole in his presence for the corpse of the prisoner whose death was already decided. He had arrogantly told the story himself to the man who repeated it to me;[223] and if the wretch has any excuse, it is that he has no earthly notion of any morality whatever. He boasts of his readiness to throw wife and children into the water if such were Bonaparte's will; and as a man who never fails to hold himself in high esteem, he has turned self-interest into zeal. But if Bonaparte lived in adversity for a year, he would learn very fast that there is no vestige of warmth in the obedience of these men. He has so carefully rid them of all generous feelings as a condition of becoming established in their positions that he would find none for himself if ever he needed them.

The newspapers dated March 20 reported the sentence of the Duke d'Enghien, handed down in consequence of the captain-judge's summary of his alleged crimes. What an oxymoron: captain-judge! It is surely enough to inspire dread of military tribunals, of the monstrous union of the peaceful and impartial office of a judge with the impulsive violence and passive obedience of a soldier! We know, and the Bonapartists have since agreed, that even from their point of view the unfortunate Duke d'Enghien was guilty in no slightest way; on the contrary. His papers show that he sang the praises of Bonaparte's military gifts. Everything attested his steadfast will to live in the most peaceable way in the world. He had chosen the neutral lands of the Margrave of Baden to withdraw from active life and be closer to the Princess de Rohan, his wife.[224]

He was the most fiery of men on the day of battle, but very calm in every other circumstance. They brought him from Strasbourg traveling day and night, and they did not give him time to recover with the sleep of exhaustion that nature bestows on us in the greatest misfortunes. They immediately summoned him before that tribunal of corporals which obeyed the signal for heinous crimes as they did the command for drill. He wanted to see Bonaparte, who refused, saying: "What good would it do? Those in power must learn that all this is not child's play";[225] and that evening, while people awaited news of the execution and the Empress Josephine wept bitterly at her inability to obtain a pardon, Bonaparte played chess with a lady of the court, saying: "He's a little weasel, shorter than I am." Then he advanced the pawn, thinking, no doubt, of the way he would have men die.

At midnight, the squad that was to shoot the Duke d'Enghien led him into the garden. It is said that they played a march from Haydn's *Creation,* where the angels thank God for creating day. What a contrast! Savary was in charge of this deed of darkness. The Duke d'Enghien approached to hand him two letters he had written, one to the Prince de Condé, the other to his wife, and asked him to be so kind as to deliver them. Savary refused, saying: "I do not deliver letters from brigands." The Duke d'Enghien threw them on the ground and pronounced these words with scorn and pride: "Some Frenchman will pick them up." Hulin was that Frenchman. Unhappy country that had no other representative then! The Duke's intrepid courage as he met his death is generally recognized, and yet we could only know it through his murderers, the sole witnesses to his death. A lock of his hair was enclosed in the letter to his wife. It all went from hand to hand at the Archchancellor's table[226] and perhaps, at last, those disdained tokens reached the person who was meant to glory in them forever.

A few days after the death of the Duke d'Enghien, a friend of mine went onto the ramparts of the dungeons of Vincennes. The earth that marked his burial place was still fresh; children were playing at quoits on that grassy knoll, the sole monument to such ashes. A disabled soldier, old and white-haired, sat nearby. He stayed to gaze at them for a while; finally he got up and, taking them by the hand, said with tears in his eyes: "Don't play there, I beg you." Those tears were the only honors paid the descendant of the Great Condé, and the earth will not bear their imprint very long.[227]

But for a few days at least, public opinion seemed to revive among the French and indignation was widespread. But once those generous flames burned out, despotism became all the more firmly entrenched for the futile attempt at resistance. For a few days the First Consul was rather anxious about people's frame of mind. Fouché himself disapproved the deed; he had used those words so characteristic of the present regime: "This death is worse than a crime, it is an error."[228] A great many thoughts are embodied in that sentence, but fortunately it can actually be turned around to affirm that crime is the greatest of errors. Bonaparte asked a senator who was a decent man:

"What do people think of the Duke d'Enghien's death?"

"General," he replied, "people are deeply grieved."

"That doesn't surprise me," he said. "A house that has long reigned over a country is always of interest," wanting thus to link with partisan interests the most natural sentiment the human heart can experience. On another occasion he posed the same question to a tribune who, anxious to please him, answered: "Well, General, if our enemies take heinous measures against us, we are right to do likewise," unaware that his words meant the measure was heinous indeed.

The First Consul pretended to consider the act as inspired by reasons of state. One day, about this time, he was discussing Corneille's theater with a man of wit:

"See here," he said, "for modern man, the public welfare, or to be more exact, reasons of state have taken the place that fate held for the Ancients. Such and such a man who, by nature, might be incapable of a crime, would be compelled to it by political circumstances. Corneille is the only one who showed in his tragedies that he understood reasons of state, and so I would have made him my Prime Minister if he'd lived in my time."

The whole aim of that seemingly guileless discussion was to prove the dispassionate nature of the Duke d'Enghien's death, and to show that circumstances, of which a head of state is exclusive judge, motivate and justify everything. That there was no passion in his decision on the Duke d'Enghien is perfectly true. Some would hold that there was rage in this crime; nothing of the kind. What grounds would there have been for rage? The Duke d'Enghien had in no way challenged the First Consul. At first he had hoped to seize the Duke de Berry, the Count d'Artois's son who, it was claimed, was to land in Normandy if Pichegru sent word that it was time. That Prince is closer in succession to the throne than the Duke d'Enghien and besides, according to French law, his coming to France would have been a criminal act. In any case, therefore, it better suited Bonaparte's purposes to have him put to death rather than the Duke d'Enghien; for want of the former, he chose the latter, discussing the matter calmly. Between the order to kidnap him and the order to have him killed, more than eight days had elapsed; and Bonaparte ordered the execution of the Duke d'Enghien well in advance and as calmly as he has sacrificed millions of men since then to the whims of his ambition.[229]

He is not even good enough to do evil with passion. People wonder now about the motives for that dreadful deed, and I think they are easily sifted out. First of all, Bonaparte wanted to reassure the revolutionary party by contracting an alliance of blood. On hearing the news, a former Jacobin exclaimed: "So much the better! General Bonaparte has joined the Convention." For a long time the Jacobins had wanted as head of the Republic a man who had voted for the King's death; it was what they called giving guarantees to the Revolution. Bonaparte fulfilled this condition of crime set in place of property as required in other countries; he offered the certainty that he would never serve the Bourbons. Royalists who threw in their lot with his thus burned all their bridges behind them and Republicans had only to sacrifice the Republic in the sure knowledge that the former masters of France would not come to punish them.

On the eve of having himself crowned by the same men who had banned royalty, of reestablishing a noble class for the supporters of equality, he thought it necessary to reassure them with the hideous guarantee of a Bourbon's murder. From the conspiracy of Pichegru and Moreau, Bonaparte had learned that Republicans and Royalists had joined against him, and he had been astonished that hatred for him was the common core of that strange alliance. Several men who owed him their positions were marked by serving the revolution that was supposed to overthrow him, and it was essential to him that, from then on, none of his agents could think they would have anywhere to turn if he were overthrown. In sum, as he was about to seize the throne, he wanted above all to inspire such terror that no one would dare resist him. In a single act he violated everything: the rights of European peoples, the Constitution such as it still was, the public's sense of decency, humanity, and religion. There were no further limits on his acts, thus there was everything to fear from the one who had committed it.

It was believed for a time that the murder of the Duke d'Enghien signaled a new revolutionary era in France and that the scaffolds would rise again. But Bonaparte wanted to teach the French just one lesson—that he was capable of anything—so that they would be as grateful to him for the harm he did not do as others would be for a good turn. They thought him merciful when he let them live so well; they had seen how easy it was for him to have people put to death! Russia, Sweden, and above all England complained at the violation of the German Empire. The German Princes themselves were silent, and the ineffectual ruler on whose territory the outrage had been committed circulated a note imploring people to refrain from speaking any further of *the event that had taken place!*[230] Is it not fair to say that this inoffensive, obscure sentence to designate such an act characterizes those contemptible Princes for whom sovereignty was no longer a matter of anything but revenues, and the State, an interest-bearing capital to be enjoyed with all possible tranquillity?

My father still had time to hear of the murder of Duke d'Enghien, and the last words I received written in his hand express his indignation at the crime.

It was in the midst of the most profound security that I found two letters on my table announcing that my father was dangerously ill. Everything was hidden from me: the messenger who had brought them, the news of death that he was entrusted to bring. I left with hope, and I clung to it despite all the circumstances that should have taken it from me. When the truth was disclosed in Weimar, my despair was compounded by a feeling of indescribable terror. I saw myself without support on this earth and forced to sustain my soul on my own. There were many objects of attachment left to me, but the tender admiration I felt for my father exerted an influence that nothing could equal. Sorrow, the greatest of prophets, warned me that henceforth I would never be happy in my heart as I had been when this man of all-powerful sensibility watched over my fate; and not a day has passed since the month of April 1804 that I have not connected all my griefs to this one. So long as my father was alive I suffered only through imagination, since for real things he always found the way to do me good. After I lost him, I had to contend with destiny directly, and yet I owe what strength I have left to the hope that he is praying for me in heaven. It is not filial love but rather intimate knowledge of his character that leads me to assert that I have never seen human nature closer to perfection than in his soul. If I were not convinced of the life to come, I would go mad at the idea that such a being could cease to exist. There was so much immortality in his feelings and thoughts that, a hundred times, when I have had impulses that lift me above myself, I believe I hear him still.

On my somber journey from Weimar to Coppet, I envied all the life flowing in nature, that of flies, of birds still flying around me. I asked for one day, one single day to speak with him again, to arouse his pity; I envied those trees in the forests that last for centuries. But the inflexibility of the grave is somehow disconcerting for the human mind, and although it is the best known of truths, the bitter intensity of the impression it produces can never grow dim. As we drew near my father's home one of my friends[231] pointed out to me, above the mountain, clouds resembling the gigantic face of a man that would disappear toward evening, and it seemed to me that heaven thus offered me the symbol of the loss I had just suffered. A giant he was in fact, this man who in no circumstance of his life put self-interest before the least of his duties; this man whose virtues were inspired by goodness to such a degree that he could have done without principles, and whose principles were so firm that he could have done without goodness. In terms of character, his is the one that stands in perfect contrast to Bonaparte's, and if I did not instinctively detest that enemy of God and men, my cult for my father would suffice to command my hatred.

When I reached Coppet I learned that throughout the nine days of the illness that took him from me, my father had worried over my fate. He blamed himself for his last book, sure that it had caused my exile, and wracked with fever, he wrote to the First Consul in a trembling hand, averring that I had had nothing to do with the publication of his last work and that, on the contrary, I had wanted it not to be printed. That voice of a dying man had such solemnity, that last prayer of one who had played so great a role in France asking as his only favor that his family might return to the place of their birth, and that the imprudent acts of a girl, then still young, be forgotten, seemed irresistible to me. And although I knew the man's character, what happened to me is, I believe, natural to those whose ardent wish is for an end to great sorrow: I hoped against all hope. The First Consul received the letter and doubtless thought me an uncommon fool for imagining that he would be touched. On this point, I agree with him.

Moreau's trial went on and on,[232] and although the newspapers maintained the deepest silence on the matter, public knowledge of the plea for the defense was enough to rouse the soul, and never has opinion against Bonaparte proved so strong in Paris as at this time. The French, more than any other people, need a certain degree of freedom of the press; they need to think and feel in common; they require the electricity of their neighbors' emotion to feel it in turn, and their enthusiasm does not thrive in isolation. Thus their tyrant is well advised to permit no kind of manifestation of public opinion. And Bonaparte has combined with this idea common to all despots, a ruse peculiar to the times, that is, the art of proclaiming a factitious opinion through newspapers which use such grandiloquent language to express what they are ordered to say that they seem to be free. None but our French writers, it must be admitted, can thus embroider the same sophisms every morning, and be so complacently diffuse even in their subjection.

Just as the judicial inquiry for those famous proceedings began, the newspapers informed Europe that Pichegru had strangled himself in the Temple.[233] All the newspapers were full of the most outrageously ridiculous surgeon's report; they did not know how to make their lie credible, so true is it that in certain cases a crime disturbs even those who, with the most perfect indifference, boast of committing it. What appears certain is that one of the Emperor's mamelukes was instructed to smother Pichegru, and that General Savary supervised the act. Imagine the fate of a brave general murdered by cowards at the back of a cell, taken by surprise and defenseless, condemned for the past few days to the solitude of prisons that breaks the soul's courage, not even knowing whether his friends will ever learn by what kind of death he has perished, whether the crime that kills him will be avenged, whether his memory will not be scurrilously attacked! Ultimately, dear Lord, You doubtless sent into his soul a ray of Your mercy, for nothing human was of any succor to him.

Pichegru had shown a great deal of courage in his first interrogation, and had threatened to give proof of Bonaparte's promises to the Vendeans on the return of the Bourbons. Some say that he was put to the question like two other conspirators, one of whom, Picot, showed his mutilated hands to the tribunal, and that they dared not expose to the eyes of the French people one of their former defenders subjected to the torture of slaves.[234] I do not believe this last conjecture. In Bonaparte's actions one must always look for the calculation that counseled them and there is none to be seen in the latter surmise, whereas it may be true that bringing Moreau and Pichegru together before the bar of justice would have inflamed public opinion at last. Already the galleries were densely packed. Several officers, headed by a loyal man, General Lecourbe, showed the strongest and most courageous interest in General Moreau.[235] When he came before the tribunal, the gendarmes designated to guard him presented arms in respect. Already people were beginning to feel that honor was on the side of the persecuted; but in the midst of all this ferment Bonaparte, by suddenly having himself declared Emperor, diverted everyone's mind with a new perspective and concealed his path through the storm surrounding him better than was possible in a period of calm.

In the tribunal, General Moreau delivered one of the best-written speeches that history can offer. He recalled, though modestly, the battles he had won since Bonaparte governed France; he apologized for having often spoken too freely perhaps, when he indirectly compared the Breton character with the Corsican.[236] In sum, he showed a great deal of wit and kept his wits about him perfectly in so dangerous a moment. Régnier[237] was Minister of Police in place of Fouché, then in disgrace. He went on to Saint Cloud when he left the tribunal. The Emperor asked what Moreau's speech was like.

"Pitiful," he answered.

"In that case," said the Emperor, "have it printed and distributed all over Paris."

Afterward, when he saw how mistaken his minister had been, he went back to Fouché, the one man who could truly help him effectively by bringing, unfortunately for the world, a kind of deft modesty to a system with no boundaries. Today, that same Régnier is called the Duke de Massa.

Réal, a former Jacobin and Napoleon's evil genius, was instructed to speak to the judges and pledge them to sentence Moreau to death.

"It is indispensable for the Emperor's reputation since he had the man arrested," he told them, "but your qualms about agreeing should be all the fewer since the Emperor is resolved to pardon him."

"And who will grant us pardon, if we cover ourselves with such infamy?" replied one of the judges, whose name we are still not at liberty to speak for fear of compromising him. General Moreau was sentenced to two years in prison, Georges and several of his friends, to death. A Polignac was sentenced to four years in prison and he is still there, as are a number of others seized by the police when the penalty ordered by the legal proceedings was carried out.[238]

Moreau wanted his prison sentence changed to perpetual exile; "perpetual" in this case, means "for life," since the world's misfortune lies on the head of Bonaparte. He agreed; exile suited his purposes in every respect. Along Moreau's route, mayors of towns responsible for stamping his exile's passport often showed him the most respectful attention. "Gentlemen," said one of them to his audience, "make way for General Moreau," and he bowed low before him as if before the Emperor. There was still a France in the hearts of these men, but the idea of acting on one's opinion was already lost, and now who knows if there is any opinion left, so smothered has it been for so long?

When he arrived in Cadiz those same Spaniards, who were to set so fine an example a few years later, rendered all possible homage to a victim of tyranny. On one occasion they threw their coats on the road Mme Moreau would cross to protect that winsome person from the damp and, through her, to honor her husband. When Moreau passed in front of the English fleet the ships saluted him as if he were a commanding general.[239] Thus did the so-called enemies of France take upon themselves to discharge her debt to one of her most illustrious defenders.

When Bonaparte had Moreau arrested, he said: "I could have sent for him and said: 'Look here, you and I can't stay on the same soil, so get out of here because I'm stronger than you are,' and I think he would have gone. But those knightly manners are infantile when it comes to public affairs." Bonaparte believes, and has had the skill to persuade several apprentice Machiavellians of the new generation, that all generous feelings are childish. It is time, no doubt, to teach him that there is something masculine in virtue too, and more masculine than himself.

Since he knew, however, that he had inspired enough horror in France, he thought it was time to soften an impression that went beyond what he wanted and could become dangerous. And so he used the Empress Josephine's kindness to have himself asked to pardon a few individuals secondary to the plot. He received the relatives of those he had chosen in advance for pardon. He did nothing spontaneous in this regard, nothing that sprang from his soul. His confederates, however, said tears had been seen in his eyes as he spoke with Mme de Polignac.[240] What a curious marvel those tears were! Bronze wept, say the Ancients, but in him it was only a sham that doubtless irritated him with the public opinion for which he made the pretense. Those same Polignacs, the occasion for the scene Bonaparte played in the eyes of France, remained in Vincennes for eight years and are still not free; for one, he increased the legal punishment; for the other, he changed it into a long torment. On other occasions he had notices put in the newspapers stating that he freed the husbands of women who threw themselves at his feet to obtain it. One of the husbands was a Swiss named Rusillon, but he has never emerged from his dungeon cell.[241] Once the newspaper article was published, what more did anyone need? I do not believe that history presents a character in which lying has so constant and varied a role as in Bonaparte's.

At his command, the motion to call him to the Empire was to be made in the Tribunate by a deputy in the Convention, the former Jacobin, Curée, supported by Jaubert, deputy for commerce from Bordeaux, and seconded by Siméon, an intelligent and sensible man, banished under the Republic as a Royalist.[242] He wanted those who were for the Revolution, those who were for the Old Regime, and those who were for the permanent interests of the nation brought together in choosing him. He told Fabre d'Aude,[243] then president: "I don't want the motion made in the Tribunate unless you are confident of unanimity. A majority is not enough." Fabre replied that he could not answer for Carnot and Moreau's brother, but that he was sure of all the others.[244] Opposition, however weak, always infuriates that man, either because he cannot endure the slightest obstacle to his omnipotence or, most important, because he relies on duplicity and fears above all the word that unmasks. Certain that Carnot would be moderate, however, he braved his protest, which was in fact couched in terms measured enough for him to be named Minister of War since that time.

It was agreed that voting registers would be opened throughout France so that the French could express their will on Bonaparte's elevation to the throne. But without waiting for the result, contrived as it was, he took the title of Emperor through a Senatus Consultum, and that wretched Senate did not even have the strength to pose constitutional limits to the new monarchy. One tribune alone, whose name I would mention if I dared,[245] had the honor of asking for them. To deflect this idea, Bonaparte cleverly called in a few leading senators and told them:

"I am reluctant to put myself forward in this way; I preferred my present situation. Nevertheless, the Republic cannot possibly go on any longer; people are weary of that kind of thing; I believe the French want royalty. I thought of calling the old Bourbons back at first, but that would only have ruined them and myself, too. My conscience tells me that we really must have one man at the head of all this, but perhaps it would be even better to wait. I've aged France by a hundred years in the last four. As for liberty, it's a good code of civil law, and modern nations don't care about anything but property. However, take my advice, appoint a committee, set up a constitution and, I tell you quite simply," he added with a smile, "take precautions against my tyranny. Take them, believe me."

That seeming guilelessness of Bonaparte's is exactly like the story they tell about the crocodile who mimics the voice of mothers to lure children. Still, it seduced the senators, who were only too willing to be seduced. One of them, François de Neufchâteau,[246] a rather distinguished man of letters, but one of those disinterested people who always find philosophical reasons to be content with those in power, said to a man who was a friend of mine:

"The Emperor's simplicity in letting one speak to him freely is just wonderful! The other day, I spent a whole hour with him proving that it was absolutely necessary to found the new dynasty on a charter guaranteeing the nation's rights."

"And how did he answer?" my friend asked.

"He slapped me on the shoulder with perfect kindness," went on François de Neufchâteau, "and he told me:'You are perfectly right, my dear senator; but trust me, this is not the time.'" And François de Neufchâteau, like many other Frenchmen, was content with the pleasure of having had his say, even though his views were in no slightest way adopted. Among the French, the requirements of self-esteem by far exceed those of character.

Two commissions were established in the Senate, one for civil liberty and the other for liberty of the press. They are still renewed every three months, and neither the titular bishoprics nor the sinecures of England have ever been so devoid of duties as they. I imagine that the senators on those committees laugh like augurs when they meet, but the Senate proceeds no less solemnly to reelect them. With respect to liberty, people play the way children in France do at being grown-up ladies, and they love ceremonies as people do in China.

A curious thing, and one that Bonaparte has very shrewdly understood, is that the French, who seize on the ridiculous so wittily, are only too willing to make themselves ridiculous the moment their vanity can turn it to account in some other way. Nothing, in fact, so lends itself to jest as the creation of a wholly new nobility such as Bonaparte is establishing as the prop for his new throne.

He was obliged to enhance the self-aggrandizement of all the revolutionaries who had wanted to take the places of the former French nobles, and of the military, who in some respects were deserving, much as he was doing for himself. Immediately, ranks and titles were decreed, the most common names were preceded by the title of count, others were disguised as foreign names—Italian, German and so forth—that those who bore them could hardly pronounce.

The princesses and the queens, citizens just yesterday, could not stifle their own laughter at hearing themselves called Your Majesty. Others, more earnest, had their title of monseigneur repeated to them from morning to night, like the *Bourgeois gentilhomme*.[247] They went through the old archives to find the best documents on etiquette; able men solemnly set up in business to design coats-of-arms for the new families; in sum, no day went by without giving rise to situations worthy of Molière. But the terror that formed the background of the picture kept the grotesqueries of the forestage from the ridicule they deserved. The glory of French generals enhanced everything, and obsequious employees crept in the shadow of soldiers who no doubt merited the sober honors of a free state, but not the futile decorations of such a court as this. Valor and genius confer ancestry from heaven, and those so endowed need no other forebears. Honors awarded in republics or in limited monarchies should be the rewards for services to the country, and everyone is equal in aspiring to them; but nothing so reeks of Tartar despotism as that mass of honors issuing from a single man whose whims are their source.

This day-old nobility was bombarded with endless puns, and people quoted a thousand remarks made by newly noble ladies that implied their scant acquaintance with the good manners of old. And what is in fact most difficult to learn is the sort of courtesy that is neither ceremonious nor familiar and seems of little consequence; but it must come from deep within ourselves, for no one acquires it unless inspired by the habits of childhood or nobility of the soul. Bonaparte himself is awkward when it comes to showing good presence, and often at home, and even with strangers, he happily reverts to the common expressions and manners that remind him of his revolutionary youth. Bonaparte knew very well that Parisians were indulging in gibes at his new nobles, but what is strange is that they expressed their opinions in wordplay and not in the expression of strong ideas. The energy of the oppressed extended no further than the ambiguity born of puns and, just as in the East they are reduced to fables, so in France have people fallen lower still, confining themselves to the rattle of syllables. However, there is a pun that does deserve to escape the genre's ephemeral success. One day at the theater, the princesses of the blood were announced, and someone in the hall shouted: *d'Enghien's blood.*" Such was, in fact, the baptism of the new dynasty.

Still, Bonaparte would have accomplished nothing had he merely surrounded himself with his new nobility. A clever caricature shows Bonaparte cutting up the Jacobins' "bonnet rouge" to make the red ribbon he wanted to use for their decorations.[248] Yet if he had not enlisted the old nobility in his government, he would hardly have done more than his colleague, the Negro Dessalines, who also had himself named Emperor in Santo Domingo and gave titles to his Blacks in imitation of Bonaparte's Whites. At first, a few nobles ruined by the Revolution agreed to receive positions at court. Bonaparte rewarded them by saying in public that he had offered them places in the army and that they had refused but eagerly accepted places in his antechamber.[249] The day after a sentence of the sort was uttered by Louis XIV, all the great men of his court would at least have sent him their resignations, but those who consented to serve in what was effectively Bonaparte's antechamber were already so debased that he could trample them underfoot without fear. They had no refuge other than his power.

One of the profound insights of his system is to do his utmost to lead every man to do something dishonorable in terms of liberty or loyalty. Thus do the English designate fidelity to their kings, so that they believe they will be utterly without resources should the order of things be changed. Several gentlemen in this situation have given the example of the noblest resistence,[250] several whose names are renowned in various ways. But there are also many who have said they were threatened before they had anything to fear, and many who have pushed themselves forward to obtain positions of squire, chamberlain, and lady-in-waiting at the palace, which all without exception should have refused. Only in the military and judicial careers can one persuade himself that he is useful to his country, whoever the leader governing it; but employment at court makes you dependent on the man and not on the State. A gentleman from one of France's oldest families replied to whoever reproached him for his position as chamberlain: "But one has to serve somebody!" Curious language for children of those knights in armor, all covered with wounds. The threat of exile, and exile itself, was one of Bonaparte's great means of obliging men and women of the old nobility to accept employment at his court.

Paris is an agreeable place, and so necessary to those who have lived there that the power to send them away was a new means of terror in Bonaparte's hands. He combined with eight hundred million in revenues and eight hundred thousand soldiers a treasury of miseries that brought into subjection the very class he needed. He wanted to gain distinction through the names of that class by degrading the individuals who composed it; he wanted to blend the aristocracy of the new regime with that of the old, to make counts of the Montmorencys,[251] to oblige the daughters of the noble caste to marry men of the Revolution whose ways were of necessity entirely foreign to them. In sum, by mixing everything together, scorning the past, dating the existence of his unfortunate subjects only from the date of his accession, he left no one the right to exercise any free choice in his own life. Never could a despotism at once so strong and so multiple, so fearful and so meticulous, have become established had the Revolution not placed all individual fortunes in the hands of the government. Bonaparte required a lavish train of life from the newly rich to dazzle the common people with ostentation, and to ensure that, unable to defray the expenses incurred at his command, they would constantly need to turn to him for gifts. The former landowners, on the other hand, enjoyed nothing except by decree of the First Consul, who returned to them what they owned in the past. It was always to reestablish order and to protect France from the Republicans or the Royalists that Bonaparte took for himself alone the right to persecute each in turn. "I retain arbitrary power out of pity," said Peter the Great in the play written by Carrion de Nisas, to show the French how they ought to be governed.[252]

We are astonished at the corruption of France, but let us reflect for a moment on the nature and circumstances of present-day power. Ordinarily, the motives of fear and hope that lead men in the path of vice or virtue are almost equally balanced. But Bonaparte has the scale weighted on the side of vice with a force of terror and magnificence of hope that totally unsettle the human mind. It is a matter of languishing in prison, dying in exile, or accepting the wealth and honors of the Empire. Without a doubt, had Bonaparte's usurpations been opposed from the start, nothing would have been easier than to stop them. He is a man who has always felt a kind of fear when faced with resistance; he recovers himself through reflection and his character takes the upper hand, but when he chances to meet an honest man, you might say he experiences a kind of shudder that forces him to give in for the moment. If, from the beginning, he had been obliged to deal with men of character, he would have been lost; but circumstances have favored him to such a degree that he has been able to cast the net of tyranny over France, and once it is allowed to be spread, nothing is more difficult than to escape it.

Registers were opened in the departments for a vote on the Empire and, just as with the Consulate for Life, all those who did not sign were counted as being in favor; the small number of individuals who took it into their heads to write "no" were dismissed from their jobs.[253] M. de Lafayette, a loyal friend of liberty, made his unswerving resistance clear once more, but his merit was all the greater since in this country of histrionics people did not know how to value courage any longer. This distinction must be made since in France we see the divinity of fear reigning over the most intrepid warriors. Bonaparte refused even the strictures of hereditary monarchy and reserved the right to adopt and choose a successor in the Eastern manner.[254] As he had no children at the time, he did not want to give his family any rights whatever. Even as he raised them to ranks beyond any of their aspirations, he enslaved them to his will with extremely well-thought-out decrees that entwined their new thrones with chains.

The fourteenth of July was celebrated again in this year of 1804 because, it was said, the Empire consecrated all the benefits of the Revolution. Bonaparte had said that the storms had strengthened the roots of the government. He declared that the throne would guarantee liberty; he repeated in every way possible that Europe would be reassured by the stable order instituted in the government of France. In fact, except for illustrious England, all Europe recognized his new rank;[255] he was called "my brother" by the former potentates of the ancient royal knighthood. We have seen how he has rewarded their fatal condescension. Had he sincerely wanted peace, the elderly King George himself, that decent man whose reign was the finest in English history, would have been forced to recognize him as an equal. But just a few days after his accession he spoke the words that unmasked all his intentions: "They make jokes about my new dynasty," he said. "Within five years, it will be the oldest in all Europe." And from then on he has not ceased to work toward this goal.

He needed a pretext to keep moving forward, and that pretext was the freedom of the seas. He knew very well that the expression was meaningless, that peace put an end to the domination of the seas which England was condemned to maintain in self-defense, and that peace depended on him since England asked no more than the independence of the continental nations. But it is extraordinary how easily the most intelligent people on earth are led to take a piece of nonsense as their banner. It is yet another of those contrasts that would be entirely inexplicable if this unhappy France had not been despoiled of religion and morality by the deadly linkage of bad principles and unfortunate events. Without religion, no man is capable of sacrifice; and since without morality no one speaks the truth, public opinion is constantly led astray. It follows then, as we have just said, that people have no courage of conscience even when they have the courage of honor and when, with an admirable understanding of how to carry out a project, they never take its goal into account.

Once he occupied the throne, Bonaparte no longer needed to try anything new to establish his tyranny within the country. France was subjugated, and if his power has grown steadily ever since, it is by the natural effect of despotism's pressure that increasingly degrades the subjects and increasingly swells the arrogance of the master. But that period marks the beginning of Bonaparte's efforts to bring all Europe under bondage to France. He once said that you had to do something new in France every three months to shake men's imaginations. I do not know whether he thought it necessary to conquer outside to maintain the servitude within and so nourish the anxiety in people's minds, but I do believe that he was mistaken in this regard, that he took his own restlessness for that of the nation. France was so thirsty for the happiness given by tranquillity that she would have accepted it with joy, even from his despotism.

From that time onward she voiced the same eagerness for peace that is felt now, after ten years of upheaval.[256] But did that man count men's wishes for anything, and was it not his mission to annihilate all the happiness of the old Europe or to regenerate it through the hate he ultimately aroused in the most demoralized souls?

There were only very decent sovereigns on the thrones of the Continent when Bonaparte made his decision to overthrow them. The political and military genius of this world was extinct, but the peoples were happy, and although the principles of free constitutions were not accepted in most of the states, the philosophical ideas widely known in France for the past fifty years had at least the advantage of stifling intolerance and despotism.

Catherine the Second and Frederick II sought the respect of French writers, and those two monarchs, whose genius could subjugate everything, lived with the opinion of enlightened men and sought to captivate it.

Twenty years ago, one traveled from one end of Europe to the other without hindrance; only the French Revolution had disturbed that happiness, but the natural bent of minds was to the pleasure and the application of liberal ideas. It can be said that there was hardly an individual who suffered in his person or in his possessions. The French revolutionaries could still say enthusiastically that personal faculties had to be given the chance to develop, that it was unjust for a whole people to live in subjugation to one man, and that national representation was the only way to guarantee the transitory benefits which a virtuous sovereign can grant but which citizens both want and have the right to possess. But what could Bonaparte say? Did he bring foreign nations greater liberty? No monarch in Europe would, in the course of a year, have allowed himself the arbitrary insolence that marks each of his days. He came only to make them exchange their tranquillity, their independence, their language, their laws, their fortunes, their blood, their children, in return for the unhappiness and the shame of being destroyed as nations and despised as men. He began, in sum, the enterprise of the universal monarchy, the greatest scourge that can threaten the human species and the certain cause of eternal warfare.

Not one of the arts of peace suits Bonaparte; he does not know how to administer except through violence and finds entertainment only in the violent crises met in the wake of battles. If there is anything spontaneous in him, it is voracious activity. The infernal deities thrust him forward and I do not know whether, ingenious as he may be, he could stop if he so wished. He has known respite, but he has never told himself seriously: "That is enough!" And his character, incompatible with the rest of creation, is like the Greek fire[257] that no force of nature could possibly extinguish.

Part Two

1810–1812

I went to an estate, Fossé by name, lent to me by a generous friend, since I could not stay longer in the one occupied now by its owners.[1] The château was the residence of a Vendean officer rather careless of its upkeep, but whose loyal kindness made everything easy, and whose original mind made everything amusing. We had hardly arrived when the Italian musician, with me to give my daughter lessons, began to play the guitar; my daughter accompanied him on the harp and my lovely friend sang in her sweet voice.[2] Peasants gathered at the windows, astonished to see this colony of troubadours come to enliven the solitude of their masters. It was there that I spent my last days in France with a few friends whose memory lives in my heart. Surely so intimate a group, so lonely a dwelling, so sweet an occupation with the arts did no one any harm. We often sang a charming air composed by the Queen of Holland, and its refrain was like the motto she had chosen: "Do what thou must, come what may."[3] After dinner, we got the idea of taking seats around a green table and writing to one another instead of speaking. Those varied and numerous tête-à-têtes were so entertaining for us all that we were impatient to leave the table where we were talking to come write to one another. When strangers happened to stop by we could not bear to interrupt our custom, and our little post office, as we called it, always maintained its pace. The people of the little town nearby were a bit surprised at these new ways and took them for pedantry, whereas our game was only an expedient against the monotony of solitude. One day a local lord, who had never thought of anything in life but hunting, came to take my sons off to his woods; he stayed a while at our busy and silent table. Mme Récamier, inclined to kindness every moment of her life, penned a little note in her pretty handwriting to this corpulent hunter so that he would not feel too much outside the group. He refused to receive it, and assured us that he could not read the handwriting in the light.[4] We laughed a bit at this setback provoked by our lovely friend's well-meant coquetry, thinking that a note from her would not always have met the same fate. And thus, if I can judge by myself, life went on without anyone's feeling time a burden.

The opera *Cinderella*[5] was creating a great stir in Paris; I wanted to see it performed in an inferior provincial production in Blois. I went on foot, and the townspeople followed me out of curiosity, more eager to know me as an exile than for any other reason. This type of success, won less by talent than by misfortune, put the Duke de Rovigo out of sorts, and shortly afterward he wrote to the prefect of Loir-et-Cher that I was surrounded by a court. "Certainly, it is not power that gives it to me at least," I answered the prefect.[6]

I was still resolved to make for England by way of America,[7] but I wanted to conclude the printing of my book on Germany. The season was wearing on; it was already September 15 and I foresaw that the difficulty of setting off with my daughter would keep me in some town or other forty leagues from Paris for another winter. I had Vendôme in mind then, for I knew a few intelligent people there and communication with the capital was easy. I, who in times past had one of the most brilliant houses in Paris, pictured settling in Vendôme as highly gratifying; fate did not grant me this modest happiness.[8]

On September 23, I corrected the last proofs of my book. After six years of work, it was a real joy for me to put the word *end* to my three volumes. I made a list of the hundred persons in different parts of France and Europe to whom I wanted to send my book. I attached great value to this book which I thought capable of introducing new ideas in France. Still, it seemed to me that it had been inspired by a feeling that was principled without being hostile, and that a language no longer spoken would be found in it. Provided with a letter from my book dealer assuring me that the censors had authorized publication of my book, I believed I had nothing to fear and left for the estate of M. Mathieu de Montmorency, five leagues from Blois. The residence on this estate is in the middle of a forest; I went walking there with the man I respect most in this world since I lost my father. The beauty of the weather, the magnificence of the forest, the historical memories called to mind by this place where Philippe Auguste and Richard the Lionhearted fought the Battle of Fréteval,[9] all conduced to put my soul into the sweetest, calmest humor. In this conversation, as in all of those we have had together, my worthy friend, who has had no other interest on earth than deserving heaven, paid no attention to the affairs of the day and sought only to do my soul good.

We set off again the following morning, and on those plains of the Vendôme where not a single dwelling is encountered and which, like the sea, seems everywhere the same, we completely lost our way. It was already midnight, and we did not know what path to follow in an unvarying countryside whose fertility is as monotonous as sterility might be elsewhere, when a young man on horseback, suspecting our difficulty, stopped our carriage and came to ask us to spend the night in his mother's château. We accepted the invitation, which was a great service, and suddenly found ourselves amid the luxury of Asia and the elegance of France. The master and mistress of the house had spent a great deal of time in India, and their château was embellished with all they had brought back from their travels. My curiosity was excited and I was marvelously comfortable there. The next day, a note from my son was brought to me, urging me to return home because my book was meeting fresh difficulties with the censors.[10] The friends with me at the château begged me to leave; I did not guess what they hid from me and, confining myself to Auguste's note, spent my time examining all the rare objects from India with no suspicion of what awaited me. Finally, I climbed into my carriage, and my good and witty Vendean, who had never flinched at his own peril, pressed my hand with tears in his eyes. Then I understood that they were keeping secret some new persecution, and M. de Montmorency, whom I questioned, informed me that General Savary—otherwise known as the Duke de Rovigo—had sent his military police to tear to pieces the ten thousand copies of my book that had been printed, and that I had received the order to leave France within three days. My children and my friends had not wanted me to hear such news in the home of strangers, but they had taken every possible precaution to save my manuscript from seizure and they managed to save it a few hours before I was asked to give it up.[11]

This new sorrow gripped my soul powerfully. I had entertained fond hopes of an honorable success through publication of my book. If the censors had refused to authorize its printing, it would have made sense to me, but after I submitted to all their comments, after I made the changes they required of me, to learn that my book was torn to pieces and that I was obliged to part with the friends who sustained my courage—all this made me weep. But I tried once again to compose myself and reflect on what must be done in a situation where my decision could so influence the fate of my family. As we drew near the house where I was living, I gave my writing-desk, which still contained a few notes on my book, to my younger son; he jumped over the wall to enter the house through the garden. An

Englishwoman,[12] my very kind friend, came ahead to greet me and advise me of all that had happened. In the distance I caught sight of the gendarmes wandering around my dwelling, but apparently they were not looking for me; they were doubtless in pursuit of other unfortunates—conscripts, exiles, persons under surveillance—in sum, persons from all the classes of oppressed people that the present regime in France has established.

The prefect of Loir-et-Cher came to ask for my manuscript; to gain time, I gave him a bad copy that I had with me and he was satisfied.[13] I have been told that he was treated very badly just a few months later because he was suspected of having shown me consideration. The grief he felt at the Emperor's disfavor was the main cause, so they say, of the fatal illness that brought about his death in the prime of life. Unhappy country, where circumstances are such that a man of his intelligence and talent sinks under the weight of disgrace!

I saw in the newspapers that American ships had put into the Channel ports, and I decided to make use of my passport for America; my intention then was to pause in England, for the season was too far along to risk the sea with a child of my daughter's age.[14] I also needed several days in any case to prepare for the trip and I was obliged to apply to the Duke de Rovigo for those few days. We have already seen that the French government is in the habit of ordering women, like soldiers, to depart within twenty-four hours.[15] Here is the reply from Savary, Duke de Rovigo; it is curious, I think, to see the style those people use.

POLICE GÉNÉRALE
OFFICE OF THE MINISTER
Paris, October 3, 1810[16]

I have received, Madame, the letter you have done me the honor of writing me. Your son must have informed you that I saw no objection to your retarding your departure by seven or eight days; I am desirous of their sufficing for the arrangements remaining for you to make, because I cannot grant you more.

You must not look for the cause of the order of which I notified you in the silence you have maintained with respect to the Emperor in your last work; that would be a mistake; he could not find a place therein that might be worthy of him. But your exile is a natural consequence of the course you have been following constantly for several years. It seemed to me that the air in this country did not suit you at all, and we are not yet reduced to seeking models in the peoples you admire.

Your last work is not at all French; I am the one who halted its printing. I regret the loss the book dealer will suffer, but I cannot possibly allow it to come out.

You know, Madame, that you were permitted to leave Coppet only because you had expressed the desire to cross over to America. If my predecessor allowed you to live in the department of Loir-et-Cher, you certainly could not have seen that tolerance as a revocation of the measures drawn up in your regard. Today you oblige me to have them executed strictly; you have only yourself to blame.

I am instructing M. Corbigny to ensure the execution of the order I have given him when the extension I grant you has expired.

I am sorry, Madame, that you have compelled me to begin my correspondence with you by a severe measure; it would have been pleasanter for me to have only to offer you the expression of the high esteem with which I have the honor of being, Madame,

Your very humble and very obedient servant,
Signed: the Duke de Rovigo

P.S.—I have reasons, Madame, for indicating to you the ports of Lorient, La Rochelle, Bordeaux, and Rochefort, as the only ports from which you may embark. I invite you to advise me of the one that you have chosen.[17]

His mawkish hypocrisy in telling me that the air of this country does not suit me, his denial of the true reason for suppressing my book, are worthy of note. Savary had, in fact, been more honest in his conversation with my son; he had asked him why I did not name either the Emperor or the armies in my book on Germany.

"But the book is purely literary," my son replied, "I do not see how she could have brought in that kind of subject."

"Do you think, Monsieur," Savary said then, "that we have waged war in Germany for eighteen years so a person with a name as widely known as your mother's can print a book without talking about us? That book will be burned and we ought to have shut its author in Vincennes."

When I received the letter from Savary, I paid attention to a single sentence—the one cutting me off from the Channel ports. I had already learned that, suspecting my intentions, they sought to prevent my going to England. This new problem was truly beyond my strength. In leaving my native country I needed the one of my choice; in leaving the friends of a lifetime, I needed at least to find those friends of all that is good and noble with whom, without knowing them personally, one's soul is always in sympathy. Suddenly, everything that sustained my imagination was crumbling before my eyes. For a moment longer I wanted to take a boat loaded with cargo for America in the hope that it would be seized on the way; but I was too shaken to make such an important decision and, since I was given America or Coppet as my only alternatives, I resolved on the latter course, for deep feeling always drew me toward Coppet despite the difficulties I was subject to there.

My two sons attempted to see the Emperor, then in residence at Fontainebleau; word was sent that they would be arrested if they remained. All the more reason for my being forbidden to go there. I was obliged to return to Coppet from Blois where I was staying, without coming closer to Paris than forty leagues. Savary had said that at thirty-eight leagues I was a lawful prize; such is his pirate-minister's way of speaking. Thus when the Emperor exercises the arbitrary right of exile, neither the exiled person nor his friends, nor even his children can approach him to plead the cause of the unhappy one who is torn from his affections and his habits. And these decrees of exile that are now irrevocable, especially where women are concerned, these decrees that the Emperor himself has rightly called "outlawing," are pronounced without its being possible to lay any justification before him, supposing that the wrong of displeasing the Emperor admits of one.

Although my order was forty leagues, I was obliged to pass by way of Orléans,[18] a rather dreary city, but occupied by very pious persons who have withdrawn to this refuge. I was not supposed to see anyone, but while walking in the city I stopped in front of the monument erected in memory of Joan of Arc. "Surely," I thought then, "when she delivered France from English power, *that* France was still far more free, far more truly France than at present." It is a strange sensation to wander in a city where you do not know anyone at all. I found a bitter joy in letting my isolation penetrate, in looking at this France that I was about to leave perhaps forever, without talking to anyone, without distraction from the impression made on me by the scene itself. From time to time passersby paused to look at me because I think that, in spite of myself, I wore an expression of pain, but they soon continued on their way, for people have long since become accustomed to the sight of suffering.

Fifty leagues from Switzerland, the border bristles with forts, with houses of detention, with towns serving as prisons, and wherever you look you see only individuals coerced by the will of a single man, conscripts of misfortune, all of them enchained far from where they would wish to live. In Dijon, Spanish prisoners who had refused to take the oath[19] came to the town square to feel the noonday sun because they took it for their compatriot, in a sense. They wrapped themselves in cloaks, often torn but which they managed to wear with nobility, and they took pride in the wretchedness that came from their self-respect; they took pleasure in the suffering that linked them to their intrepid homeland. Sometimes you saw them enter a café only to read the news sheet so they might discern the fate of their friends through the lies of their enemies; their faces were immobile, but not expressionless, and you were aware of the repressed strength of their will. Farther on, at Auxonne, resided the English prisoners who, the previous night, had saved from fire one of the city's houses where they were kept in confinement. In Besançon there were more Spaniards. Among the French exiles to be met all over France, was an angelic person who lived in the citadel of Besançon so as not to leave her father. For a long time, and through all kinds of danger, she shared the fate of the one who had given her life.[20]

As you reach Switzerland, on the summit of the mountains separating it from France, you catch sight of the Château de Joux where prisoners of state are held whose names often do not reach their families. It is in this prison that Toussaint-Louverture died of the cold; he deserved his misfortune because he had been cruel, but the man who should not have inflicted it on him was the Emperor, since he had pledged his word to guarantee his liberty and his life. The weather was horrible the day I passed beneath this château; I thought of that black man suddenly transported to the Alps and for whom this dwelling was an icy hell. I thought of nobler beings who had been confined there, of those still moaning there, and I told myself that if I were in this place I would not come out alive. Nothing can give the small number of free peoples remaining on the earth an idea of this absence of security—the habitual state of all human creatures under Napoleon's authority. In other despotic governments there are customs, laws, a religion that the master never violates, however absolute he may be. But in France and in Europe-France, since all is new the past cannot be a guarantee, and there is everything to fear as there is everything to hope, according to whether or not one serves the interests of the man who dares give himself and himself alone as the goal of the entire human race.

Returning to Coppet, like La Fontaine's pigeon with my crippled wings,[21] I saw the rainbow rise over my father's home. I dared to share in this sign of covenant; there was nothing in my sad journey to forbid my aspiring to it. I was almost resigned then to living in this château, publishing nothing more on any subject. But in sacrificing the talents I flattered myself on possessing, I needed to find happiness in my affections at least, and you will see how they arranged my private life after stripping me of my literary existence.

The first letter received by the prefect of Geneva was to notify my two sons that they were forbidden to go to Paris without new authorization from the Police.[22] This was their punishment for trying to speak with the Emperor on my behalf. Thus the morality of the present government is to undo domestic ties and substitute the Emperor's will for everything. Several generals are quoted as declaring that if the Emperor ordered them to throw wife and children into the river they would not hesitate to obey. Translated, this means that they prefer the money given them by the Emperor to the family they owe to nature. There are many examples of this way of thinking, but there are few of the shamelessness that prompts to speaking it aloud. I met with new pain in seeing my situation weigh for the first time on my sons, just entering life. One feels quite firm in one's conduct when it is based on sincere conviction, but the moment others suffer because of us, it is almost impossible not to blame ourselves. My two sons, however, generously dismissed this feeling of mine and we mutually supported one another through memory of my father.

A few days later, the prefect of Geneva wrote me a second letter, asking in the name of the Minister of Police for the remaining proofs of my book that they supposed I still had; he was well acquainted with the accounts of what I had given and retained, and his spies had served him very well. In my reply, I gave him the satisfaction of acknowledging that he had been perfectly informed, but I told him at the same time that this copy was no longer in Switzerland and that I neither could nor wished to hand it over. I added my pledge not to have it printed on the Continent, however, and I had no great merit in so promising, for at the time what continental government could have allowed publication of a book forbidden by the Emperor?

Shortly afterward, the prefect of Geneva was dismissed and it was generally thought to be because of me.[23] Nonetheless, he had not deviated in any detail from the orders he had received; and although he was one of the most upright and enlightened of Frenchmen, because he served the Emperor it was a matter of principle for him to obey scrupulously. It was yet another affliction for me to be or to pass for the cause of such a man's dismissal. Geneva in general regretted his departure, and from the moment it was thought I had played some part in his disgrace, all those aspiring to positions hurried from my house as if from some deadly contagion. Still I had more friends left to me in Geneva than any other provincial town of France would have offered, for the heritage of liberty has left a great deal of generous feeling in this city, but there can be no idea of the anxiety you feel when you are afraid to compromise those who come to see you. I made careful inquiries on all a person's relations before inviting him, for if he had just one cousin who either wanted or occupied a position, to suggest dinner was to ask for an act of Roman heroism.

At last, in the month of March,[24] a new prefect arrived from Paris, M. de Capelle. He was one of those men superlatively adapted to the present regime, that is to say, having great knowledge of facts and perfect absence of principle in matters of government, calling every fixed rule an abstraction and placing his conscience in devotion to power. The first time I saw him, he told me immediately that a talent like mine was made to celebrate the Emperor, that he was a subject worthy of the enthusiasm I had shown in *Corinne*. I answered that, persecuted as I was by the Emperor, any praise addressed to him on my part would seem like a petition, and that I was persuaded the Emperor himself would find my encomiums ridiculous in such circumstances. He fought this opinion vigorously; he came to my home several times to beg me, in the name of my own interests, to write for the Emperor, were it only a handwritten pamphlet of four pages; these would suffice, he assured me, to put an end to all my difficulties. What he told me, he repeated to everyone I knew. Finally, he came one day to propose my extolling the birth of the King of Rome;[25] laughing, I replied that I had no ideas on the subject and that I would confine myself to wishing him a good wet nurse. That joke ended the prefect's negotiations with me on the necessity of my writing in favor of the present government.

Not long afterward, the doctors ordered my younger son to take the waters. There was a spa at Aix en Savoie,[26] twelve leagues from Coppet. I chose the first days of May for the visit, a time when no one is ever there. I informed the prefect of this little journey, and I went to shut myself away in a sort of village where I did not know a single person at the time. Scarcely had I spent ten days there when a letter arrived from the prefect of Geneva ordering me back. The prefect of Mont Blanc, where I was staying, also feared that I might leave for England, he said, and write against the Emperor, and even though England did not exactly border on Aix en Savoie, he sent his gendarmes running to forbid my being given post-horses along the way.[27] Today, I am tempted to laugh at all that *prefectorial* activity against so poor and weak a thing as I, but in those days I was frightened to death at the sight of a gendarme. I lived in fear that from so rigorous an exile they might soon move to an imprisonment more terrible than death. I knew that once I was arrested, once the scandal of it was weathered, the Emperor would no longer let people speak of me to him—if anyone had the courage for it, which was hardly probable in that court where terror reigns at each moment of the day and in every detail of life.

I returned to Geneva and the prefect gave me notice that not only did he forbid my going under any pretext to the countries united to France, but that he advised me not to travel within Switzerland, and never to go farther than two leagues from Coppet in any direction. I objected that being domiciled in Switzerland and widow of a Swedish ambassador, I did not really understand by what right French authority would prohibit a foreigner from traveling to a foreign country. He no doubt thought me a bit naïve to argue a question of law in those times and repeated advice curiously bordering on an order. I stood by my protest, but the following day I learned that one of Germany's most distinguished men of letters, M. Schlegel, who for the past eight years had kindly undertaken the education of my sons, had just received orders to leave not only Geneva but even Coppet. Again I tried to point out that in Switzerland it was not for the prefect of Geneva to give orders, but I was told that I was perfectly free to have this order go by way of the French ambassador if I wished, that he would apply to the *landamman,* and the *landamman* to the canton of Vaud, which would send M. Schlegel from my home. In forcing despotism to make this detour I gained ten days, but nothing more. I tried to learn why they were taking from me the company of M. Schlegel, my friend and my children's friend. The prefect who, like most of the Emperor's agents, habitually combined sugary sentences with harsh deeds, said that it was out of concern for me that the government was sending M. Schlegel away since he was making me anti-French. Truly moved by the fatherly concern of the French government, I asked what M. Schlegel had done against France. The prefect alleged his literary opinions, and among others a pamphlet in which, comparing Euripedes' *Phèdre* with Racine's, he had given preference to the former. It took no small subtlety for a Corsican monarch thus to defend the slightest nuances of French literature.[28] But in reality, M. Schlegel was exiled because he was my friend, because his conversation enlivened my solitude, and because they were just now bringing into operation the system that would become apparent, to make a prison of my soul by tearing from me all the pleasures of mind and friendship.

Once more I resolved to depart, a decision I had often been led to forgo by the pain of leaving my friends and the ashes of my parents. But by what route? The French government set up so many impediments to a passport for America that I no longer dared look to that means. Besides, I had rea-

son to fear that just as I embarked, they would claim to have learned of my
wish to proceed to England, and that they would apply the decree sentenc-
ing to prison those intending to do so without authorization from the
French government. Thus it seemed infinitely more desirable to make my
way to Sweden, my sons' honorable native land, and the one whose new
head of state has already foretold the glorious leadership he has known
how to offer ever since.[29] But what route could I take to Sweden? The prefect had let me know in every possible way that I would be arrested everywhere that France was in command, and how could you reach a place
where she was not in command? You were forced to go through Russia,
since the Confederation of the Rhine and Denmark, those disguised
French provinces, blocked every other path. But to reach Russia you
needed to cross Bavaria and Austria; I had confidence in the Tyrol, even
though it had been joined to a Confederated State, because of the courage
its unfortunate people had displayed. As for Austria, despite the lamentable
degradation into which she had fallen, I respected her leader enough to believe that he would not hand me over, but I also knew that he could not
defend me. Since he had thought himself compelled to sacrifice the ancient
honor of his house, what strength did he have left in any domain! And so I
spent my life studying the map of Europe to escape, as Napoleon studied it
to make himself its master; and the goal of my campaign, like his, was always Russia. She was the last refuge of the oppressed, she was to be the
power that the sovereign of Europe wanted to strike down.

Resolved to depart by way of Russia, I needed a passport to enter that
country. But a new difficulty arose: one needed to write to Petersburg itself for the passport—such is the established practice; and although I was
sure of obtaining it from so generous a nature as the Emperor Alexander's,
I could rightly fear that my request would be discussed in ministry offices,
that once the French ambassador was informed, I would be arrested to
keep me from carrying out my plans. Thus I would have to go to Vienna to
request my passport from there, and to wait for it. The six weeks required
for sending my letter and getting the reply in return would have to be
spent under the protection of a ministry that had given the Archduchess of
Austria to Bonaparte.[30] Was it possible to entrust myself to these people?
Nevertheless, by remaining a hostage in Napoleon's power myself, I not
only renounced all exercise of my personal talents, but also kept my sons
from having careers; they could not serve for Bonaparte or against him. No
settlement was possible for my daughter, since I was obliged either to part
with her or confine her to Coppet. And if, however, I were arrested in

flight, it was all over for my children who would then have refused to separate themselves from my destiny.

It was in the midst of this anxiety that a friend of twenty years standing, M. Mathieu de Montmorency, wanted to visit me as he had done several times since my exile. People wrote to me from Paris, it is true, that the Emperor had expressed disapproval of any person who came to Coppet and, in particular, of M. de Montmorency should he come again. But, I confess, I was benumbed by remarks that the Emperor lavishly pronounced from time to time to frighten people, and I did not make a strong stand against M. de Montmorency who generously sought to reassure me in his letters. I was quite wrong no doubt, but who could be persuaded that it would be deemed a crime for the old friend of an exiled woman to come spend a few days at her side? M. de Montmorency's life, devoted entirely to good works or family attachments, set him at such a distance from any politics that unless you wanted to exile all saints, it seemed impossible to me that such a man might be attacked.[31] I also wondered to what purpose, a question I have always asked myself where Napoleon's behavior was concerned. I know that he will always do all the harm that may be useful to him for the slightest thing, but I do not always guess the extent in all directions, both the infinitely small and the infinitely large, of his immense egotism. Although the prefect had sent word advising me not to travel in Switzerland, I disregarded this advice that could not be an order.

I went to meet M. de Montmorency at Orbe, and as the goal of our excursion in Switzerland, I proposed returning by way of Fribourg to see the establishment for Trappist women, which is in a valley, close to the one for men.[32] We arrived in a driving rain and were obliged to go a quarter league on foot to reach the monastery. Just as we were expecting to enter, the Trappist superior who directs the women's convent told us that no woman was welcome there. I tried, however, to ring at the cloister door; a nun arrived behind the grill used by the lay sister to speak with strangers.

"What do you want?" she said in a voice devoid of inflection, like that of living ghosts, perhaps.

"I would like to see the inside of your convent," I said.

"That cannot be," she replied.

"But I am soaked," I told her, "and I need to dry off."

She released some sort of spring that opened the door of an exterior room where I was allowed to rest, but no living creature appeared. I sat there for no more than a few moments when I grew impatient at being denied access to the interior of the house and I rang again. The same lay sister returned. I asked her again whether no woman had been welcomed in the convent; she replied that one could enter when one intended to become a nun.

"But," I said, "how can I know whether I want to stay in your house if I am not permitted to become acquainted with it?"

"Oh, you needn't trouble," she answered; "I am quite sure that you have no vocation for our condition."

And with those words she closed her little window. I do not know by what signs that nun had noticed my worldly nature; it may be that a lively way of talking, so different from their own, sufficed for recognizing travelers who were merely curious. Since the hour of vespers had come, I could enter the church to hear the nuns sing; they were behind a closely woven black grill through which nothing could be seen. The only audible sounds were the sabots they wore and the wooden seats they raised to sit upon. Their singing lacked any sensitivity, and I thought I observed, either in their manner of praying, or in my conversation afterward with the Trappist father who led them, that it was not religious enthusiasm as we conceive it, but austere and solemn practices that enabled them to endure such a way of life. The softening emotion of piety itself would weaken their strength, and a kind of asperity of soul is required for so harsh an existence.

The new father-abbot of the Trappists settled in the valleys of the canton of Fribourg has added further to the austerities of the order. One cannot have any idea of the routine sufferings imposed on the religious. These go so far as to forbid their leaning against a wall when on their feet for several hours, or wiping the sweat from their brows—in sum, every moment of their lives is filled with pain, just as people in the world fill theirs with pleasure. Rarely do they grow old, and the religious to whom this lot falls consider it a punishment from heaven. Such an institution would be barbaric if one entered by force or if the suffering imposed were in any way concealed. But a printed document is distributed to whoever wants to read it in which the rigors of the order are exaggerated rather than softened, and yet novices are found who wish to devote themselves to it, and those who are received do not escape, although they could without the slightest difficulty. Everything rests, as I saw it, on the powerful idea of death. The institutions and diversions of society are intended to turn our thoughts solely toward life, but when the certainty of death penetrates man's heart to a certain depth, and he links it to that of the soul's immortality, there is no limit to the disgust he may conceive for everything that makes up earthly interests. And, as suffering seems the path to the future life, one is avid for it, just like the weary traveler who gladly tires himself to cover more quickly the route that leads to the goal of his desires. But what at once astonished and saddened me was to see children raised with this severity; their poor shaven heads, their young faces already wrinkled, the mortuary habit they wore before they became acquainted with life, before they renounced it voluntarily—everything disgusted me with the parents who had placed them there. The moment such a condition is not adopted by the free and unshaken choice of the one professing it, it arouses horror in equal proportion to the respect initially aroused. The father I conversed with spoke only of death; it was the source or the reference of all his ideas: it was sovereign monarch in this place. As we discussed the temptations of the world, I told the Trappist father how much I admired him for sacrificing everything to evade them. "We are cowards," he told me, "who have withdrawn into a fortress because we did not have the courage to fight in open country." That response was as witty as it was modest.[33]

A few days after our visit, the French government gave orders to seize the father-abbot, M. de Lestrange, to confiscate the order's holdings, and to expel the fathers from Switzerland. I do not know what they held against M. de Lestrange, but it was hardly likely that such a man would be involved in the affairs of the world, still less the religious who never left their solitude. The Swiss government searched for M. de Lestrange everywhere, and I hope for this government's honor that it took care not to find him. Nevertheless, the wretched administrators of countries called the allies of France are very often charged with arresting those designated to them, not knowing whether they are handing over innocent or guilty victims of the great Leviathan that sees fit to devour them. The Trappists' possessions were seized, that is to say their tombs, for they owned nothing else, and the order was dispersed. It is alleged that, in Genoa, a Trappist ascended the pulpit to retract the oath of loyalty he had sworn to the Emperor, declaring that since the captivity of the Pope he believed all ecclesiastics released from that oath. Immediately after that act of repentance, it is said, he was judged by a military tribunal and shot. One might think, it seems to me, that he was punished enough for the whole order not to be held responsible for his conduct. I have since learned that Abbot Lestrange and several poor religious, his brothers, had escaped to Russia, the one remaining refuge on the Continent. Perhaps they have been forced since then to go into Asia and thus carry the Christian religion toward the Orient as far as its birthplace.

We reached Vevey again by way of the mountains and proposed to ride as far as the entry to the Valais, which I had never seen. We stopped at Bex, the last town in Switzerland, for the Valais had already been joined to France. A Portuguese brigade had left from Geneva to go to the Valais; what a strange destiny for Europe that Portuguese garrisoned in Geneva should take possession of part of Switzerland in the name of France![34]

I was curious to see the cretins in the Valais whom I had often been told about. That sad debasement of man is a great subject for reflection, but it is inordinately painful to see the human face thus become an object of repulsion and horror. Still I noticed a sort of liveliness in a few of those imbeciles that has to do with the astonishment they experience at external objects. Since they never recognize what they have already seen, they are surprised each time, and the spectacle of the world is new to them every day, in every detail; it is, perhaps, compensation for their sad state, for surely there is one. A few years ago a cretin was sentenced to death for a murder he had committed; as he was led to his execution, he thought, seeing himself surrounded by many people, that they were there to pay him honor and he held himself erect and tidied his suit, laughing, to make himself worthier of the celebration. Was it admissible to punish such a creature for the crime committed by his arm?

Three leagues from Bex a famous waterfall is to be seen, where the water drops from the top of a very high mountain. I suggested to my friends that we see it, and we were back before dinner time. It is true that these falls were on the territory of the Valais, consequently on French territory, and I forgot that all I was allowed of France was the piece of ground separating Coppet from Geneva. When I returned home, the prefect not only objected to my daring to travel in Switzerland but also granted me, as a great proof of his indulgence, the silence he would maintain on the offense I had committed by setting foot on the territory of the French Empire. I could have said as in La Fontaine's fable:[35]

I cropped of this field the breadth of my tongue,

but I admitted quite simply that I had been wrong to go and see those Swiss falls without reflecting that they were in France.

This constant quibbling over life's slightest actions made it odious, and I could not distract myself with work; the memory of the wrong done to my book and the certainty of no longer being able to publish anything entirely discouraged my mind, which needs stimulation to be capable of work. Nevertheless, I could not yet decide to leave forever the borders of France and my father's home and the friends who had remained so faithful. Always I thought I would leave and always I gave myself pretexts for staying. When the last blow struck my soul, God knows what I suffered!

M. de Montmorency came to spend a few days with me at Coppet. The malice in small details of the master of so great an Empire is so well calculated that when my friend sent the letter announcing his arrival at Coppet, he received his letter of exile by return mail.[36] The Emperor would not have been satisfied had he not received the order in my home and had there not been a word in the minister's letter pointing to me as the cause of his exile. M. de Montmorency tried in every way to soften the news for me, but I say this to the Emperor so he may congratulate himself for attaining his goal:[37] I uttered cries of anguish when I learned the misfortune I had brought on my generous friend, and my heart, so sorely tested for so many years, was never closer to despair. I did not know how to deaden the succession of heartrending thoughts within me; I resorted to opium to suspend my anguish for a few hours. M. de Montmorency, calm and pious, urged me to follow his example, but he was sustained by the devotion he had so kindly shown to me while, for my part, I blamed myself for the cruel consequences of a devotion that would separate him from his family and his friends. I prayed to God without cease, but my sorrow gave me no respite and every moment of my life was painful.

Such was my state when a letter arrived from Mme Récamier, from that beautiful person who has received the homage of all Europe and who has never forsaken an unhappy friend. She announced her intention to stop at Coppet two days hence on her way to the waters at Aix en Savoie. I trembled lest Mathieu's fate strike her. However unlikely it might seem, it was prescribed for me to fear everything of a hate at once so barbaric and so meticulous, and I sent a courier to meet Mme Récamier and beg her not to stop at my home.[38] I had to be conscious of her a few leagues away, she whom I so love, she who had constantly comforted me by the noblest and most delicate attentions; I had to know that she was there, so close to my home, and that I was not allowed to embrace her again, perhaps for the last time! I entreated her but she would have none of it; she could not pass by my windows without seeing me for a few hours, and it was with convulsive tears that I saw her enter the château where her arrival was always a celebration.

She left the following day, going immediately to the home of a cousin, fifty leagues from Switzerland. It was useless; deadly exile struck her: she had intended to see me, that was enough.[39] Generous pity had inspired her; she had to be punished for it. The state of her fortune, half of which she had sacrificed to her husband's creditors, made the destruction of her personal settlement very painful. Cut off from all her friends, she spent months on end in a little provincial town, abandoned to all that is most monotonous and dreary in solitude. This is the fate that I brought on the most brilliant person of her time, and the leader of the French, so famous for their gallantry, showed no consideration for the most beautiful woman in France. On one and the same day, he struck at birth and virtue in M. de Montmorency, beauty in Mme Récamier and, if I dare say so, at a certain reputation for talent in me. Perhaps he fondly hoped he was also attacking my father's memory in his daughter, so that it might be said that, on this earth, neither the dead nor the living, nor the gently born, nor the citizens, nor piety, nor charm, nor intelligence, nor fame meant anything under his reign. You had become guilty when you fell short of the laws, of the subtle nuances of flattery, by not deserting whoever was struck with his disfavor. In his view the human race is divided between those who serve him and those who take it upon themselves, not to harm him, but to exist on their own. In all the universe, from the details of housekeeping to the direction of empires, he does not want a single will exercised without reference to his own.

"Mme de Staël," the prefect would say, "has created a pleasant life for herself; her friends and strangers come to see her at Coppet; the Emperor refuses to tolerate that." And why did he torment me thus? So that I would publish an encomium for him? And what did one more encomium mean to him among the thousands of phrases that fear and hope have made haste to offer him? The Emperor once said: "If I were given the choice between a splendid deed of my own or inducing my adversary to do something vile, I would not hesitate to select the debasement of my enemy." Here lies the whole explanation of the particular care he has shown in tearing my life apart. He knew that I was attached to my friends, to France, to my works, to my tastes, to society; in taking from me everything that made up my happiness, he meant to unsettle me enough to write some platitude in the hope of its winning my return. By refusing, I must admit, I did not have the merit of sacrifice: the Emperor wanted something contemptible from me, but futilely contemptible, for in a time when success is deified, his mockery would have been incomplete had I managed to return to Paris by any means whatever. To please our master, skilled in the art of degrading any proud souls still left, I was required to dishonor myself in exchange for my return to France so that he could mock my zeal in praising him—he who had not stopped persecuting me—and so that my zeal would prove useless. I refused him that truly refined pleasure; there lies the only merit I have shown in the long struggle that he contrived between his omnipotence and my weakness.

M. de Montmorency's family, in despair at his exile, wished, and rightly so, that he move far away from the pitiful cause of that exile, and I saw my friend leave without knowing if ever again his noble presence would honor my home on this earth. It was on August 31, 1811, that I broke the first and the last of my ties with my native land; I broke it at least in terms of the human relationships that can no longer exist between us; but I never raise my eyes to heaven without thinking of him, and I dare to believe as well that in his prayers he answers me. Destiny no longer grants me any other correspondence with him.

When the exile of my two friends was known, a host of griefs of every kind assailed me, but in great misfortune we become as if insensible of all new troubles. Rumor spread that the Minister of Police had announced his plan to have a guardhouse placed at the foot of the drive at Coppet to stop anyone who came to see me. The prefect of Geneva, charged by order of the Emperor, he said, to render me null and void—these are his expressions—did not miss an occasion to insinuate or even declare outright that all persons with something to fear or desire of the government should avoid coming to my home.

M. de Saint-Priest, the *ci-devant* King's minister and my father's colleague, was pleased to honor me with his affection; his daughters, rightly terrified that he would be sent away from Geneva, joined me in begging him not to come see me. Nevertheless in mid-winter, at the age of seventy-six, he was exiled not only from Geneva but from Switzerland as well.[40] As my example has shown, for the Emperor to exile people from Switzerland as well as from France is completely accepted; and when you object to French agents that this is, however, an issue of a foreign country whose independence is recognized, they shrug their shoulders as if you wanted to bore them with the subtleties of metaphysics. In Europe, the attempt to distinguish anything but prefect-kings or prefect-barons receiving orders from the Emperor of France requires true subtlety. If the so-called allied countries differ from the French provinces, it is because they are treated with a little less consideration. A certain memory of being called the great nation subsists in France, forcing circumspection on the Emperor at times, but this becomes less necessary with each passing day. The motive given for M. de Saint-Priest's exile is that he had not induced his sons to resign from their service to Russia. His sons had found a generous welcome in Russia during the emigration; they had risen to high position. Their intrepid courage had been justly rewarded: they were covered with wounds; they were chosen to stand among the first for their military gifts. The elder is already over thirty. How could a father have insisted that the lives of his sons, thus grounded, be sacrificed to the honor of placing themselves under surveillance on French soil? For that is the enviable fate reserved for them. When M. de Saint-Priest was exiled, I was sadly content that I had not seen him for the past four months; otherwise no one would have doubted that it was I who had infected him with my disfavor.

Not only the French, but foreigners too, were warned not to come to my home. The prefect stood as sentinel to keep even old friends from seeing me again. One unexceptional day, performing his official duty, he deprived me of the company of a German whose conversation I found especially agreeable,[41] and this time I told him that he might well have spared himself his quest of persecution:

"What!" he replied, "I acted that way as a favor to you. I gave your friend to understand that his visit compromised you." I could not help laughing at that ingenious argument. "Yes," he went on, imperturbably grave, "if the Emperor saw that people prefer you to him, he would hold it against you."

"And so," I said, "the Emperor insists that my close friends abandon me in order to gratify him, and soon my children, perhaps; that seems a bit excessive to me. Besides," I added, "I do not really see how a person in my situation might be compromised, and what you say reminds me of a revolutionary in the days of the Terror who was asked to try to save one of his friends from the scaffold. 'I would be afraid of making things worse if I spoke for him,' he answered." M. de Capelle smiled at the quotation, but the prefect went right on with arguments that, backed by four hundred thousand bayonets, always seem completely sound. A man from Geneva said to me:

"Don't you think M. de Capelle proclaims his opinions quite frankly?"

"Yes," I replied, "he says courageously that he is on the side of the greatest might and sincerely that he is devoted to the powerful man. I find it hard to see the merit of such admissions."

A few independent persons in Geneva went on giving proofs of kindness that I hold forever as deeply felt memories. But functionaries all the way down to customs clerks took themselves for diplomats in their dealings with me. And from prefects to sub-prefects and cousins of one or the other, they would have been overcome with terror if I had not spared them as much as lay in my hands the anxiety of paying or not paying me a visit. With each mail, rumor spread that other friends had been exiled from Paris for maintaining connections with me. It was my strict duty not to see a single prominent French person any longer, and frequently I was even afraid of bringing harm to people in the country where I lived, people whose courageous friendship for me never failed. I felt two contrary and, I believe, equally natural impulses: I was sad when people deserted me and cruelly anxious for those who showed attachment to me. I find it hard to believe that a situation more painful with each passing moment can be imagined in life, and for the nearly two years that it lasted,[42] I did not once see the dawn without grieving at the prospect of enduring the existence it renewed.

"But why didn't you leave?" you will say, and people never stopped saying on all sides. A man I must not name,[43] but who knows, I hope, how much I respect the nobility of his character and his conduct, said to me: "If you stay, he will treat you like Mary Stuart: nineteen unhappy years with catastrophe at the end." Another friend, intelligent but unguarded in his language, wrote to me that there was dishonor in remaining after so much ill-treatment. I did not need that advice to long for departure; from the moment that I could no longer see my friends, that I was only a hindrance in my children's lives, was I not compelled to make up my mind to leave?[44] But the prefect repeated in all sorts of ways that I would be arrested if I left, that in Vienna as in Berlin my return would be demanded, and that I could not make even the slightest preparations for travel without his being informed, since he knew everything that happened in my home. This was an empty boast, and in this respect, the event has shown him to be a fool of a spy. But who would not have been alarmed by his confident tone when he told all my friends that I could not take a step without gendarmes seizing me?

I spent eight months in a state I have no words to describe, testing my courage each day, and each day weakening at the thought of prison. Everyone dreads it, surely, but my imagination so fears solitude, my friends are so necessary to sustain me, to stimulate me, to present a new perspective when I succumb under a fixed painful impression, that death has never shown me features so cruel as prison, as the possible years of solitary confinement where not one friendly voice can reach you. I have been told that one of the Spaniards, astoundingly dauntless in the defense of Saragossa, uttered shrieks in the dungeon of Vincennes where he is confined, so harmful is that atrocious solitude to the most courageous beings! Besides, I could not pretend to myself that I was a courageous person; I am bold in imagination but timid in character, and all forms of peril seem spectral to me. The kind of talent I possess makes all images so vivid to me that, if nature's beauties are enhanced, dangers of every sort also become more fearsome. At one time I was afraid of prison; at another it was brigands, for if Russia were closed to me by some political scheme, I would be forced to cross through Turkey; at still another time, the vast sea to be crossed from Constantinople to London also filled me with terror for my daughter and me. In any event, the need to leave was unrelenting; an inner impulse of pride urged me on, but I could say like a well-known Frenchman: "I tremble at the dangers to which my courage will expose me."[45] What adds to the boorishness of persecuting women is that their nature is at once sensitive and weak; they suffer afflictions more acutely and are less capable of the strength needed to break free of them.

Another form of terror acted upon me as well: I feared that the moment my departure was known, the Emperor would have articles put in the news sheets: the kind he knows how to dictate when he wants to commit moral assassination. A senator told me one day that Napoleon was the best journalist he knew.[46] If this indeed is what the art of defaming individuals and nations is called, he is supremely possessed of it. Nations can extricate themselves, but in the revolutionary times he has lived through, he has acquired a certain feel for calumny accessible to the common people that leads him to find the remarks best suited to circulate among those whose intelligence is limited to repeating sentences the government has had published for their use. If the *Moniteur* accused someone of highway robbery, no news sheet, either French, German, or Italian, could print a vindication. Thus to the strength of the present despotism must be added the discovery of printing which used to be cited as a safeguard for liberty. In former times, cannons were called the last argument of kings.[47] News sheets must be added, for they are now among the most clever means of tyranny. The government can use them to say everything, even as it forbids any reply, any display of one's talent or character. It is impossible to imagine what it means to have one man in charge of a million soldiers and a billion in revenue, commanding all the prisons of Europe, with kings for jailers, and using the printed word to speak while the oppressed hardly have the intimacy of friendship to respond—in sum, able to make unhappiness absurd—loathsome power, ironically used as the final insult the infernal spirits can force the human race to endure!

However independent one's soul, I believe it impossible not to shudder at the idea of attracting such means against oneself. I confess, at least, that this was my reaction, and however sad my state, I often told myself that I must manage to be content with my lot: a roof for shelter, a table for eating, a garden for walking.[48] But such as this lot was, one could not be sure of maintaining it in peace; a word could slip out, a word could be repeated, and what degree of annoyance can that man not reach when his power is constantly increasing?[49] When the sun shone bright my courage revived, but when the weather turned hazy with fog, travel frightened me, and I discovered within me common tastes, foreign to my nature but fostered by fear; physical well-being seemed more important than I had thought until then and all fatigue terrified me. My health, sorely compromised by so many difficulties, weakened my soul's energy as well, and I truly made demands on the patience of my friends during that time by repeatedly bringing up my plans for deliberation, by overwhelming them with my doubts. I tried a second time to obtain a passport for America; I was made to wait until mid-winter for the answer, and in the end I was refused. I offered my pledge to have nothing printed on any subject, not even a *Bouquet to Iris,*[50] in exchange for permission to live in Rome; out of pride, I reminded them of *Corinne* when I asked permission to live in Italy.[51] No doubt General Savary judged that such a reason had never been entered in the police registers, and the South whose air was so necessary to my health was pitilessly refused; they never stopped telling me that my whole life was to be spent within the two leagues separating Coppet from Geneva. If I stayed, I would need to part with my sons, who were of an age to seek a career; I would impose the most forlorn prospects on my daughter by having her share my fate. The city of Geneva, which has preserved such noble marks of liberty, was nonetheless gradually letting herself to be won over by the interests binding her to the distributors of positions in France. Each day, the people with whom I could enjoy mutual understanding grew fewer in number, and all my feelings became a weight on my soul instead of a source of life. It was all over for my talent, for my happiness, for my existence, since it is dreadful to be of no use to one's children and to harm one's friends.

Finally, I received news from all directions announcing the Emperor's redoubtable preparations. It was clear that he meant first to make himself master of the Baltic ports by destroying Russia, and that he counted on using the remnants of that power next to drag them against Constantinople; from there, he intended to cross Africa and Asia. He had said, shortly before he left Paris: "This old Europe bores me." And it is in fact no longer enough for its master's sphere of action. But it was clear that the last ways out of the Continent could be closed from one moment to the next, and that one would find oneself in Europe as in a city at war, its gates guarded by soldiers.

And so I made up my mind to leave while there was still some way to reach England, and that way was across all of Europe. I set May 15 for my departure, having long since worked out the preparations in absolute secrecy.[52] On the eve of that day, my strength completely deserted me, and for a moment, I persuaded myself that such terror could be felt only in the face of wrongdoing. Sometimes I consulted all sorts of presages in the most senseless fashion; at other times, more wisely, I questioned myself and my friends on the morality of my decision. It seems that resignation in all matters is the most religious course, and I am not surprised that pious men come to have some form of scruples over decisions that spring from spontaneous will.[53] Necessity seems to bear a divine nature, while human resolve may stem from pride. However, not one of our faculties has been given us in vain, and that of deciding for oneself also has its place. Then again, all mediocre people are endlessly amazed that the needs of the talented are different from their own. When talent is successful, they admire it—everyone understands success, but when it causes problems, when it moves one to stray from the common path, these same people no longer consider this same talent as anything but an illness and almost as a fault. Buzzing around me I heard the platitudes to which everyone succumbs: "Doesn't she have money? Can't she live well and sleep well in a fine château?" A few persons of a higher order sensed that I lacked even the security of my dreary position, and that it could grow worse without ever improving. But the atmosphere around me counseled peace of mind because there had been no new persecution for six months, and men always believe that what is is what will be. It is amid all these oppressive circumstances that a decision was necessary, one of the most considerable that might be encountered in a woman's private life. My people, except for two who were very reliable,[54] knew nothing of my secret; most of those who came to visit suspected nothing, and by a single act, I was about to change my life and that of my children completely.

Torn by uncertainty, I wandered through the gardens at Coppet. I sat down in all the places where my father was accustomed to rest and contemplate nature; I saw once more the beauties of waves and greenery we had often admired together. I bade them farewell, commending myself to their sweet influence. The monument enclosing the ashes of my father and my mother and wherein, if the good Lord so permits, my own will be laid, was one of the main reasons for my regrets at going away,[55] but in drawing near them, I almost always found a strength of soul that seemed to come from on high. I spent an hour praying in front of the iron door that locked in the remains of the noblest of human beings, and there my soul was persuaded that I must leave.[56] I recalled those famous verses of a Latin poet, Claudius, where he expresses the kind of doubt that arises in the most religious souls when they see the earth given over to the wicked, and the fate of mortals as if floating about at the mercy of chance.[57] I felt I no longer had the strength to nourish the enthusiasm that fostered all that can be good in me, and that to have faith in my own belief I needed to hear the words of those who thought as I did. In that state of anxiety, I invoked my father's memory several times, that Fénelon of political life, whose genius was the opposite of Bonaparte's in everything. And he had genius, for as much of it is needed to be in harmony with heaven as to summon to oneself all the means unleashed by the absence of divine and human laws. I went to see my father's study again, where his armchair, his table with his papers are still in the same place. I embraced each cherished trace of him; I took his red coat that until then had been left on his chair under my orders, and I took it away with me to wrap myself in if Bonaparte's gendarmes or the messenger of death drew near me. These farewells over, I avoided to the extent possible those that hurt me too much, and I wrote to the friends I was leaving, taking care that my letters would not be delivered until several days after my departure.

The following day, at two o'clock in the afternoon, I climbed into my carriage saying that I would return in time for dinner. I took with me no package whatever; I held my fan in my hand, my daughter had hers, and only my son and a friend of his and mine[58] carried in their pockets what we needed for a few days' travel. As we went down the drive at Coppet, as we left the château that had become like an old and good friend to me, I was close to fainting. My older son took my hand and said, "Mother, *you're leaving for England, think about that.*"[59] Those words lifted my spirits. I was, however, nearly two thousand leagues[60] from this goal where the direct route would have led me so quickly, but at least each step brought me closer. After a few leagues, I sent one of my people back to my home to say that I would not return until the next day, and I went on day and night until we reached a farm on the other side of Berne, where I had arranged to meet another friend who was good enough to accompany me.[61] It was there, too, that I was to leave my older son, who was raised with the example of my father up to the age of twelve and whose features call him to mind.[62]

For a second time, my courage deserted me. This Switzerland, still so calm and always so beautiful, these people who know how to be free through their virtues, even when they have lost political independence—this whole country held me back; it seemed to be telling me not to leave. There was still time to return; I had not taken any irreparable step. Although it was the prefect's own idea to forbid me Switzerland, I saw clearly that it was for fear that I might go farther. In sum, I had not yet crossed the barrier that left me no possibility of return; it is difficult for the imagination to endure that thought. On the other hand, the decision to stay was also irrevocable, for I felt that once this moment passed, and it was certainly proved by subsequent events, I would no longer be able to escape. Besides, there is something shameful in beginning such solemn farewells all over again, and one cannot come back to life for friends more than once. I do not know what would have become of me if this uncertainty at the point of action had lasted longer, for it unsettled my head. My children, particularly my daughter, scarcely fourteen, decided me. I put myself in her hands, if you will, as if the voice of God had to make itself heard through the mouth of a child.[63] She spoke words linked to fate in my thoughts. My son went off and, when I saw him no more, I could say with Lord Russell: "The sorrow of death has come by."[64] I climbed into my carriage with my daughter; with uncertainty gone, I gathered my strength in my soul and I found for action what had been wanting in me for deliberation.

CROSSING INTO AUSTRIA

Thus it was that after ten years of ever-increasing persecution, first sent away from Paris, then relegated to Switzerland, next confined to my château, and in the end condemned to the horrible pain of being unable to see my friends any longer and having caused their exile—thus was I obliged to leave two homelands, Switzerland and France, as a fugitive, by order of a man less French than I, for I was born on the banks of the Seine where he is naturalized by his tyranny alone. He saw the light of day on the isle of Corsica, where the brutal temperature of Africa already makes itself felt; his father did not devote his fortune and his nights to preserving France from bankruptcy and famine as mine did; the air of this beautiful country is not his native air. Can he understand the pain of exile from this land, he who regards this fertile country merely as the instrument of his victories? Where is his native land? Where are his fellow citizens? His native land is the one that obeys him; his fellow citizens are the slaves who are more submissive to his orders. He complained one day that, unlike Tamerlane, he had not had under his command nations to which reasoning was foreign. I imagine that he is satisfied with Europeans now; their customs, like their armies, have drawn rather close to the Tartars.

I had nothing to fear within Switzerland since I could always prove that I had the right to be there, but to leave I had only a foreign passport. I needed to cross a Confederated State,[65] and if some French agent had asked the Bavarian government to deny me passage, who knows with what regret, but with what obedience nonetheless, it would have executed the orders it might have received?

I entered the Tyrol[66] with great respect for the country that had fought out of devotion to its former masters,[67] but with great scorn for those Austrian ministers who could advise abandoning the men compromised by loyalty to their sovereign. It is said that a certain M. Hudelist, head of the

Austrian Department of Espionage,[68] took it into his head one day during the war to maintain at the Emperor's table that the Tyroleans should be abandoned. M. Hormayr,[69] a Tyrolean and Councillor of State in Vienna who has shown a warrior's courage and a historian's talent by his deeds and by his writings, took exception to those shameful remarks with the scorn they deserved. The Emperor expressed his complete approval of M. Hormayr and in this way, at least, proved alien in his feelings to the political course he had been made to follow. Thus it is that, by the time Bonaparte made himself master of France, most of Europe's sovereigns—personally very decent men—no longer existed as kings, since for the administration of public affairs they relied entirely on circumstances and on their ministers.

In appearance, the Tyrol calls Switzerland to mind. However, the countryside does not have as much vigor or originality; the villages do not herald such plenty. It is, in sum, a country that has been governed wisely but that has never been free, and it is as a country of mountain people that it has proved capable of resistance. Almost no mention is made of remarkable men in the Tyrol. First of all, the Austrian government is hardly suited to fostering genius; further, given its customs and geographical situation, this country should be joined with the Swiss Confederation. Since incorporation into the Austrian monarchy is not consonant with its nature, it has been able to develop only the noble qualities of the mountain people in this union: courage and loyalty.

The postilion leading us pointed out a rock on which the Emperor Maximillian, grandfather to Charles V, had almost perished; swept along by the fever of the hunt, he had followed the roebuck to such heights that he could not come back down.[70] This tradition is still popular in the country, so necessary to nations is the cult of the past. But memory of the last war was still alive in the people's soul; peasants showed us the mountain summits where they had entrenched themselves; their imaginations recalled the effect produced by their beautiful martial music when it echoed from the hilltops in the valleys. Showing us the palace of the Prince Royal of Bavaria at Innsbruck, they told us that Hofer, the brave peasant who led the insurrection, had lived there. They recounted the valor shown by a woman when the French entered her château. In sum, everything about them declared the need to be a nation, even more than personal devotion to the House of Austria.[71]

An Innsbruck church holds the famous tomb of Maximillian. I went there, thinking no one would recognize me in a place so distant from the capitals where French agents reside. The bronze figure of Emperor Maximillian is kneeling on a sarcophagus in the center of the church, and forty other immense statues in the same metal—arranged on each side of the sanctuary—represent the most distinguished men, women, and princes of their time. The image of those motionless courtiers of a dead master, the etiquette maintained among the shadows, was a spectacle that induced profound reflection; one met Philip the Good, Charles the Bold, Marie of Burgundy, and Dietrich of Berne.[72] Lowered visors hid the faces of the knights, but when the visor was lifted, a visage of brass appeared under the helmet of brass and the warrior's features, like his armor, were made of bronze. Those monuments of history refresh the soul. One day, if future generations leave that man a tomb, they will pass by his ashes peacefully, whereas during his lifetime no human being has been able to enjoy either tranquillity or independence.

From Innsbruck I was to go by way of Salzburg to reach the Austrian borders. It seemed to me that all my anxieties would come to an end once I entered the territory of a monarchy that I had known to be so safe and so good. But the moment I dreaded most was crossing from Bavaria into Austria, for it was there that a courier could have preceded me to forbid my passing through. I had not gone very quickly despite that fear, for my health, damaged by all that I had suffered, did not allow me to travel at night. It was often my experience during the journey that the strongest terror could not get the better of a certain physical exhaustion that makes one dread fatigue more than death. However, I fondly hoped that I would arrive without hindrance, and my fear had already dissipated as I approached the goal I thought assured. Then, as we entered the inn at Salzburg, a man approached my traveling companion[73] and told him in German that a French courier had come to inquire about a coach arriving from Innsbruck with a woman and a girl, and that he had announced that he would pass by again for news of them. I did not miss one of the innkeeper's words and I went white with terror. My companion was alarmed for me too; he asked further questions, which all confirmed that the courier was French, that he came from Munich, that he had gone as far as the Austrian frontier to await me, and that, not finding me, he had come on ahead. Nothing seemed clearer then; it was everything I had dreaded before I left and during the journey. I could not escape any longer since the courier, said to be at the relay post already, would inevitably overtake me. I decided in a moment to leave my coach, my companion, and my daughter at the inn, go alone on foot through the streets of the city, and enter at random the first house where the master and mistress had a kind countenance. I hoped to obtain refuge with them for a few days, and meanwhile, my daughter and my companion would say that they were going to join me in Austria, and I would leave a week later disguised as a peasant woman. Whatever the risks of this course, I had no other left and as I prepared for the venture, trembling, I saw that much-feared courier enter my room: he was none other than the same Genevan friend and relative who had left Coppet with me.[74] He had passed himself off as a French courier, taking advantage of the terror inspired by that title, particularly in France's allies, to be given the swiftest horses. He had come by the road to Munich and lost no time in reaching the border of Bavaria and Austria, wanting to ensure that no one had preceded me or announced my coming. He came back to tell me I had nothing to fear and to climb into the coachman's box as we crossed the border that seemed the most formidable of my perils, but also the last. Thus did I pass from cruel fear to a very sweet feeling of security and gratitude.

We went to visit this city, once governed by an Archbishop and that, like most of the ecclesiastic principalities of Germany, has a very forsaken look. Along with this form of government ended its tranquil resourcefulness. The monastic houses were also conservators; one is struck by the number of establishments and buildings that celibate masters erected within their place of residence: all peaceable sovereigns have done their nations good. In the last century, Salzburg's ruler had built a portico at the entrance to the city that extended for several yards under a rock, like the grotto of Posilippo in Naples.[75] On the pediment of the entrance door is a bust of the Archbishop and below is the epigraph: *Te saxa loquentor* (the stones will speak of thee). There is grandeur in this epigraph.

At last I entered the Austria I had seen so happy just four years ago.[76] I was struck by the perceptible change produced by the depreciation of paper money and the fluctuations of every kind brought to its value by the uncertainties of financial speculation. Nothing so demoralizes a people as these continual fluctuations that make a speculator of each individual, and offer the entire working class a way of earning money by cunning and without work.[77] I did not find in the people an integrity that had struck me four years earlier: this vacillating paper money sets the imagination to work in the hope of rapid, easy gain, and those dangerous risks unsettle the measured and safe existence that is the foundation of honesty in the populace. During my stay in Austria, a man was hanged for making counterfeit bills at the time the old ones had been withdrawn from circulation; as he walked to his execution, he cried out that the thief was not he, but the State. And it is, in fact, impossible to make the populace understand that there is justice in hanging them for private speculation when the government practices the same speculation in its own affairs. But this government was the ally of the French government, and doubly an ally since its leader was the very patient father-in-law of a dreadful son-in-law. What resources could he have left? Marriage had won him freedom from two million in contribution at most; the rest had been exacted with the kind of justice so characteristic of Napoleon, that is, to treat his friends like his enemies, and here lay the reason for the shortage of money.

Another calamity had resulted from the last war, and above all from the last peace,[78] for peace made with that man is always more deadly than his wars, as it is far better to have his strength to deal with than his guile. Another calamity, I hold, came from the futility of the generous impulse that shed such luster on the Austrian forces in the Battles of Essling and Wagram.[79] This nation's feeling for its sovereign, once so deeply loved, has cooled. The same is true for all the sovereigns who have dealt with Emperor Napoleon: he has used them as collectors charged with levying taxes on his behalf; he has compelled them to bear heavily on their subjects to pay him the taxes he exacted, and when it has suited his purpose to remove these sovereigns, their peoples, disaffected by the harm done to them in obedience to the Emperor, have not gone to their defense. Napoleon is skilled at making the situation of countries ostensibly at peace so wretched that they find any change acceptable, and once they have been forced to give men and money to France, they hardly feel the disadvantage of being united with her. They are wrong though, for anything is better than to lose the name of nation, and since the calamities of Europe are caused by one man alone, we must carefully preserve what can rise again when he is no longer here.

Before reaching Vienna, since I was waiting for my younger son who was to join me with my people and my baggage, I stopped for a day at the abbey of Melk, located on a hilltop from which Emperor Napoleon had contemplated the twists and turns of the Danube and lauded the countryside as he was about to swoop down upon it with his armies.[80] He often likes to produce this sort of poetic piece on the beauties of the nature he is about to ravage, or on the effects of the war with which it pleases him to crush the human species. After all, according to his satanic code, he is right to enjoy himself in all sorts of ways at the expense of the human race that tolerates him. Man is stopped on the path of evil only by obstacles or remorse; no one has presented him with the one and he has readily freed himself from the other. All alone, I followed his trail on the terrace where one can look out on the countryside in the distance; I was struck by its fertility and almost distressed that heaven's gifts so quickly repaired the disasters wrought by men. It is moral wealth that does not return or that, at best, is lost for centuries. Religion, virtue, character, mind, literature, the arts: all is reduced to nothing in Europe. This age is special in that the very excess of civilization has produced the phenomenon of a satyric barbarian, charged with humiliating the human species by tearing from it all the advantages on which it arrogantly prided itself.

Fortunately I reached Vienna two hours before Count de Stackelberg, the Russian ambassador, sent a courier to Vilna where Emperor Alexander happened to be at the time. He wrote to request my passport;[81] it was June 6 and M. de Stackelberg, who treated me with the noble tact that is one of his most distinguished traits of character, assured me that I could expect the reply within three weeks. The question was where to spend those three weeks; my Austrian friends, who had welcomed me in the most amiable way, assured me that I could stay in Vienna without fear.

The court was not there at the time; it had gone to Dresden, to the grand reunion of all the German Princes who had come to pay their court to Emperor Napoleon. He had stopped in Dresden under the pretext of negotiating further from there to avoid war with Russia, that is, to obtain by politics the same result as by arms.[82] Indeed, however great he may be as a military leader, the Emperor still seems to find it less tiring to deceive than to conquer. Emperor Napoleon was unwilling, at first, to admit the King of Prussia to his banquet in Dresden;[83] he knew only too well how much that unhappy monarch's heart rebels against what he thinks he is compelled to do. M. de Metternich obtained this humiliating favor for him. M. de Hardenberg,[84] who accompanied him, pointed out to Emperor Napoleon that Prussia had paid one-third more than its promised contributions. Turning away, the Emperor replied: "You paid through the nose," for he secretly enjoys using vulgar expressions, the better to humiliate those to whom they are directed. He took pains with his behavior when he was with the Emperor and Empress of Austria because it was important to him for the Austrian government to play an active role in his war with Russia. "You see very well," he told M. de Metternich, "that it can't ever be in my interest to reduce Austria's power such as it now exists since, in the first place, it suits me to have my father-in-law a highly respected prince. Besides, I have far greater trust in the old dynasties than in the new. Didn't General Bernadotte decide to make his peace with England?"[85] And, in fact, the Prince of Sweden, as will be seen by what follows, had courageously declared for the interests of the country he governed.

When the Emperor left Dresden to review his armies, the Empress of France went to spend some time with her family in Prague. But first the Emperor himself prescribed the etiquette to be observed between father and daughter; and one must suppose that it was not easy to follow since he enjoys etiquette by distrust almost as much as etiquette by vanity, that is, as a means of isolating all individuals among themselves under the pretext of marking their ranks. The Empress travels in a gown of gold brocade and her ladies-in-waiting are obliged to do likewise. She almost always wears her tiara on her head, and since she has not received from heaven the possibility of uttering one meaningful sentence, she looks like the mannequin of a queen on which all the diamonds of the crown are placed.

The first ten days I spent in Vienna were completely unclouded. I was delighted to find myself once more in the midst of a society I enjoyed and whose way of thinking corresponded with my own,[86] for opinion was not at all favorable to the alliance with France, and the government had concluded it without the support of the nation's consent. Could a war whose ostensible object was to reestablish Poland in fact be waged by the power that had helped divide Poland and that still held one-third of Poland in its grasp more eagerly than ever?

Thirty thousand men were sent by the Austrian government to reestablish the Polish Confederation in Warsaw,[87] and almost as many spies followed every step of the Galician Poles who wanted deputies in the Confederation. An Austrian government was required to speak against the Poles even as it supported their cause and to say to its Galician subjects: "I forbid you to hold the opinion I support." What metaphysics! One would judge it quite muddled if fear were not the whole explanation. Among the nations Bonaparte trails in his wake, the only one that deserves interest are the Poles. I believe they know as well as we that they are only the pretext for war and that the Emperor does not care about their independence. Several times, he could not refrain from speaking scornfully of that nation to the Emperor of Russia for the sole reason that it wants to be free, but it suits his purposes to urge its cause against Russia, and the Poles take advantage of this expediency to restore themselves as a nation. I do not know whether they will succeed, for despotism finds it difficult to grant liberty, and what they win back for their individual cause they will lose for the cause of Europe. They will be Polish, but Poles as enslaved as the three nations—Prussian, Austrian, and Russian—in whose dependency they will no longer be. In any event, the Poles are the only Europeans who can serve under Bonaparte's banners without shame. The Confederated Princes believe their interests lie in sacrificing their honor; but Austria, by a truly remarkable scheme, is thereby destroying its honor and its interests at one and the same time. The Emperor wanted to induce Archduke Charles[88] to command those thirty thousand men whose leader, whoever he may be, is always more a courtier than a general, but the Archduke fortunately recoiled from this affront and, when I saw him in a grey suit, walking down the lanes of the Prater alone, all of my former respect for him returned.

The same M. Hudelist who had so shamefully advised surrendering the Tyroleans was in Vienna, charged in M. de Metternich's absence with surveillance of foreigners, and it will be seen how he discharged his duties. For the first few days he left me in peace. Since I had already spent a winter in Vienna, very kindly received by the Emperor and Empress and their whole court,[89] it was difficult to tell me that, this time, I was not welcome since I was in disfavor with the Emperor, particularly since the disfavor was partly caused by the praise in my book for German morality and literary genius.[90] But it was even more difficult to risk in any way displeasing a powerful nation to which, admittedly, they could well sacrifice me after all they had already done for her. Thus I believe that after my first few days in Vienna, more precise warnings reached M. de Hudelist on my position with respect to the Emperor, and he felt obliged to keep close watch over me. Here is his manner of keeping that watch: he set spies at my door to the street, who followed me on foot when my carriage moved slowly and took gigs so as not to lose sight of me when I drove to the countryside. To me, this method of police supervision seemed to combine French Machiavellianism and German clumsiness. The Austrians are convinced that they were beaten for want of as much intelligence as the French, and that French intelligence consisted of the methods of their police. Consequently, they set about practicing espionage methodically, organizing openly what at the very least must be hidden; and destined by nature to be decent people, they have made it a kind of duty for themselves to imitate a state that was Jacobin and despotic all at once.

I was bound to be troubled by this spying, however, since it took only the slightest common sense to see that I had no other goal than to flee. I was made anxious over the arrival of my Russian passport; it was claimed that I would be forced to wait for several months and that war would then prevent my going on. It was easy to judge that I could not remain in Vienna once the French ambassador returned. And what would become of me then? I entreated M. de Stackelberg to give me a way to pass by way of Odessa or Bucharest to reach Constantinople.[91] But since Odessa and Bucharest were

Russian, I needed a passport from Petersburg to get there as well. Thus only the direct route to Turkey through Hungary was left open, but this passage along the borders of Serbia was subject to a thousand dangers. One could still reach the port of Salonika by crossing the interior of Greece. Archduke Francis had built this road to go to Sardinia, but Archduke Francis was a very good horseman, which I was hardly capable of being; still less could I make up my mind to expose so young a girl as my daughter to such a journey. And so I was forced, however reluctantly, to resolve on parting with her and sending her to Denmark and Sweden in the company of reliable persons. As a precaution I arranged with an Armenian to take me to Constantinople. I proposed to go from there by way of Greece, Sicily, Cadiz, and Lisbon, and however hazardous, this journey opened a broad perspective to the imagination. At the Bureau of Foreign Affairs, directed by M. de Hudelist in M. de Metternich's absence, the Swedish envoy, under whose protection I was, requested a passport that would allow me to leave Austria by way of Hungary or Galicia, according to whether I went to Petersburg or Constantinople. Word was sent to me that I would have to decide, that it was not possible to give me a passport to leave by way of two different frontiers, and that even to go to Pressburg, which is the first town in Hungary,[92] six leagues from Vienna, authorization from the Committee of States was required. Certainly one could not help thinking that Europe, once so readily open to all travelers, has become under Emperor Napoleon's influence a great snare in which one cannot take a step without being arrested. So many constraints, so many obstacles to the slightest movement! And is it conceivable that the hapless governments oppressed by France are consoled by making the miserable remains of power left to them weigh heavily wherever possible?

Forced to choose, I decided on Galicia, which would lead me to Russia, the country I preferred. I persuaded myself that once I was away from Vienna all these annoyances, no doubt instigated by France, would come to a halt, and that if necessary I could leave Galicia to reach Hungary by way of Transylvania. The geography of "Napoleonine"[93] Europe is learned only too well through adversity; the detours required to avoid his power already amounted to almost two thousand leagues, and now, leaving Vienna itself, I would be forced to make use of Asiatic territory to escape. And so I left, still without my passport, in the hope of calming the anxieties developed at the lower level of Vienna's police over the presence of a person in disfavor with the Emperor. I begged one of my friends to travel day and night to overtake me as soon as the Russian reply arrived,[94] and I set out on my way. I was wrong to make that decision, for in Vienna I was defended by my friends and by public opinion; I could easily appeal to the Emperor or to his Prime Minister. But once I was confined in a provincial town, I had nothing left to deal with but the heavy-handed malice of M. de Hudelist, who wanted to earn credit with the French ambassador through his behavior toward me. Here is how he went about it.

I stopped for a few days in Brünn, the capital of Moravia, where they contrived to hold an English colonel in exile, M. Mills, a perfectly kind and obliging man, and to use the English expression, "harmless."[95] He was made miserably unhappy by his domestic circumstances. But the Austrian ministry is apparently convinced that taking up persecution will make it look strong. Shrewd people are not fooled, and as a witty man remarked, its method of governing as regards the police resembles the sentinels posted on the crumbling citadel of Brünn: they stand guard meticulously around ruins. I hardly arrived in Brünn when all manner of difficulties were raised over my passports, over those of my travel companions.[96] I asked permission to send my son to Vienna to provide all the necessary explanations in this respect; I was informed that my son was permitted no more than I to go back one league. Surely police administration à la Savary began rather well by preventing a young Swedish gentleman of nineteen from going to Vienna to do a service for his mother! Certainly the Emperor of Austria and even M. de Metternich were entirely unaware of all that absurd servility; but in Brünn, I encountered in a young Archduke whom I thought eminently chivalrous and in the government's employees with few exceptions a fear of being compromised that seemed to me entirely worthy of the present regime in France. And it must be admitted that even when the French are afraid, they are more excusable, for under Napoleon's rule it is at least a matter of exile, prison, or death.

The governor of Moravia, a quite respectable man it must be added, informed me that I was ordered to cross Galicia as fast as possible and that I was forbidden to spend more than twenty-four hours in Lanzut, where I planned to go. Lanzut was the estate of Princess-Marshal Lubomirska, sister to Prince Adam Czartoryski, Field Marshal of the Polish Confederation[97] which Austrian troops were going to support. Princess Lubomirska was herself widely esteemed for her personal character and, above all, for her generous benevolence in making use of her fortune. Furthermore, her attachment to the House of Austria was well known, and although Polish, she had never shared the spirit of opposition that has always been displayed in Poland against the Austrian government. Her nephew and niece, Prince Henri and Princess Thérèse, with whom it was my good fortune to have ties of friendship, were both endowed with the most brilliant and agreeable qualities; they could be deemed very attached to their Polish homeland, but it was rather difficult to make a crime of this opinion when Prince de Schwarzenberg was sent to lead thirty thousand men to restore Poland. But what have these unhappy Princes not been reduced to, they who are continually told that circumstances must be obeyed? This means proposing that they govern as the wind blows. Bonaparte's success is the envy of most German rulers; they are persuaded that they were beaten for being too decent, when it is for not being decent enough. Had they imitated the Spaniards, had they told themselves: "Whatever comes, we will not endure a foreign yoke," they would still be a nation and their princes would not loiter in salons—I do not say of Emperor Napoleon, but of all those on whom a ray of his favor has fallen.

The Archduke of Würzburg, formerly Grand Duke of Tuscany,[98] was having supper at the home of Princess Borghese one day; present as well were Mme Murat and the Princess de Piombino, now Grand Duchess of Tuscany,[99] who had in her power the beautiful country lost by this same Archduke of Würzburg. That he had taken his loss so peaceably was already an accomplishment. These ladies, who in truth have very good reasons to rejoice, wanted to dance after supper. Having learned that the Grand Duke [*sic*] of Würzburg was a musician, they gave him a violin, and there you had the *ci-devant* Duke of Tuscany in the uniform of an Austrian general, with the long face handed down from as far back as Rudolf de Hapsburg, leading the dance for the present Grand Duchess of Tuscany and her two sisters. The Emperor of Austria and his witty consort surely retain as much dignity as possible in their position, but the position is so false in itself that it cannot be restored. None of the actions of the Austrian government in favor of the French can be attributed to anything but fear, and this new muse inspires sorrowful songs.[100]

I tried to point out to the governor of Moravia that by thus pushing me so courteously toward the frontier I could not know what would become of me without my Russian passport, and that, unable either to go back or to go forward, I would find myself compelled to spend my life in Brody,[101] a city on the border of Russia and Austria where Jews have settled to lend money to foreigners crossing from one empire to the other. "What you say is true," replied the governor, "but those are my orders." For some time now, governments have skillfully argued that a civil servant was subject to the same discipline as an officer; in the latter case, reflection is forbidden or at least rarely acceptable. But to men responsible to the law, as are all civil administrators in England, it would be difficult to convey the idea that they are not permitted to judge the orders given them. And what is the consequence of this servile obedience? Were its object the supreme leader alone, it would still be conceivable in an absolute monarchy, but in the absence of this leader or even of his representative, a subaltern can misuse these police measures at will—a diabolical discovery of arbitrary governments and one that true greatness will never employ.

And so I left for Galicia[102] and this time, I confess, I was thoroughly dejected. The specter of tyranny pursued me everywhere; I saw those Germans, whom I had known to be so upright, depraved by the disastrous misalliance that seemed to have tainted the very blood of their subjects by mingling the blood of their ruler with the African race of a Corsican. I thought there was no longer any Europe except beyond the seas or the Pyrenees, and I lost hope of finding a refuge in harmony with my soul. The spectacle of Galicia was not calculated to revive hope on the fate of the human species. Austrians do not know how to inspire love in the peoples under their power. They bring a sense of justice with them, however, for this monarchy's administration within its own borders is generally equitable and its politics alone are immoral; but they understand justice itself with the help of a methodical pedantry that corresponds solely to their own character. When they came to possess Venice, the first thing they did was to ban Carnival, which had become an institution, if you will, so long had people been talking of Carnival in Venice.[103] The Austrian minister gave command over this joyous city to the most inflexible man in the monarchy, and those southern peoples almost preferred pillage by the French to regimentation by the Austrians. The Venetian Republic missed, and rightly so, its noble and prosperous government of the past.

Poles love their country like an unhappy friend. The countryside is dreary and monotonous, the people ignorant and lazy; they have always wanted liberty, they have never managed to institute it. But Poles believe they should and could govern Poland and the feeling is natural. However, education of the people is so neglected, and there is such dearth of industry that Jews have taken over all commerce and induce the peasants to sell the whole harvest of the following year for a supply of brandy. The distance between lords and peasants is so great, the luxury of the former is in such sharp contrast with the atrocious poverty of the latter, that the Austrians have probably brought them better laws than those that were in place. But a proud people, and this one is proud in its distress, does not want to be humiliated by another even in its own interests, and that is what the Austrian have never failed to do. They have divided Galicia into "circles,"[104] and each circle is under command of a German captain; occasionally a distinguished man undertakes this job, but most often it is some kind of brute taken from the lower ranks who gives orders despotically to Poland's greatest lords. The police, who at the present time have replaced the secret tribunal, authorize the most arbitrary measures. Just imagine what the police can be, that is to say, what is most cunning and arbitrary in government, when placed in the coarse hands of a circle's captain. At each relay post three types of persons would be seen running up to the travelers' coaches: Jewish merchants, Polish beggars, and German spies. The country seemed inhabited by these three classes of men alone. The beggars with their long beards and their ancient Sarmatian dress inspired deep pity; it is quite true that if they wanted to work they would not be in this state, but we do not know whether it is out of pride or laziness that they are scornful of caring for the enslaved land.

Along the major roads you meet processions of men and women bearing the banner of the cross and singing psalms, with a deeply sorrowful expression predominating on their faces.[105] I saw them, when given not money but better food than their accustomed fare, look to heaven in astonishment as if they no longer believed themselves made to enjoy its gifts. The Polish people customarily embrace the knees of nobles when they meet; you cannot take a step in a village without old people, women, and children greeting you this way. In the midst of this spectacle of wretchedness, you saw a few men in worn dress coats spying on affliction, for it was the only sight that met their eyes. Circle captains refused passports to Polish lords for fear they might see one another or go to Warsaw. They obliged these nobles to appear once a week to prove they were not away. Thus did the Austrians proclaim in every way that they knew the Poles detested them, and they divided their troops into two sections: one was charged with defending the Polish cause outside of the country, while the other was to prevent the Poles from serving this cause within. I do not think that a country has ever been so wretchedly governed, at least with respect to politics, as was Poland at that time, and it was apparently to hide this spectacle from view that they made it so difficult for foreigners to stay in this country or even to pass through.

Here, then, is how the Austrian police behaved with me to hasten my journey. Along this route you must have your passport stamped by each circle's captain, and at every third relay you came to one of the main towns where travelers went to have their passports stamped. In the offices of those towns, bills had been posted saying that I was to be kept under surveillance when I came through.[106] If it were not extraordinarily rude to so treat a woman, and a woman persecuted for her attempt to do justice to Germany, it would be impossible not to laugh at the utter stupidity that leads to posting police measures in capital letters when their effectiveness depends entirely on secrecy. It reminded me of M. de Sartine, who had proposed dressing spies in livery.[107] It is not that the man in charge of all this nonsense does not have, it is said, a kind of intelligence, but he is so eager to please the French government that he strives above all to earn its esteem as ostentatiously as possible with contemptible acts. The openly announced surveillance was carried out as subtly as it was conceived: a corporal or clerk or both together came to look at my carriage smoking their pipes and, when they had circled it, went on their way without even deigning to say whether it was in good condition; then, at least, they would have served some useful purpose.

I rode on slowly to wait for the Russian passport, my only means of safety in the situation. One morning I turned aside from my route to see a crumbling château that belonged to the Princess-Marshal.[108] To reach it, I went along roads that are unimaginable if one has not traveled in Poland. In the middle of a kind of wilderness that I was crossing alone with my son, a man on horseback greeted me in French; I wanted to answer, he was already far away. I cannot describe the effect of that friendly language at so bitter a moment. Ah! if the French stopped being Corsican, how they would be loved, and how they would be the very first to scorn their allies of the present time! I alighted in the courtyard of this château in ruins. The concierge, his wife, and his children came to meet me, embracing my knees. I had them told through a poor interpreter that I knew the Princess-Marshal; the name was enough to inspire their trust; they did not doubt what I said, although I had arrived with a very poor carriage and horses. They opened a room for me that looked like a prison, and as soon as I entered one of the women came in to burn perfumes. There was neither white bread nor meat, but a delicious wine from Hungary, and everywhere the wreckage of splendor stood side by side with the greatest poverty. This contrast is often found in Poland, even in homes where the most refined elegance reigns. There are no beds in the bedrooms—everything seems roughed out in this country where nothing is finished; but what one cannot praise too much is the kindness of the people and the generosity of the great; both are readily moved by all that is good and beautiful, and the agents sent there by Austria seem like wooden men in the middle of this volatile nation.

At last my Russian passport arrived, and I shall be grateful all my life, so intense was my pleasure.[109] At the same time, my friends in Vienna had managed to counter the malign influence of those who thought to please France by tormenting me and I fondly hoped that I was entirely sheltered from new difficulties; but I forgot that the memorandum ordering the circle captains to keep me under surveillance had not yet been revoked, and that it was directly from the minister that I had the promise to end those absurd torments.[110] I thought I could follow my original plan and stop at Lanzut, Princess Lubomirska's château, so famous in Poland for combining all the perfection that taste and splendor can offer. I was looking forward with great pleasure to seeing Prince Henri Lubomirski again, for I had spent the loveliest moments in Geneva thanks to his company and that of his charming wife. I planned to spend two days there and go quickly on my way since on all sides there was talk of war between France and Russia.[111] I do not quite see the danger in this plan for Austria's peace of mind: it was odd to fear my relations with Poles, given that the Poles now served Bonaparte. Without a doubt, and I repeat, they cannot be confused with other peoples; it is dreadful to hope for liberty only from a despot, and expect independence for your nation only from the enslavement of the rest of Europe. But still, in this Polish cause, the Austrian ministry that gave troops for its support was more suspect than I, who devoted my meager strength to proclaiming the justice of the European cause defended by Russia. But the Austrian ministry, but the governments allied with Bonaparte no longer know what it means to have an opinion, a conscience, an attachment. All they have left from their own inconsistent behavior and the skill with which Napoleon's diplomacy has ensnared them is a single clear idea, that of force, and they do everything to gratify him.

Early in July I reached the circle's chief town, three leagues from Lanzut; my carriage stopped in front of the relay post and my son went as usual to have my passport stamped. After a quarter of an hour I was surprised at not seeing him, and I sent one of my companions to find out the reason for the delay. They both returned followed by a man whose face I will remember to the end of my days: the gracious smile on his hard, stupid features gave his countenance a most unpleasant expression. My son, beside himself, advised me that the circle captain had announced that I could stay in Lanzut no longer than eight hours and that, to ensure my obedience, one of his inspectors would follow me to the château, would enter with me, and would leave only after I left. My son had explained to the captain that, exhausted as I was, I needed more than eight hours for rest, and that the sight of a police inspector in my state of suffering could cause a disastrous shock. The captain answered with a savage cruelty that one can meet only in German subalterns; further, one meets only in them the servile respect for power that follows immediately on arrogance toward the weak. Reactions in the souls of these men resemble drill exercises on the day of a parade: they make a half-turn right and a half-turn left according to the order given.

And so this inspector, charged with keeping watch over me, wearied himself with bowing and scraping but refused to change any detail of his instructions. He climbed into a gig whose horses ran immediately behind the rear wheels of my coach. The idea of arriving this way at the home of an old friend, a delightful place where I looked forward to spending a few days, brought me pain I could not master. Mixed with it, I think, was the annoyance of sensing that insolent spy behind me, a spy assuredly quite easy to fool had we so wished, but who practiced his trade with an unbearable mixture of pedantry and rigor.[112] I had an attack of nerves in mid-route, and they had to take me down from my carriage and lay me by the ditch at the side of the road. That wretched inspector imagined that it was now time to take pity on me and, without leaving his carriage himself, sent his servant to get me a glass of water. I cannot say how angry I was at my own weakness of nerves; the man's compassion was the ultimate insult, and I would have liked to spare myself that at least. He set off again at the same time as my carriage, and I entered the courtyard of the château of Lanzut along with him. Prince Henri, suspecting nothing of the kind, came to greet me with the most amiable gaiety. He was immediately alarmed by my pallor and I advised him at once of the singular guest I brought with me; from that moment on, his composure, his steadiness, and his friendship for me did not waver for an instant. But is an order of things conceivable wherein a police inspector takes his seat at the table of a great lord like Prince Henri, or rather at anyone's table without permission? I would have told him, I think, had he come into my home: "You have the right to take me to prison, but not to eat with me." After supper he came to my son and said in the mellifluous tone of voice that I particularly dislike when used to speak insulting words:

"I ought, according to my orders, to spend the night in the bedroom of Madame your mother so as to make certain that she does not confer with anyone, but out of respect for her, I will do nothing of the sort."

"You can add out of respect for yourself too," said my son, "for if you set foot in my mother's bedroom during the night, I will throw you out of the window."

"Oh! Monsieur le Baron!" answered the inspector, bowing lower than usual because the threat had a false air of power that did not fail to affect him. He went off to bed and the next day at lunch the Prince's secretary plied him so well with food and drink that I think I could have stayed a few hours longer, but I was ashamed at bringing such a scene into the Prince's home. I did not allow myself time to see the beautiful gardens that bring the southern climate to mind by presenting its products, or the house that has been the refuge of persecuted French émigrés[113] and where artists have sent the tributes of their talents in return for all the services rendered them by the lady of the château. The contrast of these sweet and brilliant impressions with the pain and indignation that I felt was intolerable; the thought of Lanzut, which I have so many reasons to love, makes me shudder when memory calls it to mind.

Thus I left that abode weeping bitter tears and not knowing what was in store for me in the fifty leagues I had still to traverse on Austrian territory. The inspector escorted me as far as the borders of his circle and, when he left me, asked whether I was satisfied with him; the man's stupidity disarmed my resentment. What is peculiar to all this persecution, which was not formerly in the nature of the Austrian government, is that, as executed by its agents, it is as coarse as it is clumsy. These *ci-devant* decent folk bring to the nasty things required of them the scrupulous rigor they once brought to the good things; and in this new way of governing, previously unknown to them, their limited minds lead them to do a hundred silly things either from awkwardness or from vulgarity. They take up Hercules's bludgeon to kill a fly, while in the course of this futile effort, the most important things might escape them.

Leaving the circle of Lanzut, I still met grenadiers stationed from relay to relay to make certain of my progress as far as Léopol, the capital of Galicia.[114] I would have been sorry for the time those good people were made to lose if I had not thought it better for them to be there than in the unfortunate army that Austria was handing over to Napoleon. When I reached Léopol, I found the old Austria once more in the governor[115] and in the commanding officer of the province, both of whom welcomed me with perfect courtesy and gave me what I most desired: an order to cross from Austria into Russia. Such was the end of my sojourn in this monarchy that I had once seen powerful, just, and upright. Her alliance with Bonaparte, for as long as it lasts,[116] reduces her to the lowest rank among the nations. History, no doubt, will not forget that she proved very bellicose in her long wars with France, and that her last attempt to resist Bonaparte was inspired by a national enthusiasm worthy of admiration; but this country's ruler, yielding to the counsel of his advisors more than to his own character, entirely destroyed this enthusiasm by thwarting it. The unfortunates who perished on the fields of Essling and Wagram so that there might still be an Austrian monarchy and a German people, hardly expected their companions-in-arms to do battle three years later so that Bonaparte's Empire might stretch to the frontiers of Asia, and so that in all Europe there would not be even a wilderness where those proscribed by the Emperor, from kings to subjects, might find refuge: such is the goal and the only goal of France's war against Russia.

CROSSING RUSSIA

It was hardly customary to think of Russia as the freest state in Europe, but the yoke made to weigh on all the states of the Continent by the Emperor of France is such that you have the sense of being in a republic the moment you reach a country where Napoleon's tyranny cannot make itself felt. It was on July 14 that I entered Russia; I was uncommonly struck by that anniversary of the day that began the Revolution. Thus closed for me the circle of France's history that had begun on July 14, 1789;[117] and when the barrier separating Austria from Russia opened to let me pass, I swore never to set foot again in a country that was in any way subject to Emperor Napoleon.[118] Will this vow permit me to see lovely France ever again?

The first man to welcome me in Russia was a Frenchman, a clerk in my father's office in days gone by; he spoke of him with tears in his eyes, and that name thus pronounced seemed a happy augury to me. In this Russian Empire so wrongly called barbaric, I have experienced only noble and pleasant impressions; may my gratitude draw further blessings upon this people and upon their sovereign! I was leaving countries that claimed to be at peace, or that at least provided only auxiliaries for Napoleon's army, and you could not take a step without showing passports, without having to deal with the police.

When I entered Russia, the French Army had already penetrated deeply into Russian territory, and yet no persecution, no constraints stopped the foreign traveler for a moment. Neither I nor my companions knew one word of Russian; we spoke only French, the language of the enemies devastating the Empire. Through a series of unlucky accidents, I did not have even one servant who spoke Russian, and but for a German physician (Doctor Renner),[119] who with the greatest generosity gladly served as our interpreter as far as Moscow, we would have truly deserved the name of deaf-mutes, which the Russians use for foreigners in their language. At all events, our journey in these circumstances would still have been safe and easy, so great is the hospitality of the nobles and of the people in Russia! As soon as we set out, we learned that the direct route to Petersburg was already occupied by the armies and that we would need to reach it by way of Moscow. This meant a detour of two hundred leagues, but we were already doing fifteen hundred, and I congratulate myself now on having seen Moscow as well.

The first province we needed to cross, Volhynia,[120] is part of Russian Poland: it is fertile country, flooded with Jews like Galicia, but much less wretched. I stopped at the château of a Polish noble to whom I was recommended; he advised me to hasten forward because the French were marching toward Volhynia and could well arrive within a week. Poles in general prefer Russians to Austrians. Russians and Poles are Slavs by race; they have been enemies but they respect one another, while the Germans, more advanced than the Slavs in European civilization, do not know how to do them justice in other respects. It was easy to see, however, that the Poles in Volhynia did not dread the entry of the French, but although their opinion was known, they were not subjected to the petty persecutions that only excite hatred rather than contain it. Yet the spectacle of one nation subjected by another was always a painful sight; it takes several hundred years for unity to be established so that the names of victor and vanquished are forgotten.

At Jitomir, the chief town of Volhynia, I was told that the Russian Minister of Police[121] had been sent to Vilna to learn the reason for Emperor Napoleon's unprovoked assault and to protest, according to procedure, his entry into Russian territory. It is in fact difficult to believe the innumerable sacrifices Emperor Alexander had made to preserve the peace. He should rather have been reproached for being overly scrupulous in implementing the disastrous Treaty of Tilsit; it was Alexander who could have made war on Napoleon for being the first to break it. For while Russia was closing her ports to the English, Emperor Napoleon was awarding licenses to bring goods from the colonies into France; and it may be said in truth that the principal aim of France and Europe against Russia was to ensure exclusive rights to English merchandise for the House of Bonaparte and Co.—a fine motive for stirring up all the peoples of the Continent![122] Emperor Napoleon, in his conversation with M. de Balachoff, indulged in inconceivable indiscretions that would be taken for lack of reserve if one did not know that it suits him to increase the terror he inspires by showing himself to be above every kind of calculation: "Do you think," he told M. Balachoff, "I care about those Polish Jacobins?" And there in fact exists a letter from M. de Champagny to Chancellor de Romanzoff, in which Napoleon proposed several years ago to erase the words Poland and Polish from all European records.[123] What a calamity for this nation that in accepting the title of

King of Poland, Emperor Alexander did not join this nation's cause to the cause of all generous souls! The Emperor asked M. de Caulaincourt[124] in front of M. de Balachoff, Minister of Police, if he had ever been to Moscow and what the city was like. He answered that to him it had seemed more a big village than a capital.

"And how many churches are there?" Emperor Napoleon continued.

"About sixteen hundred,"[125] answered M. de Caulaincourt.

"That's inconceivable," Napoleon went on, "in an age when people aren't religious any more."

"Pardon, Sire," said M. de Balachoff, "Russians and Spaniards still are."

An admirable reply, and a sign that the Muscovites will be the Castillians of the North.

Nevertheless, the French Army was advancing rapidly, and one is so used to seeing the French triumph over everything outside of France—although at home they do not manage to resist any kind of yoke—that I had good reason to fear meeting them already along the road to Moscow. A strange fate to flee from the French among whom I was born and who had carried my father in triumph, and to flee them to the borders of Asia! But after all, what fate, great or small, is not profoundly shaken by the man chosen to humiliate man? I thought I was obliged to go to Odessa, a city now prosperous through the enlightened administration of the Duke de Richelieu,[126] and from there I would have gone to Constantinople and Greece. I consoled myself for that grand journey with a poem on Richard the Lionhearted, which I plan to write if God gives me the strength. The poem is meant to portray the customs and nature of the Orient, and to consecrate a great epoch of English history when enthusiasm for the Crusades gave way to enthusiasm for liberty. But since one can portray only what one has seen, just as one can express only what one has felt, I must go to Constantinople, Syria, and Sicily to follow in Richard's steps.[127] My travel companions, better judges of my strength than I, advised against such a plan, assuring me that if I hurried I could travel by post faster than an army. It shall be seen that in fact I did not have much time to spare.

Resolved to continue my journey in Russia, I entered Ukraine, whose capital is Kiew, as it was for Russia in an earlier day, and this Empire began by establishing its center in the South. At the time, the Russians had continual dealings with the Greeks settled in Constantinople and with the peoples of the Orient in general, taking on their customs in many respects. Ukraine is a very fertile country, but in no way pleasant; you see great fields of wheat that seem as if cultivated by invisible hands, so sparse are habitations and inhabitants. When you approach Kiew, or most of what are called cities in Russia, you must not expect to see anything resembling the cities of the Occident; the roads are kept no better and the country houses do not herald a more populous region ahead. As I arrived in Kiew, the first object to catch my sight was a cemetery: thus did I learn that I was close to a place where living people were gathered. Most of Kiew's houses resemble tents, and from a distance the city gives the impression of a camp; it is impossible to keep from thinking that the homes of the nomadic Tartars were their model for building wooden houses that do not give an impression of great stability either. It takes only a few days to build them; frequent fires consume them, and people send to the forest to order a house as to the market for winter supplies. In the midst of these huts, however, palaces rise up and, above all, churches whose green and gilded domes are singularly striking to the eye. In the evening, when the sun reflects its rays on these dazzling vaults, it is as if you are seeing the illuminations for a fête rather than a solid building.

Russians never pass by a church without making the sign of the cross, and their long beards add a great deal to the religious expression of their countenance. For the most part, they wear a wide blue robe, bound tight at the waist with a red belt. There is something Asiatic about women's dress as well, and it shows the taste for bright colors that comes to us from countries where the sun is so beautiful that one enjoys bringing out its luster on the striking objects it illuminates. In a very short time I developed such a taste for these Oriental clothes that I did not like to see Russians dressed like the other Europeans—then it seemed to me that they were about to enter into the grand uniformity of Napoleon's despotism which makes to all nations a gift of conscription first, then war taxes, then the Napoleonic Code to rule entirely different nations in the same way.

The Dnieper, called the Borysthenes by the Ancients, runs through Kiew, and the ancient tradition of the country assures us that it was a boatman who, when he crossed it, found its waters so pure that he decided to found a city on its banks. Indeed, the greatest natural beauties of Russia are its rivers. You hardly ever come upon rivulets, so heavily does sand obstruct the flow. There is almost no variety in trees. The dreary birch grows endlessly in this largely uninventive nature. You might even wish for stones, so wearying is it to encounter neither hills nor valleys and always to move forward without ever seeing new objects. The rivers rescue the imagination from this fatigue. Therefore priests bless the rivers. The Emperor, the Empress, and the whole court attend the ceremony of blessing the Neva at the height of the cold season. It is said that in the eleventh century Wladimir declared that all the waters of the Borysthenes were holy and that to be a Christian one had only to plunge into them. Since the Greek baptism was done by immersion, thousands of men went into this river to abjure their idolatry. This same Wladimir sent representatives to Constantinople to learn which of all the cults practiced in that capital suited him best; he decided on the Greek rite because of the pomp of its ceremonies. He preferred it, perhaps, for still more important reasons; by excluding the influence of the Pope, the Greek rite effectively gave both spiritual and temporal powers to the sovereign of Russia.

The Greek religion is inevitably less intolerant than the Catholic religion for, accused of schism, it can hardly complain of heretics. Moreover all religions are accepted in Russia and, from the banks of the Don to those of the Neva, the brotherhood of the native land joins all men together even when their theological opinions separate them.

The ceremonies of the Greek religion are at least as beautiful as those of the Catholics, and their chants are spellbinding.[128] Everything about this cult induces reverie. But it seems to me that it captivates imagination more than it directs behavior. Priests are married, and gentlemen almost never take up this life. As a result, the clergy does not have a great deal of political influence; it affects the people but is very submissive to the Emperor. There is something poetic and sensual in the Greek religion that calls to mind the Orient of its origins. When the priest emerges from the sanctuary where he remains confined while he receives Holy Communion, you would think that the gates of day are opening before your eyes. The cloud of incense encompassing him, the silver, the gold, and the precious stones sparkling on his vestments and in the church seem to come from the country where the sun was worshiped. The contemplative feelings inspired by Gothic architecture in Germany, in France, and in England can in no way be compared to the effect of these churches; they suggest the minarets of the Turks and Arabs rather than our temples. Nor can one expect to find the luxury of the fine arts as in Italy. The most remarkable ornaments are the virgins and saints crowned with diamonds and rubies. Magnificence characterizes everything one sees in Russia; neither man's genius nor nature's gifts create its beauty.

The ceremonies for marriage, baptism, and funerals are noble and moving; parts of them go back to ancient customs of pagan Greece, but only those with no connection to dogma and which can enhance our reaction to the three great scenes of life: birth, marriage, and death. Among Russian peasants it is still customary to speak to the dead person before parting forever with his remains. "Why in the world did you leave us?" they say. "So were you unhappy on this earth? Wasn't your wife beautiful and good? So why did you leave her?" The dead man makes no reply, but the value of existence is thus proclaimed in the presence of those who are still alive.

In Kiew, you are shown catacombs somewhat reminiscent of those in Rome, and people come there on foot as pilgrims from Kazan and other cities bordering on Asia; but these pilgrimages are less costly in Russia than anywhere else although the distances are far greater. It is in the nature of these people to fear neither fatigue nor physical suffering. There is a mixture of patience and activity in this nation, of gaiety and melancholy. The most striking contrasts in all things are to be seen brought together here, and this may portend great things for, ordinarily, superior beings alone possess opposing qualities; the masses, for the most part, are uniform in color.

In Kiew, I put Russian hospitality to the test in the military commandant of the province, General Miloradovitch. He lavished the most agreeable attentions on me. He was an aide-de-camp to Souvoroff, and equally intrepid.[129] He inspired greater confidence in the military success of Russians than I had yet entertained. Until then, I had met only a few officers of the German school who placed no value on the Russian character. In General Miloradovitch I saw a true Russian: impulsive, brave, confident, and in no way led by the spirit of imitation that sometimes robs Russians even of their national character. He recounted stories about Souvoroff which proved that this man studied a great deal, although he retained the fundamental instinct that depends on direct knowledge of men and things. He hid his learning the better to strike the imagination of his troops by assuming an air of inspiration in all situations.

Russians, as I think will be clear later in my account of the journey, are far more closely connected to the peoples of the South, or rather to the Asiatic character, than to those of the North. What is European in them has to do with court manners, the same in every country, but by nature they are Oriental. I shall attempt to expand further on this observation eventually. General Miloradovitch told me that a regiment of Kalmucks had spent the winter in Kiew, and that one day the Prince of the Kalmucks had come to confide to him that he was suffering greatly from spending the winter shut up in a city and that he would like permission to camp in the nearby forest. He could hardly be refused so simple a pleasure, and so he went with his troops into the snow to settle in wagons that also served as cabins.

Russian soldiers endure equally well the strain and suffering of the climate and of war, and the people of all classes have a scorn for obstacles and physical pain that can carry them to the greatest things. The Kalmuck

Prince, who found wooden houses too elaborate a dwelling in mid-winter, gave diamonds to women who pleased him at a ball, and since he could not make himself understood, he substituted gifts for compliments, as happens in India and in the silence of those lands of the Orient where the spoken word is less powerful than in our countries. General Miloradovitch invited me to a ball in the home of a Moldavian Princess for the very night of my departure. I was truly sorry that I could not go. All those names of foreign countries, of nations that are almost not European, stir the imagination extraordinarily. In Russia you sense that you are at the gateway to another land, close to the country where Christianity emerged and that still locks in its bosom unbelievable treasures of perseverance and reflection.

Approximately a thousand versts[130] still separated Kiew from Moscow. My Russian coachmen drove like lightning, singing as they went, and I was assured that the words of those songs were blandishments to encourage their horses: "Come on, my friends" they said; "we know each other, go to it, get along." I have seen nothing barbaric in this people; on the contrary, there is something elegant and gentle in their manners not to be found anywhere else. Never does a Russian coachman pass by a woman of whatever age or condition without bowing, and the woman responds with a nod that is always noble and gracious. An old man, who could not make himself understood to me, pointed to the ground and then to the sky to show that for him the one would soon be the way to the other.[131] I am well aware that there is reason to take issue with me, given the great atrocities committed in the course of Russian history; but I would begin by accusing the boyars,[132] depraved by the despotism they practiced or that they suffered, rather than the nation itself. Besides, political dissension, everywhere and in all times, distorts the national character, and nothing is more deplorable in Russian history than the series of masters elevated and overthrown by crime; but such is the ineluctable condition of absolute power on this earth. Civil servants from a lower class, all those who expect to make their fortune by their pliability or by their intrigues, bear no resemblance to country people. I understand all the ill that is and must be said of them; but one must seek to understand a bellicose nation through its soldiers and through the class from which soldiers are drawn: the peasantry.

Although they drove very rapidly, it seemed to me that I was not going forward, so monotonous was the countryside. Sand-covered plains, a few birch forests, villages far apart and made up of wooden houses all cut from the same pattern: these were the only sights that endlessly greeted my eyes. It was like the kind of hideous dream that sometimes seizes you in the night when you think you are walking endlessly and never moving ahead. It seemed to me that this country was the image of infinite space and that it would take all eternity to cross. At every moment you saw couriers go by at an incredible speed; they were seated on wooden benches placed on small carts drawn by two horses, and nothing stopped them for a moment.[133] The roads were bad, and at times the jolts sent them jumping several feet in the air. With the energy displayed by the French on the day of battle, they would fall back down with astonishing skill and immediately say: "get along there" in Russian. The Slavic language is particularly resonant; I would almost say there is a metallic ring to certain sounds. When Russians pronounce certain letters of their language, entirely different from the ones used by the dialects of the Occident, it sounds as if they are striking on brass.

Halfway between Kiew and Moscow, horses began to grow scarcer since we were now close to the armies. We were kept waiting several hours at the relay posts. We saw reserve units pass by, hurrying to the aid of the Russian Army. One by one, without order and without uniforms, Cossacks made their way to the army, great lances in hand and wearing a kind of grayish cloak, its full hood covering their heads. I had formed a completely different idea of those peoples; in fact, they lived beyond the Dnieper, independent in the way of savages; but in war they let themselves be governed despotically. We are accustomed to the sight of beautiful uniforms, brilliant in color, on an army's most redoubtable troops. The dull colors worn by the Cossacks inspire another kind of fear: it is as if ghosts are swooping down on you.

I began to fear that my journey would come to a halt at the very moment haste became more urgent. One of my companions, struck by the rapid success of the French, was quite concerned lest there be a dearth of horses for me as the armies approached. And when I spent five or six hours in front of a relay post, as there was rarely a room where one might wait, I trembled at the thought of the army that could overtake me at the far edge of Europe[134] and render my position both tragic and ridiculous. For thus it is with non-success in this kind of enterprise; since the compelling circumstances were not generally known, I would have been asked why I had left my home—even though it had been made a prison for me—and decent enough people would not have failed to look solemn and say that it was quite unfortunate but that I would have done better not to leave. If tyranny had only the direct support of its partisans, it would never last; the astonishing thing, and one that shows human wretchedness above all else, is that most mediocre men serve the event. They do not have the strength to think beyond an accomplished fact, and when an oppressor has triumphed, when a victim is ruined, they hasten to justify, not precisely the tyrant, but the destiny that has made him its instrument. Weakness of intelligence and character is no doubt at the root of this servility, but there is also a certain need in man to declare that fate, whatever it may be, is in the right, as if this were a way of making peace with it.

At last I reached the part of my route leading away from the theater of war and I entered the administrative district of Orel and Toula, which figure so much in the bulletins of the two armies. I was welcomed into these isolated dwelling places—for such is the look of provincial towns in Russia—with perfect hospitality. Several gentlemen of the surrounding area came to my inn to compliment me on my writings, and I confess that I was flattered to find I had a literary reputation so far from my native land. The governor's wife received me in the Asiatic manner with sorbet and roses. Her chamber was elegantly decorated with musical instruments and paintings. In Europe, the contrast of wealth and poverty is visible everywhere. But in Russia, neither is noticeable, if you will. The people are not poor; nobles manage to live the same life as the people when necessary; it is the contrast between the most rigorous hardships and the most refined pleasure that characterizes this country. When they travel, the same lords whose homes assemble the most splendid luxury from the different parts of the world, eat far less well than our French peasants, and are able to endure very unpleasant physical conditions not only in war but in a number of life's circumstances. The harshness of the climate, the swamps, the deserts, the forests that form a large part of the country make human life a struggle with nature. Fruits and flowers themselves come only from hothouses; vegetables are generally not grown; there are no vineyards anywhere. In Russia, the way of life customary to French peasants can be had only through very large expenditures. It is only through luxury that one has the necessities there; consequently, when luxury is impossible, one forgoes even the necessities. What the English call comfortable and what we express as well-being is hardly to be found in Russia. For his bed-curtains, a French general requested a fabric so magnificently embroidered that it was impossible to procure in the quantity he wanted: "Well!" he said, "since you can't find me that fabric, put a bundle of straw over there, in the corner of the room, I'll sleep very well on that."[135] The story can be applied to the great lords of Russia. You will never find anything perfect enough to satisfy their imagination in every type of thing; but when the poetry of wealth fails them, they drink hydromel, lie down on a board, and ride in an open wagon day and night with no regrets for the luxury one would think their custom. They love the magnificence of a fortune rather than the pleasures it affords, similar also in this to the Orientals who practice hospitality to strangers, lavish gifts on them, and often neglect their own well-being. This is one explanation for the splendid courage of the Russians as they withstood the devastation of the burning of Moscow. It might be said that for them, wealth is an honor guard they have sent to their country's defense with no regrets, and more accustomed to outward display than attention to themselves, they are in no way softened by luxury, and sacrificing money satisfies their pride as much and more than the magnificence with which they spend it. Something gigantic characterizes this people in every area; ordinary dimensions apply to nothing about them. I do not mean to say that neither true grandeur nor equilibrium are ever encountered here, but the daring, the imagination of Russians know no bounds; everything is colossal rather than in proportion, audacious rather than considered, and if the goal is never reached, it is because it is exceeded.

I came ever closer to Moscow and nothing presaged a capital. The wooden villages were at an equal distance from one another; one saw no greater movement along the vast plains called highroads; country houses were no less infrequent. There is so much space in this country that everything vanishes into it, even the châteaux, even the people. It is as if one were crossing a country whose population had just gone away, so few are the houses and so few the men to be seen, so few the sounds to be heard. The absence of birds adds to the silence; cattle too are seldom seen, or are at least far removed from the travelers' path. The vast expanses obliterate all but the expanse itself, which haunts the imagination like certain metaphysical ideas the mind cannot shake off once they take hold.

Just before I reached Moscow, on the evening of a very hot day, I stopped in a rather pleasant meadow. As peasant women in the picturesque dress of the region returned from their work, they sang those Ukrainian melodies whose words praise love and liberty with a sort of melancholy tinged with regret. I asked them if they would kindly dance and they agreed. I know nothing more graceful than those country dances that all have the originality that nature accords the arts; a certain modest sensuality is noticeable; the bayadères of India must have something akin to this mixture of indolence and vivacity, the charm of Russian dance. This indolence and vivacity betoken revery and passion, two aspects of character that civilization has so far neither shaped nor tamed. I was struck by the gentle gaiety of those peasants just as I had been, in subtly different ways, by the common people of Russia with whom I'd had dealings. I think they are dreadful when their passions are aroused, and as they have no education, they do not know how to control their violence. In consequence of that very ignorance, they have few moral principles and theft is very common—but so is hospitality; they give to you as they take from you, according to whether their imagination is excited by guile or generosity. Both excite their admiration.

To a degree, this way of living corresponds to that of savages, but at present it seems to me that European nations are vigorous only when they are what is known as barbaric—that is unenlightened—or when they are free. But nations which have learned no more of civilization than indifference to this or that yoke—provided that their own chimney corner be undisturbed, nations which have learned no more of civilization than the art of explaining power and rationalizing servitude are made to be conquered. I often picture what those tranquil places I saw must be like now: those likeable girls, those long-bearded peasants[136] who acquiesced so calmly in the fate meted out to them by Providence: they have perished or they are in flight, for not one among them has gone into the conqueror's service.

One thing worthy of remark is the degree of public spirit found in Russia. The reputation for invincibility given this nation by manifold success, the pride natural to the nobility, the devotion to duty in the character of the people, the profoundly powerful religion, the hatred of foreigners that Peter I tried to eradicate in order to enlighten and civilize his people, but that has nonetheless remained in the blood of Russians: all of these elements combine to make of this nation a highly energetic people the moment a circumstance awakens public spirit. A few unpleasant anecdotes on earlier reigns, a few Russians who have accumulated debts on the paving stones of Paris, a few of Diderot's jokes have put in French minds the notion that Russia consists of nothing more than a corrupt court, officer-chamberlains, and a population of slaves. This is a grave error. Ordinarily, this nation can in truth be known only on prolonged examination, but her situation when I was there brought out everything in her, and one never sees a country in a more advantageous light than in a time of trouble and courage. It cannot be repeated too often: this nation is composed of the most striking contrasts. Perhaps the reason lies in the mixture of European civilization and Asiatic character.

Russians welcome you so kindly that, from the first, you would think yourself bound to them in friendship, and perhaps ten years later this would not be the case. Russian silence is altogether extraordinary; it is a silence that bears solely on what is of vital interest. Generally, they talk as much as you could want, but their conversation acquaints you with nothing but their courtesy; it betrays neither their sentiments nor their opinions. They have often been compared to Frenchmen, which seems to me the falsest possible comparison. Because their vocal organs are so flexible, they find every sort of imitation easy. Their manners are French, English, German, as circumstances demand, but they never cease being Russian—that is, both impetuous and reserved, more capable of passion than friendship, more proud than refined, more religious than virtuous, more brave than knightly, and so violent in their desires that nothing can stand in the way of their satisfaction. They are far more hospitable than the French, but their society, unlike ours, does not consist of a circle of intelligent men and women who enjoy conversing with one another. They meet as they would attend a party, to be with a great many people, to taste unusual fruit and other products of Asia and Europe, to hear music, to gamble—in sum, to procure vivid emotions through exterior objects rather than through the mind and the soul: both of these are reserved for deeds, but are not for use in society. Further, as they have very little education in general, they take little pleasure in serious conversation and do not pride themselves on shining through the wit that can be displayed in such interchange. Wit, eloquence, literature are not yet found in Russia; luxury, power, and courage are the principal objects of pride and ambition. All other ways of distinguishing oneself still seem effeminate and futile to this nation that is closer to the customs of Asia than of Europe.

But, it will be said, the people are enslaved; what, then, can be assumed about character? I surely need not say that all enlightened persons want the Russian people to emerge from this state, and the one who wants it most perhaps, as will be seen by what follows, is Emperor Alexander. But in its effects, this Russian slavery does not resemble slavery as we conceive of it in the Occident. It is not, as under feudal rule, the victors who have imposed harsh laws on the vanquished; in their relations, however, the nobility and the people resemble what was called the family of slaves among the Ancients, rather than the condition of serfs among the moderns.[137] That the Third Estate does not exist in Russia is a great disadvantage for the progress of letters and the arts, for ordinarily it is in this class that enlightenment develops. But the absence of intermediaries between the nobility and the people leads them to like one another more. The distance from the people to the nobility seems greater because there are no gradations between the two extremes, and in fact they are in closer contact for not being separated by intermediaries. It is a social organization entirely inimical to enlightenment in the upper classes but not to the happiness of the lowest. Moreover, where there is no representative government, that is, in enlightened countries where the monarch nevertheless still decrees the law he is to execute, men are often more degraded by the sacrifice of their very reason and their character than in the vast Empire where a few simple ideas of religion and country influence a great mass guided by a few leaders. There is in Asia a certain dignified repose, a certain mute grandeur, more pleasing to me than the mongrel nations of the European Occident, and I call by this name all those that do not have a free government. Given the great expanse of the Russian Empire, the despotism of the nobles does not weigh on the people in details. Most important, in sum, the religious and military spirit so dominate the nation that many failings may be forgiven in the light of these two grand sources of fine human deeds. A very intelligent man[138] said that Russia resembled the plays of Shakespeare, where whatever is not a fault is sublime and whatever is not sublime is a fault. Nothing could be more accurate than this observation, but in Russia's critical situation when I crossed through, one could note only the forceful resistance and the uncomplaining sacrifice displayed by this nation; and in the light of such virtues, one hardly dared to take notice of what one would have condemned in other times.

Gilded domes herald Moscow from afar.[139] Yet since the city is built on a plain, and the surrounding countryside, like all of Russia, is nothing but a plain, the great city can be entered without one's being struck by it in advance, and it was only from a tower that one admired it in all its splendor. Someone rightly said that Moscow was rather a province than a city. In fact you see huts, houses, palaces, a bazaar as in the Orient,[140] churches, public institutions, lakes, woods, parks. The diversity of customs and nations of all Russia was displayed in this vast place of residence. In the Tartar district I would be asked: "Do you want to buy cashmere shawls?" "Have you seen the Chinese city?" Asia and Europe found themselves joined in this city. Its people enjoy greater liberty than in Petersburg, where the court necessarily wields great influence. The great lords settled in Moscow were not in search of positions; but they proved their patriotism with immense gifts to the state, either as public institutions in time of peace, or as assistance in time of war. The immense fortunes of the great Russian lords are used for collections of every kind, for enterprises, for festivities modeled on the *Thousand and One Nights,* and those fortunes are also very often lost through the unbridled passions of those who possess them.

This time, when I came to Moscow, the only matter at hand was sacrifices being made for the war. A young Count de Mamonoff was raising a regiment for the state and wanted to serve in it only as a second lieutenant. A Countess Orloff, charming and wealthy in the Asiatic manner, was giving three-fourths of her income.[141] When I passed by those palaces surrounded by gardens as spacious in the city as elsewhere in the middle of the countryside, I was told that the owner of this superb dwelling had just given a hundred thousand peasants, and another, two hundred.[142] I found it difficult to get used to the expression *to give men,* but they offered themselves fervently, and their lords were but their interpreters in this war.

As soon as a Russian becomes a soldier his beard is cut off, and from then on he is free. People wanted all those who had marched off as soldiers to be considered free, but then the whole nation would have been free since it rose up almost as one man. Let us hope that this desired emancipation can be achieved without upheaval. But meanwhile, one would like to see those beards retained, so great are the strength and dignity they give to the physiognomy. Bearded Russians never go by a church without making the sign of the cross, and their trust in the visible images of religion is very moving. They also bring into their churches the taste for luxury they get from Asia; only ornaments of gold, silver, and rubies are seen there. It is said that a man in Russia had proposed making an alphabet with precious stones and writing the Bible with them. He understood the best way of interesting the Oriental imagination of Russians in reading. As yet, however, that imagination has not been displayed through the arts or poetry. They reach a certain point in everything very quickly and go no further. They take the first step out of impulse, but the second step pertains to reflection, and these Russians, totally unlike the peoples of the North, still have very little capacity for meditation.

The most beautiful palaces in Moscow are made of wood so that they can be built more quickly and so that the nation's natural inconstancy in everything outside of religion or country may be satisfied by the ease of changing dwelling places at will. Several of these beautiful palaces were built for a fête; they were meant for the glitter of a day, and the treasures decorating them have ensured their lasting until this era of universal destruction. A great many houses are colored in green, yellow, and rose, and sculpted in detail like ornaments on a dessert. From afar, these Arabesque-like ornaments seem like edging at the foot of great churches.

The Kremlin, the citadel where Russia's emperors defended themselves against the Tartars, is surrounded by a high wall with a notched cornice that calls to mind a Turkish minaret rather than a fortress like most of those in the Occident. Nonetheless, though the outward nature of the city's buildings may be Oriental, the sense of Christianity is in the multitude of greatly revered churches that attracted the eye at every step. Seeing Moscow, one thought of Rome, certainly not because the monuments were of the same style, but because the mixture of isolated countryside and magnificent palaces, the grandeur of the city and the infinite number of temples give the Asian Rome some resemblance to the European Rome.[143] It was reserved for one man to profane them both.

In the first days of August I was shown the interior of the Kremlin. I reached it by way of the staircase Emperor Alexander had climbed but a few days earlier, surrounded by an immense gathering of people who gave him their blessing and promised to defend his Empire at all costs.[144] This people has kept its word. The rooms holding the arms of Russia's ancient warriors were opened for me first of all.[145] Arsenals of this type are worthier of interest in the other countries of Europe. Russians did not take part in the times of chivalry; they did not wear swords before Peter the Great; they did not join in the Crusades. Constantly at war with Tartars, Poles, and Turks, the military spirit was shaped in Russians amid the atrocities of every kind attendant on the barbarity of the Asiatic nations and of the tyrants who governed Russia. Thus it is not the generous gallantry of the Bayards and the Buckinghams, but the boldness of fanatical courage that has been displayed in this country for the past several hundred years. In the Kremlin's arsenal, the quivers still seen among the arms seem to differ from cold steel[146] as do Tartar wars from those of knights. In the social relations so new to them, Russians are not renowned for the spirit of chivalry as Occidental peoples conceive it, but they have always proved implacable against their enemies. So many massacres took place in Russia's interior up to and beyond the reign of Peter the Great that the nation's morality, and particularly that of the great lords, must have been seriously affected. Those despotic governments, curbed only by assassination of the despot, unsettled the principles of honor and duty in the minds of men, but love of country and religion has been maintained in its full vigor through the wreckage of that bloody history, and the nation that keeps such virtues alive can astound the world still.

I was escorted from the old arsenal into the chambers once occupied by the czars, where the clothing worn on their coronation day is preserved. Although bereft of any kind of beauty, these rooms correspond very well to the hard life the czars once led and still lead today. The greatest splendor reigns in Alexander's palace, but he himself sleeps on bare boards and travels like a Cossack officer. What probably keeps the military spirit alive in Russia is that wealth is used for ostentation and not well-being. This way of life has been much faulted and, in fact, is not the most agreeable, but you will see on reflection that it eases the sacrifice of wealth. The indifference displayed by the great Russian lords when Moscow burned shows well enough that they can do without the pleasures of life when they so desire.

In the Kremlin, I was shown a double throne that was occupied at first by Peter I and his brother, Ivan. Princess Sophie, their sister, took her seat behind Ivan's chair and dictated to him what he should say;[147] but this borrowed strength did not long resist the native strength of Peter I, and soon he reigned alone. Dating from his reign, the clothing shown to us was no longer of the same design. Until then, czars dressed in the Asiatic fashion. The great wig of the age of Louis XIV came in with Peter I, and without casting aspersions on the respect due this great man, there is a contrast, unpleasant but hard to define, between the ferocity of his genius and the formal correctness of his dress. Was he right to eradicate the Oriental ways of his nation as far as possible? Should he have set his capital in the northernmost extreme of his Empire? This important question has not yet been resolved; the centuries alone can pass judgment on such serious thoughts. Finally, I climbed to the top of the Ivan Veliki Tower that looks down on the whole city.[148] From there I saw the palace of the czars who conquered the crowns of Siberia, Kazan, and Astrakan by force of arms. I heard the chanting from the church where the Catholicos, Prince of Georgia, officiated amid Moscow's inhabitants and created a Christian union between Asia and Europe. Fifteen hundred churches bore witness to the piety of the Muscovite people.

Commercial establishments bore an Asiatic stamp: men in turbans, others dressed in the varied costumes of every country, displayed the rarest merchandise; furs from Siberia and fabrics from India offered all the pleasures of luxury to the great lords whose imagination enjoys Samoyed sables as much as Persian rubies. Here, the Rasoumovsky[149] palace and garden contained the most beautiful collection of plants and minerals. Farther on, a Count Boutourline had spent thirty years of his life assembling a beautiful library;[150] among the books in his possession were some that bear notes in the hand of Peter I. This great man did not suspect that the very European civilization he so envied would come to ravage the very institutions he had created to establish it in his Empire. The goal of a constantly improving university was to stabilize the impatient Russian mind through study.

Farther on was the Foundling Home, one of Europe's most admirable institutions;[151] hospitals for all classes of society drew one's attention in the various sections of the city. In sum, the eye could fall on nothing but wealth or benevolence, charitable or sumptuous buildings, and churches or palaces that spread happiness or luster over a vast portion of the human species. One caught sight of the loops of the Moskva, the river that had not flowed with blood since the last Tartar invasion. It was a glorious day; the sun seemed to delight in pouring its rays on the sparkling temples. I recalled the elderly Archbishop Plato, who had just written a pastoral letter to Emperor Alexander and whose Oriental style had moved me deeply. He sent the image of the Virgin from the borders of Europe to plead, far from Asia, with the man who wished to make Russians feel the full weight of the nations enslaved in his wake.[152] For a moment it occurred to me that he might walk on this same tower from which I was admiring the city that his presence would destroy; for a moment I thought that he would be proud to take the place of the leader of the Great Horde, who also managed to seize hold of it for a time; but the sky was so beautiful that I pushed my fear aside. One month later, this beautiful city was in ashes, so that it might be said that every country allied with that man was ravaged by the fires of Hell at his command.[153] But how well the Russians and their monarch have redeemed that error! Moscow's calamity has in itself resurrected the Empire, and this devout city has perished like a martyr whose blood gives new strength to the brothers who survive him.

The famous Count de Rostopchine, whose name has filled the Emperor's bulletins, came to visit and invite me to dine at his home.[154] He had been Minister of Foreign Affairs under Paul I; his conversation had originality and one could readily perceive that, should circumstances so require, his character would come markedly to the fore. I went to see him in his country home within Moscow; to reach it, one had to cross a lake and a woods. Count Rostopchine himself set fire to his house, one of the most agreeable places to live in Russia, when Napoleon drew close. Even enemies should have admired such a deed. The Emperor, however, compared Count Rostopchine to Marat,[155] forgetting that the former sacrificed his own property while the latter set fire to that of others, which makes a difference all the same. Count Rostopchine could have been criticized for concealing bad news from the armies for too long, either because he deceived himself or because he thought it necessary to deceive others. The English, with the admirable candor that distinguishes everything they do, give as truthful an account of their reverses as of their success, and their enthusiasm is sustained by the truth, whatever it may be. Russians cannot yet achieve this moral perfection that derives from a free constitution. But no civilized nation includes so many primitive members as the Russian people, and when nobles are vigorous they also approximate the faults and the qualities of this unbridled nature. Much praise has been accorded to Diderot's famous line: "Russians are rotten before they ripen."[156] I know of nothing more erroneous; with but few exceptions, even their vices relate to violence, not to corruption. "A Russian wish," said a superior man, "would blow up a city."[157] They are alternately seized with rage and guile when they want to implement any decision, good or bad, but their nature remains unchanged by the rapid civilizing given them by Peter I: as yet it has shaped their manners alone. Fortunately for them, they are still what we call barbarians, that is, led by an often generous, always involuntary instinct that admits of reflection only in the choice of means and not in the consideration of ends. I do not say "fortunately for them" from any wish to praise barbarity; rather do I designate by this name a certain primitive vigor that alone can stand in place of the surprising power of liberty in nations.

Countess de Rostopchine was kind enough to give me a book she had written on the triumph of religion, very pure in its style and morality.[158] I saw the most enlightened men in the domains of science and letters; but there, as in Petersburg, it was almost always Germans who directed public education. There is a great dearth of educated men in Russia in every area, and particularly in the sciences: for the most part, young men go to university only to enter the military profession more quickly. Civil office in Russia confers a rank corresponding to military rank in the army; national spirit is directed entirely to war. Everywhere else—administration, political economy, public education, etc.—the other peoples of Europe surpass the Russians so far. Nevertheless, they are trying their hand at literature. Even those who do not understand their language are attracted by the sweetness and brilliance of its sounds; it must be quite suited to music and to poetry. But Russians, like so many other countries on the Continent, err by imitating French literature, which in its very beauties is appropriate to the French alone.[159] To my way of thinking, Russians should base their literary studies on the Greeks rather than the Romans. The characters of Russian handwriting, so similar to the Greek, Russia's ancient lines of communication with the Byzantine Empire, its future fortunes that will lead perhaps toward the renowned monuments of Antiquity, should all incline Russians to the study of Greek. But at the very least their writers must draw their poetry from what is most personal in the depths of the soul. As yet their works have been composed from the tips of their tongues, if you will, and so vehement a nation can never be stirred by such thin melodies.

I left Moscow reluctantly.[160] I stopped for a while in a woods near the city where, on festival days, Muscovites come to dance and celebrate the sun whose splendor is short-lived even in Moscow. What is it like then to move steadily northward? Even those unending birch trees grow very sparse, they say, when you draw near Archangel; they are cosseted like orange trees in France. Those unending birches are wearying in their monotony. The road from Moscow to Petersburg is nothing but sand at first, and then marshland. The moment it rains, the soil turns black and you no longer know where to find the highway across the vast plains they call roads. Still, the homes of peasants signal well-being everywhere; they decorate their houses with columns; swirls of flowers carved in wood frame their windows in arabesques. Yet even though I crossed through this region in summer, I sensed the threatening winter that seemed to be hiding behind the clouds. When fruits were offered to me, they tasted acrid because their ripening had been too hurried. A rose stirred feelings in me akin to a memory of our beautiful lands, and it seemed that flowers themselves carried their heads with less pride, as if the glacial hand of the North were already about to seize hold of them.

I went by way of Novgorod which was a republic three hundred years ago, allied with the Hanseatic cities. It fought tenaciously in the war against Pontusson de la Gardie, the renowned Swedish gentleman who commanded his nation's troops shortly after Christina's abdication.[161] People like to say that only in the last century has liberty been demanded in Europe; rather is despotism a modern invention. Even in Russia, enslavement of peasants was established only in the sixteenth century. Until the reign of Peter I, the standard form of all *ukases*[162] was: "The boyars have decided, the czar will command." Although in many respects Peter I did Russia infinite good, he humbled the nobles and took into his hands both temporal and spiritual power so that he would meet no obstacles to his despotism. Richelieu acted likewise in France, therefore Peter I admired him greatly. It is said that on seeing his grave in Paris he exclaimed: "Great man! I would give half my Empire to know how to govern the other half like thee." Peter was too modest on that occasion for, to begin with, he had the advantage over Richelieu of being a great warrior and, what is more, of founding the navy and commerce in his country, whereas Richelieu merely governed tyrannically within France and astutely outside.[163]

But let us return to Novgorod. Ivan III seized it in 1470 and destroyed the city's liberty; he had the great bell of Vetchevoy transported to the Kremlin in Moscow: when it rang, citizens gathered on the square to deliberate on public interests. Its liberty gone, Novgorod saw its population, its commerce, its wealth dwindle with each passing day—so desiccating and destructive is the breath of arbitrary power, says Russia's finest historian! Even today, the city of Novgorod strikes one as remarkably dreary. A vast enclosed space proclaims that the city was once large and densely populated, and all you see are scattered houses whose inhabitants seem placed there like figures weeping over tombs. This may be the sight that beautiful Moscow[164] now offers the beholder, but public spirit will rebuild her just as it has won her back.

From Novgorod as far as Petersburg there is nothing but marshland, and when you come into one of Europe's most beautiful cities, it is as if a sorcerer had suddenly brought forth all the wonders of Europe and Asia from the depths of the wilderness. The foundation of Petersburg is the greatest proof of the passionate Russian will that recognizes nothing as impossible. The surrounding countryside is altogether horrible. The city is built on a marsh and even marble stands on wooden pilings, but on seeing those splendid buildings, one forgets their fragile foundations and cannot but admire the miracle of so beautiful a city built in so short a time.

When I reached Petersburg,[165] my first reaction was to thank heaven for being on the shore of the sea. I saw the English colors floating over the Neva as a sign of liberty, and I felt that by entrusting myself to the ocean I could come once more under the immediate power of the Divinity. It is an inescapable illusion to believe oneself more fully in the hands of Providence when one is at the mercy of the elements rather than of men, and above all of the man who seems a revelation of the principle of evil on this earth.

It was rightly claimed that in Petersburg one could not say of a woman that she was as old as the streets, so modern were the streets themselves. The buildings are still a dazzling white and, at night, lit by the moon, you seem to see great white ghosts, motionless as they watch the rapid course of the Neva. I do not really know what is so especially beautiful about this river, but never have the waters of any stream looked so limpid to me. Granite quays thirty versts long[166] border its waves, and this magnificent work of man is worthy of the transparent water it ornaments. Had Peter I directed such works toward the south of his Empire, he would not have obtained the navy he wanted, but perhaps he would have conformed more closely to his nation's character.

The Russians living in Petersburg have the look of a southern people condemned to life in the North and bending all its efforts to contend with a climate not in harmony with its nature. Northern peoples are very reclusive as a rule and dread the cold precisely because it is their daily enemy. The Russian populace has adopted none of these habits. Coachmen wait at the door for twelve hours in winter without complaint; they lie down to sleep on the snow under their carriages and transplant the ways of the Neopolitan *lazzaroni* to the sixtieth degree of latitude.[167] You see them settled on the steps of a staircase like Germans in their down quilts; sometimes they sleep on their feet, their heads leaning against a wall. Alternately apathetic and impulsive, they devote themselves in turn to sleep or to unbelievable labors. Some become intoxicated, differing in this from the peoples of the South, who are quite sober, but so are Russians, and in a scarcely credible way when the difficulties of war require it. This people, which can never be portrayed except by contrasts, shows an implausible perseverance against nature or against enemy armies. Necessity always finds Russians patient and invincible, but in the ordinary course of life they are very erratic. The same men, the same masters do not inspire their enthusiasm for long; reflection alone can ensure the lasting quality of the same affections and the same judgment in the customary tranquillity of life; and Russians, like all peoples subjected to despotism, are more capable of dissimulation than of reflection. The great lords in their own way also show the tastes of southern peoples. One must go into the various country houses they have built for themselves in the middle of an island formed by the Neva, almost within the confines of Petersburg. The plants of the South, the perfumes of the Orient, the sofas of Asia embellish these dwellings. The fruits of every country ripen in immense greenhouses that create an artificial climate. The great Russian lords try not to lose the slightest sunbeam while it appears on their horizon; they celebrate it like a friend who is to leave them soon, but whom they once knew in a happier land.

Opposite the house where I lived in Petersburg was the statue of Peter I; he is shown on horseback, climbing a steep mountain amid serpents trying to impede his horse's progress. Those serpents are in truth put there to support the immense bulk of horse and rider. The idea is not felicitous, however, for in reality it is not envy that can alarm a sovereign; those who grovel are not his enemies either, and Peter I in particular had nothing to fear in his lifetime but Russians who longed for their country's old customs. Nevertheless, the admiration still felt for him is evidence of the good he did for Russia, since a hundred years after their death despots have no one to flatter them. On the pedestal you see the words: "To Peter the First, Catherine the Second." This simple yet arrogant inscription has the merit of truth, however. These two great men lifted Russian pride very high,[168] and knowing how to place in a nation's mind the idea that it is invincible is to make it so, at least within the confines of its own borders, for conquest is a stroke of luck that depends still more on the faults of the vanquished perhaps than on the genius of the victor.[169]

The day after my arrival, I went to dine at the home of one of the city's most respected merchants, and one who practiced Russian hospitality; that is, he placed a banner on the roof of his house to announce that he was dining at home, and this invitation sufficed for all his friends and for the friends of his friends. He had dinner served out-of-doors, so happy were people with those meager last days of summer that we would hardly have so named in the south of Europe. The garden was very pleasant, adorned with trees and flowers, but just a few steps from the house, wilderness or marshland resumed. Nature on the outskirts of Petersburg has the look of an enemy who reclaims her rights as soon as man stops fighting her for an instant.

The next morning I made my way to the church of Kazan, built by Paul I and modeled after Saint Peter's in Rome.[170] The interior of the church, decorated with a great many granite columns, is supremely beautiful, but the building itself fails to please precisely because it recalls Saint Peter's, and differs from it all the more for the attempted imitation. What cost the foremost artists of the universe one hundred fifty years cannot be done in two. Russians would like to escape both time and space through speed, but time conserves only what it has founded, and in any event, the arts, whose primary source seems to be inspiration, need reflection above all else.

From Kazan I went to the monastery of Saint Alexander Newski, a place devoted to one of Russia's heroic sovereigns who extended his conquests as far as the banks of the Neva.[171] Empress Elizabeth, daughter of Peter I, had a silver casket made upon which people customarily lay a coin as a token of the wish they commend to the saint.

It was for the Emperor who bore his name that I invoked him. I had not yet seen this Alexander, his Empire's finest citizen, but I was already aware that the happiness of the world, and of France in particular, depended upon his success on the battlefield. What would Europe be, what would poor France be if she had triumphed once again under that man?[172] Instead of reigning as a nation as she once did in the midst of Europe, she would serve as one more slave amid the throng of peoples—Germans, Italians, Croats, Illyrians—that she is commanded to consider as compatriots.

Souvoroff's grave is within this monastery of Alexander's, but his name is its sole ornament; that is enough for him, but not for the Russians whom he so notably served. Moreover, this is so warlike a nation that it wonders less than another at valorous deeds of this kind. The greatest Russian families have built tombs for their relatives in the cemetery attached to the Newski Church, but none of these monuments is worthy of note; they are not beautiful in terms of art and no great idea strikes the imagination. Moreover, the thought of death has very little effect on Russians; be it courage, be it insta-bility of reactions, prolonged sorrows are scarcely in character for them; they are more capable of superstition than of piety. Superstition relates to this life and religion to the other; superstition is linked to fatality and religion to virtue. The acuteness of earthly desires makes us superstitious, but it is the sacrifice of these same desires that makes us religious.

M. de Romanzoff, the Russian Minister of Foreign Affairs, had showered me with the most amiable courtesies and, I thought reluctantly, he had been so much a part of Emperor Napoleon's system that, like English ministers, he should have stood down when the system was rejected. No doubt, in an absolute monarchy the master's will explains everything, but a Prime Minis-ter's dignity perhaps requires that contradictory words not emanate from the same mouth. The sovereign is the State and the State can change its policy as circumstances require, but the minister is only a man, and a man, on ques-tions of this importance, should have only one opinion in the course of his life. At all events, it is impossible to have better manners than M. de Romanzoff and to welcome foreigners more nobly.

I was at his home when the English minister, Lord Tyrconnel, and Admi-ral Bentinck were announced;[173] both of them, remarkable in bearing, were the first Englishmen to reappear on this Continent from which one man's tyranny had banished them. After ten years of so terrible a struggle, after ten years whose successes and reverses had always seen the English faithful to conscience—the compass of their politics—they returned at last to the first country to wrest itself free of the universal monarchy. Everything about them—their tone, their simplicity, their pride—stirred within the soul the sentiment of truth in all things that Napoleon has found the art of obscur-ing in the eyes of those who have read only his bulletins and heard only his agents. I do not even know whether Napoleon's adversaries on the Conti-nent, constantly beset with false opinion that relentlessly dizzies them, could comfortably trust their own opinion. If I can judge by my own example, I know that often, after I heard all the advice on caution or baseness that en-gulfs a person in Napoleon's ambiance, I no longer knew what to think of my own opinion. My blood forbade me to give it up, but my reason did not always suffice to protect me against so much sophistry. Blessed be Russia, where I could hear once more the voice of England with which one must agree if one is to deserve the respect of decent people and of oneself.

Count Orloff invited me to spend the following day on the island bear-ing his name. It is the most agreeable of all those formed by the Neva: oak trees, a rare species in this region, shade Count Gregory Orloff's garden.[174]

He and Countess Orloff devote their fortune to offering foreigners a welcome as simple as it is sumptuous; one is at ease there as in a rustic retreat while enjoying all the luxuries of cities. Count Orloff is one of the most highly educated of the great lords to be met in Russia, and one cannot help being moved by the depth of his love for his country. On the first day I spent in his home, peace with England had just been announced. It was a Sunday and in his garden, open that day to people coming to stroll, one saw a great number of the bearded merchants who in Russia retain the moujik, that is peasant, dress. Several of them gathered to hear the excellent music Count Orloff had arranged to have performed. The musicians played *God Save the King,* the song of liberty in a country whose king is its foremost guardian.[175] All of us were moved and we vigorously applauded this national anthem for all Europeans, as there are only two kinds of men in Europe now: those who serve tyranny and those who can hate it. Count Orloff went over to the bearded Russian traders and told them that we were celebrating peace between England and Russia; they made the sign of the cross and thanked heaven that the sea was open to them once more.

Orloff Island is at the center of all those chosen for summer residence by the great lords of Petersburg and by the Emperor and Empress themselves. Not far from there is Stroganoff Island, whose wealthy owner sent to Greece for highly valuable works of art from ancient times.[176] His house was open every day of his life, and whoever had been introduced there once could return; he never invited to dinner or supper for a specific day: it was understood that, once admitted, one was always welcome. He often did not know half the persons dining in his home, but this profuse hospitality gave him the same pleasure as every other form of splendor. Many houses in Petersburg have much the same custom. One may readily infer that what we understand in France by the pleasures of conversation cannot be found there: society is too numerous for discussion of a certain depth ever to develop. All well-bred people have perfect manners, but there is neither enough education among nobles, nor enough trust between individuals living constantly under the influence of a court and of a despotic government, for them to know the pleasures of intimacy.

Most of Russia's great lords express themselves with such grace and decorum that, at first sight, one has illusions on the degree of intelligence and knowledge of one's interlocutors. The first appearance is almost always of a very intelligent man or woman, but occasionally one is left in the long run with only that first appearance. In Russia, people are not accustomed to speak from the depths of the soul or of the mind; in earlier times, people so feared their masters that they have not yet been able to get used to the judicious liberty they owe to Alexander's character.

Russians, as I have said, almost never speak of what interests them personally. They enjoy literature, and several of the great lords have already demonstrated talent;[177] but in this respect enlightenment is not spread widely enough for there to be any public judgment based on the opinion of each individual. The national character is too passionate to enjoy thoughts at all abstract—only facts entertain them; they have not yet had the time or the taste for generalizing ideas from facts. Then again, any significant thought is more or less dangerous in a court where everyone watches everyone else, more often than not with envy. It follows from these different causes that the charm of society in Russia does not lie in conversation or intimacy, but in elegance of customs and courtesy of manners.

The silence of the Orient is turned into language that is agreeable but does not ordinarily probe the depths of things further than the silence itself. Yet although one enjoys this pleasant and brilliant ambience that squanders life agreeably, one learns nothing new in the long run, one's faculties do not expand, and men who spend their time this way acquire no capacity for serious matters. This was not so in Parisian society. There one saw men—educated solely by the stimulating and serious conversations occasioned by the interchange of nobles with men and women of letters—learn through conversation what they had not been able to draw from books.[178]

At last I saw the monarch, absolute by law and by custom, and so moderate by his own inclination.[179] I was presented first to Empress Elizabeth; she appeared to me as the guardian angel of Russia; one glance from her would suffice to punish or reward the most guilty or the most illustrious. Her manner is very reserved, but what she says is full of life, and it is at the hearth of all generous thoughts that her sentiments and opinions have derived strength and warmth. In speaking with her, I was enchanted by something I cannot describe that was not related to her majesty but to the harmony of her soul. It had been such a very long time since I had seen power and virtue in harmony.

While I was being honored by a visit with the Empress, the door opened and Emperor Alexander was kind enough to come speak with me. What struck me about him straight away is an expression of kindness and dignity such that he seems to have made one quality of the two, so indivisible do they appear. I was also very moved by his noble simplicity in broaching the most important questions from the very first sentences he was so good as to address to me. I have always judged the fear of discussing the bedrock of matters that has been inspired in most of Europe's sovereigns as a sign of mediocrity; they are afraid to pronounce words that might have serious and real meaning. Emperor Alexander, on the contrary, conversed with me as would English statesmen who place their strength in themselves and not in the barriers a person can erect around himself. Napoleon tried to disparage Emperor Alexander in the eyes of others, but he is a man both intelligent and remarkably learned, and I do not think he can find any minister in his Empire more capable than he in everything related to the judgment and management of affairs. He did not conceal his regret for yielding to enthusiasm in his relations with Napoleon.[180] In the same way, a forebear of Alexander's had felt great enthusiasm for Frederic II. In these sorts of illusions that a great warrior can inspire, there is always a noble motive, whatever the resultant errors.

Yet Emperor Alexander was quite astute in his portrayal of the effect of those conversations wherein Bonaparte said the most conflicting things, as if one were supposed to wonder at each without realizing that they were contradictory. He also related some of the Machiavelli-style lessons that Napoleon had deemed suitable to give him: "Look here," he said, "I am careful to set my ministers and generals at odds with one another so that each of them reveals to me what the others are doing wrong. That way, I foster unremitting jealousy around me by how I treat those who surround me: one day this person thinks he is preferred, the next day it's the other, and not one of them can ever be sure of my favor." What a theory, vulgar and evil at one and the same time! And will there never come a man superior to that man who will prove its futility? What the sacred cause of morality requires is that it be strikingly useful to great success in the world; the person who feels the full dignity of this cause will gladly sacrifice success. But those arrogant persons who believe depth of thought resides in the soul's vices must still be taught that even though there is sometimes intelligence in immorality, there is genius in virtue.

Once I was convinced of Emperor Alexander's good faith in his relations with Napoleon, I was also persuaded that, given the example of Germany's unfortunate sovereigns, he would sign no peace treaty with the man who is as much the enemy of peoples as he is of kings. A soul that is sincere and firm cannot be fooled twice by the same person. Alexander gives and withdraws his trust upon the most thorough reflection. Only his youth and outward advantages could have opened him to suspicion of frivolity in the early days of his reign, but in his soul he is as serious as a man might be who has known misfortune. Alexander voiced his regret to me at not being a great general. In response to that noble modesty, I said that a sovereign was rarer than a general, and that to sustain the public spirit of his nation by his example was to win the greatest battle and the first of its kind to be won. Emperor Alexander spoke enthusiastically to me of his nation and what it was capable of being. He mentioned his wish, known to everyone, to improve the conditions of peasants still subject to serfdom.

"Sire," I said, "your character is your Empire's Constitution and your conscience is its guarantee."

"Even were that true," he replied, "a man is never more than a happy accident."[181]

Splendid words—the first of their kind, I believe, that an absolute monarch has uttered! How many virtues it requires to judge despotism when one is a despot, and how many virtues never to misuse it when the nation governed is almost astonished by such rare moderation!

In Petersburg above all, the great lords are less open-minded in their principles than the Emperor himself. Accustomed to being absolute masters of their peasants, they want the monarch in his turn to be all-powerful so as to maintain the hierarchy of despotism. The status of bourgeois does not yet exist in Russia, but it is beginning to take form; sons of priests,[182] those of traders, a few peasants who have won freedom from their lords to become artists, may be considered a third order in the State. The Russian nobility, moreover, does not resemble that of Germany or France. One is noble there the moment one has military rank. One is noble the moment the Emperor wills it so. No doubt the great families, like the Narychkines, the Dolgoroukys, the Golitzines, etc. will always be foremost in the Empire, but it is no less true that the advantages of aristocracy belong to men whom the Prince's will has turned into nobles overnight, and the whole ambition of the bourgeois is to make their sons officers so they may be in the privileged class. That is why all education ends at age fifteen; they rush headlong into the military career at the first possible moment and all the rest is neglected. This is most certainly not the moment to criticize an order of things that has produced such splendid resistance, but were an era of peace to return in Europe, one might truthfully say that there are great gaps in administration for the interior of Russia. This nation is imbued with vigor and greatness, but order and enlightenment are still often missing both in the government of the interior and in the private conduct of individuals. In making Russia European, Peter I undoubtedly gave her great advantages; the price exacted, however, was the establishment of a despotism rough-hewn by his father but consolidated by him alone. Catherine the Second, on the contrary, tempered the use of the absolute power that she had not created. If the political circumstances of Europe restored peace, that is if a single man no longer meted out evil upon the earth, we would see Alexander solely occupied with bettering his country and exploring for himself what laws could ensure for Russia the happiness that is hers without question only during the lifetime of her present master.

When I left the Emperor I went to see his esteemed mother, she to whom calumny has never been able to impute a sentiment unfavorable to her husband, her children, or the family of unfortunates whose protector she is.[183] Farther on I shall relate her way of directing the charitable Empire she governs within her son's omnipotent Empire. She resides in the Taurida Palace,[184] and to reach her apartments, one must cross through a room built by Prince Potemkin: it is of incomparable size. A winter garden occupies one part; you see its plants, its trees through columns surrounding the space in the center. Everything is immense in this dwelling. The Prince who constructed it had strangely gigantic ideas. He had towns built in the Crimea only for the Empress to see as she went by; he ordered a town attacked to please a beautiful woman, Princess Dolgorouky, who had spurned his compliments. His sovereign's favor created him such as he appeared; but, in most of Russia's great men, such as Menchikoff,[185] Souvoroff, Peter I himself, and far earlier still, Ivan Vassilievitch,[186] there is nevertheless something strange, violent, and ironic all together. For them the mind was a weapon rather than a pleasure, and they were led by imagination. Generosity, barbarity, unbridled passions, superstitious religion: all came together within the same character. Even today civilization has not penetrated to the depths of Russia, even among the great lords. Some outwardly resemble the French, others the Germans, still others the English. But all are Russian in their souls and from this come their strength and originality, with love of country, after love of God, the most beautiful that man can experience. To inspire marked attachment, it is imperative for a country to be thoroughly distinct from the other lands surrounding it; nations that blend into one another by way of nuances, or that are divided into several states detached from one another, do not dedicate themselves with real passion to the philosophic fellowship to which they have attached the name of country.

I went to spend a day at the country estate of M. de Narychkine,[187] grand chamberlain of the court, a pleasant man, polite and easy to get on with, but who does not know how to live without a fête. It is through him that one truly gains understanding of the vividness in tastes that explains the defects and the qualities of the Russians. M. de Narychkine's house is always open, and when there are only twenty people at his country estate, he is bored with this philosophical retreat. Obliging to foreigners, always in motion, and yet very capable of the forethought needed for behaving properly at a court, preferring to give away all he has rather than pay his debts, avid for the pleasures of imagination, finding these pleasures only in things and not in books, impatient everywhere but at court, witty when being so is to his advantage, magnificent rather than vain, and seeking in everything a certain Asiatic grandeur in which wealth and rank stand out rather than the advantages particular to his person. His countryside is as pleasant as possible where nature is created by the human hand; all the surrounding land is arid and swampy, with his dwelling an oasis. Going up on the terrace you glimpse the Sea of Finland, and in the distance you glimpse the palace that Peter had built on its shores.[188] But the space separating the sea and the palace is almost uncultivated, and there are only M. de Narychkine's gardens to delight the eye. We went to dine in the Moldavian house, that is, a room built according to the taste of this people. It was laid out to give shelter from the sun's heat, a rather useless precaution in Russia. The imagination, however, is so struck by the idea that one is living in a country northern only by chance, that it seems natural there to revert to the customs of the South, as if the Russians would one day have the climate of their former country brought to Petersburg. The table was covered with fruits of all lands, following the Oriental practice of displaying only the fruit, while a multitude of servants bring each guest the meats and vegetables required for nourishment.

The horn music peculiar to Russia, and often talked about, was played for us. Each of twenty musicians sounds one and the same note every time it recurs, thus each man bears the name of the note he is charged with executing. Seeing them walk by, one says: "Here's M. de Narychikine's sol, mi, or re." The horns increase in size and volume from row to row, and someone rightly called this music a "living organ." From a distance the effect is very beautiful; the precision and beauty of the harmony give rise to the noblest thoughts. But when one draws near those poor musicians standing there like pipes that yield but one note and unable to participate through their own emotion in the emotion they evoke, the pleasure cools; one does not like to see the arts transformed into mechanics and capable of being learned under compulsion like exercise.

Next, inhabitants of Ukraine, dressed in red and with Oriental features, came to sing singularly pleasing songs of their land for us, some joyous, some melancholy, and some both at once. At times these songs break off suddenly in the midst of the melody, as if the imagination of this people

had wearied at finishing what gave it pleasure at first, or found more piquancy in suspending the charm just when most effective. Thus does the
sultana of the *Thousand and One Nights* always interrupt her tale when the
interest is at its height.

In the midst of these varied pleasures, M. de Narychkine proposed a toast
to the success of the combined Russian and English armies. At the same moment, he signaled for his artillery, which was almost as loud as a sovereign's.
All the guests were seized with the intoxication of hope; for my part, I felt
bathed in tears. Did it take an African tyrant to reduce me to wanting the
French vanquished? "Let us wish," I said then, "let us wish for the Corsicans'
defeat, for true Frenchmen will triumph if the Corsicans are repulsed." The
English and the Russians, with M. de Narychkine in the lead, applauded my
view and the name of France—once equivalent to Armida—found favor
once more with the knights of the Orient and of the seas[189] who were to
fight her, or rather free her from hell's witchcraft now holding her in chains.

Kalmucks with flattened features are raised among Russian lords as if to
preserve a sampling of those Tartars vanquished by the Slavs. In Narychkine's
palace, two or three of those wild, pagan Kalmucks ran about. They are very
agreeable as children, but lose all of youth's charm by the age of twenty.
Stubborn, although slaves, they entertain their masters with their resistance
like a squirrel flinging itself against the bars of its cage. I did not much like
this sample of debased humanity. It seemed to me that amid all the pomp of
luxury I saw an image of what human nature can become when it has no
dignity either through religion or through laws, and this spectacle humbled
the pride that the pleasures of splendor can inspire in man.

Long barouches drawn by white horses took us into the gardens after
dinner. It was the end of August; yet the sky was pale and the lawns an almost artificial green because they were maintained only by dint of care.
Even the flowers seemed an aristocratic pleasure, so great was the cost of
having them. We heard no birds warbling in the woods: they did not trust
that fleeting summer's moment; nor did we see any cattle in the meadows:
to let them graze on plants raised at the cost of such pains was unthinkable.
Water barely flowed, and then only with the help of machines that guided it
into the garden. In its every aspect, nature had the look of party ornaments
that would disappear once the spectators were gone. Our barouches stopped
at a little structure in the garden depicting a Tartar camp. There, we began to
hear all the musicians together again, and the horns and cymbals gently
numbed our thought. To lose ourselves the more completely, we imitated in
summer the sleighs whose swiftness consoles Russians in winter; we rode on

planks from the top of a mountain to the bottom with the speed of lightning. The game charmed the women as well as the men and let them share something of those pleasures of war that come from the emotion of danger and the spirited quickness of every gesture. Thus time went by, for what seemed a fête to me recurred almost every day.

With but few differences, most of Petersburg's great houses have the same way of living. Surely, then, there can be no question of any kind of sustained conversation, and education is of no use in this kind of society, but when one's purpose is to bring a great many persons together at home, fêtes are, after all, the only way to stave off the boredom that crowded salons always evoke.

"Amid all this noise, is there any love?" Italian women would ask, hardly imagining any other interest in society than the pleasure of seeing the one whose love they wish to win. I have spent too little time in Petersburg to have an accurate idea of life within the family. It seemed to me, however, that on the one hand there was more domestic virtue than reported, but that on the other hand sentimental love was rarely experienced there.

The Asiatic customs one meets at each step ensure that women have nothing to do with their domestic arrangements; it is the husband who controls everything, and the woman merely adorns herself with his gifts and receives the guests he invites. Respect for morals is already greater in Petersburg than it was in the days of those sovereigns, men and women, who by their example depraved opinion in this regard. The present two Empresses exemplify the virtues they have brought others to love.

Yet in this regard, as in many others, the principles of morality are not firmly established in Russian minds. The master's influence has always been so strong that, from one reign to the next, all maxims on all subjects may be changed. Russians, men and women, ordinarily bring their native impetuosity to love, but their changeable disposition also allows them to give up their choices easily. A certain disorder of imagination does not allow them to find enduring happiness in anything. Cultivation of mind, which multiplies sentiment through poetry and the arts, is very rare among Russians, and in these odd and vehement natures, love is rather a feast or a frenzy than a deep and considered affection.

Good company in Russia is thus a perpetual whirlwind, and it may be that one result of the extreme caution to which a despotic government accustoms Russians is their delight that society does not expose them to talk on subjects that might have some sort of consequence. Indeed, the untruthfulness they are accused of must be attributed to the reserve they have found only too necessary under various reigns. The courtier's cast of mind corrupts sincerity of character in every country, but when the sovereign has the authority to commit great evil—to exile, imprison, send to Siberia, etc.—his power over most men is too strong. One may have encountered men proud enough to scorn favor, but it requires heroism to brave persecution, and heroism cannot be a universal quality.

None of these reflections, as we know, applies to the present government since its leader is perfectly just as Emperor and unusually generous as a man. But subjects retain the faults of slavery long after the sovereign himself would like to remove them. We have nevertheless seen by the war's progress how many virtues even Russian courtiers have displayed. When I was in Petersburg, virtually no young men were to be seen in society. Even those who were married, only sons, or lords possessed of immense wealth were in the army as simple volunteers, and when they saw their lands and houses ravaged, they thought of those losses only to take revenge and never to compromise with the enemy. Such qualities override everything that a still faulty administration, a new civilization, and despotic institutions can have brought about by way of abuses, disorders, and irregularities.

We went to see the natural history collection, which is remarkable for the products of Siberia. That country's furs have excited greed in Russians as Mexico's gold excited greed in Spaniards.[190] There was a time in Russia when the coin of exchange still consisted of marten skins and squirrel heads, so universal was the need for protection against the hoar-frost. What is most remarkable in the Petersburg museum is the skeleton of the great mammoth, a gigantic animal whose remains were found in Siberia. It appears, according to the observations of the wittiest of scholars, M. Cuvier,[191] that the world has a history far more ancient than the one we know: infinity frightens us in all things. At the present time, the inhabitants and even the animals of this extreme end of the inhabited world seem permeated with the cold that brings death to nature a few leagues from their country; the color of animals blends with that of snow, and the earth seems to vanish into the ice and fog that bring creation to a close here on earth.

I was struck by the faces of the inhabitants of Kamchatka, whose perfect likeness is found in the Petersburg collection. In that country there are improvisators of a sort, called shamans, who wear on their bark tunics a kind of steel mesh from which hang several pieces of iron that make a loud noise the instant the improvisator moves. He has moments of inspiration that closely resemble hysterics, and it is rather by witchcraft than by talent that he impresses his people. In countries as dreary as this, imagination can scarcely be moved except through fear, and earth itself seems to reject man through the terror she causes him.

Next I saw the citadel[192] with the church alongside where the caskets of all the sovereigns since Peter the Great are laid. These caskets are not shut away in monuments; they are displayed as on the day of the funeral ceremony, and one feels quite close to these dead, who seem separated from us by a mere wooden board. When Paul I succeeded to the throne he had his father's remains crowned, for Peter III had not received this honor in his lifetime and so could not be placed in the citadel. By his order, the burial ceremonies for his father and his mother, Catherine the Second, were begun again.[193] Both were displayed once more; once more four chamberlains stood guard over their bodies as if they had expired the night before, and the two caskets are placed side by side, compelled to live in peace under the sway of death.

Among the sovereigns who held the despotic power transmitted by Peter I, several were overthrown by bloody conspiracies.[194] The same courtiers who lack the strength to tell their master the slightest truth know how to plot against him; and the most profound dissimulation necessarily accompanies this form of political revolution, for respect must be showered on the person one means to assassinate. And yet what would become of a despotically governed country if a tyrant above all laws had nothing to fear from daggers? A horrible alternative, and sufficient in itself to show what it means to have institutions where crime is introduced for the balance of powers.

I paid homage to Catherine the Second by visiting her country home, Tsarkoïé-Selo.[195] The palace and garden are laid out with a great deal of skill and magnificence, but the air was very cold already, though it was barely the first of September, and those southern flowers made a strange contrast with the north wind blowing them about. It can be compared to the Russian nation, itself transported into a climate foreign to its ways. All the stories told about Catherine the Second as sovereign fill one with admiration for her; and I do not know whether Russians do not owe still more to her than to Peter I the conviction that they are invincible—the conviction responsible for their success. A woman's charm tempered the exercise of power and blended courtly attentiveness with the success for which she is paid homage. Catherine the Second had supremely good sense in governing. A more brilliant mind than hers would have resembled genius less, and her strong capacity for reason[196] inspired great respect in those Russians who distrust their own imagination and want it guided wisely. Close by Tsarkoïé-Selo is the palace of Paul I, a charming residence because it is the setting chosen by the Dowager Empress and her daughters for the masterpieces of their talents and good taste.[197] It calls to mind the admirable patience of this mother and these daughters whom nothing has been able to distract from their domestic virtues.

I let myself indulge in the pleasure inspired by the new objects I visited each day, and I do not know how I forgot the war that was to determine the fate of Europe. It gave me such vivid pleasure to hear everyone express the sentiments I had stifled for so long in my soul that it seemed to me that there was nothing more to be feared, and that such truths were all-powerful the moment they were known. Nevertheless, reverses followed one upon the other without the public's being informed. A witty man has said that everything was a mystery in Petersburg although nothing was a secret, and in fact one does ultimately discover the truth; but the habit of silence among Russian courtiers is such that they conceal in the evening what will be known the next day, and it is always involuntarily that they reveal what they know. And so it was a foreigner who told me that Smolensk was taken and Moscow in the gravest danger.[198] Despair took hold of me. I thought I was seeing anew the lamentable story of the peace concluded by Austria and by Prussia following on the conquest of their capitals. It was the same trick played for the third time, but it might still succeed. I did not perceive the public spirit; the apparent instability of Russians kept me from noticing it. Despondency had frozen all minds, and I was unaware that, in these violently impressionable men, despondency is prelude to a fearful awakening. In like fashion, men of the people show an unbelievable inertia up to the moment their activity resumes; then it knows no obstacle, dreads no danger, and seems to triumph over the elements as over men.

I knew that the administration of the interior often fell into the most venal hands in matters of war as of justice, and that the thefts ventured by minor officials in consequence of that peculation made it impossible to have any precise idea either of the number of troops, or of the measures taken to furnish them with supplies. The fact is that lies and theft are inseparable, and in a country where civilization is so new, the intermediate class has neither the simplicity of peasants nor the grandeur of boyars, and no public opinion yet restrains this third class[199] so recently come into being and which has given up religion without having learned the point of honor. Feelings of envy were visibly developing among the army's leaders. In the first place, a despotic government by nature develops jealousy among those in its circle, even in spite of itself: since the will of a single man can entirely change the fate of each individual, the margin for fear and hope is too great for them not to be constantly in play. This jealousy was stimulated by another impulse as well, hatred of foreigners. The commander of the Russian Army, M. Barclay de Tolly, although born on the Empire's soil, was not purely Slavic by race, and this sufficed to keep him from leading the Russians to victory. Further, he had turned his distinguished talents to the development and system of advanced camps, maneuvers, and positions, whereas the military art suited to Russians is the attack. To have them retreat, even by wise and well-reasoned calculation, is to chill the impetuosity whence all their strength derives.[200]

Thus the omens for the campaign were the sorriest possible, and the silence maintained in this regard was more frightening still. In their public news reports, the English give the most exact accounting of each engagement, man by man, of the wounded, the prisoners, and the dead: noble candor of a government that gives as sincere an accounting to the nation as to its sovereign, acknowledging for both the same rights to know the state of the public welfare. I was profoundly sad as I walked through that beautiful city of Petersburg that could become spoils for the conqueror. In the evening, when I returned from the islands and saw the tip of the citadel's silvery spire like a flash of fire shooting into the air, when the Neva reflected the marble quays and palaces surrounding it, I pictured all of these marvels withered by the arrogance of one man. He would say, like Satan on the mountaintop: "The kingdoms of Asia are my own."[201] All that was good and beautiful in Petersburg seemed faced with impending destruction, and I could take no pleasure in it without this painful thought.

I went to see the educational institutes founded by the Empress[202] and there, still more than amid palaces, my anxiety deepened, since that man's breath has only to draw near institutions to improve the human species for them to be poisoned forever. [In] two houses, each with a capacity for two hundred fifty, noble or bourgeois girls are brought up [sic] under the supervision of the Empress with care beyond all that a wealthy family could give its children. Order and elegance are evident in all the details of this institute, and the purest sentiment of religion and morality governs all the charm that the arts can foster. Russian women have such natural grace that on entering a room where all the girls greeted us, I did not see one who did not endow her curtsy with all the politeness and modesty this simple act could express. These young women were invited to show us the various talents that distinguish them, and one who knew passages from the best French writers by heart recited for me one of my father's most eloquent pages in his *Course on Religious Morality*.[203] That very sensitive thoughtfulness came from the Empress herself perhaps; in any event, I felt the most intense emotion at hearing this language that, for so many years, had no other refuge than my heart.

Beyond Bonaparte's Empire, in every country, posterity begins and justice is shown toward those who have felt the impact of his imperial calumnies even in the tomb. The young women of the Institute of Saint Catherine sang psalms in chorus before sitting down at table; those many voices so pure and so sweet moved me to a pity tinged with bitterness. What would the war do to such peaceable institutions? Where would these doves flee the savage and profane weapons of such a conqueror?

After the meal, the young ladies gathered in a magnificent room where all of them danced together. There was nothing striking in the beauty of their features, but their grace was extraordinary; they are daughters of the Orient with all the decorum introduced among women by Christian manners. First, they performed an old dance to the tune of *Long Live Henri IV, Long Live that Valiant King!* How far from the present were the days called to mind by this tune! Two round-faced little girls, ten years old, ended the ballet with the Russian step. At times this dance takes on the sensuality of love, but performed by children, the innocence of their age blended with the originality of the nation. One cannot describe the interest inspired by all those charming talents, cultivated by the sensitive and generous hand of a woman and a sovereign. An institute for the deaf and mute, another for the blind are likewise under the Empress's supervision.[204] For his part, the Emperor pays great attention to the school for young men, directed by a man of superior mind, General Klinger.[205]

The government must be praised for these truly useful institutions, which might, however, be criticized for their ostentation. At the least, it should be possible to establish in various parts of the Empire not such elegant schools but a few institutions to give the rudiments of knowledge to the people. Everything in Russia has begun with luxury, and the pinnacle, if you will, has preceded the foundation.

There are only two large cities in Russia, Petersburg and Moscow. The others barely deserve the name of city; they are, it must be added, at very great distances from one another. Even the châteaux of the great lords are so far apart that they can hardly ever see one another. The inhabitants are in fact so widely scattered in this Empire that the store of knowledge acquired in one place can scarcely be useful to the others. Peasants count only with wooden balls and postal clerks also use this method.[206] Greek popes are far less enlightened than Catholic parish priests and than Protestant ministers especially; Russian priests are thus not fitted to instruct the people as in the other countries of Europe. The nation is bound into one by religion and patriotism, but there is still no center of enlightenment whose rays can spread to all parts of the Empire, and the two capitals still cannot communicate to the provinces what they have gathered by way of literature and the arts. Had this country been able to enjoy peace, it would have experienced all kinds of improvements under Alexander's beneficent reign. But who knows whether the virtues developed by such a war are not precisely those which are to regenerate nations?

Russians have had men of genius only in the military career up to now; in all the other arts they merely imitate, but printing was introduced among them only one hundred and twenty years ago. Other European peoples were all civilized in approximately the same era and they have been able to blend their native genius with their acquired knowledge; among Russians, this blending has not yet been effected. Just as one sees rivers flow side by side without mingling their waters,[207] so nature and civilization come together in Russians without being identified with one another, and according to circumstances, the same man presents himself now as a European who seems composed of social manners alone, and now as a Slav who is prompted by the wildest passions alone. Genius will come to them in the arts and, above all, in literature when they have found the way to bring their true nature into language just as they demonstrate it in deeds.

I saw a Russian tragedy entitled *Dimitry Donskoj,* whose subject was the deliverance of the Russians when they pushed the Tartars back beyond Kazan.[208] The Prince of Smolensk and the Prince of Tver appeared in the ancient dress of the boyars, and the Tartar Army was called the *Golden Horde.* That name could well fit the Corsican Army and I saw the audience shudder at the performance of the play. It was written almost entirely according to the rules of French dramatic art; the rhythm of the verses, the declamation,[209] the way scenes were divided—everything was French. Only one single situation referred to Russian customs: a young girl's profound terror of her father's curse. Paternal authority is almost as strong in the Russian people as in China, and it is always to the people that one must look for the essence of national genius. Good company is alike in all countries, and nothing is less suited than this elegant world to furnish subjects for tragedy. Among all those offered by Russian history, one particularly struck me. Ivan the Terrible, already an old man, was laying siege to Novgorod. The boyars, seeing him weakened, asked if he did not want to give over command of the assault to his son. His rage at the proposal was so great that nothing could appease him. His son prostrated himself at his feet; he repelled him with so violent a kick that, two days later, the unfortunate man died. The despairing father, indifferent now to both war and power, survived his son by only a few months. In that despotic old man's revolt against nature's law, there is something grand and solemn, and the tenderness that follows the rage in that fierce soul portrays man as the Creator has made him, sometimes prodded by selfishness, sometimes conquered by affection.

One Russian law imposed the same punishment on the person who crippled the arm of a man as on the one who murdered him. The fact is that in Russia, military strength in particular constitutes manhood; all other forms of energy are related to customs and institutions that, in her present state, Russia has not yet developed. Women in Petersburg, however, seemed imbued with the patriotic honor that creates the moral power of a state. Princess Dolgorouky, Baroness Stroganoff, and several others of equally high rank,[210] already knew that part of their fortunes had sustained serious loss from the havoc wrought on the province of Smolensk, and they seemed to hold it of little account except to encourage their peers to sacrifice everything as they had done. Princess Dolgorouky told me that an old man with a long beard, seated on a hilltop overlooking Smolensk, his grandson on his knee, wept as he said: "In the old days, my child, Russians went to the ends of Europe reaping victories. Now foreigners come to attack them in their own country." That old man's sorrow was not in vain, and we shall soon see how well those tears were redeemed.

LEAVING FOR SWEDEN

Rumor spread through Petersburg that the Emperor had gone to Åbo,[211] where he was to see General Bernadotte, Crown Prince of Sweden. From that moment on, there was no further doubt on the course the Prince had resolved to take in the present war, and there was none more important then for the salvation of Russia and, consequently, for that of Europe. We shall see his influence grow as this narrative continues. News of the fall of Smolensk arrived during the meeting between the Prince of Sweden and the Emperor of Russia; there, Alexander pledged to himself and to his ally the Prince-General never to sign a treaty of peace.

"Were Petersburg taken, I would withdraw to Siberia. I would resume our old ways, and like our ancestors with their long beards, we would come back again to reconquer the Empire."

"That resolve shall set Europe free!" exclaimed the Prince of Sweden. And his prediction shall come to pass.

I saw Emperor Alexander for the second time on his return from Åbo, and the conversation it was my honor to have with him so convinced me of his firmness of will that, despite the fall of Moscow and all the ensuing rumors, I never believed he would yield. He was good enough to tell me that after the fall of Smolensk, General Berthier[212] had written to the Russian general with regard to a few military matters, and that he ended his letter saying that Emperor Napoleon still felt the most affectionate friendship for Emperor Alexander, a revolting mockery received by the Emperor of Russia exactly as it deserved. Napoleon had given him lessons on politics and lessons on war, tacitly assenting in the first to the imposture of vice, and in the second to the pleasure of showing scornful unconcern. He had misread the character of Emperor Alexander; he took the nobility of his character for credulity and was unable to perceive that, if the Emperor of Russia had let himself be carried too far by enthusiasm for him, Napoleon, it is because he thought him an advocate of the principles of the French Revolution, which are in accord with his own opinions. But it was never Alexander's idea to ally himself with Napoleon to enslave Europe. Napoleon believed, in this circumstance as in all others, that his false representations would surely blind a man with his own self-interest, but he met with conscience and his plans were all thwarted, for this is an element whose strength he does not know and that he never brings into his schemes.[213]

M. Barclay de Tolly was a very respected officer, but since he had suffered reverses at the beginning of the campaign,[214] opinion designated a highly renowned general to replace him: Prince Koutousoff. He was appointed fifteen days before Moscow fell, and managed to reach the army only six days before the great battle fought at the gates of that city, at Borodino.[215] I went to see him on the eve of his departure. He was an elderly gentleman with charming manners and a lively countenance, although he had lost an eye from the incredible wounds he had received over the fifty years of his military career. Nevertheless, looking at him, I feared he might be unequal to fighting the ruthless young men swooping down on Russia from the four corners of Europe. But while Russians are courtiers in Petersburg they become Tartars again in the army, and Souvoroff's example has shown that neither age nor honors can weaken their physical and moral energy. I was moved when I took leave of the illustrious Marshal Koutousoff; I did not know whether I was embracing a victor or a martyr, but I saw that he understood the full grandeur of the cause entrusted to him.[216] It was a question of defending, or rather of reestablishing, all the moral virtues man owes to Christianity, all the dignity he holds from God, all the independence permitted him by nature; it was a question of retrieving all these treasures from the claws of a single man, for the French must not be accused, any more than the Germans and the Italians who followed him, of the outrages of his armies. Providence meant all men to learn what the human race of the oppressors as of the oppressed would be like without religion.

Before he left, General Koutousoff went to pray in the Church of Kazan and all the people followed in his footsteps, crying out to him to save Russia. What a moment for a mortal being! His dedication cost him his life. But he found a certain sweetness in sacrificing it to the enthusiasm he felt. There are times when man must die to satisfy his soul.

Certain of the generous judgment and noble conduct of the Prince of Sweden, I was strengthened more than ever in the decision to have my sons return to their father's country by attaching them to the service of Sweden, and toward the end of September,[217] I left Petersburg to go on to Sweden by way of Finland. My new friends, those drawn close to me by empathy of feeling, came to bid me farewell: Sir Robert Wilson,[218] who goes everywhere seeking the chance to fight and to set souls ablaze with his spirit; M. de Stein, a man of the old school, who would not have lived had Germany not been free;[219] the Spanish envoy, Don Bermuda, working every day for his cause; the English Minister, the noble Lord Tyrconnel; the witty Admiral Bentinck;[220] Tettenborn, Prince Schwarzenberg's aide-de-camp,[221] who left him at the right moment and so had the good fortune to enter Hamburg; Alexis de Noailles,[222] tyranny's only French émigré, who was, like me, alone in testifying for France; Colonel Dörnberg, that bold Hessian whom nothing deterred from his goal; Arndt,[223] a German writer ever devoted to the good cause; and a number of Russians whose exploits have since made their names famous. Never had the world's cause faced more dangers; no one dared admit it to himself but everyone knew. I alone, as a woman, was not at risk, but I could count what I had suffered for something. As I bade farewell to those worthy knights of the human race, I did not know whom among them I would see again, and already, two of them are no longer alive.[224]

When men's passions rise up against one another, when nations attack one another in rage, people moan but they recognize human destiny in humanity's disasters. But when a single small being, hardened to life, callous of soul, like the idols to whom terror-struck Laplanders burn incense, spreads a deluge of catastrophe over the earth, we feel an indefinable dread that leads us to consider decent people as victims.

When you enter Finland,[225] everything proclaims that you have crossed into another country and that you are dealing with a race other than Slav. It is said that the Finns come directly from the north of Asia, and that their language is totally unrelated to that of the Swedes, which is almost entirely composed of English and German. Finnish faces, however, are entirely Germanic for the most part; their blond hair, their white complexions bear no resemblance to the liveliness of Russian faces, but their customs are also gentler. The common people show a deliberate probity that they owe to Protestant education and to purity of customs. On Sunday, you see the young girls come home from the sermon on horseback, followed by the young men. Hospitality is often found in the homes of Finland's pastors who consider it their duty to lodge travelers, and nothing is purer or sweeter than the welcome one meets in families. There are virtually no châteaux or great lords in Finland, so that pastors are ordinarily foremost among the country's inhabitants. There are Finnish songs in which girls offer to sacrifice the pastor's dwelling for their lover, even when it is offered to them as their portion. This brings to mind the words of a young shepherd: "If I were king, I would guard my sheep on horseback." Imagination itself scarcely goes beyond what one knows.

In Finland, nature's aspect is very different from that of Russia. Instead of the bogs and plains surrounding Petersburg, one comes upon boulders—well-nigh mountains—and forests, but in the long run one sees that the mountains are monotonous, the forests composed of the same trees—firs, pines, and birches. The enormous blocks of granite scattered in the countryside and beside the main roads lend a vigorous look to the landscape, but there is scant life around these great bones of the earth, and vegetation begins to decline from the latitude of Finland to the ultimate degree of life-giving earth. We crossed a forest half-consumed by fire; the north winds increase the potency of flames and the frequency of fires both in the cities and in the country. In every way, it is extremely hard for man to live in the Arctic zone.

One encounters few cities in Finland, and those are sparsely populated. There is no center, no stimulation, nothing to say, and very little to do in a northern province of Sweden or Russia, and for eight months of the year all living nature falls into sleep. The proportion of the country's population to its expanse differs so markedly between the North and the South that public opinion must necessarily be less intense in this country where men come upon one another intermittently, like inhabitants remaining behind from weariness or indolence at the time of the great migration of northern or southern peoples.

Emperor Alexander seized Finland after the Treaty of Tilsit and at a time when the clouded faculties of the reigning Swedish King, Gustavus IV,[226] made him totally unfit to defend his country. His moral character deserved respect, but even as a child he recognized himself that he could not hold the reins of government. The Swedes fought with the greatest courage in Finland, but without a warrior on the throne, a scantly populated nation could not triumph over its enemies. Emperor Alexander seized Finland by conquest and treaties based on force, but in all justice it must be said that he treated this new province as a sovereign who knows how to respect the liberty it once enjoyed. He left to the Finns all their privileges relative to levying taxes and troops. He was generous in coming to the aid of cities set on fire, and to a certain degree, his favors compensated for what the Finns possessed by right if, however, free men can voluntarily accede to this sort of exchange. Ultimately, the great idea of the century, natural borders, made Finland as necessary to Russia as Norway to Sweden, and it may be said in truth that wherever these natural borders do not exist, they have been the object of never-ending wars.

I embarked at Åbo, Finland's capital city.[227] There is a university in the city and they do make some effort to cultivate the mind; but with bears and wolves so close by in winter, all thought is absorbed in the need to ensure an endurable physical life, and the pains that must be taken for this purpose in northern countries consume a large part of the time devoted elsewhere to the pleasures of the arts and the mind. It may also be said that the very difficulties with which nature encircles men instill their character with greater firmness and close their minds to all the disorders caused by idleness. Nevertheless, I constantly felt the lack of the rays of the southern sun that had penetrated deeply into my soul.

The mythological ideas of the North's inhabitants endlessly portray specters and ghosts; daytime there is as propitious as night for apparitions. Something pale and clouded seems to call the dead back to earth, to breathe the air, cold as the tomb, that surrounds the living. In these lands, the two extremes are usually manifest rather than the intermediate degrees: one is either solely involved in conquering his life over nature, or the mind's labors readily become mystical because man draws everything from within and is in no way stirred by exterior objects.

Ever since I have been so cruelly persecuted by the Emperor, I have lost every form of confidence in fate; yet I believe all the more in the protection of Providence, but not in the guise of happiness on this earth. Thus it follows that, while all action frightens me, exile often compels one to resolve upon it. I was afraid of the sea and everyone told me: "Everybody crosses here. Nothing happens to anyone." Such words reassure almost all travelers, but imagination does not let itself be curbed by this kind of consolation, and when you are separated from this abyss by so frail an obstacle, it fills you with thoughts of all the likelihood of peril. M. Schlegel noticed the fear I suffered on the boat taking us to the ship. He pointed to the prison near Åbo, where one of Sweden's most unfortunate kings, Eric XIV, had been confined for some time before he died in another prison near Gripsholm.[228] "If you were there," he said, "how you would long to cross this sea that terrifies you now!" This sound reflection quickly set my thoughts on another course, and the first days of our sail were pleasant enough. We passed among the islands, and although there is far greater danger near the shore than on the open sea, one never feels the terror inspired by the sight of the waves meeting the sky. As we went on, I had them show me the land on the horizon from as far as I could glimpse it: infinity frightens our eyes as much as it pleases our souls. We passed Åland Island, where the plenipotentiaries of Peter I and Charles XII negotiated for peace[229] and tried to set limits to their ambition on this frozen earth, which, for a brief moment, the blood of their subjects alone had managed to warm. We expected to reach Stockholm the following day, but a decidedly adverse wind forced us to drop anchor off the coast of an island that was all rocks interspersed with a few trees standing scarcely higher than the stones out of which they grew. Still we hastened to take a walk on the island and feel solid earth underfoot.

I have always been quite prone to boredom, and far from knowing how to fill these completely empty moments that seem meant for study[230]

Appendix I

Auguste de Staël's Commentaries
as Editor of the 1821 Edition

Preface

The book that you are about to read does not constitute a finished work and should not be judged as one.[1] These are fragments of memoirs that my mother planned to complete in her leisure hours, and that would perhaps have undergone changes of a nature I do not know, had a longer span of life allowed her to revise and to conclude them. This reflection was enough for me to consider scrupulously whether I was justified in publishing them. No fear of any kind of responsibility may arise in the mind when our most cherished affections are concerned; but the heart is beset with painful anxiety when one is reduced to guessing wishes that, manifested, would be a sacred and immutable ruling. However, after serious reflection on what duty required of me, I was convinced that I had complied with my mother's intentions in pledging not to omit from this edition of her *Works* any text admitting of publication. My fidelity in honoring this pledge gives me the right to disavow in advance all that anyone might claim to add, at any time whatever, to a collection that, I repeat, includes everything whose publication my mother has not expressly forbidden.

The title, *Ten Years of Exile,* was chosen by the author herself; I was obliged to retain it even though the book, unfinished as it was, includes a period of only seven years. The story begins in 1800, that is, two years before my mother's first exile, and stops in 1804, after the death of M. Necker.[2] The narrative resumes in 1810,[3] and stops abruptly with my mother's arrival in Sweden in the fall of 1812.[4] Thus between the first and second parts of these memoirs there is a gap of almost six years. The explanation will be found in the faithful account of the way they were composed.

I shall not broach the story of my mother's persecution under the imperial government; that persecution, as petty as it was cruel, forms the object of the volume you are about to read, and whose interest I could only weaken. It suffices to recall that after they exiled her from Paris first, then expelled her from France after suppressing her book about *Germany*[5] on the most arbitrary whim, and made it impossible for her to publish anything—even on subjects entirely foreign to politics—they went so far as to make a prison of her home, forbid her every kind of travel, and take from her the pleasures of social life and the consolations of friendship. Such was my mother's situation when she began her memoirs, and her frame of mind in those days may well be imagined.

While this was being written, the hope of bringing it out one day was hardly foreseeable in the most distant future. Europe was still so bent under Napoleon's yoke that no independent voice could make itself heard: on the Continent the press was in chains, and the most rigorous measures excluded any writing printed in England. And so my mother thought less of composing a book than of preserving the trace of her memories and her thoughts. Even as she recounted her personal circumstances, she set down the various reflections prompted, from the beginnings of Bonaparte's power, by the state of France and the march of events. But if printing such a work then would have been an incredibly reckless act, the mere fact of writing it required a great deal of courage and caution, especially in my mother's position. She could not doubt that her every step was subject to police surveillance. The prefect who had replaced M. de Barante in Geneva[6] claimed to be informed of everything that went on in her home, and the slightest pretext sufficed for seizing her papers. The greatest precautions were therefore advisable, and so scarcely had she written a few pages than she had them transcribed by one of her closest friends, being careful to replace all proper nouns with names drawn from the history of the English revolution.[7] It was under this disguise that she took her manuscript with her in 1812 when she resolved on flight to escape increasingly severe measures.

Arriving in Sweden, after crossing Russia and just barely avoiding the armies advancing on Moscow, my mother attended to making a fair copy of this first part of her memoirs which, as I have said above, stop in the year 1804. But before going on in chronological order, she decided to take advantage of the moment when her memories were completely sharp to write the story of the remarkable circumstances of her flight, and of the persecution that had made it, if you will, a duty. Thus she resumed the story of her life in the year 1810, at the time her book about *Germany* was suppressed, and got as far as her arrival in Stockholm: hence the title *Ten Years of Exile.* This also explains why, in speaking of the imperial government, my mother sometimes speaks as though she were living under its power and at other times as if she had escaped it.

Ultimately, when she conceived the plan for her work on the *French Rev- olution,* she took from the first part of *Ten Years of Exile* the historical pas- sages and generalizations that fit her new framework, reserving the personal details for the time when she expected to complete the Memoirs of her life, and when she imagined she could name all the persons who had given her generous proof of friendship, without fear of compromising them with her expression of gratitude.

The manuscript entrusted to my care was thus composed of two distinct parts. The first, necessarily of less interest to the reader, included several pas- sages already incorporated in *Considerations on the French Revolution;* the other formed a kind of journal, no part of which was known as yet to the public.[8] I followed the path traced out by my mother, removing from the first part of her manuscript all the passages that, with slight modification, had already been placed in her great political work. This is the extent of my work as editor, and I have not ventured the slightest addition.[9]

As for the second part, I offer it to the public without any change what- ever, and I found it hard to make even slight corrections in style, so impor- tant did it seem to me to preserve for this draft all the vivacity of its original character. Readers will be convinced of my scrupulous respect for my mother's manuscript when they see the judgments she brings to bear on the political conduct of Russia; but without speaking of the power that gratitude exerts on noble souls, it will doubtless be recalled that the sovereign of Rus- sia was fighting then for the cause of independence and liberty. Was it possi- ble to foresee that in the course of so few years, the immense forces of this Empire would become instruments of oppression for unhappy Europe?[10]

If one compares *Ten Years of Exile* with *Considerations on the French Revo- lution,* one may find that the reign of Napoleon is judged with greater severity in the first of these writings, and that he is attacked with an elo- quence not always free of bitterness. The difference is easily explained: one of the works was written after the despot's fall, with a historian's compo- sure and impartiality; the other was inspired by a courageous sentiment of resistance to tyranny, and the imperial power was at its height when my mother composed it.

I have not chosen one moment rather than another to publish *Ten Years of Exile;* chronological order has been followed in this edition,[11] and the posthumous works naturally came at the end of the collection. Moreover, I have no fear of claims that it is ungenerous to publish attacks on Napoleon's power after his fall. She whose talent was always devoted to the defense of the noblest causes, she whose home was successively the refuge of the oppressed of all parties would be too far above such a reproach. It could, in any case, be addressed only to the editor of *Ten Years of Exile,* but I confess it would hardly affect me. We would accord despotism undue favor if, after imposing the silence of terror while he was triumphant, the despot could still ask history's forgiveness after his defeat.

No doubt memories of the former government have served as pretext for a great deal of persecution; no doubt decent people are revolted by the cowardly invective still ventured against those who, having enjoyed the favors of that government, have enough dignity not to disavow their past conduct; no doubt, in fact, fallen grandeur can captivate the imagination. But the issue is not simply the person of Napoleon, nor is it he who can be the object of reproof for generous souls today; nor is it those who under his reign served their country usefully in the different branches of public administration; what one cannot stigmatize too strongly is the system of egotism and oppression whose author is Bonaparte. Now, does this lamentable system not reign in Europe? Do the powerful of the earth not carefully reap the shameful heritage of the man they overthrew? And if we cast our eyes on our own country, how many of those instruments of Napoleon do we not see who, after wearying him with their servile compliance, come to offer their petty Machiavellianism to a new power? Does not the whole structure of their wretched knowledge rest today, as it did then, on vanity and corruption? And is it not from the traditions of the imperial regime that the counsel of their wisdom is drawn?

Thus in portraying that disastrous regime in the most vivid colors, a defeated enemy is not insulted; rather is a powerful adversary under attack, and if, as I hope, *Ten Years of Exile* is destined to increase the horror of arbitrary governments, I can indulge in the pleasant thought that, by publishing it, I serve the holy cause to which my mother was ever faithful.

FOREWORD TO PART TWO

There is a gap here, in my mother's manuscript that I have already explained[12] and that I would not know how to try to fill. But to enable the reader to follow my mother's story, I shall quickly review the main circumstances of her life during the five years separating the first part of these Memoirs from the second.

Returning to Switzerland after M. Necker's death, his daughter's primary need was the attempt to assuage her grief by drawing the portrait of the one she had just lost, and assembling the last traces of his thought. In the fall of 1804, she published her father's manuscripts with a preface on his character and private life.[13] My mother's health, weakened by unhappiness, obliged her to take the southern air. She left for Italy.[14] The beautiful Neopolitan sky, the reminders of Antiquity, the masterpieces of art opened sources of pleasure unknown to her until then. Her soul, weighed down with sorrow, seemed to revive with these new impressions, and she regained the strength to think and to write. During this journey my mother was treated without favor, but without injustice, by the diplomatic agents of France. She was forbidden to stay in Paris, she was separated from her friends and her accustomed ways; but then, at least, tyranny did not pursue her beyond the Alps; persecution was not yet systematic as it became later. I am pleased to recall that letters of recommendation, sent by Joseph Bonaparte to my mother, contributed to making her stay in Rome more agreeable.[15]

She returned from Italy in the summer of 1805 and spent a year, either at Coppet or in Geneva, where a number of her friends were gathered. During this time she began to write *Corinne*.

The following year her love of France, a feeling with such power over her heart, led her to leave Geneva and draw closer to Paris, at the distance of forty leagues allowed her. At the time I was studying for admission to the Ecole Polytechnique;[16] and, in her perfect goodness to her children, she wanted to supervise their education from as close-by as her exile permitted. Thus she went to settle in Auxerre, a small town where she knew no one, but whose prefect, M. de la Bergerie, was very obliging and tactful in his conduct toward her.[17]

From Auxerre she came to Rouen, thus drawing several leagues closer to the center of all the memories, all the affections of her childhood. There, at least, she could receive letters from Paris every day. She had penetrated, unimpeded, the area forbidden to her; she could hope that the fatal circle would progressively shrink. Only those who have suffered exile will understand what was unfolding within her heart. M. de Savoye-Rollin was then prefect of the Seine-Inférieure. It is known by what rank injustice he was dismissed several years later, and I have reason to believe that his friendship for my mother and the interest he showed her during her stay in Rouen were not irrelevant to his becoming the object of harsh measures.[18]

Fouché was Minister of Police. He had made it his system, as my mother says, to do the least harm possible, given the admitted goal. The Prussian monarchy had just succumbed;[19] no enemy on the Continent fought Napoleon any longer; no internal resistance blocked his advance, or could offer a pretext for arbitrary measures. What motive was there for sustaining the most gratuitous persecution against my mother? And so Fouché gave her permission to take up residence twelve leagues from Paris on an estate belonging to M. de Castellane.[20] There she completed *Corinne* and supervised its printing. Moreover, her secluded life on that estate, the extreme caution of her every move, the very small number of those undeterred from visiting her by fear of disfavor, should have sufficed to reassure the wariest despotism. But that was not enough for Bonaparte; he wanted my mother to give up all exercise of her talent, and refrain entirely from writing, even on subjects most foreign to politics. It will be seen that later this abnegation would not suffice to protect her from ever-increasing persecution.

Corinne had hardly come out[21] when a fresh exile began for my mother, and all the consoling hopes of the past few months vanished before her eyes. By an unhappy coincidence that made her grief the more bitter, it was on April 9, the very day of the anniversary of her father's death, that she was served with the order separating her from her native land and from her friends. Broken-hearted, she returned to Coppet, and the immense success of *Corinne* brought but little diversion from her sadness.

However, where literary glory was unable to help, friendship succeeded; and thanks to the proofs of affection she received on her return to Switzerland, summer went by more pleasantly than she could have hoped.[22] Some of her friends left Paris to visit her; and Prince Auguste of Prussia, restored to freedom by peace, paid us the honor of stopping at Coppet for several months, before returning to his country.[23]

After her trip to Berlin, so cruelly interrupted by her father's death, my mother had not suspended her study of German literature and philosophy, but she needed another stay in Germany to complete the portrait of that country which she planned to offer France. In the fall of 1807 she left for Vienna, where, in the company of the Prince de Ligne, Princess Lubomirska, etc., she found once more the urbane manners and the easy conversation she thought so charming. The Austrian government, exhausted by the war, did not have the strength to be an oppressor in its own right, and yet it retained an attitude toward France that was not without independence and dignity. Those pursued by Napoleon's hatred could still find refuge in Vienna; thus the year my mother spent there was the most tranquil she had enjoyed since her exile.[24]

When she returned to Switzerland, where she devoted two years to writing her reflections on Germany,[25] it did not take her long to observe the daily progress of the imperial tyranny, and the contagiously rapid spread of the passion for positions and the fear of disfavor. Without doubt, a few friends in Geneva and in France maintained courageous and constant fidelity to her in her misfortune; but all those who favored the government or aspired to employment began to keep their distance from her home, and to dissuade the timid from coming. My mother suffered from all these symptoms of servitude that she was incomparably astute at discerning. But the unhappier she was, the greater her need to spare those around her from the difficulties of her situation, and to spread in her circle the life, the intellectual activity that seemed to exclude solitude.

Her gift for the art of declamation was her own most powerful means of distraction, even as it varied the pleasures of her society. It was precisely then, as she worked on her great book about *Germany,* that she composed, and performed in the theater at Coppet, most of the playlets that I have collected in the sixteenth volume of her *Complete Works* under the title of *Dramatic Sketches.*[26]

At last, early in the summer of 1810, with the three volumes of *De l'Allemagne* complete, she decided to supervise the printing forty leagues from Paris, a distance still allowed her, and where she might hope to see those of her friends whose affection had not wavered in the face of the Emperor's disfavor.

And so she went to take up residence near Blois in the old château of Chaumont-sur-Loire, where Cardinal d'Amboise, Diane de Poitiers, Catherine de Médicis, and Nostradamus once lived. The present owner of this romantic abode, M. Le Ray, with whom my parents were connected by relations of business and friendship, was then in America. But he returned from the United States with his family while we were living in his château, and although he certainly urged us to stay, the more courteously he insisted, the more distressed we were by the fear of inconveniencing him. M. de Salaberry extricated us from this difficulty with the most amiable kindness by putting his estate of Fossé at our disposal. At this juncture, my mother's narrative resumes.

CONCLUSION

Here the manuscript breaks off.[27]

After a crossing that was not without danger, my mother landed safely in Stockholm. She spent eight months in Sweden, where she was welcomed with perfect kindness, and it was there that she wrote the journal you have just read. Shortly afterward she left for London, and there published her work on *Germany*,[28] which the imperial police had suppressed. But with her health already cruelly impaired by Bonaparte's persecution, and having suffered from the strain of a long journey, my mother felt obliged to undertake the story of M. Necker's political life, and to postpone all other work until she had completed the one commanded by daughterly affection. She then conceived the plan for *Considerations on the French Revolution*. She was unable to complete even this work, and the manuscript of her *Ten Years of Exile* has remained in her portfolio just as I publish it today.

Appendix II

THE DISGUISED MANUSCRIPTS DECODED

A SAMPLE

*Excerpts from unpublished memoirs from the time
of Queen Elizabeth of England drawn from a manuscript
in the Edinburgh library.*

ELIZABETH AND MARIE STEWART[1]

I was living on the quai in *Edinburgh* and my window was almost at street level. One morning, at one o'clock, I was told that *Lord Arundal* was at my window on horseback asking to speak with me. I was astonished by his visit at that hour. I hurriedly rose to go see him; he was a singularly graceful horseman and his emotion at that moment added to the nobility of his form.

"Do you know," he said," that *Marie Stewart* was *beheaded* at *Fotheringay* castle three days ago?"

"That's insane," I answered. "Don't you think it's a fairy tale circulated by the *English Queen's* enemies?"

"Those enemies," he told me, "are *she herself*. I shall send you the article from the *court newsletter* that begins with these words: '*Marie Stewart, commonly known as Queen of Scotland.*' I too am threatened," said *Lord Arundel*, "and all [of us] can expect the same fate one of these days." With those words he left, and his horse seemed to take from his master's noble indignation a kind of impetuous fervor that hurled him several months later into the ranks of the enemy. I stood there dumbfounded. I had observed in *Elizabeth's* character all that is most incompatible with generous natures, but so great a crime far exceeded any imaginable hatred.

Lord Arundel sent me *the newsletter,* and there I saw the article recounting the torture and execution *of the most illustrious queen of the Scottish monarchy* like that of a slave whose duty might not have been suitably performed. The *forty* men composing the tribunal that judged *her* were for the most part not from the noble classes, and it was said that this was meant as a kind of mockery. They began by announcing that they had no need to recuse themselves since they were not *Catholic.* Ah, I believe that is so! You were not of the same *religion,* you who condemned *her* to that unjust execution by order of the *woman* who understood the secret of your characters and who knew so well how to transform your military courage into political cowardice. The *woman* known as *Marie Stewart* called *herself Queen of Scotland, when Brantôme portrayed her at the head of her troops, beautiful and generous like a second Zenobia.*[2] And you *Englishmen,*[3] you allow the descendant of *Henry VII to be designated* as an unknown *woman.* This victim was innocent not only in the eyes of the nation, but in the very eyes of those who murdered *her,* for [*she* was] solely concerned with the desire to *succeed Elizabeth, and not to overthrow her.* Among *her* papers were found only expressions of respect for the talents of the *woman* who, after a captivity *of nineteen years,* sentenced *her* to die on *the scaffold.*[4] On the eve of the so-called trial of the *Queen of Scotland, Lord Drury*[5] sent for *a man to make a coffin in the room beneath the one occupied by Marie Stewart;* he measured the length, etc., and since then he has told the story as a proof of his vigor. I heard it from the very man whom he considered it appropriate to tell. It might be imagined that there are few *Drurys* in *England,* but even at the time of Marie Stewart's trial, a young man from a noble family[6] said: "Good Lord! I'm glad I was away when that tribunal of nobles was convened. After all, I could have been called and I would have been obliged to judge exactly like the others."

BONAPARTE AND THE DUKE D'ENGHIEN

I was living on the quai in *Berlin* and my window was almost at street level. One morning at one o'clock, I was told that *Prince Louis* was at my window on horseback asking to speak with me. I was astonished by his visit at that hour. I hurriedly rose to go see him; he was a singularly graceful horseman and his emotion at that moment added to the nobility of his form.

"Do you know," he said, "that *the Duke d'Enghien* was *shot* at the château of *Vincennes* three days ago?"

"That's insane," I answered. "Don't you think it's a fairy tale circulated by the *First Consul's* enemies?"

"Those enemies," he told me, "are him*self*. I shall send you the article from the *Moniteur* that begins with these words: *'Louis Antoine Henri de Bourbon, commonly known as the Duke d'Enghien.'* I too am threatened," said *Prince Louis*, "and all [of us] can expect the same fate one of these days." With those words he left, and his horse seemed to take from his master's noble indignation a kind of impetuous fervor that, a few months later, hurled him into the ranks of the enemy. I stood there dumb-founded. I had observed in *Bonaparte's* character all that is most incompatible with generous natures, but so great a crime far exceeded any imaginable hatred.

Prince Louis sent me the *Moniteur,* and there I saw the article recounting the torture and execution of *the Duke d'Enghien* like that of a slave whose duty might not have been suitably performed. The *seven* men composing the tribunal that judged *him* were for the most part not from the noble classes, and it was said that this was meant as a kind of mockery. They began by announcing that they had no need to recuse themselves since they were not *related to the accused*. Ah, I believe that is so! You were not of the same *family,* you who condemned *him* to that unjust execution by order of the *man* who understood the secret of your characters and who knew so well how to transform your military courage into political cowardice. The *man* known as *Louis de Bourbon* called *himself Duke d'Enghien*. And you, *Frenchmen,* you allow the descendant of *the Grand Condé* to be designated as an unknown *man*. This victim was innocent not only in the eyes of the nation, but in the very eyes of those who murdered *him,* for [*he* was] solely concerned with the desire to *praise Bonaparte* and not to overthrow *him*. Among *his* papers were found only expressions of respect for the talents of the person who, after *having him kidnapped,* sentenced *him* to be *shot* to death. On the eve of the so-called trial of the Duke d'Enghien, *General Savary* sent for a *gardener who dug the grave in a ditch* [*under the walls of the château* crossed out]; he measured the length, etc., and since then he has told the story as a proof of his vigor. I heard it from the very man he considered it appropriate to tell. It might be imagined that there are few *Savarys* in *France,* but even at the time of *the Duke d'Enghien's* trial, a young man from a noble family said: "Good Lord! I'm glad I was away when that tribunal of nobles was convened. After all, I could have been called and I would have been obliged to judge exactly like the others."

Notes

The following abbreviations are used in the notes:

Carnets   Simone Balayé, *Les Carnets de voyage de Madame de Staël* (Geneva: Droz, 1971)

C.G.   Mme de Staël, *Correspondance générale,* ed. Béatrice Jasinski (Paris: J. J. Pauvert, then Hachette, then Klinckieck, 1960 ff.)

Considérations   Mme de Staël, *Considérations sur la Révolution française,* ed. Jacques Godechot (Paris: Tallandier, 1983)

[Trans]   Translator's note; all others are by Simone Balayé

INTRODUCTION

1. Letter to Mme de Berg, London, May 5, 1814 (A. Goetz, "Sechs unveröffentliche Briefe der Frau von Staël an Frau von Berg und Gräfin Voss," *Archiv fur das Studium der neueren Sprachen und Literaturen* 202 [June 1965], p. 51).

2. *Considérations,* pt. 4, chap. 8.

3. This paragraph and the next are largely based on Avriel Goldberger's introduction to her translation of Mme de Staël's *Delphine* (DeKalb: Northern Illinois University Press, 1995), p. xviii [Trans].

4. When Albertine Necker de Saussure "complimented her on her daughter's distinction of mind," [Mme Necker replied]: "It is nothing, absolutely nothing, next to what I wished to make of her" (Madelyn Gutwirth, *Madame de Staël, Novelist: The Emergence of the Artist as Woman* [Urbana: University of Illinois Press, 1978], p. 35) [Trans].

5. M. Gutwirth, *Madame de Staël, Novelist,* p. 77 [Trans].

6. Quoted by Ghislain de Diesbach, *Madame de Staël* (Paris: Librairie Académique Perrin, 1983), p. 19 [Trans].

7. Quoted by Simone Balayé in draft sections of the biography she is preparing and has kindly lent to me [Trans].

8. On September 21, the deputies to the new National Convention declared royalty abolished. On September 22, they proclaimed the First Republic.

The National Convention replaced the National Assembly and governed France from September 21, 1792, to October 26, 1795. Controlled increasingly by its extremist members, the Jacobins, it voted on January 17, 1793, to execute the King. It declared war on England and Holland on February 1, and created the Revolutionary Tribunal and the Committee of Public Safety on April 6, launching the infamous Reign of Terror. Just over a year later, on July 22, 1794—Thermidor 9th—the so-called Thermidorean reaction to the Terror began. Robespierre and Saint-Just were executed, and the Jacobins were hunted down. In 1795, under the Constitution of the Year III, the Convention was replaced with a legislative body composed of the Council of Five Hundred and the Council of the Ancients and with an executive branch that gave the government its name: the Directory. The Directory consisted of five directors, each to serve in turn as the presiding officer for three months [Trans].

9. Mme de Staël's nationality poses a problem. Genevan by birth to Swiss parents, Swedish by marriage, she was French only by virtue of her birth on French soil. She could have been recognized as French, and she tried repeatedly to achieve this status officially. However, her enemies, including Napoleon, found it convenient to maintain her classification as foreign since this allowed them to expel her from France as often as they wished, and they very often so wished.

10. Auguste was born on July 14, 1790. Albert was born on November 20, 1792. She broke with Narbonne in July 1794 [Trans].

11. Margaret Anne Doody, *Frances Burney: The Life in the Works* (New Brunswick, N. J.: Rutgers University Press, 1988), p. 410 n.1 [Trans].

12. Avriel Goldberger's introduction to her translation of Mme de Staël's novel *Delphine* (DeKalb: Northern Illinois University Press, 1995), p. xxii [Trans].

13. Simone Balayé, *Madame de Staël, Lumières et liberté* (Paris: Klincksieck, 1979), p. 226. Quoted from Stendhal, *Rome, Naples et Florence* [Trans].

14. Baron de Staël died in March 1802 [Trans].

15. Health was only part of Browning's motivation, and her narrative poem *Aurora Leigh* is modeled on the novel. Men too were influenced, as can be seen in Walter Scott's *Waverly Novels* and Nathaniel Hawthorne's *Marble Faun* [Trans].

16. The astonishing extent of police surveillance of Mme de Staël under the Revolution and the Empire has been fully documented in an issue of *Cahiers staëliens*, prepared by Simone Balayé and Norman King and devoted exclusively to the subject. It shows the aptness of the word "prisoner" here and documents the examples given in the next paragraph (*Cahiers staëliens* 44 [1992–1993]) [Trans].

17. Simone Balayé and Norman King, "Madame de Staël et les polices françaises sous la Révolution et l'Empire," *Cahiers staëliens* 19 (December 1974), pp. 105–7.

18. John Isbell has written an informative essay on the little-known memoir and shows how it reveals Rocca's essentially romantic temperament. "Espagne ro-

mantique et résistance nationale: John Rocca, Mme de Staël et *Les Mémoires sur la guerre des Français en Espagne,*" in *C'est la faute à Voltaire, c'est la faute à Rousseau,* Recueil anniversaire pour Jean-Daniel Candaux, ed. Roger Durand (Geneva: Droz, 1997), pp. 197–206 [Trans].

19. This statement is based on audience reaction to the translation of *La Signora Fantastici*—performed at Rutgers University in 1988 for the conference on Mme de Staël and at Hofstra University in 1990, where it was staged for an audience of faculty, students, and people from the community—and to scenes from *Captain Quarterdec* (a translation of *Le Capitaine Kernadec*), performed in 1990 at the Santa Cruz conference on "Translating for Performance." Both plays were translated by Avriel Goldberger [Trans].

20. "Textes de présentation d'Auguste de Staël," in Mme de Staël, *Dix années d'exil,* ed. Simone Balayé and Mariella Bonifacio (Paris: Fayard, 1996), pp. 524–25.

21. On March 17, 1809, she wrote to Prince Charles de Schwarzenberg, whom she had met in Vienna a year earlier, asking for information on going to England via Riga or Saint Petersburg: "A family very close to me would like to make the journey, and I take the liberty of asking if you might use your influence to make it possible" ("Histoire de l'oeuvre," in Staël, *Dix années d'exil,* ed. Balayé and Bonifacio, p. 14 n.2).

22. Police reports and Capelle's letter are evidence of these efforts [Trans].

23. When I asked a present-day member of her family how she paid the day-to-day expenses of the trip across Europe, he replied with the trace of a smile: "She was not a banker's daughter for nothing." In point of fact, she was what we would call an excellent business woman today. Moreover, not only did she make use of bank drafts throughout the journey, she also used banks to leave letters for transmission to those at home and to pick up correspondence from them [Trans].

24. This paragraph is based on material in S. Balayé's draft biography [Trans].

25. Baby Alphonse Rocca was placed in the care of the pastor of a Vaud mountain village.

26. This is true wherever she can rely on her own observation, on the accuracy of what she is told and what she reads. Readers aware of her open-mindedness—in *Corinne,* for example, she explicitly includes Jews—will be surprised by what she says about them in the account of the journey through Galicia and Poland. The only Jewish people she saw there crowded travelers at frontier posts to change money. She had no sources to inform her about the extremely severe limits imposed on what they were allowed to do in order to survive (for example, the interdict on owning property) [Trans].

27. Although they were there on official business they did not have official status as their country's emissaries, since relations between the two countries were not yet regularized [Trans].

28. Not until 1834 when Count Adolphe de Custine wrote his work on Russia was a book of the quality of hers written on the subject.

29. *Madame de Staël, ses amis, ses correspondants: Choix de Lettres,* ed. Georges Solovieff (Paris: Klincksieck, 1970), pp. 495–437 n.395 [Trans].

30. P. Zaborov, "Mme de Staël et ses correspondants russes," *Cahiers staëliens* 13 (1971), p. 16. She does not mention that she is already working on such a project.

31. Her son Auguste de Staël and her son-in-law, Victor de Broglie, prepared and published *Considérations* in 1818, a year after her death.

32. S. Balayé, "La Bibliothèque de Mme de Staël: Les livres sur la Suède et l'Europe orientale," *Cahiers staëliens* 11 (December 1970), pp. 48–54.

33. Claude Hochet, Benjamin Constant, and Madame de Staël, *Lettres à un ami,* ed. Jean Mistler (Neuchâtel: La Baconnière, 1949), p. 226. She mentioned the embryonic book again in *Considérations,* pt. 4, chap. 19.

34. Zaborov, p. 16.

35. John Rocca died on January 30, 1818, six months after his wife.

36. See S. Balayé, "Le deuxième voyage en Italie," chap. 6 of *Carnets.*

37. Unprecedented also was the Protestant chapel Victor had built for his wife on his family estate. From the union of these two remarkable people has come a long and distinguished line of writers, statesmen, mathematicians, and physicists—one of whom, Louis Duke de Broglie, won the Nobel Prize in 1929 [Trans].

38. "De l'esprit des traductions" was published in *Biblioteca italiana* under the patronage of the normally astute Austrian Count Saurau. It did not occur to him that translation, by its nature, is a political act. For example, in the sixteenth century, Protestant and Catholic Bible translators risked death at the stake for the smallest error real or supposed; more recently, translators of Salmon Rushdie have been attacked, one fatally.

39. Although the ruling junta has changed Burma's name to Myanmar, Suu Kyi insists on Burma, which is retained here in deference to her courage.

40. Mme de Staël's will was published in 1916 in Pierre Kohler's *Madame de Staël et la Suisse* (Lausanne-Paris: Payot, 1916), pp. 672–75. Auguste, Albertine, and August Schlegel worked together on the forewords to the complete works of the author and her father.

41. In 1903 he published his *Madame de Staël and Napoléon.*

42. The problems confronting the editors were delicate, and the process of solving them was arduous. One measure of the editors' success is the prestigious Louis Barthou medal of achievement in the field of history, awarded to them for their work by the French Academy in 1997.

43. There are also notes ("mémentos") that Mme de Staël wrote on the manuscripts themselves and in travel notebooks; a necessary part of the critical edition, they are referred to only in notes in the present book.

44. N. King and J.-D. Candaux, "La Correspondance de Benjamin Constant et de Sismondi, 1801–1830," *Annales Benjamin Constant* 1 (1980), p. 34.

45. The letter is dated May 5 (*Lettres à un ami,* p. 211).

46. See Auguste de Staël's preface in Appendix I. It is because Auguste used

the word "disguised" that the term "disguised manuscripts" has been adopted here.

47. Carl Gustav von Brinkman, "Lettre sur l'auteur de *Corinne*," ed. Simone Balayé, *Cahiers staëliens* 39 (1987–1988), p. 156.

PART ONE: 1797–1804

1. This point will be called to mind in *Considérations*, pt. 3, chap. 16: "On the Government Called the Reign of Terror."

2. The future *Considérations*, pt. 1, chap. 4, "On the Character of M. Necker as a Public Man."

3. Here Mme de Staël begins a violent attack on the Directory, which she examines in several chapters of *Considérations* (see pt. 3, chaps. 11, 24, and 25).

4. Mme de Staël deals with this subject in *Considérations* (pt. 3, chap. 23, "On the Army of Italy," and chap. 26, "The Treaty of Campo Formio"). During the Italian Campaign she is said to have written Bonaparte a few letters "highly intelligent, fervent, and metaphysical," which the general interpreted as love letters (Count Emmanuel de Las Cases, *Mémorial de Sainte-Hélène*, ed. Marcel Dunan, vol. 1 [Paris: Flammarion, 1983], p. 358 [hereafter cited as *Mémorial*]). See the introduction for discussion of how Mme de Staël's view of Napoleon evolved.

5. Mme de Staël first met Bonaparte in the home of Talleyrand, then in charge of foreign relations. The general had arrived from Italy on December 5, 1797; the minister received him at eleven o'clock the following morning and invited Mme de Staël (see Jean Tulard and Louis Garros, *Itinéraire de Napoléon au jour le jour, 1769-1821* [Paris: Tallandier, 1992], p. 104; *Mémoires du prince de Talleyrand*, ed. Duke de Broglie, vol. 1 [Paris: Calmann-Lévy, 1892], p. 259; and *Considérations*, pt. 3, chap. 26). In *Considérations*, Mme de Staël adds: "I was young then [thirty-three], which can excuse my emotion, but it was so strong that I found no words to answer him when he came to tell me that he had looked for my father at Coppet and regretted crossing Switzerland without seeing him."

6. This expression appears in *On Germany*: "If the objects we see and the beings whom we love are nothing but the product of our ideas, then man himself may be considered the world's great celibate.'" She borrowed it from Chateaubriand (*Le Génie du Christianisme*, 1st edition (1802), t. 1, p. 270). Faced with controversy over the expression, Chateaubriand removed it for the next edition.

7. Mme de Staël is not alone in emphasizing this vulgarity as it can be felt by a society, like that of the eighteenth century, which prizes good manners. For example, at the grand reception held for Bonaparte by Talleyrand, he is said to have replied to Mme de Staël's question: "General, what kind of woman has the greatest merit?" with "Madame, the one who has the most children" (*Mémorial*, vol. 2, p. 189). In his memoirs, Chateaubriand says that women did not like Bonaparte and that he was not well-bred (*Mémoires d'outre-tombe*, ed. Maurice Levaillant and Georges Moulinier [Paris: Gallimard, 1946–1951], vol. 5, pp. 54–55; and *Mémoires d'outre-tombe*, 2d ed.,

ed. Jean-Claude Berchet [Paris: Bordas, 1989–1992], vol. 2, p. 380).

8. The scene is a reception given by the Minister of the Interior, Charles Louis François Honoré Le Tourneur (1751–1817), former member of the Legislative Assembly, the Convention, and the Council of Ancients. He was Minister of the Interior from September 1797 to July 1798.

9. Emmanuel Joseph Sieyès (1748–1836) was long a friend of Mme de Staël's. As a deputy of the Third Estate he played a major role in transforming the Estates General into the National Assembly in June 1789. He favored a constitutional monarchy but as a member of the Convention he voted for the execution of Louis XVI. As a member of the Directory he helped Bonaparte effect the coup of 18 Brumaire, and helped write the constitution of the year VIII (1790), which Bonaparte would quickly modify for his own ends.

10. Mme de Staël had known Dominique Joseph Garat (1749–1833) for a long time; a lawyer and man of letters, he was friend of the Neckers from before the Revolution. Active in politics from 1789 on, he supported the coup of 18 Brumaire and became a senator in 1800. He kept Mme de Staël informed of the First Consul's attitude toward her and tried to help her (C. G., vol. 5, no. 2, p. 545).

11. This took place at the same dinner with Sieyès. The woman referred to is Sophie Condorcet (1764–1822).

12. The French generals plundered Bern's treasury. Out of ten million francs, three million were used to finance the Egyptian Expedition. The plan was also to create a Helvetic Republic to protect French borders (Jacques Godechot, Les Commissaires aux armées sous le Directoire, vol. 2 [Paris: Presses universitaires de France, 1941], pp. 57–65, 126–31).

13. Armand Jean du Plessis, Cardinal, Duke de Richelieu (1585–1642), was the de facto ruler of France from 1624 until his death, during the reign of Louis XIII. He spent only a few months in Rome in 1607. The Cardinal is one of the main characters in Mme de Staël's very early tragedy, Montmorency. Giulio Mazarini, Cardinal Mazarin (born in 1602 in Italy, died in 1661). He ruled France during the minority of Louis XIV. Catherine de Medicis was the Italian-born wife of Henri II, mother to a succession of ineffective short-lived kings, and thought responsible for the Saint Bartholomew Day Massacre of Protestants in August 1572.

14. Venice was ceded by the Treaty of Campo Formio, October 17, 1797, in exchange for the left bank of the Rhine (Georges Lefebvre, Le Directoire [Paris: A. Colin, 1958], p. 92).

15. The advice was probably given during a secret meeting he had with envoys of the Republic of Genoa on the eve of signing a secret agreement with Genoa in Montebello on June 6, 1797.

16. Between 1762 and 1763, a Scottish man of letters, James MacPherson (1736–1796) published what he said were translations from the Gaelic of epic poems by the bard Ossian. They were immensely popular and much imitated in all of pre-Romantic Europe. "Their wild, romantic qualities served to emphasize Mme de Staël's distinction between les littératures du Nord and du Midi." Only much later

was it discovered that they were a hoax (*Oxford Companion to French Literature* [1959], p. 531).

17. A field for military exercises in Paris.

18. Bonaparte, named commander-in-chief of the Army of England, showed little enthusiasm for the projected invasion. On February 8, 1798, he left for Dunkerque, Boulogne, Calais, Ostend, and Brussels. He returned on February 20 convinced that the invasion could not succeed as he reported to the Directory on February 23 (Tulard and Garros, pp. 108ff.).

19. Bernadotte was sent to Vienna in January 1797 and stayed until April 15. Talleyrand and Bonaparte criticized him severely and unjustly to the Directory. Diplomatic relations with Austria bordered on a break (T. T. Höjer, *Bernadotte, maréchal de France,* tr. Lucien Maury [Paris: Plon, 1943], pp. 106 ff.). Charles Jean Baptiste Jules Bernadotte (1763–1844) became a general in 1794. He refused to participate in the coup of 18 Brumaire, although he was Joseph Bonaparte's brother-in-law, and so won the admiration of the Republicans. Despite his cautious opposition, he was named marshal in 1804 and Prince of Ponte Corvo in 1805. On August 21, 1810, the Diet of Orebo elected him Prince and heir to the Swedish throne.

Paul Jean François Nicolas, vicomte de Barras (1755–1829), was present at the fall of the Bastille, voted for the abolition of the monarchy and the death of Louis XVI in 1792, was a member of the Committee of Public Safety, helped to overthrow Robespierre, and was a Director. During that time he took under his wing the young General Bonaparte who married Barras' former mistress, Josephine de Beauharnais. When his protégé became First Consul he retired permanently from public life (*Oxford Companion to French Literature,* p. 49).

20. Barras probably described the scene, which took place around January 4, to Mme de Staël the following day. The anecdote is also found in his *Mémoires* (quoted by Louis Garros, *Itinéraire de Napoléon au jour le jour, 1769–1821* [Paris: Editions de l'Encyclopédie française, 1947], p. 124).

21. Charles Pierre François Augereau, a general who came out of the Revolution, had fought in the Italian Campaign. Bonaparte had him appointed commandant of the Paris military division and he took part in the coup of 18 Fructidor (September 4, 1797) against the Royalists, who had become a threat. Hostile at first to the coup of 18 Brumaire, he rallied to the Consulate and was named marshal in 1804. A chapter in *Considérations* is devoted to him: "On the Introduction of Military Government in France by the Eighteenth of Fructidor" (pt. 3, chap. 28).

22. She left Paris between January 6 and 8, 1798. General Ménard invaded the Vaud on January 27. Necker was wrongfully considered an émigré since he was not French and had left France in September 1790, with authorization from the Constituent Assembly. Mme de Staël had won his provisional elimination from the list on July 20, 1797. Her children Auguste and Albert were seven and five; Albertine was eighteen months old.

Gabriel Suchet (1770–1826) was on the staff of General Brune when

French troops entered Switzerland. He became a general that same year, fought in numerous campaigns, including the war in Spain, and was named marshal in 1811 and Duke d'Albufera.

French troops entered Switzerland during the night of January 25, 1798. On January 22 Mme de Staël was still writing to Barras to save Switzerland from invasion (*C.G.,* vol. 4, no. 1, pp. 111–13). Troops reached Coppet on January 27. Geneva was occupied on April 24, 1798, and its annexation voted by an extraordinary commission on January 26. It became the Department of the Léman in the summer of 1798.

23. Allusion to Leonidas I, King of Sparta, who fought Xerxes at Thermopylae in 480 B.C. with four thousand men.

24. In fact, only the mountain cantons responded (see Ernest Fischer, *Histoire de la Suisse des origines à nos jours* [Paris: Payot, 1946], pp. 307–8). The Bern government itself was divided on the issue, and on March 4 the troops from the small cantons withdrew. Bern fell on March 5, 1798.

25. The cantons of Uri, Schwyz, Glarus, and Zug refused to accept the constitution France meant to impose. They were defeated on May 3 at Morgarten, near the lake of the Four Cantons, but remained restive (Jacques Godechot, *La Grande Nation, l'expansion révolutionnaire de la France dans le monde de 1789 à 1799,* 2d ed. [Paris: Aubier-Montaigne, 1983], pp. 198–200; A. Rufer, *La Suisse et la Révolution française* [Paris: 1974], pp. 78–80; Fischer, p. 312). "Freedom of the seas" alludes to the British blockade of the continent.

26. On September 9, 1798, the people of Nidwalden defended themselves against French troops, inflicting heavy losses. The victors "pitilessly killed and burned even the tiniest hamlet"; 712 buildings burned down, 386 people perished, one-third of whom were women and children (Fischer, p. 314).

27. As early as 1776, Necker advocated suppression of feudal rights and other privileges on condition that the privileged be indemnified and pay taxes like everyone else. Thus he was not prepared to give up his own rights without a quid pro quo (*Considérations,* pt. 1, chap. 4). Like him, Mme de Staël planned to have the tithes and ground rents declared redeemable (Kohler, p. 237).

28. On October 21, 1776, Necker became Deputy Director of Finance. Three years later he became the first Director-General of Finance, and served from June 29, 1777 to May 19, 1781. Recalled on August 25, 1788, he retained the post until July 11, 1789, was recalled once more on July 29, and resigned on September 4, 1790. Merlin de Douai and Treilhard were both jurists and former members of the Convention. The vote took place on July 31, 1798.

29. Béatrice Jasinski has clarified the matter of the loan of two million often mentioned in this text (*C.G.,* vol. 1, no. 1, pp. XVI–XIX). In 1777 Necker deposited 2.4 million *livres* in the Treasury, approximately half his fortune, in the form of a loan at 5 percent interest. He withdrew 400,000 *livres* in September 1790 when he left France, leaving the remainder in guarantee of his administration until his accounts were audited. Interest was paid until May of 1793, and Necker had no fur-

ther income from this money that Napoleon refused to return. The money was not reimbursed until the Second Restoration, and even then not fully.

30. This famous banking house, founded in the eighteenth century in Amsterdam and Rotterdam, conducted a great deal of business between France, the United States, and various European countries, even under the Empire.

31. The coup d'état of 18 Fructidor (September 4, 1797).

32. This "harem revolution" took place on 28 Prairial (June 16), 1799.

33. Jean Victor Moreau (1763–1813), promoted to general in 1793, conquered Holland in 1796 on orders from Pichegru. He had close ties with Mme de Staël, and would later join the opposition to Bonaparte. The use of the present tense here shows that he was still alive when this was written. He was killed in the Battle of Dresden in August 1813, fighting with the allied armies. Charles Pichegru (1761–1804) had fought in the American War of Independence, had a fine military career during the Revolution, and had been one of the most popular generals. For Bernadotte, see note 19 above.

34. Lucien became a deputy. Supported by the left, he moved toward the moderates and grew wealthy during his ambassadorship to Spain. Joseph became established in society, surrounding himself with liberals (Louis Madelin, *Histoire du Consulat et de l'Empire,* vol. 4, [Paris: Hachette, 1937–1954], p. 96). Each man had his coterie. Mme de Staël knew them well and later had occasion to show the fidelity of her friendship when they were no longer in a position to help her. News from France reached Bonaparte, who had lost in the Syrian Campaign after defeating the Turks at Aboukir, July 25–27, 1797.

35. He was elected to the Institute on December 25, 1797 in the area of science and mathematics. If Bonaparte expressed his respect for Islam to the Mufti at the pyramid of Cheops, he never declared his intention of converting. He received newspapers and letters again on August 10, but it is quite unlikely that his decision to return was precipitous (Tulard and Garros, pp. 129–30). He embarked during the night of August 22–23 (ibid., p. 130).

36. The Jacobins had made great advances in the year VII; they began to frighten people and create disturbances in the streets (Albert Vandal, *Napoléon et Alexandre Ier, l'alliance russe sous le Premier Empire,* vol. 1 [Paris: Plon, 1894–1897], pp. 103 ff.). This led to the day of 27 Fructidor (September 13) when Sieyès skillfully thwarted their machinations.

37. Bernadotte was Minister of War from July 2 to September 14, 1797. Sieyès forced him to resign after the day of 27 Fructidor (September 13) when the Jacobins offered him "authority" were he to intervene on their behalf (Lefebvre, *Le Directoire,* pp. 181–82). Vandal says that he showed "remarkable qualities of intelligence and diligence, but the situation was insurmountably chaotic (*L'Avènement de Bonaparte,* vol. 1 [Paris: Plon, 1903], p. 97).

38. A port in the south of France. He landed on October 9 at noon (Tulard and Garros, p. 132).

39. The people along the coast said: "We prefer the plague to the Austrians" (Vandal, *L'Avènement*, vol. 1, p. 238).

40. Jean François Reubell (often spelled Rewbell) (1747–1807), deputy to the Estates General and then to the Convention, and Director from November 1795 to May 1799. He collaborated with Bonaparte in revolutionizing Switzerland in 1798. He unsuccessfully tried to prevent the Egyptian Campaign and himself relates that when Bonaparte threatened to resign, he handed him the pen. Barras and François de Neufchâteau intervened.

41. Bonaparte went through Lyons on October 13, 1797, reaching Paris on the sixteenth.

42. On October 15 she wrote to Meister: "it is a great event and, what is more, this man is worth a whole army. His destiny is invincible" (*C.G.*, vol. 4, no. 1, p. 243). At the time, she believed that he came to support the Republic. On October 24, preparing to leave for Paris, she wrote to Pierre de Rochemont: "What shall I tell the hero on your behalf? The Republic is saved" (*C.G.*, vol. 4, no. 1, pp. 244–45).

43. It was truly a coincidence. Her letters show the date of her departure had been set several weeks earlier (*C.G.*, vol. 4, no. 1, p. 246). .

44. Along with Gohier, he had been kept out of the plot. He signed his resignation at noon on the eighteenth, certainly for a price (Vandal, *L'Avènement*, vol. 1, p. 325), and asked to leave for Grosbois. Bonaparte sent a hundred dragoons to keep him under surveillance (ibid., pp. 325–27).

45. The woman is unidentified, but her plight was a common phenomenon.

46. Allusion to 18 Fructidor (September 4, 1797).

47. Allusion to Bernadotte's future role: in 1812 he became Napoleon's enemy and the ally of Russia and England. Bonaparte met him on 6 Brumaire—October 28 (Tulard and Garros, p. 134) and exaggerated the country's ills. Looking him straight in the eye Bernadotte said: "I do not despair of the Republic and I am convinced that it will resist its enemies from within and from without" (Vandal, *L'Avènement*, vol. 1, p. 306; Höjer, p. 191). Mme de Staël does not point out here that most of the generals rallied to Bonaparte, including Moreau, who was angry with the Directory.

48. Section 5, article 102 of the Constitution of the Year III. The Legislative Body consisted of two councils: The Council of Ancients and the Council of Five Hundred.

49. This was one of the most important phases of the plot to isolate the Assemblies outside of Paris. The most hostile Ancients were not notified (Vandal, *L'Avènement*, vol. 1, pp. 300–301). The decree passed without difficulty. Its execution was confided to Bonaparte, whom the Council of Ancients placed in command of troops in Paris for the task (ibid., p. 303). Mme de Staël forgets to point out that the decision was illegal since this was the prerogative of the Directory, according to section 5, articles 144–45 of the Constitution of the year III (Georges Lefebvre, *La France sous le Directoire, 1795–1799* [Paris: Editions sociales, 1983], p. 725).

50. The friend was Constant, who writes in his "Souvenirs historiques": "The morning of the eighteenth [*sic* for nineteenth], rather a spectator than an accomplice, I ran to Saint Cloud not without uncertainty and sorrow, and I watched as representative government collapsed for fourteen years."

51. Barthélemy Aréna, Corsican deputy to the Five Hundred, would be wrongly accused of having tried to assassinate Bonaparte (Vandal, *L'Avènement,* vol. 1, p. 374). It was Deputy Destren's heavy hand that fell on his shoulder. The dagger is a myth.

52. Mme de Staël minimizes Lucien's decisive role. On horseback he harangued the soldiers along with his brother, denouncing the seditious deputies (Vandal, *L'Avènement,* vol. 1, pp. 375–76).

53. The word "senatorial" is inexact since there were no senators.

54. Actually, as she said above, she was afraid of a Jacobin return. She does not include all the details of this fateful day; in particular, she does not mention the Assembly's nomination of three provisional consuls: Bonaparte, Sieyès, and Roger Ducos (see Vandal, *L'Avènement,* vol. 1, pp. 391, 395–96).

55. On December 18, 1801, she wrote to Joseph Bonaparte that Thibeaudeau "told her that one must be resigned to the loss of the Revolution's ideas provided that Bonaparte protected the men of the Revolution. This outlook cannot be accused of ardent emotion" (*C.G.,* vol. 4, no. 2, p. 450). Antoine Clair Thibeaudeau (1765–1854) was a member of the Convention who voted for the King's death. He became a Thermidorian; then he was elected to the Five Hundred, and was ultimately named prefect of Bouches-du-Rhone. Mme de Staël had known him under the Directory (*C.G.,* vol. 4, no. 2, p. 98 and passim), but their relationship ended with the Consulate.

56. Napoleon's conqueror in Spain and at Waterloo became a friend of Mme de Staël's and they maintained an important political correspondence.

57. She does not mention her satisfaction at the time with the positive steps taken to restore civil peace. It is also true that she rapidly discerned the rise of the dictatorship. Constant's first speech to the Tribunate, which classed them both in the opposition, is dated January 7, 1800, and at the same time she herself began to speak and to record in letters the views expressed here.

58. That is twenty-five from each council formed two commissions charged with preparing a new constitution (Jacques Godechot, *Les Institutions de la France sous la Révolution et l'Empire,* 4th ed. [Paris: Presses universitaires de France, 1989], pp. 549–50). As Mme de Staël had friends among them, she was well informed.

59. Mme Balayé points out the concurrence between Mme de Staël's assessment and that of the great historian Georges Lefebvre (*Le Directoire,* pp. 199 ff.).

60. That is, by popular election. The role of the Tribunate was confined to discussion.

61. On December 21, Bonaparte had a law voted giving Sieyès the estate of Crosnes in Seine-et-Oise, of a worth estimated at 480,000 francs, a poisoned gift

that discredited the recipient forever (Jean-Denis Bredin, *Sieyès* [Paris: Fallois, 1988], pp. 488–89). Note that Constant was named to the Tribunate by Sieyès and not by Bonaparte, as the latter claimed (Etienne Hofmann, *Les Principes de politique de Benjamin Constant* [Genève: Droz, 1988] vol. 1, pp. 190 ff.).

62. Before 1789, Jean Jacques Régis de Cambacérès (1753–1824) was councillor to the Court of Aids (now called the Board of Customs and Excise) in Montpellier, where Mlle Necker met him while spending several months there with her parents in 1785. Elected to the Convention, then a Thermidorian, he sat on the Council of Five Hundred and became Minister of Justice in 1799. Named Archchancellor of the Empire in 1804, he later became Prince and Serene Highness.

63. Charles François Lebrun (1739–1824) had been elected to the Estates General and then to the Council of Ancients. Bonaparte appointed him at the urging of Cambacérès. In 1804 he was named Arch-treasurer (a court title) and Duke de Plaisance. He joined Napoleon during the Hundred Days.

René Nicolas Charles Augustin Maupeou (1714–1792), magistrate, chancellor, and Keeper of the Royal Seals (Minister of Justice) from 1768 to 1774.

64. The great English statesman William Pitt (1759–1806) was among Bonaparte's opponents.

65. Bonaparte moved into the Tuileries on February 19 (see Vandal, *L'Avènement,* vol. 2, pp. 147 ff.).

66. Bonaparte met the Vendean leaders after 18 Brumaire, late in 1799 and early in 1800. He left them no hope. Many Vendeans resigned themselves to his authority, but not Georges Cadoudal, of whom more will be said later (Vandal, *L'Avènement,* vol. 1, p. 489; vol. 2, pp. 2–16, 27 ff.).

Abbé Etienne Bernier (1762–1806) mediated the renewal of negotiations with the Vendeans in January 1800. A non-juring priest, he had joined the Vendean armies. He negotiated Napoleon's Concordat with Rome in 1801, and attended to the reorganization of dioceses and the naming of bishops. He was Bishop of Orleans.

67. The decree of January 7, 1800, did in fact reduce the number of newspapers to fourteen; those abolished were mostly on the political right. Those that survived needed to be very cautious (André Cabanis, *La Presse sous le Consulat et l'Empire, 1799–1814* [Paris: Société des études robespierristes], pp. 12 ff., 240 ff.).

68. André Périvier, *Napoléon journaliste* (Paris: 1918); A. Guillois, *Napoléon, l'homme, le politique, l'orateur, d'après sa correspondance et ses oeuvres* (Paris: Parrin, 1889). Before the archives of the *Moniteur* were destroyed in a fire, Guillois saw many articles written or edited by Napoleon (*Histoire générale de la presse française,* ed. Jacques Godechot, vol. 1 [1914; reprint, Paris: Presses universitaires de France, 1969], p. 557).

69. Pierre Louis Roederer (1754–1835), a former member of the Constituent Assembly, owner and manager of the *Journal de Paris* under the Directory, had been on good terms with Mme de Staël since 1795. He succeeded in reconciling Bonaparte and Sieyès. When he had a role to play under the Consulate he distanced himself from her. He would be senator, Finance Minister to King Joseph

in Naples, Count of the Empire, and Peer of France at the time of the Hundred Days (see Jean Ménard, "Madame de Staël et Roederer," *Revue de l'Université d'Ottawa*, April–June, 1961).

70. Maurice Jean Madeleine de Broglie (1776–1821), uncle to Victor, Duke de Broglie, Mme de Staël's future son-in-law, had lived in emigration. He became Napoleon's chaplain, bishop of Acqui, in 1805, and of Ghent from 1807 to 1821. Enthusiastic about the Emperor at first (Madelin, *Histoire du Consulat et de l'Empire,* vol. 8, p. 145), he joined the opposition in 1811, was suspended, and then imprisoned until January 1813. She omitted this anecdote from *Considérations* in 1815, since she feared he might oppose her daughter's marriage while she was seeking a dispensation from Rome (Albertine was Protestant and Victor, Catholic).

Bonaparte's remarks are a parody of Brennus the Gaul's famous "Vae victis" (Woe to the vanquished!) when Rome fell.

71. Public opinion turned against the Tribunate and the Legislative Body because too many men sat in them who had stood against the general will: members of the Convention, Thermidorians, and Fructidorians. Further, Jullien de Paris recorded remarks of Bonaparte's that make clear his opposition to large legislative bodies, as well as his determination to treat opponents as enemies of the nation. Thus from the start Mme de Staël, Constant, and their friends fought a losing battle.

A minority of fairly numerous opponents had formed; they met in the home of Mme de Staël, whose other guests included ministers, councillors of state, and Bonaparte's brothers. Her father warned her in vain to be on her guard.

72. He was to make this speech on 15 Nivoise of the Year VIII (January 5, 1800); the subject was the government's plan to regulate discussion of drafted legislation. The speech made Bonaparte furious, whence the tale of Mme de Staël's subsequent woes.

73. "I am French only through this great city, great in inhabitants, great in happiness" (Michel de Montaigne, *Les Essais,* vol. III, chap. IX [London: A. Murray & Co., 1872]). The quote also appears in one of Mme de Staël's letters to Gouverneur Morris in 1807.

74. Michel Louis Etienne Regnaud de Saint-Jean-d'Angély (1762–1819) had been a deputy to the Estates General, known Bonaparte in the Army of Italy, participated in the coup of 18 Brumaire, and became Councillor of State. He was among the best of Napoleon's collaborators and protected Mme de Staël as much as he could. Ségur was probably Louis Philippe, Count de Ségur.

75. Constant.

76. Mme de Staël apparently confused the *commissaires des guerres, military* administrators under the Old Regime with roughly the functions of an American quartermaster, and the *commissaires aux armées* who supplanted them under the Directory in 1795, and were *civil* administrators. Responsible for such matters as authorizing armistices and collecting contributions for war, they were often in conflict with generals, as seems to be the case here [Trans].

77. On January 28, Necker wrote to her that Roederer had told the banker Biderman that the order to leave France had been sent and then revoked (*C.G.*, vol. 4, no. 1, pp. 252, 254).

78. Expelled from England in February 1794, Talleyrand had sought refuge in the United States. In June 1795, he petitioned the Convention for authorization to return. Thanks to Marie Joseph Chénier and Mme de Staël, it was granted and he was back in Paris on September 20, 1796 (Georges Lacour-Gayet, *Talleyrand* [Paris: Payot, 1990], p. 222).

Mme de Staël wrote to Wellington on November 23, 1816: "Last night I went to Talleyrand's so that I might teach him how one should behave with one's unfortunate friends; since he deserted me under Bonaparte, I enjoyed the contrast and it was as good a revenge as any" ([Wellington Duke de], V. de Pange, *Madame de Staël et le duc de Wellington, correspondance inédite, 1815–1817* [Paris: Gallimard, 1962], p. 68).

79. In a note (*C.G.*, vol. 4, no. 1, pp. 76–77), B. Jasinski cites several convincing passages of a text on Choiseul read by Talleyrand at the Institute on July 3, 1797. Mme de Staël is also said to have collaborated with him on his *Report on Public Education* (1791) and to have written his speech on the death of Mirabeau (see J. Isbell, *Madame de Staël, Ecrits retrouvés* [*Cahiers staëliens*, Nouvelle Série, no. 46 (Paris: Touzot, 1994–95)], pp. 11–17). On Talleyrand's secretaries, see Madelin, *Histoire du Consulat et de l'Empire*, vol. 6, p. 40.

"Conversing with Mme de Staël in Stockholm, Bernadotte said: I recall that when [M. de Talleyrand] was called upon to announce Mirabeau's death to the Consituent Assembly, his highly praised speech was composed by you, Madame.' . . . B. Jasinski notes that Mme de Staël apparently did not refute this assertion" (*Madame de Staël: Ecrits retrouvés*, #41, "Collaboration: Talleyrand, Discours sur la mort de Mirabeau, April 3, 1791," *Cahiers staëliens*, Nouvelle Série, no. 46 [Paris: Touzot, 1994–95], pp. 11 pp. 11–12).

80. The Jacobins [Trans].

81. Bertrand Barère de Vieuzac (1755–1841), a former member of the Constituent Assembly, then of the Convention, a Montagnard skilled as an orator, a member of the Committee of Public Safety, had escaped deportation after 9 Thermidor. Although he had saved many outlawed people, he was scorned for his role in the Revolution. Granted amnesty in 1805, he wrote for a few newspapers. In 1805 the Senate refused his candidacy for the Legislative Body. He was a low-level policeman until his dismissal in 1807.

82. To be exact, Edmund Burke called him "the Anacreon of the guillotine."

83. Mme de Staël sometimes referred to England with this image or as the "holy ark."

84. Glory, for Mme de Staël, is to be understood as the recompense awarded by humanity to the man of genius who has led to its progress (see Simone Balayé, "Le génie et la gloire dans l'oeuvre de Madame de Staël," from *Convengo internazionale su Madame de Staël e il suo gruppo*, Pisa, 1967, in *Rivista di*

letterature moderne e comparate, September/December, 1967].

85. *On Literature Considered in Its Relations to Social Institutions,* published in April 1800, was the century's first book of major importance.

86. These two commissions were created by the Organic Senatus Consultum that established the Empire on May 18, 1804. The commission on individual freedom was given 585 cases of arbitrary detention for consideration, but its objections were rarely effective. The role of the other commission was even more insignificant since periodicals were excluded from its charge: eight cases in ten years (Godechot, *Les Institutions,* pp. 584–85).

87. The campaign began in Germany at the end of April. Placed at the head of a strongly Republican army, Moreau defeated the Austrian army at Stockach on May 3, 1800, and went on to further victories.

88. Bonaparte reached Geneva at three o'clock A.M. on May 9. He stayed with the Saussure family whose daughter, a close friend to Mme de Staël, had married a nephew of Necker's. Necker visited Bonaparte there on May 10.

89. Mme de Staël presents a somewhat different picture in *Considérations:* "During the conversation, which lasted two hours, the First Consul's confidence in speaking of his future plans made an agreeable impression on my father" (pt. 4, chap. 7). On Saint Helena, Napoleon would write: "I had wanted to see him while I was there, . . . and found only a dull, bloated schoolmaster" (*Mémorial,* vol. 2). Necker, ill and already heavy, had gained a great deal of weight.

90. General Michael Friedrich Benedikt von Melas (1729–1806) took command of the Austrian army in Italy in 1799. His orders were to enter Provence, which was impossible for lack of British reinforcements. He besieged Massena in Genoa, forced him to surrender, and threw Suchet back to the Var. At that point, Bonaparte decided to cross into Italy.

91. Unidentified verse. Paul Emile was defeated and killed by Hannibal in Apulia in 216 B.C.; the companion was Varron, the other consul, who fought the battle in spite of Paul Emile.

92. Leaving Lausanne on May 16, he crossed the Saint Bernard Pass on the twentieth (Tulard and Garros, pp. 156–57). He won the Battle of Marengo on June 14.

93. Mistakes were made during the battle fought on June 14 (see Madelin, *Histoire du Consulat et de l'Empire,* vol. 3, pp. 261 ff.). Melas went back to Alexandria. Desaix (who was killed) and Kellermann won the battle (Georges Lefebvre, *Napoléon,* 6th ed. [Paris: Presses universitaires de France, 1969], p. 99).

94. The armistice was signed on June 15. The Austrians retained Tuscany and the Papal States. The winter campaign of 1800–1801, led by Moreau in the north and Macdonald in the south, ended with the defeat of the Austrians. The Treaty of Lunéville confirmed their defeat and completed their loss of Italy.

95. By his break with Austria and England late in 1799 and rapprochement with Bonaparte, becoming his ally against England in 1901, after the Peace of

Lunéville. His father was Peter III, grandson of Peter the Great and husband of Catherine II.

96. The Czar was assassinated during the night of March 23–24, 1891. Russian nobles were incensed at his behavior with them. The conspirators were in complicity with Alexander, who did not, however, want his father murdered, and they acted in spite of him (Lefebvre, *Napoléon*, p. 108).

97. The pamphlet, entitled *Parallèle entre César, Cromwell, Monk et Bonaparte, fragment traduit de l'anglais,* was published on November 1, 1800. It was attributed to various authors; Lucien was certainly one of them. In the First Consul's entourage, the reestablishment of a hereditary regime was desired. Fouché was against it, and Bonaparte himself thought it was premature. Lucien was disgraced and named Ambassador to Madrid on November 6 (Lefebvre, *Napoléon,* p. 120; N. Alcer, *Louis de Fontanes, 1757–1821, homme de lettres et administrateur* [Frankfurt/Main: P. Larq, 1994], p. 242).

98. Battles Moreau won.

99. That is, "the friends of liberty," as Mme de Staël called her friends of 1789.

100. Hydrophobia, with its connotation of "mad dog."

101. The attack on the rue Saint Nicaise took place on the evening of December 14, 1800, as Bonaparte was on his way to hear Haydn's oratorio, *The Creation,* at the Theater of the Republic. There were a good many people injured or killed. The main perpetrators were Chouans, Cadoudal's agents. The public was horrified, and Mme de Staël too spoke of it as a "heinous event" in a letter to Joseph Bonaparte (*C.G.,* vol. 4, no. 2, p. 343). The arsonists were burnt at the stake, others had their bones broken on a cross.

102. Actually, although he remained calm at the Opera, he unleashed his violent anger at the Tuileries (Henri Gaubert, *Conspirateurs au temps de Napoléon Ier* [Paris: Flammarion, 1962], p. 90).

103. Allusion to Voltaire's tragedy, *The Death of Caesar* (act 3, scene 3). Antony's speech shows him prepared to succeed Caesar.

104. The historian Lefebvre agrees with Mme de Staël's estimate, and quotes this sentence in his *Napoléon* (p. 122).

105. It was signed on February 9, 1801. Austria lost the whole left bank of the Rhine. France gained the north and center of Italy. Venice was to be annexed to France in 1805, and Napoleon proclaimed himself King of the Lombards in violation of this treaty.

106. Jerome, Marquis de Lucchesini (1751–1825), who frequented her salon, had been the King of Prussia's envoy extraordinary to Paris since October 1800, and is said to have inspired her comical portrait of the prototypical courtier in *Delphine,* the Duke de Mendoce, as Mme Balayé points out in her introduction to *Dix années,* p. 36.

107. Count Louis de Cobenzl (1753–1809) the Emperor's minister plenipotentiary, a talented diplomat, had been ambassador to Russia from 1779 to 1797. He

negotiated the treaties of Campo Formio and of Lunéville. He remained in Paris until September 1801 and frequented Mme de Staël's salon. He was Foreign Minister until Austria signed the Treaty of Pressburg with France in 1805, following its defeat by the French at the Battle of Austerlitz (*Mémorial,* vol. 1, p. 420n.). He wore the costume of the Countess d'Escarbagnas. This well-known anecdote is also found in C. F. P. Masson, *Mémoires secrètes sur la Russie pendant les règnes de Catherine II et Paul Ier* (ed. F. Barrère [Paris: F. Didot, 1863], p. 84), that Mme de Staël had read and used. Chrysale is a character in Molière's *Femmes savantes.*

108. Gérard Christophe Michel Duroc (1772–1813) had been Bonaparte's aide-de-camp in the Egyptian and Italian campaigns, and was entrusted with diplomatic missions. He was made general in 1801, and Grand Marshal of the Palace, Duke de Frioul in 1807.

109. In 1799 Joseph bought the Condé's former château de Mortefontaine, near Senlis, and put in magnificent gardens. A contemporary speaks of the "noble and honorable" hospitality shown by Joseph and his wife, whose "natural courtesy and simple, affectionate manners" delighted their guests (Baron Claude-François de Méneval, *Mémoires pour servir à l'histoire de Napoléon Ier depuis 1802 jusqu'en 1815,* vol. 1 [Paris: Dentu, 1893–1894], p. 66). Mme de Staël visited Mortefontaine several times.

110. The friendship between Louis Alexandre Berthier (1753–1815) and Bonaparte began in the Army of Italy. Brave, a good diplomat, Minister of War from 1799 to 1807, he played an important role and became Prince de Wagram and Marshal of France.

111. It was at this reception that he is said to have asked her if she had breast-fed her babies. The Prince de Ligne also spoke of Bonaparte's adopting the Bourbon style in his way of talking and carrying himself (see *Oeuvres choisies,* 2d ed., ed. G. Charlier [Brussles, 1944], p. 25).

112. They numbered one hundred as she says correctly later.

113. Mme de Staël returns to the subject at length in discussing the military commission that "judged" the Duke d'Enghien.

114. In this paragraph, Auguste de Staël omitted, as too critical, from "Bonaparte" to "the eighteenth of Brumaire," from "The French are" to "before the law." He eliminated the following two paragraphs in their entirety.

115. As a result of the amnesty (Senatus Consultum of October 20), many émigrés sought to have their names struck from the list. Fouché did so for a number of them at the entreaty of Mme de Staël.

116. The Institute was then dominated by Ideologues: Destutt de Tracy, Daunou, Cabanis, Volney. Bonaparte reorganized it in 1803, eliminating the division of moral sciences and politics where they were entrenched. Like Mme de Staël and her friends, they were heirs to the eighteenth century but, as she explains, were separated from her by their ideas on religion.

117. Juliette Bernard, who became Mme Récamier (1777–1849), a banker's wife, met Mme de Staël in the summer of 1799 at her château de Clichy as B.

Jasinski shows (*C.G.,* vol. 4, no. 1, p. 213 n.9). She dates the beginning of their enduring friendship from the winter of 1800–1801.

118. Napoleon greatly overestimated the wealth of Spain. When Lucien Bonaparte went there as ambassador, he was charged with getting Spain to send an expedition against Portugal, which was an English fief. Prime Minister Manuel de Godoy waged a war that was pure sham and ended in May 1801. Lucien brought enormous plunder back to Paris, as did Talleyrand and Berthier (Lefebvre, *Napoléon,* p. 104).

119. By the Treaty of Lunéville Napoleon took the grand duchy of Tuscany from Archduke Ferdinand III. The Treaty of Aranjuez, March 21, 1801, transformed it into the Kingdom of Etruria and gave it to Louis de Bourbon, now Louis I, from whom he had taken the duchy of Parma by the Treaty of Madrid, and who was married to the Infanta Marie-Louise of Spain. In gratitude for this gesture, her father Charles IV agreed to make war on Portugal, retroceded Louisiana to France, and gave up his portion of Elba.

120. Voltaire, *Oedipe* (act 2, scene 4).

121. The Museum of the Arts (the present Louvre) and the Museum of Natural History. In his *Mémorial,* Norvins cites his many blunders (Jacques Marquet de Montbreton de Norvins, *Souvenirs d'un historien de Napoléon: Mémorial . . . ,* ed. L. Lanzac de Labory, vol. 2 [Paris: Plon, 1896–1897], pp. 73–74). Fugier reports that he was rather good-looking but not very intelligent, and that his wife was ugly "with one hip lower than the other and round-shouldered [. . .], sly, treacherous, and dangerous" (*Napoléon et l'Italie* [Paris: J.-B. Janin, 1947], p. 135).

122. The "ladies" are the women who will become the new aristocracy [Trans]. The Minister of the Interior's mistress was a dancer.

123. This is an error. The last celebration was in 1804. In 1803 there was no celebration at the Tuileries, which may account for Mme de Staël's mistake.

124. The state prisons were reinstituted by decree on March 10, 1810.

125. The island was governed by Toussaint-Louverture under the nominal authority of France. Bonaparte wanted to reconquer it along with other Antillean islands for its produce. General Victor Emanuel Leclerc (1772–1802) was Pauline Bonaparte's husband. He died in Santo Domingo of yellow fever. On May 20 Bonaparte reestablished slavery in the colonies, setting off a revolt. The French were badly defeated by Dessalines and the English. Mme de Staël was doubtless well acquainted with the details of this disaster since her friend Norvins had lived through it (see his *Mémorial,* vols. 2 and 3). Pauline, later Princess Borghese, found life on the island hard to bear, but the tales of Bonaparte's mistreatment of his sisters are simply gossip.

126. She saw the Mint in the Citadel of Saints Peter and Paul in Saint Petersburg late in August of 1812 (*Carnets,* p. 309). Thus this was written after her visit to that city.

127. She left Paris on May 19 and reached Coppet around May 25, 1801 (*C.G.,* vol. 4, no. 2, p. 375 n.5 and pp. 377–78).

128. Voltaire, *Rome Saved* (act 5, scene 2). Cicero speaks. The correct quote is:

"Romans, I love glory and refuse silence on that score. / For human labors, it is the fitting payment."

129. *Last Views on Politics and Finance,* published early in August 1802.

130. They were signed on October 1, 1801 after the death of Paul I and Bonaparte's failure in Portugal. Bonaparte was obliged to heed the urging of Alexander and accept the situation achieved by Paul I in the Mediterranean. On October 9, Mme de Staël wrote to Joseph Bonaparte: "Peace with England is the joy of the world" (*C. G.,* vol. 4, no. 2, p. 415). In reality, the situation was neither so easy nor so brilliant for Bonaparte as was thought.

131. Cairo fell to the combined Anglo-Turkish forces on June 28, 1801, and Alexandria on August 30.

132. General Jean Baptiste Kléber (1753–1800), who had assumed command in Egypt when Bonaparte left, was indeed assassinated on June 14, but by a fanatic from Syria who had come to kill him.

133. The siege of Acre lasted from March to May 1799. Plague struck Jaffa after the massacres committed by French soldiers. A hospital was set up on Mount Carmel to take care of the plague-stricken. At the time of the retreat, Bonaparte gave precise orders to evacuate the sick and wounded. Desgenettes himself told Mme de Staël the story related here and dates Bonaparte's proposal as made on April 28, 1799. Not surprisingly, a whole controversy developed.

134. Mme de Staël, who had been in Switzerland since May 1801, decided in June to leave on November 10 (*C. G.,* vol. 4, no. 2, p. 425). She left on November 13. Although this was not to avoid the celebration, the fact that she did so doubtless made her decision seem all the better. The fête took place on the tenth (Tulard and Garros, p. 177).

135. Pacts had been signed with the Pasha of Tripoli in 1801 and the Bey of Tunis in 1802. In August, a French fleet forced the Dey of Algiers to do likewise (Lefebvre, *Napoléon,* p. 167). The Dey freed captives from France or its allies.

136. The Treaty of Mortefontaine had been signed on September 30, 1800.

137. Robert R. Livingston (1746–1816), the American minister plenipotentiary, was presented to the First Consul on December 6, 1801 (*C. G.,* vol. 4, no. 2, p. 457 n.2).

138. Bastien Horace François Sébastiani (1772–1851), Corsican like Bonaparte but not a relative, had supported him on 18 Brumaire by commanding the charge that cleared the Legislative Body from the orangery at Saint Cloud. Allied with Talleyrand, he fought in Spain, Russia, and France. He became an opposition deputy under the Restoration, minister in the July Monarchy, and marshal in 1840.

139. There were former Jacobins on the Tribunate who were eliminated at the same time as Constant.

140. Pierre Claude François Daunou (1761–1840), a moderate in the Convention, a member of the Council of Five Hundred and the Institute, presided over the Tribunate until he was eliminated in 1802. In 1805 he became conservator of

the French Archives. Mme de Staël probably met him in 1797.

On January 7, 1802, the Council of State approved renewal of one-fifth of the Tribunate. The Senate, probably under coercion, did so, not by lot, but by naming those to be eliminated. The Tribunate itself disappeared on April 19, 1807.

141. Mme de Staël is biased here. She is more exact in a letter to Joseph Bonaparte of December 8, 1801, saying that "it is impossible not to admire the First Consul's facility and perspicacity" (*C. G.,* vol. 4, no. 2, p. 440).

142. The Cisalpine Republic was reestablished and enlarged on June 25, 1800, after Marengo. Charged with organizing it was a 450-member *consulta* headed by Count Francesco Melzi d'Eril (1753–1816), who set its meetings in Lyons. On January 11, Bonaparte arrived to settle everything and, on the twenty-fifth, was elected president of the Italian Republic that was proclaimed the following day. Melzi became vice-president (Fugier, chap. 3). Mme de Staël knew him well. He was a grandee of Spain and later, Duke de Lodi. Bonaparte had great respect for him and entrusted him with major responsibilities in the Republic, and then in the Kingdom of Italy. Often dissatisfied with Napoleon, Melzi always kept his distance, even when covered with honors.

143. Copied from that of France, the government having the same prerogatives.

144. The three electoral colleges were to present candidates for the Legislative Council. Bonaparte, of course, shaped everything himself.

145. Francis James Jackson (1771–1814) was England's minister plenipotentiary to Paris from November 1801 to April 1802. He numbered among the diplomats received by Mme de Staël.

146. The Peace Treaty of Amiens was signed on March 25, 1802. Besides Malta, England abandoned Minorca, Elba, and the French Antilles. Bonaparte gave up Egypt, lost in any case, and retained his conquests on the continent. The treaty left too many problems unsolved for it to last, but it was greeted warmly on both sides of the Channel (Lefebvre, *Napoléon,* p. 111). General Louis Charles Antoine des Aix, called Desaix (1768–1800), had a brilliant career in the revolutionary armies, became Bonaparte's friend in Italy, went to Egypt with him, and took part in the capture of Malta. He was killed at Marengo on June 14, having played a major role in the French victory.

147. This was on September 11, 1802. Piedmont was divided into departments with the same administrative and financial systems as France (Fugier, pp. 127 ff.).

148. On August 21, 1802, the consuls went to the Luxembourg Palace to receive the oath of the senators. The First Consul presided for the first time. Auguste omitted this paragraph on the Senate.

149. What had to be done was to reconcile the Church with the State and have it accept the constitutional clergy; the refractory priests had also to be brought back. After difficult negotiations, the Concordat was signed in Paris on July 15. It then faced strong opposition in the Council of State and in the assemblies, but was finally promulgated and celebrated in Notre Dame cathedral on Easter Sunday, April

18, 1802. Mme de Staël and her friends understood that this event consecrated Bonaparte's triumph.

150. The reference is to Louis Philippe, Count de Ségur (1753–1830). He had fought in the American Revolution, and been ambassador to Russia in 1785. He had been an intimate friend of the Neckers and Mme de Staël, whom he had courted. Under the Consulate, he was a member of the Legislative Body and then the Council of State. He became a senator in 1813, rallied to Napoleon during the Hundred Days, and offered to follow him to Saint Helena. Mme de Staël was well informed on the strange adventure of his "lost" eldest son, Octave, who had abandoned career (deputy prefect of Soissons), wife, and family in 1802 to join the army under an assumed name. He came home in 1809 and ultimately killed himself. According to Méneval (*Mémoires,* vol. 1, pp. 338–43), when he was thought dead, in 1802, Bonaparte—who respected him—wrote a touching letter to his father. He does not mention the sentence reported here.

151. Mgr. Jean de Dieu-Raymond de Boisgelin (1732–1804), Archbishop of Aix before the Revolution, had pronounced the homily at Louis XVI's coronation, had been a member of the French Academy and president of the Constituent Assembly of 1789. He emigrated to England in 1792. Back in France, he became Bishop of Tours under the Concordat in 1802 and Cardinal in 1803.

152. Msgr. Jean-Baptiste de Belloy (1709–1808), Archbishop of Marseilles before the Revolution, who had refused to swear allegiance to the Revolutionary government, saw his position eliminated but had not emigrated. Dean of the French episcopate, he was ninety-three at the time of the Concordat, and was made Archbishop of Paris in 1802. By the time he died, he was senator, Count of the Empire, and Grand Eagle of the Legion of Honor (*Mémorial,* vol. 2, p. 85).

153. Mme de Staël writes that the remark is hers and that the general to whom she made it then took it as his own. That could only have been Bernadotte. Several dissatisfied generals behaved quite badly at the ceremony. Bonaparte sent away the main instigators. Bernadotte was sent to the Army of the West, which he had temporarily left to come to Paris. From that time on his attitude seemed very ambiguous; Bonaparte was already talking of having him court-martialed, but was dissuaded by his brother Joseph, brother-in-law to Bernadotte through their wives, who were sisters.

154. LaFayette voted "no" in 1802 and did not vote in 1804. He never concealed his hostility to the regime and refused to be a senator.

155. *The True Meaning of the National Vote for the Life Consulate* was a violent critique published in July 1802 by Camille Jordan, former deputy to the Five Hundred, friend and confidant to Mme de Staël who had saved him from the Temple Prison during the Terror. The first edition was seized, and the second circulated clandestinely. Jordan had emigrated after the Lyons Revolt in 1793 and did so again after 18 Fructidor. He went to Germany, studied German language and literature, and was one of those who intitiated Mme de Staël in this domain. He maintained close ties with the Coppet Group and became a deputy under the Restoration.

156. Except for a few minor players, they were dealt with gently. General Simon, Bernadotte's chief of staff, sent proclamations to the army that were intercepted by Prefect of Police Dubois. Bonaparte hushed up the affair and sent a number of generals away. Mme de Staël was also exiled from Paris. She surely knew more than she says here, but Mme Jasinski, who sheds new light on her role (*C.G.,* vol. 4, no. 2, pp. 483–85), does not think that Mme de Staël was a conspirator, and refutes Napoleon's accusations in the *Mémorial* (vol. 2, pp. 189–90). What is important is that he thought she was or made a pretense of so thinking.

157. She left Paris on May 5 or 6 with her son Albert and her husband (*C.G.,* vol. 4, no. 2, pp. 490, 502). M. de Staël died at Poligny during the night of May 8 or 9, and was buried at Coppet on May 11 (see ibid., pp. 502 ff.).

158. The First Consul.

159. William of Nassau (1772–1843), son of William V, Stadtholder of the Netherlands, Prince of Orange. Although the First Consul welcomed him nicely in Paris, he refused to join the Confederation of the Rhine and lost all his states. In 1813 he returned to the Netherlands to reign as King William I.

160. When Mme de Staël speaks of the people's party, she refers to the Jacobins [Trans].

161. Allusion to the murder of the Duke d'Enghien.

162. The Senatus Consultum of August 2, 1802, proclaimed the Consulate for Life, and the body of laws extending the First Consul's powers was enacted on August 4 (see *C.G.,* vol. 4, no. 2, pp. 543, 548). The "Body of Laws" referred to in the next paragraph is art. 44 of this Senatus Consultum.

163. The Convention created the Ecole Polytechnique in 1794. Mme de Staël does not mention the Museum of Natural History, the Museum of the Arts (later the Louvre), or the Ecole Normale Supérieure, which with Polytechnique is the basis of the system of "Grandes Ecoles" that still form the top echelons of France in government, technology, university teaching, etc. Mme de Staël was understandably bitter when her son, Auguste, came to Paris for the competitive entrance examination for Polytechnique and passed it, but was refused admission by the express order of Napoleon himself.

164. The law of 11 Floréal of the year X (May 1, 1802) created lycées to replace the Central Schools instituted under the Revolution. Mme de Staël had her son Auguste privately tutored in Greek.

165. This is repeated in Part Two. The sentence is Napoleon's, except that he uses the Arabs as his point of comparison, not Tamerlane.

166. The English word "possessionary," like its French equivalent, is no longer in use. The meaning is "with possessions" [Trans]. In this less than clear sentence, Mme de Staël refers to the Congress of Rastatt, which was projected by the treaty of Campo Formio to negotiate German affairs and met from December 1797 to April 1798.

167. The Tories were the governing party, the Whigs were the opposition.

Charles James Fox (1749–1806) came to Paris early in 1802. Leader of the Whig faction that favored the Revolution, then Bonaparte, he had contributed to the Peace of Amiens. Mme de Staël had met him in London in 1793, and she admired his gifts as an orator. He quoted her *Reflections on Peace* in a speech to Parliament in 1806.

168. "Never," he had shouted, "will Necker's daughter return to Paris!" (Pierre-Louis Roederer, *Oeuvres,* ed. A.-M Roederer, vol. 5 [Paris: 1853–1859], p. 104).

169. Auguste was then thirteen, Albert eleven, and Albertine six.

170. As is said in a variant, the people carried him through the streets on June 23, 1789, when the King recalled him.

171. Lebrun's letter is dated April 5, 1803.

172. An association of ideas surely evoked in Sweden, which would show that this draft dates from her stay in that country (1812).

173. Necker died on April 9, 1804, less than fifteen months later.

174. In 1801, Bern had promulgated a constitution with little success. A new one was promulgated by the "unitaires," proponents of rule by leading citizens, under federalist Colonel Reding in February 1802. Civil war broke out, and was stopped by Bonaparte's imposed mediation on September 30, backed by his army under General Ney (see Edouard Guillon, *Napoléon et la Suisse, 1803–1815* [Paris: Plon; Lausanne: Payot, 1910], pp. 70 ff.).

175. One of the terms Bonaparte imposed as mediator was four regiments of four thousand men each (Guillon, p. 118).

176. In December 1802, Bonaparte convened forty-five centralists (aristocrats) and eighteen federalists (democrats), who worked virtually at Bonaparte's dictation. The meeting described here took place at the Tuileries on December 23 between 1:00 and 8:00 P.M. The constitution, called the Act of Mediation, was completed in February 1803. Reaction triumphed almost everywhere; the unity of the cantons disappeared (Lefebvre, *Napoléon,* pp. 115–16, 162–63).

177. This term died out in Switzerland along with the office it designated. In the pre-Napoleonic era, the *landamman* was the chief officer of the court as well as the chief legislator in a town, village, or rural area. Once Napoleon occupied Switzerland in 1803, the *landamman* assumed both legislative and executive functions. He was the representative of the Swiss parliament and in charge of foreign and diplomatic relations. (This information was kindly provided by Patricia Schramm, Cultural Attaché at the Swiss Consulate General in New York.) [Trans]

178. Roederer was one of the four senators named to write the Act.

179. Bonaparte undeniably provoked the break, notably in Germany. But England broke the treaty the moment she was assured of Russia's cooperation. It was a conflict of two imperialisms on land and on the seas. That England was fighting an undeclared war served the First Consul's purposes (Lefebvre, *Napoléon,* pp. 166–68).

180. The Bank of France, founded in February 1800, was the only agency entitled to issue bank notes in April 1803.

181. Lord Whitworth (1752–1825), future viceroy of Ireland, a man of perfect

manners, had participated in the plot against Paul I. His appointment to Paris testified to the British government's hostility toward Bonaparte. This scene took place in the Tuileries in front of numerous witnesses (*Mémorial,* vol. 1, p. 705 n.; Méneval, *Mémoires,* vol. 1, pp. 237–38; Tulard and Garros, p. 193).

182. General Mortier entered Hanover, a hereditary fief of England's King, in May 1802. Bonaparte took over the kingdom with the idea of eventually giving it to Prussia, which indeed took possession in 1806 (Madelin, *Histoire du Consulat et de l'Empire,* vol. 5, pp. 8–9).

In its struggle against Turkey, Malta was important to Russia, which preferred to see it in English rather than French hands. In February–March, Bonaparte had stormy meetings with Whitworth to no avail. England refused to leave Malta.

183. This pastoral letter is dated December 30, 1802. It salutes the Consulate as "the legitimate government, both national and Catholic, without which we would have neither worship nor country." On Archbishop Boisgelin, see Part One, note 151.

184. Jean Etienne Marie Portalis (1746–1807) had been a member of the Council of Ancients. An eminent jurist, he played a preponderant role in drafting the Civil Code and negotiating the Concordat. Mme de Staël wrote to her father that he was "one of the most rapacious" in a very corrupt milieu (*C. G.,* vol. 5, no. 1, p. 28). The "friend" is Trophime Gérard, Marquis de Lally-Tolendal. Deputy to the Estates General, whose brilliant oratory Mme de Staël praises in *Considérations* (pt. 2, chap. 6), he supported Necker, was arrested after the Tenth of August (when the monarchy fell), and was another whom she saved.

185. Mme de Staël does not mention that Britain, displeased with Bonaparte's activities in Germany, had placed an embargo on French and Dutch ships in English ports, but without declaring war. In reprisal, Bonaparte seized land in Hanover and Portugal. On May 22, he decreed that all British citizens in French territory would be arrested, even Lord Elgin, ambassador to Turkey, who was passing through France. Public opinion in France approved (Madelin, *Histoire du Consulat et de l'Empire,* vol. 5, p. 8). The news came to Geneva on May 27. Several of Mme de Staël's friends left in the morning; by afternoon it was already too late. (*C. G.,* vol. 5, no. 1, pp. 623, 626–27, 646–47, 649).

186. Preparations began as early as 1801 when Bonaparte set up the camp at Boulogne after the Treaty of Lunéville, in February 1801. They were interrupted by the Treaty of Amiens; once it was broken, Bonaparte resumed plans for the invasion, which was supported by public opinion (Madelin, *Histoire du Consulat et de l'Empire,* vol. 5, pp. 9–10). The death of Admiral Latouche-Tréville in August 1804, and the naval superiority of the English definitively compromised the project (Lefebvre, *Napoléon,* pp. 173 ff.). While Britannia effectively ruled the seas, its own territory was relatively undefended. Bonaparte, however, lacked the necessary money to carry out his plans (see *Considérations,* pt. 4, chap. 13).

187. Prussia had occupied Hanover, a British possession, in 1801. Although France took it over in May 1803, Prussia never gave up her claims.

188. Mme de Staël alludes to the convention signed by the Spanish ambassador, Azara, and Talleyrand on October 19, 1803. Spain was to remain neutral and remit a subsidy of six million francs to France (letter to Necker, October 2, *C.G.,* vol. 5, no. 1, p. 37).

189. Such a union was finally realized: "On March 1, 1813, the Treaty of Kalisz, the cornerstone of the final alliance against Napoleon, was ratified" by Prussia and Russia (Leo Gershoy, *The French Revolution and Napoleon* [N.Y.: Crofts, 1947], p. 503).

190. She left on September 16 or 17, traveling with Mathieu de Montmorency and her children, Auguste and Albertine (letter to her father, dated September 17, 1803 in *C.G.,* vol. 5, no. 1, p. 17). According to the diary of Constant, who joined her on the twenty-first, she visited LaFayette, and shortly thereafter settled in an estate belonging to the Marquis's notary. Montmorency (1767–1826) was one of Mme de Staël's oldest and dearest friends, and guardian to her children. He had fought in the American Revolution and been elected to the Estates General. She had saved him from the massacres in August and September 1792. He kept aloof from the imperial court.

191. He was not yet Emperor, and he left her in peace for barely two weeks.

192. The friend was Constant. Montmorency, charged officially with bringing the message, refused (letter from Mme de Staël to her father, October 8, 1803, *C.G.,* vol. 5, no. 1, p. 52).

193. The man was Regnaud de Saint Jean d'Angély, and he intervened for her with Bonaparte.

194. Her chambermaid, Olive Uginet, married to her valet, Eugène Uginet, who had become her business manager.

195. Sir James Mackintosh defended Peltier in proceedings brought against him after the Treaty of Amiens, for the violent attack against Bonaparte in his newspaper. The trial was held in London in February 1803. Contemporaries said that Mme de Staël had translated the plea, but no copy has been found. Peltier had to pay costs, damages, and interest, but a public subscription was taken up on his behalf. Jean Gabriel Peltier (1760–1825) emigrated to London in 1792 where he founded a journal, *L'Ambigu, variétés atroces et amusantes,* that was hostile to the Revolution and insulting to Bonaparte.

196. Actually, this happened about noon on October 13 when she returned to Maffliers from Saint-Brice (*C.G.,* vol. 5, no. 1, p. 63). Napoleon was not yet Emperor. The letters in the National Archives are from the Minister of Police to the prefect of police and General Moncey, instructing that an officer of the Gendarmerie inform Mme de Staël of her exile from France, under the escort of a gendarme if necessary (Henri Welschinger, *Le duc d'Enghien* [Paris: Plon-Nourrit, 1888], p. 331).

197. On October 7 she told her father of four such sentences that had been ratified by the Council of State. These are enumerated in *C.G.* (vol. 5, no. 1, p. 51).

198. General Andoche Junot, future Duke d'Abrantès (1771–July 29, 1813),

was Bonaparte's aide-de-camp and followed him to Italy and Egypt. Appointed governor of Paris, he earned Napoleon's disfavor several times because of his friendship with Mme Récamier. He eventually lost his mind and killed himself. Thus this was written before 1813.

199. Mme de Staël stayed there from October 15 to October 19, approximately.

200. On October 17, she wrote to her father: "Joseph, the admirable Joseph, has just invited me to Mortefontaine" (*C.G.,* vol. 5, no. 1, p. 69). She left Paris to go there on October 19. Julie Clary (1771–1845), sister to Bernadotte's wife, Désirée, married Joseph in 1794 and reduced her official duties to a minimum so as to live at her country estate.

201. Auguste was then thirteen. What follows on Joseph Bonaparte suggests that Mme de Staël was unaware of his ambition: he wanted to be a King and he was, first in Naples, then in Madrid.

202. She spent the first night (October 21) in an unidentified inn, and the second at Bondy, a small town east of Paris. From there she left for Germany.

203. They reached Metz on October 26 (*Carnets,* p. 24). Charles de Villers (1765–1815) had emigrated to Germany in 1792 and set out to study German literature and philosophy. He had published a book on Kant's philosophy in France where it was not well understood (*Philosophie de Kant ou Principes fondamentaux de la philosophie transcendentale* [Metz, 1801]). Mme de Staël, on the contrary, judged it very important and entertained an extended correspondence with him.

204. Albertine, then six and a half, fell ill with scarlet fever on November 19 (*C.G.,* vol. 5, no. 1, p. 85), a serious danger to children until the development of modern antibiotics. Mme de Staël and the doctor spoke English. She did manage to visit the city, which she judged too commercial and uncultivated. She saw art collections that interested her, however, and met the painter Rehberg, who did her portrait (*Carnets,* pp. 37, 41, 42–43). Constant, who shared his friend's concern for their daughter, went on to Weimar with them (letter to her father, November 25, *C.G.,* vol. 5, no. 1, p. 120).

205. The travelers left Frankfort on December 3 and reached Weimar on December 14. On the way, she had seen Grimm again on December 10 (*Carnets,* p. 61). She had begun to learn German in February 1800 with Wilhelm von Humboldt (*C.G.,* vol. 4, no. 1, p. 269), who hoped she would spread the knowledge of German literature and philosophy in France.

Charles-Auguste, Duke de Saxe-Weimar (1757–1828), invited men like Goethe, Schiller, and Wieland to his court. He had frequented the Necker salon in 1775, as Mme de Staël reminds her father (*C.G.,* vol. 5, no. 1, p. 151).

206. Mme de Staël had left Weimar with Constant on March 1. At Leipzig, on the evening of the sixth, he left her to return to Switzerland. She set out for Berlin, arriving on the eighth (*C.G.,* vol. 5, no. 1, pp. 256, 258). The Queen is Louise (1776–1810), who was both cultivated and beautiful, and exercised strong influence over her husband. After Austerlitz, she remained in the part of Prussia hostile to

Napoleon and pushed for the Third Coalition, finally coming to Tilsit, where she was near Napoleon, whom she detested. She died in 1810 at the age of thirty-four, a symbol of Prussian patriotism; Mme de Staël mourned her death.

207. Cadmus, the legendary Greek hero protected by Athena, killed a dragon from whose teeth sprang armed men who set about killing each other. He founded Thebes with the five survivors. The story has nothing to do with the Argonauts.

208. She develops these ideas fully in *De l'Allemagne*.

209. This nephew of Frederick II was killed at the start of the campaign in the Battle of Saalfeld on October 10, 1806, at the age of thirty-four (Madelin, *Histoire du Consulat et de l'Empire*, vol. 6, p. 191). Mme de Staël paid homage to his heroism in *On Germany* in a passage the censors told her to omit. Her judgment on the Prince was more mixed than she could show here; in letters she speaks of his lack of self-control and calls him "the German Lovelace" (see *Carnets*, pp. 444–45; *C.G.*, vol. 5, no. 1, p. 307).

210. Georges Cadoudal (1771–1804), a leader of the Chouans, counter-revolutionary Royalists who engaged in guerilla warfare in northwest France from 1793. He reached Paris on August 20, 1803. No prince supported the conspirators, nor did the Count d'Artois, who had irresponsibly encouraged them, nor did the Duke de Berry. Mme de Staël usually refers to him by his first name, as did everyone else for some unexplained reason. See Part One, note 33 for Moreau and for Pichegru.

211. Jean-Claude-Hippolyte Méhée de La Touche (1760–1826), a secret agent before and during the Revolution. Deported to the Isle of Oléron in the Atlantic, he got to England where he was hired by Francis Drake, a major "spymaster" of the day, who sent him to Paris. He then sold his services to Bonaparte, who used him against Drake. To the Count d'Artois, he posed as the agent of a party bent on overthrowing the First Consul. Through his work as a double agent, the vast spy network developed by Drake and Spencer Smith was dismantled, and the English government made to look ridiculous. (The Greek, Sinon, got the Trojans to admit him into Troy and convinced them to let in the famous Trojan horse.) Note that Francis Drake had been Minister Plenipotentiary to Munich since July 1803, as well as spymaster.

212. In fact, the plotters meant to kill Bonaparte and Moreau knew it. As Mme de Staël says, he thought he would succeed Bonaparte, but he had no interest in conspiring for the Royalists (see Gaubert, pp. 182, 184; and Madelin, *Histoire du Consulat et de l'Empire*, vol. 5, chap. 4).

213. "The new era and the new year were designated as beginning on September 22, 1792, the day following the abolition of the monarchy and [. . .] the day of the autumnal equinox. [. . .] The names of the months were changed to substitute "the truths of nature and the realities of reason for sacerdotal prestige and visions of ignorance." Thus for example, March is *Ventôse* or windy. "The new calendar was in official use until January 1, 1806" (see Gershoy, p. 286 n.11).

214. From 1795 on, Pichegru conspired with the Royalists. Deported to Guyana after 18 Fructidor, he escaped, met Royalist agents in London, notably

Cadoudal with whom he returned to Paris to stir up the army. Public opinion turned against him when his treason was discovered. He was given up by an informer and imprisoned in the Temple, where he was discovered strangled on April 7, 1804.

215. Another conspirator who detested Moreau informed on him. He was arrested on February 15 and put into the Temple prison (Gaubert, p. 193). Bonaparte, shocked by Moreau's presence among the conspirators, took two days to order his arrest. Then, to get rid of an obstacle on his march to the throne, he made a great stir about the popular Moreau's supposed role in a Royalist plot (Gaubert, pp. 199 ff.). Mme de Staël and Constant learned about it in Weimar through French newspapers.

216. For example, barriers were set up in streets, homes were searched, trial by jury was suspended (Madelin, *Histoire du Consulat et de l'Empire,* vol. 5, p. 42). Pichegru fell into a trap set up by a disguised policeman who wanted the bounty (Gaubert, pp. 203–205). Cadoudal, constantly running from one hiding place to another, was arrested in a rented tilbury (Gaubert, pp. 206 ff.) at the cost of a bloody fight, which left one man dead and another critically injured. For the Legion of Honor, Mme de Staël confuses the arresting officer here with the one in the Pichegru case.

217. The date was March 23, since the Prince specifies that the event took place three days earlier.

218. Louis-Antoine de Bourbon (1772–1804) was the only son of Louis Henri Joseph, Prince de Condé, the last of the line. Kidnapped during the night of March 14–15, the Duke was sent from Strasbourg to Paris on the seventeenth, brought before a military tribunal at 11:00 on the night of the twentieth, and shot three hours later. News spread rapidly.

219. The date is actually 1 Germinal (March 22).

220. General Pierre Augustin Hulin (1758–1841) was one of the French guards who revolted in July 1789. He fought in Bonaparte's Italian Campaign, and was a division general in command of the Consular Guard in 1803. The other members of the "tribunal" were five regimental colonels stationed in Paris. It was Savary who kept the Prince's request to see Bonaparte from being forwarded to the First Consul. See Madelin, *Histoire du Consulat et de l'Empire,* vol. 5, pp. 71, 73.

221. In the *Moniteur* of 31 Ventôse (March 21) he is said to be "commonly known as Louis Antoine Henri de Bourbon, Duke d'Enghien."

222. Victories of the Grand Condé in 1643 and 1648. He was Louis II de Bourbon (1621–1686) and led Louis XIV's armies to triumphs that none of the King's other generals could replicate after his death.

223. Savary (1774–1833) was then Napoleon's aide-de-camp. While the head of the prison at Vincennes chose the site for the Duke d'Enghien's grave, Savary was in charge of the execution. Pichegru, desperate and depressive, probably (but not certainly) committed suicide. Savary announced his death to Bonaparte, who had planned to exile him. In May of 1808 he took part in trapping Ferdinand VII (the as yet uncrowned successor to Charles IV, who had abdicated). He was sent with his

brother, Don Carlos, to the château of Talleyrand who, now in disfavor, became their jailer. This act provoked the Spanish uprising. Mme de Staël's friend Prosper Barante heard Savary boast about it (*Souvenirs,* ed. Claude de Barante, vol. 1 [Paris: Calmann-Lévy, 1890], pp. 275–76). Savary was named ambassador to the Czar of Russia after Tilsit, and Duke de Rovigo in 1808. He replaced Fouché as Police Minister in 1810, and always executed Napoleon's wishes with brutal zeal, notably in the destruction of *De l'Allemagne.*

224. The marriage has not been proved. Cardinal de Rohan, the Princess's uncle, is said to have performed it; the Condé family, wanting a royal match for the Duke, never recognized it. Princess Charlotte de Rohan-Rochefort (1767–1841) remained faithful to the Duke's memory.

225. These words also figure in his speech to the Council of State: "We had to make clear [. . .] to all the courts of Europe that this is not child's play" (Madelin, *Histoire du Consulat et de l'Empire,* vol. 5, p. 77). Note: Josephine was not yet Empress. The Duke was 1.70 meters in height (about 5'8"), according to the description in the *Moniteur* of March 21. The scene in Josephine's apartments could not have taken place before the execution, since no one knew about it beforehand, but it could have happened the next day.

226. Before the execution, the Duke cut a lock of his hair that he added to a ring and a letter for Princess de Rohan-Rochefort. He gave these items to Lieutenant Noirot (Welschinger, *Le Duc d'Enghien,* p. 190), who gave the packet to Hulin, who in turn gave it to Réal. The Arch-chancellor was Cambacérès. This incident seems highly unlikely.

227. This anecdote is not reported by any other historian of the Duke's death.

228. Generally attributed to Fouché, this was said by the jurist Antoine Jacques Claude Joseph, Count Boulay de la Meuthe (1761–1840). Rallying to Bonaparte, he was a member of the Council of State and played an important part in drawing up the Napoleonic Code. Very close to Napoleon, he was exiled after the Hundred Days.

229. Bonaparte made his decision on March 10, and immediately issued orders to kidnap the Duke (Welschinger, *Le Duc d'Enghien,* p. 197). More than one thousand men were mobilized for the operation.

230. The elector of Baden refrained from complaining to the diet at Ratisbonne. He confined himself to a colorless letter sent to Paris. Even the three Bourbon courts, in Spain, Naples, and Etruria, did not protest (Madelin, *Histoire du Consulat et de l'Empire,* vol. 5, pp. 91–92).

231. More likely Constant than Schlegel, who still did not know her very well. She had left Weimar on May 1 and reached Coppet on May 19, according to Constant's journal.

232. The trial lasted from May 25 to June 10 (Gaubert, pp. 238–50). The accused numbered forty-five and included Cadoudal. Moreau did not speak at all. Mme Récamier, a childhood friend of Mme Moreau's, attended part of the trial,

and no doubt described it to Mme de Staël, who had other informants as well.

233. Mme de Staël did not believe he had killed himself, and echoes the rumors then circulating. Savary himself announced the event to Bonaparte, who sent him to the Temple prison to investigate. The autopsy was performed by two surgeons, and the official verdict of suicide does not seem suspect, particularly since the general was very depressive and since Bonaparte only wanted him exiled.

234. Pichegru was interrogated from February 27 to March 15, and threatened to give proof of Bonaparte's treason at Campo Formio and of his promises to Louis XVIII (Gaubert, p. 221). The documents from the interrogation have disappeared.

Louis Picot, Cadoudal's servant, had been arrested on February 8, 1804 (Gaubert, p. 191), and tortured under orders from Savary, whose subordinates pounded his hands with a rifle but. Consequently he revealed the plot to assassinate Bonaparte (Madelin, *Histoire du Consulat et de l'Empire,* vol. 5, p. 41).

235. Claude Jacques Lecourbe (1758–1815), a brilliant general who had served under Moreau, took his side with other generals, notably Massena. At the trial he lifted Moreau's son in his arms, shouting: "Soldiers! Here is your general's son!" All the soldiers present rose and presented arms. He was removed from office after the trial.

236. Moreau was a Breton, born in Morlaix, son of a lawyer, and related to Chateaubriand.

237. Claude Ambroise Régnier (1746–1814), a lawyer before the Revolution, deputy to the Estates General and member of the Council of Ancients, supported Bonaparte on 18 Brumaire, was named Councillor of State, and was head judge and Minister of Justice from September 14, 1802 to July 10, 1804, after Moreau's trial. When Fouché's ministry was eliminated, Régnier was given his duties which, given his lack of competence, were in fact exercised by the Jacobin, Pierre François Réal (1757–1834), virtual Vice-Minister of Police from 18 Brumaire on, who conducted the investigation for the Moreau trial. A Count in 1808 and prefect of police during the Hundred Days, he went into voluntary exile to the United States until 1827.

238. Twenty were acquitted, twenty condemned to death. Twelve, including Cadoudal, were executed, the others (all noble) pardoned. Pardoned or not, however, none of them were freed until the fall of the Empire.

239. Napoleon wanted Moreau to leave the country, and Fouché persuaded him through his brother, the tribune. Mme Moreau, born in Mauritius, was beautiful and talented. At this time Spain was blockaded by the English fleet.

240. The Empress Josephine and Mme de Rémusat intervened for the Duchess de Polignac, who managed to see the Emperor. Mme de Rémusat believes that he did not want to cast a pall over his accession with too many executions (see her *Mémoires,* ed. Paul de Rémusat, vol. 2 [Paris: Calmann-Lévy, 1879–1880], pp. 12 ff.).

241. François Louis Rusillon (1751–1821) was arrested on March 6, two days after the Polignacs and three days before Cadoudal. He was the Count d'Artois's aide-de-camp, and had landed secretly in France with Pichegru, Jules de Polignac, Moreau's former aide-de-camp, and others.

242. Jean François Curée (1756–1835) proposed that Bonaparte become Emperor and that a hereditary monarchy be established (Madelin, *Histoire du Consulat et de l'Empire,* vol. 5, pp. 99 ff.). He had supported 18 Brumaire, became tribune in 1800, senator in 1807, and Count in 1808. François Jaubert (1758–1822), a lawyer from Bordeaux, was a tribune, became Councillor of State in 1806, and showed special competence when the Civil Code was under discussion. He became head of the Bank of France in 1807, Count in 1808, and finished his career on the Court of Appeals. Joseph Jérome Siméon (1749–1842) was Royalist, jurist, deputy to the Five Hundred, and tribune in 1800. He became Councillor of State, then minister to King Jerome in Westphalia, retiring in 1813. He had an important career under the Restoration and the July Monarchy.

243. Jean Pierre Fabre d'Aude (1755–1832), a lawyer, elected to the Estates General, member of the Five Hundred, supporter of Brumaire, senator in 1807, Count in 1808. He voted for Napoleon's deposition in 1814, became Peer of France under the First Restoration, rallied to Napoleon for the Hundred Days, and devoted himself thereafter to financial matters.

244. Grégoire resisted as did Carnot. Lajunius, who had refused, was absent for the vote. Cabanis and Choiseul–Praslin abstained (Madelin, *Histoire du Consulat et de l'Empire,* vol. 5, p. 101). Joseph-Marie Moreau, who had welcomed the coup d'état of Brumaire, protested the indictment of his brother and resigned from the Tribunate.

245. The new constitution was drafted between May 16 and May 18, and that same day became Senatus Consultum by acclamation. Napoleon submitted the measure to a plebiscite, which ratified it.

Note by Auguste de Staël: "M. Gallois." The courageous tribune was Jean-Antoine Gauvin, known as Gallois (1755–1828), a member of the Tribunate and an excellent orator closely connected to the Ideologues. Constant said of Gallois that he loved liberty.

246. Nicolas Louis François de Neufchâteau (1750–1828) was a poet before the Revolution, deputy to the Legislative Body, Minister of the Interior in 1797 (and again from 1798–1799), a director, senator after Brumaire, and Count in 1808.

247. Molière's hilarious satire of the parvenu bourgeois, *The Would-Be Gentleman,* of 1670.

248. Mme de Staël speaks here of the Legion of Honor, created on May 19, 1802. The new members were sworn in on July 15, 1803. Crosses were distributed to the army on August 16 at the Boulogne camp. The caricature referred to was English. The red cap, similar to one worn by the ancient Phrygiens, was worn by the revolutionaries of 1789. Marianne, the French equivalent of Uncle Sam and John Bull, depicted as wearing this hat, is the emblem of the Revolution. In the well-known painting of 1831 by Eugène Delacroix, she is shown as "Liberty Leading the People" [Trans].

Jean-Jacques Dessalines (1750–1806) was a leader in his country's revolt. Appointed general by Toussaint-Louverture, he fought General Leclerc, surrendered, and was named general by the French. Taking up the fight against them, he defeated Rochambeau in 1803, had many Whites massacred, and proclaimed the independence of Haiti on January 1, 1804. Mme de Staël sent the text of the proclamation to her father. Dessalines had himself proclaimed Emperor of Haiti in 1804; his despotism led to his assassination (*C.G.*, vol. 5, no. 1, p. 245).

249. A recurrent idea in Mme de Staël's writings. Although the remark seems doubtful (Madelin, *Histoire du Consulat et de l'Empire,* vol. 9, p. 116), as early as the Consulate people with no resources had to seek jobs in the administration, as did Mme de Staël's future son-in-law, Victor de Broglie, who entered the Council of State. When Napoleon's court was set up, some young men took positions there, but many preferred the army (ibid., pp. 16 ff.).

250. Chateaubriand resigned on March 22, as soon as he heard of the Duke d'Enghien's death.

251. Each person chose his position. The title is ludicrous given that the Montmorency family was of the oldest nobility: the medieval nobility of the sword. Mme de Staël's friend Mathieu de Montmorency refused and persuaded most of the men of his family to do likewise.

252. The Marquis de Carrion de Nisas, a former cavalry officer, Bonaparte's comrade at military school and a tribune, wrote two tragedies, *Montmorency* and *Peter the Great* (1803 and 1804), which were performed at the Comédie Française. The latter, performed on May 18, was hissed and the performance was not completed; the play was withdrawn the following day. (Information kindly provided by J.-P. Perchellet.)

253. The results were announced on November 6, 1804: 3,572,329 "yes" and 2,569 "no."

254. See Article II of the Constitution: "On Heredity." Having no sons, Bonaparte reserved the right to adopt whom he wished. Failing that, the heir would be his brother Joseph, then Louis. Lucien, eliminated from government for refusing to divorce his wife, went into exile in Italy.

255. George III refused to call Napoleon "my brother." In an unpublished note by Albertine de Staël, we read that the Prince of Wales calls the Crown Prince of Sweden (Bernadotte) *"my dear brother."*

256. Taking us back to the Treaty of Amiens, this passage would date from 1813.

257. Greek fire, invented by the Arabs in the Middle Ages, is an incendiary mixture composed of saltpeter, sulfur etc. that cannot be put out with water. It was used in warfare and led to the invention of powder for firing canons.

PART TWO: 1810–1812

1. Her hosts, M. and Mme Leray de Chaumont, had returned in mid-August. Fossé, located near Blois, is both immense and pretty; it belonged to Count Charles Marie Irumberry de Salaberry (1766–1847), of Basque descent, who had fought in

Condé's army and in the Vendée, and who had traveled in Italy, Germany, and Turkey.

2. The musician was Pertosa, a Neopolitan, who had come to Chaumont in June. The "beautiful friend" is Mme Récamier, who occasionally accompanied him on a Basque drum.

3. Queen Hortense wrote songs. The refrain of this one circulated among Mme de Staël's friends, and she quotes it in *De l'Allemagne* (ed. Countess Jean de Pange with Simone Balayé, vol. 4 [Paris: Hachette, 1959–60], p. 313, var. A and B). She wrote to the Queen: "I spent part of the summer singing Your Majesty's songs and, often, in these family concerts, our refrain was Do what thou . . .'" The "green table" in the next sentence is a table covered with a green cloth [Trans].

4. He was most probably illiterate [Trans].

5. A comic opera in three acts with a libretto by Etienne and music by Isouard, known as Nicolo. It was performed for the first time at the Opéra Comique in Paris on February 22, 1810, and was a great success.

6. Note by Auguste de Staël: "M. de Corbigny, a man of amiable and enlightened mind." Louis Antoine Chicoilet de Corbigny (1771–1811), a protégé of Condorcet, was now prefect of Loir-et-Cher. Numerous letters testify to his kindness to Mme de Staël. He was a frequent visitor at Chaumont and Fossé (Simone Balayé, "Mme de Staël et le gouvernement impériale en 1810, le dossier de la suppression de *De l'Allemagne*," *Cahiers staëliens* 19 [December 1974], pp. 12 ff.).

She was the object of numerous police reports, and the one referring to her visit to the theater reveals that the police spy thought her entourage suspect (for the year 1810, ibid.).

7. Necker had made investments in the United States which his daughter continued. Over a period of years she had indeed thought of going to America, but in 1810, the plan truly took shape and Chaumont was doubtless a step on the route to England as the police understood.

8. On October 4, Corbigny forwarded Mme de Staël's request to remain in Vendôme until her book was published (Balayé, "Mme de Staël et le gouvernement impériale en 1810," p. 49).

9. Philippe Auguste lost to the English King at Fréteval on July 5, 1194. We know that Mme de Staël worked on an epic entitled *Richard the Lionhearted,* which was to include a scene with the two Kings as well as the Emperors Frederick Barbarossa and Saladin. She planned to travel to the Near East for the background. As far as we know, however, there is no extant manuscript of the work.

10. Auguste de Staël adds this note: "Worried when my mother did not arrive, I mounted my horse and rode off to meet her so that I might soften, as much as was in my power, the news she would hear when she returned; but, like her, I lost my way on the unvarying plains of the Vendôme, and it was the middle of the night before a happy chance led me to the door of the château where she had been given hospitality. I had M. de Montmorency awakened, and after I advised him of the added persecution directed at my mother by the imperial police, I set off again to

finish removing her papers to a safe place, leaving it for M. de Montmorency to prepare her for the new blow that threatened her." On September 24, Minister of Police Rovigo had had seals placed on the plates and pages of *De l'Allemagne*.

11. Mme de Staël telescopes a number of events here. They could only have told her of the seizure and affixing of seals. A week later, she was informed that, as ordered on October 3, all copies of her book were to be crushed into pulp, The order to leave France had been given on September 24. During the night of August 26–27, Miss Randall, companion to Mme de Staël, and Prefect Corbigny himself did everything they could to save the manuscript and the proofs. Mme de Staël deleted references here to Corbigny's role so as not to compromise him. As for the manuscript, she could only have had that of the third volume, which was used for printing and survives in its entirety.

12. Note by Auguste de Staël: "Mademoiselle Randall." Frances (Fanny) Randall, born in Norwich, England, in 1777, died in Paris at the home of the Broglies in 1833. Engaged as Albertine's governess in December 1808, she became a confidant of Mme de Staël's and followed her everywhere except for the journey across Europe from 1812 to 1814. When Mme de Staël died, she went to live with Albertine and Victor de Broglie and took care of Alphonse Rocca, Mme de Staël's son with John Rocca, who was born in April 1812.

13. He also informed her of the orders of the Minister of Police. She declared that she was leaving for the United States, that she would hand over to him what remained of her book, and asked for an extension of two or three days to put her affairs in order. On the twenty-ninth, he wrote to Rovigo that she had given him the proofs and that the manuscript was in Paris at the printer's (Balayé, "Mme de Staël et le gouvernement impériale en 1810," pp. 39–40). She was granted an extension of a week (ibid., p. 49). In actual fact, Mme de Staël and her friends used the time to put a major portion of the manuscripts and proofs of her book into safekeeping.

14. Albertine was thirteen.

15. An allusion to her exile of October 1803.

16. Note by Auguste de Staël: "This letter is the same as the one printed in the preface of *De l'Allemagne*," that is, the preface of the 1813 edition printed in London. The "Police Générale" was the Ministry of Police for all of France.

17. Mme de Staël's note: "This postscript is easily understood: the aim was to keep me from going to England." The original of this letter, which is not in this manuscript, is to be found in the archives at Broglie.

18. Mme de Staël arrived in Orleans, twenty-five leagues from Paris, on October 7. She met Constant in Briare on the tenth and was in Auxerre on the twelfth and Avallon on the fourteenth. That evening she reached Dijon, where she apparently stayed for about two days; on the seventeenth she reached Dôle, Salins around the twentieth, Lausanne on the twenty-first, and Coppet on the twenty-fifth (see [Count de Balk] "Un amour inconnu de Mme de Staël," ed. Simone Balayé, *Cahiers staëliens* 2 [1964], pp. 44 ff.).

19. Houses of detention were for prisoners awaiting trial. This passage has led to a misunderstanding. Mme de Staël did not go through Besançon on this trip, but she had precise information on prisons from Mathieu de Montmorency and his cousin, Adrian de Laval, who made an official tour of inspection in 1811. There were approximately fifty thousand Spanish prisoners by the end of the Empire. It was customary for prisoners-of-war to take an oath of allegiance to France, which many of them undoubtedly refused to do.

20. Note by Auguste de Staël: "Mademoiselle de Saint-Simon." Her father Claude-Anne, Marquis de Saint-Simon, deputy to the Estates General, had emigrated and served Spain as a general, defending Madrid against the French in 1808. Taken prisoner, he was condemned to death, but the sentence was commuted when his daughter threw herself at Napoleon's feet. He was confined in the citadel until 1814. Mathieu saw the Marquis and his daughter in 1811 when he made his tour of prisons. (The citadel was built by Louis XIV's great military architect, Vauban, in 1674, and was used as a state prison from the Reign of Terror to the Restoration.)

21. The reference is to La Fontaine's fable "The Two Pigeons."

22. Rovigo wrote to the prefect, Barante, that Mme de Staël and her children were forbidden to go into France, which then included Geneva. The prefect immediately asked if Geneva was included in the interdiction. The minister granted "Geneva only," and Mme de Staël settled there for the winter on November 26 (Balayé, "Mme de Staël et le gouvernement impériale en 1810," pp. 59 ff.).

23. Auguste de Staël's note: "M. de Barante, Prosper de Barante's father, a member of the House of Lords." Baron Claude Ignace Brugière de Barante (1755–1814) was a longtime friend of Mme de Staël, and his son was in love with her. He was dismissed at the end of November and sent into forced retirement. He, too, believed it to be her fault (ibid., p. 75).

24. Auguste adds "1811" here. Guillaume Antoine Benoît Capelle (1775–1843) was named prefect on November 30, 1810, and was installed late in February 1811 (Kohler, p. 583). He zealously persecuted Mme de Staël and made himself thoroughly detested by Genevans. A prefect under the Restoration, he became a minister in the Polignac government in 1830 and, as Mme Balayé writes in her note, "ended his life in the obscurity he should never have left."

25. He was born on March 20, 1811.

26. The present Aix-les-Bains.

27. On May 22, Capelle informed Rovigo that he had given Mme de Staël formal notice to return, and he wrote to the prefect of Mont Blanc to refuse her post-horses if she wanted to go farther in France. In the same letter he asked that Schlegel be sent back to Germany (Balayé and King, pp. 102–3).

28. Schlegel's *La Comparaison entre la Phèdre d'Euripide et celle de Racine,* published in Paris in the fall of 1807, had provoked numerous reactions (see M. de Rougemont, "Hellénique ou romantique: les enjeux du drame sous l'Empire").

29. Mme de Staël's sons, Albert and Auguste, whose father was actually Louis de Narbonne, bore her husband's name and therefore had Swedish as well as French nationality. The remark about Bernadotte as the "new head of state" shows that the passage was written in Stockholm, or even London, when this Prince, heir to the Swedish throne, decided on an alliance with the Czar.

30. The ministry was headed by Metternich, who had no liking for Mme de Staël but would do his duty to her.

The archduchess is Marie Louise de Hapsbourg-Lorraine, who was married to Napoleon on April 1, 1810, and became Empress of the French [Trans].

31. Mme de Staël is far from bearing sole responsibility for his exile since there were political reasons for the exile imposed on Montmorency by order of Napoleon. With his cousin Adrian, future Duke de Laval, he made an official tour of state prisons, not only out of philanthropic motives but also for intelligence work among the officers. (See Part Two, note 32 below.)

32. She left early in August, since Sismondi wrote to her from Coppet on the sixth (Jean-Charles-Léonard Simonde de Sismondi, *Epistolario,* ed. Carlo Pellegrini, vol. 1 [Firenze: La Nuova Italia, 1933], pp. 338–40). Pursuing his own political ends, Mathieu went to the Trappist monastery, for the monks there served as intermediaries between the French clergy and the imprisoned Pope. For her part, Mme de Staël managed a discreet meeting with Schlegel (Countess Jean de Pange, *A.-G. Schlegel et Mme de Staël* [Paris: Albert, 1938].

33. Note by Auguste de Staël:

> I accompanied my mother on the excursion she describes here. Struck by the primeval beauty of the place, and interested by the witty conversation of the Trappist who received us, I asked to stay until the following day, with the idea of crossing the mountain on foot to see the great monastery of Val-Sainte, and to rejoin my mother and M. de Montmorency at Fribourg. The religious, with whom I went on conversing, had no difficulty in seeing that I hated the imperial government, and I could guess that he shared my feeling. Moreover, after I thanked him for his kindness I completely lost sight of him, and I did not think he retained any memory of me.
>
> Five years later, in the first months of the Restoration [this would be three or four years according to whether Auguste is thinking of the First or Second Restoration, or else in 1816], it was with no small surprise that I received a letter from this same Trappist. He did not doubt, he told me, that with the legitimate King back on his throne, I had a great many friends at court, and he entreated me to use their influence to have his order's holdings in France returned. The letter was signed Father A . . ., priest and bursar of the Trappist order. He added a postscript: "If twenty-three years of emigration and four campaigns in a light cavalry regiment of Condé's army give me any right to royal favor, I beg you to make the most of it." I could not help laughing both at the influence this good religious presumed I had, and at the use of it he requested of a Protestant. I sent his letter on to M. de Montmorency, whose influence was greater than my own, and I have reason to believe that the petition was successful.

Moreover, those Trappists, withdrawn to the high valleys of the canton of Fribourg, were not the strangers to politics that their place of residence and their habit were meant to suggest. I have since learned that they served as intermediaries for the correspondence of the French clergy with the Pope, then a prisoner in Savona. Surely this fact does not excuse Bonaparte's harshness to these religious, but it does offer an explanation.

It is obvious that this information came to him from Mathieu.

34. By the imperial decree of November 12, 1810, the Valais was joined to France as the department of Simplon. Led by a French general (César Berthier), a corps of twelve hundred Portuguese stationed in Geneva and fifteen hundred men from army bases in Piedmont entered Sion on November 14 (Guillon, p. 201).

35. *Les Animaux malades de la pesta.*

36. Mathieu left Coppet on August 31 for exile in Montmirail, the estate of his daughter's father-in-law, the Duke de la Rochefoucauld.

37. Thus this was written before Napoleon's fall.

38. Mme Récamier left for Coppet on August 23. A letter of warning from Mathieu did not reach her, but Mme de Staël's message did. She disregarded it, however, and spent three days at Coppet (Edouard Herriot, *Madame Récamier et ses amis,* vol. 1 [Paris, Hachette, 1904], pp. 263–64, 165).

39. Mme Récamier was about to return to Paris when, on September 2, M. Récamier was notified of the order for her exile; he went to Dijon to tell her the news. Thus she was made to pay for sympathizing with Napoleon's enemies, and for refusing his offers of a position at his court (Herriot, vol. 1, pp. 126 ff.). Copelle wrote to Rovigo: "Coppet is in mourning; so much the better" (Balayé and King, pp. 105–7).

40. François Emmanuel Guignard, Count de Saint-Priest (1735–1821), had been an officer in the army, then a diplomat in Turkey and Russia; he served in Necker's last ministry. Emigrating in 1790, he joined Louis XVIII in Verona, and then came to Switzerland. His sons were in the service of the Russians, and this, as Mme de Staël says a few lines further on, was the true reason for his exile. Schlegel wrote to her from Bern his conviction that the letters of the Count's sons were the cause: "They fear a former diplomat's view of the interior situation and the information that he might send to the North" (J. de Pange, *A.-G. Schlegel et Madame de Staël,* pp. 342–43).

41. Baron Caspar von Voght (1752–1839), son of a rich Hamburg merchant, was a philanthropist whom Mme de Staël respected. In 1809 she had his report on the poor of Hamburg translated, and it won him a European reputation. It was put out by Paschoud, the publisher of many works by Mme de Staël and the Coppet Group. Prefect Capelle dissuaded him from going to Coppet and boasted of it in a letter to Rovigo (Balayé and King, pp. 107–9).

42. From October 1810 to May 1812, about twenty months.

43. Note by Auguste de Staël: "Comte Elzéar de Sabran." Louis Marie Elzéar de Sabran (1774–1846) was the older brother of Mme de Staël's friend Delphine de

Custine (whose name became the title of the author's first major novel). His love for Mme de Staël was not reciprocated, although rumors of their marriage circulated from time to time. He was arrested on April 20, 1813, partly for his close friendship with her, and partly for refusing any position at court.

44. Her letters of the time to close friends like Sismondi frequently speak of departure. Schlegel grew impatient. The fact is that no one knew she was pregnant with John Rocca's child (born April 7, 1812), and so could not travel until she gave birth. Further, she had good reason to fear that Napoleon would order her imprisoned.

45. Spoken by the abbé d'Espagne (René Sahuger d'Amarzit, 1751–1794), canon of Paris. In charge of supplies for the Army of the Alpes, he was denounced by a member of the Committee of Public Safety and sent to the guillotine.

46. The senator was Roederer.

47. *Ultima ratio regum* was the motto Louis XIV had engraved on his cannons.

48. She repeats here what Chateaubriand wrote to her in October 1810.

49. The use of the present tense here shows that Napoleon was still in power when this was written, and "increasing" power suggests that it was before the retreat from Russia.

50. Inconsequential little poem in praise of the charms of its object.

51. Mme de Staël had written to Rovigo on November 12. Capelle enclosed the letter with his own requesting the authorization (Balayé and King, p. 116).

52. Schlegel worked on the plans with her from Bern. This sentence shows how carefully she organized her departure in spite of her difficulties. She left on May 23. Capelle did not inform Rovigo until June 4 (ibid., pp. 123–26).

53. This is an allusion to the Pietism practiced in Lausanne under the leadership of a cousin of Benjamin Constant's, and in Geneva under a cousin of Mme de Staël's.

54. Her confidential agent, Joseph Uginet, known as Eugène, and his wife, Anne-Olive, Mme de Staël's personal maid.

55. The use of the present and future tenses here shows that she is neither at Coppet nor in France when she writes these words.

56. Fanny Randall would tell Sismondi on August 8: "On the morning she left, she told me that she wanted to take me with her to her father's tomb. Once we were there, she said: It is here in this solemn place that I wanted to assure you of my affection, which nothing but you yourself could ever shake'" (Biblioteca municipale di Pescia, arch. Sismondi).

57. Claudius Clauianus, *In Rufinum,* lib. 1, verses 370–404.

58. The son was Auguste who left her near Bern. The friend is John Rocca. He returned to Coppet that evening to take care of some business, and joined her at Innsbruck. (This is the first time that he appears in the book. See introduction for details on Rocca.) Albert left Coppet on May 27 with servants and the travel coach and met his mother in Vienna.

59. Note by Auguste de Staël: "At the time, England was the hope of whoever

suffered for the cause of liberty. Why, after the victory, did her ministers find it necessary to betray the expectations of Europe so cruelly?"

60. Eight thousand kilometers!

61. This is Schlegel who, from Bern, had prepared his friend's flight (J. de Pange, *A.-G. Schlegel et Mme de Staël,* pp. 374 ff.; *Carnets,* p. 265). Auguste went to Bern to get the passports from the Austrian minister, M. de Schraut (ibid.).

62. Auguste, born on August 31, 1790, was thirteen and a half when his grandfather died in April 1804.

63. Albertine, born June 8, 1797, was almost fifteen at the time. Auguste de Staël's note:

> It was simple enough to leave Coppet by eluding the surveillance of Geneva's prefect; but then we still needed to obtain passports to cross through Austria, and under a name that would not attract the attention of the various police forces that shared Germany [the pseudonym used is unknown]. My mother entrusted me with this task, and the emotion I felt will never cease to be present in my thoughts. It was, indeed, a decisive step. Once the passports were refused, my mother would fall into a far more grievous situation: her plans would be known; all flight would become impossible from then on, and the severity of her exile would be more intolerable with each passing day. I thought that I could not do better than address myself to the Austrian minister, with the confidence in the sentiments of one's fellow men which is the first impulse of every gentleman. M. de Schraut did not hesitate to give me those much desired passports, and I hope he will allow me to express here the gratitude that I bear him. In an epoch when all Europe was still bent under Napoleon's yoke, when the persecution practiced against my mother estranged from her persons who perhaps owed the preservation of their fortunes or their lives to the courageous zeal of her friendship, I was not surprised, but deeply moved by the generous conduct of the Austrian minister.
>
> I left my mother and returned to Coppet, recalled by the interests of her fortune; and a few days later a brother, taken from us by a cruel death at the very start of his career, went to join my mother in Vienna with her people and her travel coach. It was only this second departure that alerted the prefect of Léman's police, so true it is that along with the other qualifications for spying, stupidity must also be added. Fortunately, my mother was already beyond the gendarmes' reach, and she was able to continue the journey whose next part follows.

When the family reached Sweden, Albert de Staël entered that country's army; he was killed in a duel in 1813 at Doberan in northern Germany, where he is buried.

64. Mme de Staël frequently quoted this line. She wrote to her father: "I might well say that *sorrow has come by.* All the rest is nothing after what I have lost" (December 18 or 19, 1796, *C.G.,* vol. 4, no. 1, p. 16. See also, *Carnets,* pp. 263–64). Lord Russell, unjustly accused of conspiracy against Charles II, was beheaded in 1683. For Mme de Staël, he was a hero of liberty.

65. The Confederation of the Rhine, established in 1806. The kingdoms of Bavaria and Würtemberg, the grand duchies of Baden, Hesse-Darmstadt, Berg, and the archbishopric of Mainz were the largest and most important of the fifteen states that entered the Confederation imposed by Napoleon. Prussia and Austria were excluded. All this was part of the plan to dismember the Holy Roman Empire and re-make the map of Germany (Gershoy, p. 408) [Trans].

66. The itinerary was Zurich in the evening, followed by Winterthur and Saint Gall on the twenty-sixth and twenty-seventh. On the twenty-eighth they entered the Tyrol, which was then annexed to Bavaria and allied with France after Austerlitz (*Carnets*, p. 266).

67. Allusion to the Tyrol's insurrection of 1809, which occurred with the complicity of the Austrian government as a diversionary action against the French and Bavarian troops.

68. Joseph, Baron de Hudelist (1759–1818) led the secret services of court and state from 1803 to 1818. In Metternich's absence, he raised great difficulties for Mme de Staël after she left Vienna.

69. Joseph, Baron de Hormayr (1782–1848), accompanied Archduke Jean to the Tyrol, where he organized and supported his and Andreas Hofer's insurrection (see note 71 below). He became the historiographer of the Empire in 1815. Patriot and Habsburg propagandist, he was named director of the state archives in 1808. Emperor Francis I did not like intellectuals to meddle in politics and, with Metternich's help, dismissed him and had him imprisoned (A. Robert, *L'Idée nationale autrichienne et les guerres de Napoléon, l'apostolat du Baron de Hormayr et le salon de Caroline Pichler* [Paris: Alcan, 1933], pp. 231–33).

70. This is the rock of Martinswand, near Zirl. The spot where the Emperor was saved by a hunter is designated by a small cross in a grotto.

71. Built in 1400 for Duke Leopold of Austria, the palace of the Prince Royal was redone several times over the years, notably by Emperor Maximillian and Empress Maria Theresa. After the Peace of Pressburg in 1809, it became the property of the Prince Royal of Bavaria, the future Louis I, a friend of Mme de Staël's.

Andreas Hofer, an innkeeper, led the Tyrolean Insurrection, which broke out April 11, 1809. He held out against Marshal Lefebvre for months, but was captured on January 8, 1810, and shot at Mantua on February 20.

Maria Theresia von Sternbach (1775–1829) rode armed through the villages on horseback to maintain order and summon her compatriots to their duty. When he occupied Innsbruck, Marshal Lefebvre had her arrested and then imprisoned in Munich. She was detained in Strasbourg until the treaties of Vienna. Her journal was published in 1844.

72. Maximillian's cenotaph, not his tomb, is set in the chapel of the imperial palace.

There are actually twenty-eight statues, slightly larger than life-sized, plus twenty-three small saints and twenty busts of Roman emperors. Either Mme de

Staël was mistaken or the attributions have changed; on recent lists are found two dukes of Burgundy, and Marie, daughter of Charles, but not Dietrick of Bern.

73. Schlegel.

74. John Rocca.

75. Mme de Staël describes this ancient tunnel in *Corinne,* bk. 13, chap. 3. The Neuthor (modern spelling: Neutor) is a path cut through the Mönchsberg between 1765 and 1767 by the Prince Archbishop Sigismund III.

76. During her stay, mainly in Vienna, from December 1807 to June 1808. Since that time war had intervened, in particular the battles of Essling and Wagram, and the peace of 1809, which was ruinous for Austria.

77. In 1808, Sismondi came to join Mme de Staël in Vienna. A specialist in economic and social matters, he passed on to the Minister of Finance a "Memorandum on Paper Money in the Austrian States and the Means of Abolishing It," and had it published in Weimar in 1810. The crisis was chronic, the state deficit had increased between 1805 and 1809, and war had made it worse. Paper money was printed for expenditures within the country. Bankruptcy was finally declared on February 20, 1811. The Hungarian diet protested and was dissolved. Thus things were going badly when Mme de Staël returned in 1812.

78. The peace of Schönbrunn, October 14, 1809.

79. Essling: May 21–22, 1809. Wagram: July 6, 1809.

80. Napoleon reached Melk on May 7, 1809 and spent the night in the famous Benedictine abbey. The following day he left for Vienna, which capitulated on the thirteenth (Tulard and Garros, p. 315).

81. She reached Vienna on June 6 (*Carnets,* p. 270). Gustav, Count de Stackelberg (1766–1850) was the Russian ambassador to Vienna in 1812 and remained so until 1816. He came to see Mme de Staël as soon as she arrived. The courier left an hour later for Saint Petersburg. They had to wait three weeks for the reply (undated letter to Rocca, "Lettres de Mme de Staël à John Rocca," ed. Edouard Chapuisat, *Bibliothèque universelle et Revue de Genève,* [1929], p. 264).

82. Napoleon decided on war upon the return of a special mission to the Czar at Vilna on May 26, 1812 (Tulard and Garros, p. 369). The mission had been entrusted to Count Narbonne, his aide-de-camp since 1809. Displeased with the alliance concluded at Tilsit, the Czar was determined to break it.

83. King Frederick-Wilhelm III of Prussia, who arrived with a small escort and without pomp, was not treated on an equal footing with the Emperor of Austria. Napoleon gave a kindly welcome to the Crown Prince, and appearances were saved (Vandal, *Napoléon et Alexandre Ier,* vol. 3, pp. 424–25). He had signed a humiliating treaty in Paris on February 24, 1812. One-fourth of his officers resigned their commissions. Metternich, on the other hand, had signed a treaty in Paris on March 14. By its terms he furnished the Grand Army with a contingent of thirty thousand men—half of what had been demanded—under the command of Prince Schwarzenberg rather than of Archduke Charles, so as not to humiliate the imperial

family even further. Meanwhile, Metternich negotiated secretly with England and Russia (Guillaume de Bertier de Sauvigny, *Metternich et la France après le congrès de Vienne, I: Napoléon à Decauzes* [Paris: Hachette, 1968], p. 139).

84. Karl August von Hardenberg, future Hanoverian Prince (1750–1822). He served as principal minister to Frederick Wilhelm III of Prussia until Jena. Mme de Staël had met him in Berlin. Chancellor of Prussia from 1810 on, he was one of Napoleon's powerful enemies, and was also a social reformer in a Prussia that was far behind Western Germany in this respect (Lefebvre, *Napoléon,* pp. 490 ff.).

85. Because of the Russian conquests, a large segment of Swedish public opinion was favorable to Napoleon. Sweden did not respect the continental blockade and pursued active trade relations with England. Bernadotte turned to Russia, and Swedish public opinion followed him, in spite of its hostility to the Russians, when Napoleon invaded Pomerania to prevent smuggling. The break took place in 1812. A first mutual aid pact between Russia and Sweden was concluded on April 5, and in the summer of 1812, peace was made between Sweden and England.

86. This was not true of everyone, it seems. Baroness du Montet, a not impartial witness, says: "She is not satisfied with the scant enthusiasm shown her. She is writing the story of Richard the Lionhearted, who fascinates her. A lot of things are said: there is talk of dropsy, pregnancy, a M. de Rocca, a secret marriage" (*Souvenirs* [Paris: Plon, 1914], p. 70).

87. This was the contingent to the Grand Army agreed to by Austria and commanded by Prince von Schwarzenberg.

88. Archduke Charles (1771–1847), son of Emperor Leopold III, was a military genius who took part in the wars of the Revolution and the Empire. Hostile to Napoleon, he founded a party of belligerents with his brother Jean, Hormayr, and others. He resigned his commission in disgrace after Wagram and the Armistice of Znaim. Prince Charles von Schwarzenberg (1771–1820) took over his command. He had fought in the wars of the Revolution and the Empire as a general at the Archduke's side. Named ambassador to France after the marriage of Marie-Louise, he was obliged to accept command of the Austrian contingent in the Grand Army in 1812. Commander-in-chief of the allied armies in 1813, he was victorious at Leipzig and entered Paris on March 28, 1814. (The Prater is a formal public garden where the Archduke liked to walk without escort.)

89. See Auguste de Staël's Preface to Part Two in appendix I.

90. *De l'Allemagne (On Germany)* [Trans].

91. Mme de Staël seriously considered going to England via Turkey and the Mediterranean. She made inquiries among the noted Orientalists in Vienna and wrote for information to her friend Count de Balk, who was then in Constantinople (unpublished paper presented to the Staël Society by S. Balayé).

92. Pressburg is the German name for Bratislava, which was then in Hungarian territory and is in Slovakia today.

93. *Sic* for Napoléonienne (Napoleonic). Mme de Staël's word-play.

94. She left Vienna with Rocca and her children on June 22 at five o'clock in the afternoon, as we read in a spy's report (Jean Mistler, *Madame de Staël et Maurice O'Donnell* [Paris: Calmann-Lévy, 1926], pp. 291). The Emperor referred to is Napoleon. She had left Schlegel and Uginet in Vienna to bring her the precious document. The letter advising Mme de Staël of the arrival of the Russian passports was sent on June 30, but it did not reach her before she left Brünn [the German name for Brno] on July 1.

95. This is surely George Mills, secret agent of the British government whom Mme de Staël had met in Vienna (Mistler, *Mme de Staël et Maurice O'Donnell,* p. 78). Expelled toward the end of 1808, he came to Switzerland in January 1809 and stayed at Coppet during the spring of that year. In 1810, he was in Berlin, then Vienna, before he was detained in Brno (N. King, "Coppet en 1809–1810," *Cahiers staëliens* 24 [1978], p. 39). The "witty man" referred to later in the paragraph may be Schlegel.

96. The problems raised were for Rocca's passport. The order came from Vienna to separate him from Mme de Staël and oblige him to go through Prussian Silesia. He caught up with her at Olomouc (*Olmütz* in German) on July 2, and was then obliged to proceed by way of Opava; he joined her again only at Brody, on the border of the Austrian and Russian Empires (*Carnets,* p. 274). Ironically, the travel authorization for Mme de Staël was handed down in Vienna on that same July 2 (ibid., p. 275). She had left the previous day. The papers reached her several days later. The stay in Brno was very unpleasant. On March 12, 1813, she would write to Mme de Humboldt: "Through Gentz I received M. de Metternich's apologies for the way I was harassed in Vienna. He claims that M. de Hudlitz [*sic*] alone was responsible. I rather doubt it, but that stay in Brünn was one of the most difficult moments of my life" (copied from the original by Heinzmann).

97. Prince Adam Casimir Czartoryski (1734–1823) had been a candidate for the throne. He was a general in the Austrian army after the division of Poland, and Napoleon made him Marshal of the Polish Confederation. The estate of Lanzut is *Lańcut* in Polish.

98. The future Ferdinand III of Hapsberg (1769–1824), brother to Emperor Francis I, Grand Duke of Tuscany, lost his states under the Treaty of Lunéville. In compensation he was named Grand Duke of Würzburg in 1805 and so remained until 1814 when he recovered Tuscany. Chateaubriand heard him sing at Fontainebleau at concerts sponsored by Empress Josephine (*Mémoires d'outre-tombe,* 2d ed., vol. 2, p. 374).

99. Napoleon's three sisters: Pauline, Princess Borghese; Caroline Murat, afterwards Queen of Naples; and Elisa Bacciochi, who was still only Princess de Lucques, and was to become Grand Duchess of Tuscany.

100. Rudolf I of Hapsberg (1218–1291) became the first emperor of this dynasty in 1273.

Maria Ludovica (Marie Louise) d'Este (1787–1816), Maria Theresa's granddaughter, third wife of Emperor Francis I. Mme de Staël had attended their wedding in Vienna in 1808. "The young Empress," she wrote in *De l'Allemagne* (vol. 1, pp. 123–24), "brought up in cruel times, had about her the double aura of grandeur and adversity." Her father, Hercule Renaud III, last Duke of Modena, and deprived of his states by the Treaty of Campo Formio, had taken refuge in Vienna and was an implacable enemy of Napoleon, as was his daughter. She scarcely hid her feelings at Dresden.

101. Brody was an important commercial center.

102. The travelers left on the afternoon of July 1 and met again in Olomouc. They left immediately for Wadowice, southeast of Cracow. Schlegel joined them on July 7 at Gdów, and they reached Lanzut on July 8. Thus Mme de Staël saw only a small area of Poland, south of Cracow.

103. Attributed to the Austrians by the Treaty of Campo Formio in 1797, Venice was awarded to the French by the Treaty of Pressburg in 1805. Venetians did not like the Austrians and remembered them unfavorably; thus they cheered Napoleon on November 29, 1807. Certain nobles in particular detested the Austrians, and Mme de Staël may have met them in 1805. As for Carnival, the festival itself was not prohibited, but face masks were not allowed in the streets from 1801 on.

104. Mme de Staël translates the German *Kreis* as *cercle;* it is an administrative division.

105. From Wadowice, on July 5, Mme de Staël wrote to Mme Récamier: "Along the road, I met long processions of humble people going in their misery to beg of God, not hoping for anything from men, wanting to address a higher power. . . . From time to time a few melancholy songs declare the laments of suffering beings who sigh even as they sing" (*Lettres à Madame Récamier,* ed. Emmanuel Beau de Loménie [Paris: Domat, 1952], p. 236).

106. This calls to mind her adventure of 1796. By the Directory's decree, she was to be arrested if she entered France, and her name was to be displayed at frontier posts (Balayé and King, pp. 46 ff.).

107. Antoine de Sartine, Count d'Alby (1729–1801). As an effective lieutenant general of police in Paris from 1759 to 1774, he used lower level policemen in civilian clothes for surveillance at night and had numerous informers in all milieux. Thus Mme de Staël's joke here seems rather surprising.

108. Near Spitzgowitz (*Carnets,* p. 276). The Princess-Marshal is Mme Lubomirska.

109. Schlegel brought the passports when he rejoined her at Gdów (*Carnets,* p. 277).

110. Mme de Staël was unaware that orders had been given not to let her stop and visit her various princely friends any longer than strictly necessary for rest. When Metternich lifted the restriction, it was too late. This was doubtless fortunate since the Grand Army was advancing inexorably toward Russia and she would have found it very difficult to reach Moscow two weeks later.

111. The war began in June. Napoleon left Dresden on May 29, and crossed

the Vistula on June 6. His troops crossed the Nieman on the twenty-fourth or twenty-fifth of that month.

112. Auguste de Staël's note. "To explain the strength and validity of my mother's anguish during the journey, I must say that the attention of the Austrian police was not directed at her alone. M. Rocca's description had been sent along the whole route, with orders to arrest him as a French officer; and although he had resigned his commission, although his wounds made him unfit for further military service, there is no doubt that had he been handed over to France, he would have been treated with the utmost severity. He had therefore traveled alone and under an assumed name, and it was at Lanzut that he had arranged to meet my mother. Since he arrived before her, and did not suspect that she might be escorted by a police inspector, he came to meet her, confident and joyous. Frozen with terror at the danger he risked all unknowingly, my mother barely had time to signal to him to retrace his steps; and but for the generous presence of mind of a Polish gentleman who furnished M. Rocca with the means of escape, he would inevitably have been recognized and arrested by the inspector.

"Unable to foresee the fate of her manuscript, and under what public or private circumstances she might publish it, my mother thought it best to omit these details that I am allowed to make known today."

113. "Faithful to the Bourbons, Princess Lubomirska wore mourning for the Duke d'Enghien and showered with kindness all the émigrés she could collect along the main roads" (Countess Anna Potocka, *Mémoires 1794–1820,* ed. Casimir Stryienski [Paris: Plon, 1897], p. 55). She detested Napoleon. Mme de Staël met her during her stay in Vienna in 1808, along with her nephew, Prince Henri Lubomirski (1777–1850), and his wife, Thérèse, whom she had received at Coppet where she put on plays with them.

114. Lemberg, Lvov in Polish; it is now in Ukraine. She left Lanzut on the morning of the ninth. It was thirty kilometers to Lemberg, which she probably reached on the same day. She was certainly there on the eleventh (Norman King, "Un récit inédit du grand voyage de Madame de Staël," *Cahiers staëliens* 4 [May 1966], p. 18).

115. Count Jean-Pierre Goëss (1774–1846), whose name figures several times in police instructions and reports.

116. The use of the present tense shows that Napoleon still reigned when this was written.

117. Note by Auguste de Staël: "It was on July 14, 1817 that my mother was taken from us and that God received her into His bosom. What soul would not be struck with religious emotion, meditating on the mysterious juxtapositions offered by human destiny?"

118. She crossed the border between the two empires at Brody (*Carnets,* p. 279), east of Lemberg. There she made the decision to head for Sweden and give up the idea of Turkey, just as Auguste advised. Since the direct route was cut off, the

travelers crossed Volhynia, Ukraine, and Russia by way of Jitomir, Kiev, and Tula, a journey of over one thousand kilometers, and more than six hundred from Moscow to Saint Petersburg. [The text retains the author's spelling of Russian names of people and places, which represents nineteenth-century European usage. However, modern English spelling is used in the notes, e.g. Kiew / Kiev—Trans]

119. It should be remembered that Schlegel obviously spoke German, as did Mme de Staël and her son, Albert.

120. Volhynia had been annexed by Russia in 1778.

121. Alexander had sent General Balachov to Napoleon on June 28 with a letter from the Czar. The meeting took place on July 1 at Vilna. Napoleon spoke violently of the Czar whose empire he was invading. Alexander insisted that the French army cross back over the Niemen, and Napoleon refused. Mme de Staël surely met the general in Saint Petersburg, then in Paris. Alexander Dimitrievich Balachov (1770–1837) was Minister of Police from 1810 on. He accompanied Alexander on the French campaign.

122. Allusion to the blockade of the continent.

123. Jean-Baptiste Nompère de Champagny, Duke de Cadore (1756–1834), had fought in the American Revolution and served as deputy in the Estates General. Minister of the Interior in 1804, he succeeded Talleyrand at Foreign Affairs in 1807 and defended the continental blockade. Surprised by Napoleon's change of policy toward Russia in 1810, he clumsily reminded the Emperor of his anti-Polish remarks of 1809, and so lost his portfolio on April 16, 1811.

Count Nicolaï Petrovich Rumiantsev (1754–1826) had been Foreign Minister since 1807. He served as ambassador to Paris after Tilsit. Favoring the French and hostile to England, he resigned in 1812. Mme de Staël met him in Saint Petersburg on August 14. Chateaubriand quotes this passage in *Mémoires d'outre-tombe,* 2d ed., vol. 1, pp. 789–90.

124. The emperor in this sentence is Napoleon. Armand Augustin, Marquis de Caulaincourt, Duke of Vicenza, had a brilliant military career. From 1802 on, he was Bonaparte's aide-de-camp and was made brigadier general in 1803. It has been seen that he was implicated in the death of the Duke d'Enghien. He was ambassador to Saint Petersburg from 1807 to May 1811. He fought in the Russian campaign and was at Napoleon's side during the retreat.

125. The number varies greatly in Mme de Staël's writings as in those of other travelers, but it is always given as well over a thousand.

126. Armand Emmanuel du Plessis, Duke de Richelieu (1762–1822), with the permission of the National Assembly fought in the Russian and Austrian armies during the Revolution. Beginning in 1790 he served in Russia. In 1803, Alexander I named him governor of Odessa. He too hated Napoleon. Returning to France under the Restoration, he became Prime Minister in 1815 and was influential in arranging the departure of the allied armies in 1818.

127. Mme de Staël did not abandon this project. She planned on making the

trip in 1817, which was to be the year of her illness and death. It was in part because of this idea that she hesitated in Vienna and again in Jitomir between the North and the South, between Sweden and Turkey.

128. Mme de Staël heard them for the first time in Jitomir.

129. Mikhaïl Andreievich, Count Miladorovich, born in Saint Petersburg in 1771 of a Serbian family, had fought in several campaigns against the Turks and the French, notably in Italy under Suvorov in 1799. He fought brilliantly at Borodino, and was instrumental in the burning of Moscow. He became governor of Saint Petersburg and was assassinated in 1825 in the revolt that followed the accession of Nicolas I. Mme de Staël wrote to Princess Kutosov from Stockholm on October 6, 1812: "Would you be kind enough to send word to General Miladorovich that I am making a crown of laurels for him, since he has been a worthy aide-de-camp to his general [Kutosov]?" (letter quoted in P. Gautier's edition of the present book). Suvorov was one of the greatest Russian generals and strategists.

130. About 960 kilometers. The travelers left Kiev on July 21.

131. She records this in her notebook, but in Finland (*Carnets,* p. 334). We do not know whether this happened in Finland or is a memory of Russia.

132. The old aristocratic class whose power was destroyed by Ivan the Terrible and Peter the Great.

133. The *feldjaeger* were official couriers who traversed the country at high speed under very difficult conditions.

134. On July 24, Napoleon entered Vitebsk. The Russians fell back to Smolensk, which Napoleon would reach on August 16.

135. The key to the story is found in the last manuscript of *Considérations* (pt. 4, chap. 14) when the general's name appears. He was Jean Lannes, Duke de Montebello (1769–1809), Marshal of France, who became a general during the Revolution, and was one of the greatest military men of the time. He gradually came to detest the savagery of war and, fatally wounded at Essling, he died on May 31, 1809.

136. Pushkin relates that in response to jokes about the long beards worn by Russians, Mme de Staël retorted: "The common people who managed to defend their beards a hundred years ago will manage to defend their heads" (A. S. Pushkin, *Roslavlew: Polnoïé sotchinenij* [Leningrad, 1978], vol. 6, p. 135). (Information provided to Mlle Balayé by V. Milchina.)

137. The Genevan Jean Louis Mallet heard Mme de Staël talk about the serfs in the spring of 1813 in London. In reply to a Russian woman who wanted to prove to her that they were free and happy, she said: "Happy is all very well, but free? Among all the definitions of liberty, I have never encountered slavery" (Kohler, p. 623). Simone Balayé remarks: "This is probably far closer to her true thinking."

138. Perhaps Schlegel, who translated Shakespeare into German, or Joseph de Maistre.

139. Mme de Staël reached the city on August 2 and left on the August 7 (*Carnets,* p. 439). She wrote to F. Randall on the third and the sixth. Albertine also

wrote, saying that her mother was improved in health and spirit. This information was included in a letter from Miss Randall to Sismondi on September 21 (Biblioteca municipale di Pescia, arch. Sismondi).

140. She probably saw Kitai-Gorod, near the Kremlin, which is much more centrally located than the other bazaars. *Kitai* means "Chinese," and she speaks of the Chinese city several lines further on.

141. Count Matvei Alexandrovich Dmitriev-Mamanov (1790–1863), son of a lover of Catherine the Great, offered millions of rubles in silver, diamonds, and real estate. The Czar accepted only the formation of a cavalry regiment and named the Count brigadier general. Turgenev tells the story in *Russia and the Russians* (Paris: 1847, vol. 1, p. 223). The Countess in the next sentence is quite probably Anna Alexeevna Orlova-Chesmenskaya (1785–1848), daughter of a favorite of Catherine II.

142. For the army. (In the first notebook, she writes "a thousand.")

143. In variants of *Ten Years,* Mme de Staël expands this idea, unfortunately discarding here the expression "Tartar Rome." Besides the great number of churches and the great solitary expanses that remind her of Rome, she may be referring to the very Russian idea of the "third Rome": the one that succeeded Rome and Byzantium.

144. Alexander had come to Moscow on the evening of July 23 amid an immense gathering of people.

145. Mme de Staël saw this arsenal-museum in the Kremlin's barracks, where it had been stored in 1806. All of this can be seen now in the Palace of Armor, along with the crown of Siberia and Astrakhan, which she discusses further on.

146. The steel of swords, that is, not firearms or bows and arrows.

147. Ivan and Peter shared the throne. But Ivan V (1666–1696) was in very poor health. Their older sister, the Regent Sophie (1657–1704), was exiled to the Novodevichy Convent in Moscow, where she died.

148. She went to the top of the Kremlin's highest tower, ninety-seven meters tall, built by Boris Godunov in 1600.

149. Count Alexei Kirillovich Razumovsky (1748–1822), ambassador to Austria until 1807, francophobe, and Minister of Public Education from 1810 to 1816. In her notes, "La Retraite de Russia vue par Albertine de Staël" (*Studi in onore di Mario Matucci* [Pisa: Piacini, 1993], p. 117), Albertine writes that the French laid waste to this garden, and that Minister Markoff's home was destroyed by cannon fire.

150. Count Dmitri Petrovich Buturlin, Alexander's aide-de-camp (1763–1829), senator, and director of the Hermitage, wrote a *History of the Campaign of 1812*. His library, looted by the French as Mme de Staël says further on, was taken back by the Russians at Beresina (*Dix années d'exil,* ed. Paul Gautier [Paris: Plon-Nourrit et Cie, 1904], according to Langeron's *Mémoires*).

151. It was the largest establishment of its kind in Europe. Alexander I had placed it under the patronage of his mother, the Dowager Empress Maria Feodorovna. It was saved from the fire, along with its two hundred children, by her close

friend, the elderly director of the home, Ivan Akinfievich Toutolmin, to whom Napoleon entrusted a message for the Czar (Curtis Cate, *1812: le duel des deux empereurs,* tr. Claude Yelnik and Jean d'Hendecourt [Paris: Laffont, 1987], pp. 316 ff.).

152. The Archbishop, former tutor to Paul I, had anointed him Emperor as he did for Alexander I. Born Piotr Levchin in 1737, Archbishop of Tver, then of Moscow, Metropolitan of Moscow from 1787 on, he was to die on November 11, 1812. Too ill to come in person, he sent the Czar an icon, not of the Virgin but of Saint Serge (Cate, p. 223), which had accompanied the conquering Czar Alexei Mikhaïlovich and his son, Peter the Great. He compared Alexander to David and Napoleon to Goliath.

153. On September 16, Napoleon did in fact climb this tower with Berthier and Caulaincourt (Tulard and Garros, p. 290) to watch Moscow burn in the fire that had started the previous night. The Great Horde is the name of the most western Mongol kingdom, founded in 1223. The Mongols conquered the Russians, and the great princes of Moscow and Kiev became their vassals, but after 1391 their empire fell apart and the various kingdoms were gradually integrated into Russia. Mme de Staël draws on the historian Levesque here.

In *Considérations* (pt. 4, chap. 14) she writes: "I was in Moscow one month to the day before Napoleon's army entered the city, and already fearing his arrival, I dared remain only a short time. As I walked atop the Kremlin, palace of the ancient czars that overlooks Russia's vast capital and its eighteen hundred churches, I reflected that it was given Bonaparte to see empires at his feet, as Satan offered them to Our Lord. But when nothing was left for him to conquer in Europe, destiny lay hold of him so that he fell as rapidly as he had risen." Mme Balayé points out the biblical tone of this variant.

154. Count Feodor Rostopchin (1765–1826) was appointed to high office under Alexander I.

155. Jean Paul Marat (1743–1793) was a Jacobin of the extreme left. This so-called "Friend of the People" is considered one of those responsible for the September Massacres of 1792 that inaugurated the Reign of Terror. He was assassinated by Charlotte Corday [Trans].

156. Unidentified quotation attributed to Diderot without proof.

157. Count Joseph de Maistre, whom Mme de Staël had known since 1794 in Lausanne (*Carnets,* pp. 320 ff.). The sentence figures in his *Cinq lettres sur l'éducation publique en Russie* (*Oeuvres Complètes,* vol. 8 [Lyon: Vitte et Perrussel, 1886], p. 288).

158. Countess Ekaterina Rostopchina was converted to Roman Catholicism in 1806 or 1810 and practiced it with fanatical strictness. In 1810 she published her *Recueil de preuves sur la vérité de la religion.* This is surely the book she gave to Mme de Staël.

159. This opinion is often repeated in *De l'Allemagne* with respect to writers like Wieland, for example. The translator would add that it is also discussed at length in the chapter on Italian literature in Book VII of the novel *Corinne* (1807), and is

taken up again in the essay "On the Spirit of Translations" of 1816 (see A. Gold-berger, "Madame de Staël, De l'esprit des traductions,'" in *Le Groupe de Coppet et l'Europe 1789–1830* [Paris: Touzot, 1994], pp. 345–59).

160. All the more regretfully for being obliged to leave without her son Albert, who was ill. During this extension of his stay, he witnessed an atrocity committed by Rostopchin, who flogged his French cook and sent him to Siberia. Albert and several others gave the cook money for sustenance (King, "Un récit inédit," pp. 11–13).

161. That Mme de Staël is mistaken here explains Auguste's deletion of the passage. It was during a war waged by Charles IX of Sweden that Jakob Pontusson de la Gardie took Novgorod and entered Moscow in 1610.

162. A ukase is an edict of the Russian government [Trans].

163. "Russia, although different from other European empires in its institutions and its Asiatic customs, underwent the second crisis of European monarchies under Peter I with the humbling of the nobility by the monarch" (*Considérations,* pt. 1, chap. 1).

Under the date June 14, 1717, Saint-Simon wrote: "On the day he visited the Sorbonne, he displayed greater regard for the statue of Cardinal de Richelieu than he had shown the person of Mme de Maintenon. The moment he saw the Cardinal's tomb, he ran to kiss that minister's face, addressing these words to him: "I would give half my kingdom to such a man as thee so that he might help me govern the other half" (*Mémoires de Saint-Simon,* ed. Arthur A. G. M. Boislisle, in "Les Grands écrivians de France" vol. 31 [Paris: Hachette], p. 383). Mme de Staël detested Richelieu, in whom she saw the founder of monarchical tyranny and an enemy of Protestants. She also speaks of him harshly in *Considérations* (pt. 1, chap. 2).

164. This was written in Stockholm after the burning of Moscow.

165. The travelers reached Saint Petersburg on August 13. On Friday the fourteenth, she began her tour of the city. She was presented to Czar Alexander on the seventeenth.

166. About 32 kilometers.

167. Masson describes these coachmen in the snow (*Mémoires secrets sur la Russie pendant les règnes de Catherine II et Paul Ier* [Paris: Didot, 1863], p. 407), a sight she could not have seen. On the *lazzaroni,* see *Corinne,* bk. 11, chap. 2.

168. Mme de Staël considers Catherine a man in the sense that she exercised political power, a function then reserved exclusively to men [Trans].

169. Clearly an allusion to the weakness of Napoleon's adversaries.

170. The church was built between 1802 and 1811.

171. The monastery *(lavra)* of Saint Alexander Nevsky was founded by Peter the Great. On this site, Catherine II rebuilt it between 1779 and 1790 as the Cathedral of the Trinity (*Carnets,* pp. 295, 325).

172. "That man" is, of course, Napoleon. This seems to have been written after the defeat in Russia, given the use of the past tense, But her use of the present tense a few lines later ("is commanded") shows that Napoleon's defeat was not yet total.

173. They arrived at around the same time as Mme de Staël. George, Count of Tyrconnel, an Irish peer (1788–1813) sent to Russia by the British government as aide-de-camp to General Robert Wilson, became military advisor to the Russian armies. Admiral William Bentinck (1764–1813) enjoyed the confidence of Alexander and Bernadotte; he also exercised great influence over Mme de Staël at this time. They had no official diplomatic mission but were welcomed as if they had.

174. She dined at Count Orlov's on the eighteenth, the day after her presentation at court (*Carnets,* p. 298 n.194). Count Vladimir Grigorievich Orlov (1743–1831), and not Gregory—as she calls him in the following sentence—was the director of the Academy of Sciences. In 1817, the Czar bought back the island. Great chestnut trees stood there in Mme de Staël's time.

175. The poet Ernst Moritz Arndt, companion to the exiled Prussian statesman Baron Heinrich von Stein, describes this evening. Mme de Staël read the chapter "On Enthusiasm" from *De l'Allemagne.* "What an intoxicating draught she pours for these listeners burning with fever, ablaze with martial fervor! Leaning toward her, they listen to that eloquent voice that resounds like a call to arms." Stein was very much taken with her and met her often (Ernst Moritz Arndt, *Erinnerungen aus dem äusseren Leben* [Leipzig: Weidmann, 1840], pp. 312–13).

176. She went there on August 22 (*Carnets,* p. 304). The Greek artifacts she saw have since been brought to Saint Petersburg.

177. Pushkin cites this idea in his essay "A Journey from Moscow to Petersburg" (1834): "Among us, as Mme de Staël has observed, literature in most cases has been an occupation for nobles. In Russia, a few gentlemen have taken up literature." This last sentence is in French in the Russian text (Alexandre Pushkin, *Oeuvres* [Paris: Gallimard, 1990], p. 747).

178. As has been seen in Part One, Mme de Staël says this of Talleyrand's education.

179. Mme de Staël gets the chronology wrong here. She was presented to the sovereigns on August 17. Empress Yelisaveta-Alekseyevna, née Louise Marie Auguste of Baden (1779–1826), daughter of the Margrave of Baden, married Alexander in 1793. Through her mother, she was niece to Grand Duchess Louise of Saxe-Weimar, to whom Mme de Staël later wrote from Stockholm: "I saw your illustrious niece who inspired my deepest interest. I was accorded the most flattering welcome by her august husband, and I foresaw his conduct through his way of expressing himself" (*Coppet et Weimar: Madame de Staël et la grande-duchesse Louise . . .),* ed. Amélie Lenormant [Paris: M. Lévy frères, 1862], p. 243).

180. He refers to the meeting at Tilsit between June 25 and July 8. Napoleon's recollections of the meeting are recorded in his *Mémorial* (vol. 1, pp. 740–41). There follows in our text an allusion to Paul I, a great admirer of Frederick II of Prussia.

181. Auguste de Staël's note: "These words have already been cited in the third volume of *Considérations sur la Révolution française,* but they are worth repeating. All of this, moreover, I must remind [the reader], was written at the end of

1812." In *Considérations* (pt. 6, chap. 6) Mme de Staël writes: "'You are not unaware,' the Emperor of Russia told me, that Russian peasants are slaves. I do what I can to improve their lot gradually in my own estates, but elsewhere I meet obstacles that the peace of the Empire commands me to deal with carefully.' 'Sire,' I replied, I know that Russia is happy now, although she has no constitution other than Your Majesty's personal character.' 'Even were there some truth in the compliment you pay me,' the Emperor replied, I would never be more than a happy accident.'" The Czar's efforts were genuine, but he confronted immense obstacles.

182. Mikhaïl Mikhailovich Speransky (1772–1839) is a notable example. Beginning in 1796, this son of a Pope rose rapidly in the bureaucracy and continued to do so under Alexander I, becoming his executive secretary in 1807. He reorganized the whole central administration. Abruptly dismissed in March 1812, he slowly regained his power without ever retrieving his previous position. He had tried to prevent the war (Vandal, *Napoléon et Alexandre Ier*, vol. 3, pp. 364–69).

183. Empress Maria Fedorovna, widow of Paul I, née Dorothy de Wurtemberg-Montbéliard. Her son had entrusted her with official functions at court and with charitable functions, and her influence was strong (Vandal, *Napoléon et Alexandre Ier*, vol. 1, pp. 120–22).

184. This immense palace, built in 1783, was the imperial family's residence during August and September (*Carnets*, pp. 312–13).

185. Alexander Danilovich Menshikov (1673–1729) had been Peter I's friend and Catherine I's favorite. Through his efforts she ascended the throne when her husband died. Exiled to Siberia by Peter II, he died there.

186. Ivan IV Vassilyevich, known as Ivan the Terrible (1530–1584), drove the Tartars from Kazan, capital of the Golden Horde, in 1522, and from Astrakhan in 1554. He is mentioned several times in *Ten Years*.

187. Alexander Lvovich Narychkin, grand marshal of the court (1760–1826), was also superintendent of the theater. The visit took place on August 21 (*Carnets*, pp. 301–2). Note the characteristic Staëlien addition of the particle.

188. The "sea" she mentions is actually the *Bay* of Finland. My thanks to Jacob N. Oppenheim for providing this information [Trans]. Peterhof, between Oranienbaum and Saint Petersburg, was begun by Peter I in 1709. The Grand Palace and surrounding parks date from the 1720s.

189. The "knights of the Orient and of the seas" refer to the Russians and the English. Armida is the beautiful and deceitful sorceress in Tasso's *Jerusalem Delivered* who sows discord in the Christian camp and holds Tancred captive for a time [Trans].

190. She went there on August 20 at the suggestion of Count Orloff, director of the Academy. (The "squirrel heads" mentioned in the next sentence—the French is "squirrel *foreheads*"—are perhaps the equivalent of the squirrel neckpieces worn by Western women in the 1920s and 1930s) [Trans].

191. Georges Cuvier (1769–1832), a Protestant and member of the Collège de France, was named to the Institute in 1796, and named professor at the Museum

of Natural History in 1802. He founded the discipline of paleontology. From the way she speaks of him, it seems that Mme de Staël had met him, which was entirely possible when she lived in Paris.

192. The Citadel of Saint Peter and Saint Paul, begun by Peter the Great, housed a cathedral, state prisons, the arsenal, and the mint, which she visited. There she saw metal cast: "The mint: brilliance of the silver. Enormous machines. Poverty of those who work to make silver. 60 rubles a minute. Blackened faces of these men and their thick gloves make them blend with the heavy machines" (*Carnets,* pp. 309, 321). From this sight she drew the image applied to Napoleon's tyranny in Part One of *Ten Years.*

193. Catherine II had overthrown her husband, Peter III. Paul I, who may not have been the murdered Czar's son, detested her.

194. Ivan VI, overthrown in 1741, was assassinated under Catherine II's rule in 1764. Peter III, her husband, had been assassinated in 1762.

195. Monday, August 24, not September 1. She wrote: "The palace is decorated with tasteful luxury, particularly the rooms Catherine II occupied. One would prefer to see simpler rooms, however, for they would seem to reveal more clearly the soul of the person who lived there. But those beautiful rooms seem never to have witnessed other than [. . .] ceremonial words" (*Carnets,* pp. 323–24).

196. As a young woman, Mme de Staël had appreciated Catherine less because of the difficulties she had brought to M. de Staël's career. On the other hand, the Empress had held Necker in high esteem and proposed his coming to Russia when he fell out of favor in 1781. Other European sovereigns, such as Marie Caroline, Queen of Naples, made similar offers.

197. This is the Pavlovsk Palace.

198. Smolensk fell after two days of fighting, August 17 and 18.

199. The bourgeoisie, intermediate between the people and the aristocracy [Trans].

200. Prince Mikhaïl Bogdanovich Barclay de Tolly (1761–1818) came from a Scottish family settled in Finland since the beginning of the eighteenth century. Governor of Finland in 1810, he became Minister of War that same year and was the only victorious Russian general at Borodino. He led a splendid campaign in 1813 and was named field marshal in 1814 in Paris. His idea of retreating deep into Russia to draw Napoleon into a trap won him widespread hostility (Madelin, *Histoire du Consulat et de l'Empire,* vol. 12, pp. 160–87); however, it was by following this system until Moscow fell that the Russians trapped Napoleon in the Russian winter. It must be noted that Mme de Staël represents the thinking of her time and place.

201. Allusion to the temptations of Christ in the Gospels of Luke and Matthew.

202. Mme de Staël visited the Institute of Saint Catherine on August 22 (*Carnets,* p. 308).

203. Published in 1800, and for which she had a marked preference.

204. Mme de Staël went there on September 2. In her notebooks we read: "Intelligent faces of the girls and boys. Possibility of being mistaken on their account when one enters. Their facility for writing, their minds and gestures, a little deaf-mute girl's pretty face. Beautiful eyes. Curiosity of the deaf. While elsewhere they sing before dinner, prayer signed for them all by a girl and a boy while they all make signs of the cross, signs of the cross that they make without understanding them!" (*Carnets,* pp. 313–14).

205. Friedrich Maximillian von Klinger (1752–1831), an important German poet and playwright, finished his career in Russia where he held a high position in the army and was director of the Cadet School in Saint Petersburg. He had married an illegitimate daughter of Catherine II. The famous *Sturm und Drang* school took its name from one of his plays in 1775. Mme de Staël speaks of him in *De l'Allemagne* (vol. 3, pp. 174 ff.).

206. The counting frame, or abacus.

207. Allusion to the confluence of the blue Rhone and the gray Arve at Geneva known as the Junction.

208. A tragedy by V. A. Ozeroff, first performed in 1807, and revived in 1812 with great success, due to the circumstances at the time.

209. At the time, "declamation" meant both diction and gestures [Trans, with thanks to J. P. Perchelet].

210. Princess Catherine Feodorovna Dolgoruki was a friend of Mme Vigée-Lebrun and Mme Récamier. In Saint Petersburg, Mme de Staël frequented Countess (not Baroness) Stroganova, daughter of Natalia Petrovna Golitzina, whom Mme de Staël had known in Paris before the Revolution.

211. The Swedish name for Turku, a seaport in southwest Finland [Trans].

212. Berthier, whom she had known as a general, was now a marshal.

213. Allusion to the meeting at Erfurt. As for the principles of the Revolution, Mme de Staël refers to the ideas of 1789.

214. He had evacuated Vitebsk and Smolensk. Paradoxically, as has been noted previously, it was this retreat that led to the final defeat of the French.

215. Mikhaïl Larinovich Kutusov (1745–1813) had fought victoriously against the Turks. Soon to be victor at Borodino and Smolensk, pursuing the Grand Army in retreat, he would receive the title of Savior of Russia. The Battle of the Moskva, or Borodino, was fought on September 5. Considered a victory by both sides, it served the Russian cause better than the French.

216. There is an account of the interview: "'I come to salute the estimable leader on whom the destiny of Europe depends,' said Mme de Staël. 'Madame, you give me the crown of immortality,' he replied." On October 5, 1812, she wrote to Princess Kutusov: "Your husband was Fabius [Cunctator] against that African" (Gautier, p. 411). Thus she compares Hannibal's conqueror to that of Napoleon, whom she calls "African" on several occasions. Kutusov died in January 1813, in Poland. His career was glorious except for Austerlitz, a battle fought without his approval.

217. September 7, to be precise.

218. Colonel Sir Robert Thomas Wilson (1777–1849) had fought Bonaparte in Egypt; he had served in the Russian Army while also serving as his country's diplomatic agent in Saint Petersburg until war was declared with England. He went to Portugal, where he organized resistance to Napoleon, and returned to Russia in 1812. He fought the French in Lützen at the head of the Prussian reserves (Vandal, *Napoléon et Alexandre Ier*, vol. 1, pp. 152–54). For a time he served under Bolívar, and finished his career as governor of Gibraltar. On December 12, 1812, Mme de Staël sent him a highly laudatory letter from Stockholm, for which he thanked her (V. de Pange, "Madame de Staël et ses correspondants anglais" [diss. Oxford University, 1955], pp. 298–99).

219. Heinrich Friedrich Karl, Baron von Stein (1757–1831), an important member of the Prussian administration, was dismissed in 1807 and recalled after Prussia was defeated. He effected major economic and social reforms. Napoleon insisted on his dismissal in November 1808, when his secret preparations for revenge were discovered. In 1812 he was an advisor to Alexander I and worked for the rapprochement of Prussia and Russia. He had just arrived in Saint Petersburg, where Mme de Staël saw him frequently.

220. The English ambassador, William Shaw, Earl of Cathcart (1755–1843), arrived on September 4. Mme de Staël invited him on the sixth, according to John Quincy Adams, whose father was then President of the United States. He was at Mme de Staël's for the first time with fifteen or twenty people, and gives his father a detailed account of the visit (*Writings of John Quincy Adams,* ed. Worthington Chauncey Ford [New York: MacMillan Co., 1913–1917], vol. 4, pp. 450 ff.).

221. General Baron Friedrich Karl von Tettenborn (1778–1845) had a command in the Russian army and besieged Hamburg where the French held out for a year (May 30, 1813–May 27, 1814).

222. Count Louis Adolphe Alexis de Noailles (1783–1835) had a role in propagating Pius VII's Bull of Excommunication for Napoleon. Arrested, then freed, he left France for Switzerland, then Sweden, and became a secret agent for Louis XVIII. Aide-de-camp to Bernadotte, he fought in the campaigns of 1813 and 1814. Mme de Staël, who knew his father (the Duke de Noailles) well, had met him in Geneva in 1811. He returned to France with the Count d'Artois, the future Charles X.

223. Ernst Moritz Arndt (1768–1860), a writer much involved in politics, accompanied Stein to Saint Petersburg. He was thus able to meet Mme de Staël. His *Erinnerungen* contain his portrait of her and an anecdote relating that she wept when she heard that a Russian audience hissed Racine's *Phèdre* with Mlle George, a famous actress of the time.

224. Tyrconnel died at Vilna on December 10, 1812; Bentinck died of pleurisy on February 21, 1813. Thus this passage was written after the latter date.

225. The Russians took Finland from Sweden after Tilsit in 1808, whence Bernadotte's difficulties in making an alliance with Russia. Mme de Staël was in

Åbo (Turku), then Finland's largest city, on September 15.

226. Gustavus IV Adolph (1778–1837), son of Gustavus III, had already lost Swedish Pomerania in August 1807. When his madness intensified, he was deposed by a military coup on March 13, 1809, and exiled. He died poor and obscure in Switzerland.

227. Since she was in Finland only one day, September 15, she was there too briefly to acquire any real knowledge of the country or its society.

228. From 1569 to 1571 Eric XIV, imprisoned by his brother John III, lived in this château built on a cape at the mouth of a river. Poisoned on John's orders, he died on February 25, 1577 at Örbyhus.

229. Negotiations between Sweden and Russia took place unsuccessfully on one of the Åland Islands in May 1718. Charles XII was killed on the following November 30. The Ålands are a group of Finnish islands in the Baltic Sea between Sweden and Finland.

230. The draft of the text breaks off abruptly here. Despite travel notebooks and some separate passages and notes, it was not resumed. In her note at the end of the uncompleted sentence, Simone Balayé writes:

> On December 21, 1838, a few months after Albertine's death, August Schlegel wrote to her husband, the Duke de Broglie, that there had been a storm and that Albertine had shown great courage. (See Countess Jean de Pange, *A.-G. Schlegel et Mme de Staël*, p. 397. For the events of the forced stay on the island, see *Carnets* [pp. 332–33]. On the actress: K. Gram Holmström, *Monodrama, Attitudes, Tableaux Vivants . . . Studies on Some Trends of Theatrical Fashion, 1770–1815.*)
>
> Traveling with Mme de Staël and her entourage were the actress Henrietta Hendel-Schütz and her husband, professor of philosophy and history at the University of Jena. Mme Schütz was famous for her art of the "attitude," a form of dramatic expression of great interest to Mme de Staël. For her companions, she performed "The Paintings and Statues of Glorious Rome." Schlegel wrote verses for the occasion, and Mme de Staël said later: "She comforted me on the deserted Åland Island where I was virtually shipwrecked" (*Briefe von Karl Viktor von Bonstetten an Friedrike Brun*, hrsg. von F. Mathisson [Frankfurt am Main: W. Schefer, 1829], vol. 2, p. 45).

APPENDIX I: AUGUSTE DE STAËL'S COMMENTARIES AS EDITOR OF THE 1821 EDITION

1. Auguste de Staël's notes commenting on his mother's text are included among the explanatory notes with his name appended.

2. Auguste makes a number of errors here. Given its primary aim, the narrative begins in December 1797 when she met Bonaparte for the first time. As abridged by Auguste, it covers barely six years, not seven. Necker died on April 9.

Mme de Staël goes beyond that date and shows the rise of Napoleon to the throne in the course of 1804.

3. At the end of August 1810.

4. Mid-September.

5. While the title of the book is *De l'Allemagne,* referencs such as this appear in Auguste's text as "sur *l'Allemagne*" and the translator has followed Auguste.

6. The new prefect was Capelle.

7. These are the disguised manuscripts, copied by Fanny Randall. The reference to the English Revolution is inexact, as there are the so-called narratives of the death of Mary Stuart as well as episodes from the Middle Ages and from the reign of James I.

8. This is partly true. See the introduction to this volume.

9. He also changed many details of word and fact. See the introduction.

10. Auguste de Staël alludes to the consequences of the Holy Alliance in the course of different congresses, notably those of Aix-la-Chapelle, Troppau, and Laibach in 1820.

11. Of his mother's *Complete Works.*

12. See Auguste de Staël's preface above.

13. *Manuscrits de M. Necker,* published by his daughter (Geneva: J. J. Pachoud, year XIII), and preceded by Mme de Staël's splendid text, "On M. Necker's Character and Private Life."

14. This is the journey she made from December 1804 to June 1805 in order to write *Corinne.*

15. We know of at least one, sent to Cardinal Fesch (see S. Balayé's article on the subject in *Cahiers staëliens* 10 [June 1970], pp. 25–26).

16. See Part One, note 163.

17. Nicolas Jean Marie Rougier de la Bergerie (1784–1857), elected deputy to the Legislative Assembly from Yonne, was named prefect there by Bonaparte in 1800. Mme de Staël stayed in Auxerre from mid-April to mid-September 1806. From September 18 to the end of November, she lived in Rouen.

18. Jacques-Fortunat de Savoye-Rollin (1754–1823) was prefect of the Seine-Inférieure beginning in March 1806. He welcomed Mme de Staël nicely ("Lettres de Mme de Staël aux Savoye-Rollin"). N. King gives the details of his dismissal for negligence in 1812; he was acquitted by the Imperial Court and named prefect of Deux Nèthes.

19. Victory over Prussia and entrance into Berlin at the end of October 1806.

20. The eighteenth-century château d'Acosta, since destroyed, was near Melun. It belonged to Boniface Louis André Marquis de Castellane-Navejan, (1758–1837), an old friend of Mme de Staël. A deputy for the nobility to the Estates General, he had joined forces with the Third Estate. He had been prefect for the Basses-Pyrénées since 1802. Mme de Staël lived in his château from November 29, 1806, until her departure for Coppet on April 27, 1807 (for further details, see *C.G.,* vol. 6, p. 179).

21. On May 1, Paris: Nicolle.

22. It was one of the most brilliant summers of those she divided between Coppet and Ouchy (in the hills beneath Lausanne). She performed in several plays at large gatherings there (see Martine de Rougemont, "L'activité théâtrale dans le Groupe de Coppet: la dramaturgie et le jeu," *Le Groupe de Coppet,* 2nd Coppet Conference, July 10–13, 1974 [Genève: Slatkine; Paris: H. Champion, 1977]; J.-D. Candaux, "Le théâtre de Madame de Staël au Molard, 1805–1806" *Cahiers staëliens* 14 [September 1972], pp. 19–32; and Danielle Johnson-Cousin, "La société dramatique de Madame de Staël de 1803 à 1816," *Studies on Voltaire and the XVIIIth Century,* vol. 296 [Oxford: Votaire Foundation, 1992)].

23. The Prince's visit was marked by the inception of his love for Mme Récamier, whom he desperately wanted to marry. A prisoner, released on his own recognizance, he was freed by the Treaty of Tilsit (July 1807).

24. See the chapters on Austria and Vienna in *De l'Allemagne;* Mistler, *Madame de Staël et Maurice O'Donnell;* "Lettres inédites du prince de Ligne," ed. Simone Balayé in *Bulletin de l'Académie royale de langue et de littérature françaises de Belgique* (1966). See also E. Tunner, "Ce que Madame de Staël savait des écrivains autrichiens," and articles by N. King and G. Solovieff in *Cahiers staëliens* 41 (1989–1993).

25. She began drafting her book in July 1808 and finished it in 1810.

26. Auguste omitted four tragedies, which will appear in D. Cousin-Johnson's forthcoming collection of Mme de Staël's plays.

27. In this "conclusion" to <u>Ten Years of Exile</u> Auguste de Staël summarizes the end of the Great Journey and the reasons for the interruption of the book.

28. *De l'Allemagne* was published in London on November 3, 1813.

Appendix II: The Disguised Manuscripts Decoded: A Sample

1. Italics designate the disguised words and their equivalents in the decoded text. The Elizabeth and Mary Stuart characters stand for Bonaparte and the Duke d'Enghien. It was natural for Mme de Staël to use Mary Stuart's death here, for it was much on her mind and she referred to it in *Considérations.* That Schiller's play on the subject was a favorite of hers, one that she chose to analyze in *De l'Allemagne,* must have strongly influenced her choice.

2. Zénobia is mentioned in *Corinne:* "In adversity she did not manage to die for glory like a man, nor, like a woman, to die rather than betray her friend" (bk. 8, chap. 4).

3. Here the story of the Duke d'Enghien is intermixed with that of his ancestor the Grand Condé (1621–1686). Allusion is made both to the latter's military glory and to the gallantry shown by the Duke d'Enghien when he fought in the Condé army. This consisted of a small group of nobles assembled by the émigré Prince de Condé in 1792 in the Rhineland to fight the Republican armies.

4. From here on, the stories of Mary Stuart and the Duke d'Enghien encroach on one another.

5. General Savary. Note the rhyme with Drury, who is one of Mary Stuart's guards in Schiller's play; the choice of name is not gratuitous.

6. This was a Corbert who figures in a number of Mme de Staël's notes on this anecdote.

Selected Bibliography

WORKS BY GERMAINE DE STAËL

Books

Oeuvres complètes de Madame la Baronne de Staël-Holstein. 17 vols. Vol. 15, *Dix années d'exil.* Edited by Auguste de Staël. Paris: Treuttel et Würtz, 1820–1821.

Considérations sur la Révolution française. Edited by Jacques Godechot. Paris: Tallandier, 1983.

Corinne ou l'Italie. Edited by Simone Balayé. Paris: Gallimard, 1985.

De l'Allemagne. 5 vols. Edited by Countess Jean de Pange with Simone Balayé. Paris: Hachette, 1959–60. (Les Grands écrivains de France)

De la littérature considérée dans ses rapports avec les institutions sociales. 2 vols. Edited by Paul Van Tieghem. Geneva: Droz; Paris, Jean Minard, 1959. Re-edited by Jean Goldzink and Gérard Gengembre, Paris: Flammarion, 1991, GF.

Des circonstances actuelles pour terminer la Révolution. . . . Edited by Lucia Omacini. Geneva: Droz, 1979.

Dix années d'exil. Edited by Paul Gautier. Paris: Plon–Nourrit et Cie, 1904. Reprinted in 1966 in 10.18 collection with preface and notes by Simone Balayé.

Du caractère de M. Necker et de sa vie privée, which serves as an introduction to *Manuscrits de M. Necker, édité par sa fille.* Geneva: J.J. Pachoud, an. XIII.

Ed. *Lettres et pensées du Prince de Ligne.* Paris, Geneva: J. J. Pachoud, 1809.

Modern Translations

Corinne, or, Italy. Translated and with an introduction by Avriel H. Goldberger. New Brunswick, N.J.: Rutgers University Press, 1987.

Delphine. Translated and with an introduction by Avriel H. Goldberger. DeKalb: Northern Illinois University Press, 1995.

An Extraordinary Woman: Selected Writings of Germaine de Staël. Translated and with an introduction by Vivian Folkenflick. New York: Columbia University Press, 1987.

Correspondence

By Mme de Staël

Correspondance générale. Edited by Béatrice Jasinski. 6 vols.– Paris: J.J. Pauvert; Hachette; Klincksieck, 1960ff.
"Correspondances suédoises de Germaine de Staël." Edited by Norman King. *Cahiers staëliens* 39 (1987–1988):11–137.
Lettres de Madame de Staël conservées en Bohème . . . Edited by Maria Ullrichová. Prague: Editions de l'Académie tchècque des sciences, 1959.
"Madame de Staël et ses correspondants russes." Edited by Piotr Zaborov. *Cahiers staëliens* 13 (1971): 44–54.
"Quelques lettres inédites de Madame de Staël." Edited by Kurt Kloocke. *Cahiers staëliens* 23 (1977): 57–75.
"Théâtre et société, la correspondance des Staël et des Odier." Edited by Jean-Daniel Candaux and Norman King. *Cahiers staëliens* 38 (1987): 1–111.

With Mme de Staël

[Balk, Count de]. "Un amour inconnu de Mme de Staël." Edited by Simone Balayé. *Cahiers staëliens* 2 (1964).
[Devonshire, duchesse de]. *Le plus beau de toutes les fêtes, Madame de Staël et Elisabeth Hervey, duchesse de Devonshire, d'après leur correspondance inédite, 1804–1817.* Edited by Victor de Pange. Paris: Klincksieck, 1980.
[Du Pont de Nemours, Samuel]. *De Staël–Du Pont Letters.* Edited and translated by James F. Marshall. Madison: University of Wisconsin Press, 1968.
[Hochet, Claude]. *Lettres à un ami [par] Benjamin Constant et Madame de Staël.* Edited by Jean Mistler. Neuchâtel: La Baconnière, 1949.
[Mackintosh, James]. "Lettres de Madame de Staël à Sir James Mackintosh." Edited by Norman King. *Cahiers staëliens* 10 (June 1970).
[Meister, Henri]. *Lettres inédites de Madame de Staël à Henri Meister.* Edited by Paul Usteri and Eugène Ritter. 2nd ed. Paris: Hachette, 1904.
[Napoléon Ier]. "Un projet de lettre de Madame de Staël à Napoléon, sept. 1810," 113–21. *Occident* and *Cahiers staëliens,* 1938.
[O'Donnell, Comte Maurice]. *Madame de Staël et Maurice O'Donnell.* Edited by Jean Mistler. Paris: Calmann-Lévy, 1926.
Récamier, Juliette. *Lettres à Madame Récamier.* Edited by Emmanuel Beau de Loménie. Paris: Domat, 1952.
[Rocca, John]. "Lettres de Madame de Staël à John Rocca." Edited by Edouard Chapuisat. In *Bibliothèque universelle et Revue de Genève,* 1929.
[Savoye-Rollin (famille)]. "Lettres de Madame de Staël aux 1929, Savoye-Rollin." Edited by Norman King. *Cahiers staëliens* 21 (1976): 39–50.

[Saxe-Weimar, Louise, duchesse de]. *Coppet et Weimar: Madame de Staël et la grande-duchesse Louise* . . . Edited by Amélie Lenormant. Paris: M. Lévy frères, 1862.

[Villiers, Charles de]. *Madame de Staël, Charles de Villiers, Benjamin Constant, Correspondance*. Edited by Kurt Kloocke et al. Frankfurt am Main: P. Lang, 1993.

[Wellington, duc de]. *Madame de Staël et le duc de Wellington, correspondance inédite, 1815–1817*. Edited by Victor de Pange. Paris: Gallimard, 1962.

CONTEMPORARY WORKS, MEMOIRS, AND CORRESPONDENCE

Arndt, Ernst Moritz. *Erinnerungen aus dem äusseren Leben*. Leipzig: Weidmann, 1840.

Barante, Prosper Brugière, Baron de. *Souvenirs*, vol. 1. Edited by Claude de Barante. Paris: Calmann-Lévy, 1890.

Bonaparte, Lucien. *Lucien Bonaparte et ses mémoires, 1775–1840*. Edited by Th. Iung. Paris: G. Charpentier, 1882–1883.

Brinkman, Carl Gustav, Baron. "Lettre sur l'auteur de *Corinne*." Edited by Simone Balayé. *Cahiers staëliens* 39 (1987–1988).

Chateaubriand, François René, vicomte de. *Correspondance générale*, vol. 1, 1789–1807. Edited by Béatrix d'Andlau, Pierre Christophorov, and Pierre Riberette. Paris: Gallimard, 1977.

———. *Mémoires d'outre-tombe*. 1st ed. 5 vols. Edited by Maurice Levaillant and Georges Moulinier. Paris: Gallimard, 1946–1951.

———. *Mémoires d'outre-tombe*. 2d ed. 2 vols. Edited by Jean-Claude Berchet. Paris: Bordas, 1989–1992.

Constant, Benjamin. *Ecrits et discours politiques de Benjamin Constant*. Edited by Olivier Pozzo di Borgo. Paris: J. J. Pauvert, 1964.

———. *Lettres à Madame Récamier, 1807–1830*. Edited by Ephraïm Harpaz. 1977. Reprint, Paris: H. Champion, 1992.

———. *Oeuvres*. Edited by Alfred Roulin. Paris: Gallimard, 1957.

———. *Portraits, mémoires, souvenirs*. Edited by Ephraïm Harpaz. Paris: H. Champion, 1992.

Custine, Astolphe, marquis de. *La Russie en 1839*. 2 vols. Preface by d'Hélène Carrère d'Encausse, postface by Julien Tarn, notes by Michel Parfenov. Paris: Solin, 1990.

Du Montet, Marie Prévost de la Boutetière de Saint-Mars, Baronne du Fisson. *Souvenirs*. Paris: Plon, 1914.

Joseph [Bonaparte], King of Spain. *Mémoires er correspondance politique et militaire*. Edited by A. Du Casse. Paris: Perrotin, 1853–1854.

Las Cases, Emmanuel, Comte de. *Mémorial de Sainte-Hélène*. Edited by Marcel Dunan. Paris: Flammarion, 1983.

Lévesque, Pierre Charles. *Histoire de la Russie, tirée des chroniques originales, de pièces historiques de la nation*. Yverdon, 1783.

Maistre, Joseph, Comte de. *Oeuvres complètes.* Nouvelle ed. Lyon: Vitte et Perrussel, 1886.

Masson, C. F. P. *Mémoires secrets sur la Russie pendant les règnes de Catherine II et Paul Ier.* Edited by F. Barrère. Paris: F. Didot, 1863.

————. *Memoirs of Catherine II and the Court of St. Petersburg During Her Reign and that of Paul I.* New York: Merrill and Boice, 1903.

Méneval, Claude-François, Baron de. *Mémoires pour servir à l'histoire de Napoléon Ier depuis 1802 jusqu'en 1815.* 5 vols. Paris: Dentu, 1893–1894.

————. *Memoirs of Napoleon Bonaparte, the Court of the First Empire.* 3 vols. Edited by Baron Napoléon Joseph de Méneval. New York: P. F. Collier, 1910.

Napoléon Ier. *Correspondance.* Edited by L. Lecestre. Paris, 1897.

Norvins, Jacques Marquet de Montbreton de. *Souvenirs d'un historien de Napoléon. Mémorial . . .* 3 vols. Edited by L. de Lanzac de Laborie. Paris: Plon, 1896–1897.

Potoka, Anna, Comtesse. *Mémoires 1794–1820.* Edited by Casimir Stryienski. Paris: Plon, 1897.

Pouchkine, Alexandre Sergueiévitch. *Oeuvres.* Paris: Gallimard, 1990.

Remâcle, Comte. *Relations secrètes des agents de Louis XVIII à Paris sous le Consulat, 1802–1805.* Paris: Plon, 1899.

Rémusat, Claire-Elisabeth-Jeanne Gravier de Vergennes, Comtesse de. *Mémoires de madame de Rémusat, 1802–1808.* 3 vols. Edited by Paul de Rémusat. Paris: Calmann-Lévy, 1879–1880.

Roederer, Pierre-Louis. *Oeuvres.* 8 vols. Edited by A. M. Roederer. Paris: 1853–1859.

Sismondi, Jean-Charles-Léonard Simonde de. *Epistolario:* Vol. 1, *1799–1814.* Edited by Carlo Pellegrini. Firenze: La Nuova Italia, 1933.

Talleyrand, Charles-Maurice de, prince de Bénévent. "Lettres de M. de Talleyrand à Madame de Staël." Edited by Albert, duc de Broglie. *Revue d'histoire diplomatique,* 1890.

WORKS ABOUT MADAME DE STAËL

Balayé, Simone. *Les Carnets de voyage de Madame de Staël, contribution à la genèse de ses oeuvres. Le Séjour en Angleterre, 1813–1814.* Preface by Comtesse Jean de Pange; essay by Norman King. Genève, Droz, 1971.

————. "*Delphine* de Madame de Staël et la presse sous le Consulat." *Romantisme* 51 (1986).

————. "Le génie et la gloire dans l'oeuvre de Madame de Staël." *Rivista di letterature moderne e comparate* (September/December 1967).

————. "Madame de Staël et le gouvernement impériale en 1810, le dossier de la suppression de *De l'Allemagne.*" *Cahiers staëliens* 19 (December 1974).

————, with Marie-Laure Chastang. *Madame de Staël et l'Europe.* Preface by Etienne Dennery. Paris: Bibliopthèque nationale, 1966.

————, and Norman King "Madame de Staël et les polices françaises sous la Révolution et l'Empire." *Cahiers staëliens* 44 (1992–1993).

Blennerhassett, Lady Charlotte Julia von Leyden. *Madame de Staël et son temps, 1766–1817.* . . . Translated by Auguste Dietrich. Paris: L. Westhausser, 1890.

Gautier, Paul. *Madame de Staël et Napoléon.* Paris: Plon–Nourrit et Cie, 1903.

————. *Mathieu de Montmorency et Madame de Staël.* Paris: Plon–Nourrit et Cie, 1908.

Gram Holström, Kirsten. *Monodrama, Attitudes, Tableaux Vivants . . . Studies on Some Trends of Theatrical Fashion, 1770–1815.* Stockholm: Almqvist och Wiksell, 1967.

Gutwirth, Madelyn. *Madame de Staël, Novelist: The Emergence of the Artist as Woman.* Urbana: University of Illinois Press, 1978.

Haussonville, Comte d'. *Madame de Staël et l'Allemagne.* Paris: Calmann–Lévy, 1928.

————. *Madame de Staël et M. Necker.* Paris: Calmann–Lévy, 1925.

Hawkins, R. L. *Madame de Staël and the United States.* Cambridge, Mass.: Harvard University Press, 1930.

Johnson-Cousin, Danielle. "La société dramatique de Madame de Staël de 1803 à 1816." *Studies on Voltaire and the Eighteenth Century,* vol. 296. Oxford: Voltaire Foundation at the Taylor Institution, 1992.

King, Norman. "Un récit inédit du grand voyage de Madame de Staël." *Cahiers staëliens* 4 (May 1966).

Kohler, Pierre. *Madame de Staël et la Suisse.* Lausanne–Paris: Payot, 1916.

Levaillant, Maurice. *Une amitié amoureuse, Madame de Staël et Madame Récamier.* Paris: Hachette, 1956.

Martin, Xavier. "Bonaparte méridional dans le propos staëlien." In *Le Groupe de Coppet et l'Europe: 5e Colloque de Coppet, Tübingen, juillet, 1993.* Lausanne: Institut Benjamin Constant; Paris: J. Touzot, 1994.

Ménard, Jean. "Madame de Staël et Roederer." *Revue de l'Université d'Ottawa* (April–June 1961).

Pange, Comtesse Jean de. *A.-G. Schlegel et Madame de Staël.* Paris: Albert, 1938.

Pellegrini, Carlo. *Madame de Staël e il Gruppo di Coppet.* Rev. ed. Bologna: Patròn, 1974.

Pingaud, Léonce. "Madame de Staël et le duc de Rovigo." *Revue de Paris* (December 1, 1903).

Rougemont, Martine de. "L'activité théâtrale dans le Groupe de Coppet: la dramaturgie et le jeu." *Le Groupe de Coppet, 2è Colloque de Coppet, 10–13 juillet, 1974.* Genève: Slatkine; Paris: H. Champion, 1977.

Solovieff, Georges. "Madame de Staël et la police autrichienne." *Cahiers staëliens* 41 (1989–1990).

Vianello Bonifacio, Mariella. "Contributo alla genesi delle *Dix années d'exil.*" *Saggi di linguistica e di letteratura,* 1991.

Welschinger, Henri. *La Censure sous le Premier Empire.* Paris: Charavay frères, 1882.

WORKS ABOUT THE PERIOD

Bertier de Sauvigny, Guillaume de. *Le Comte Ferdinand de Bertier et l'énigme de la Congrégation*. Paris: Les Presses continantales, 1948.

Bredin, Jean-Denis. *Sieyès*. Paris: Fallois, 1988.

Cabanis, André. *La Presse sous le Consulat et l'Empire, 1799–1814*. Paris: Société des études robespierristes.

Cate, Curtis. *1812: le duel des deux empereurs*. Translated by Claude Yelnik et Jean d'Hendecourt. Paris, Laffont, 1987. The original is *The War of the Two Emperors: The Duel between Napoleon and Alexander*. New York: Random House, 1985.

Dictionnaire Napoléon. Edited by Jean Tulard. Paris: Fayard, 1987.

Fischer, Ernest. *Histoire de la Suisse des origines à nos jours*. Paris: Payot, 1946.

Fugier, André. *Napoléon et l'Italie*. Paris: J.-B. Janin, 1947.

Gaubert, Henri. *Conspirateurs au temps de Napoléon Ier*. Paris: Flammarion, 1962.

Gershoy, Leo. *The French Revolution and Napoleon*. New York: Crofts, 1947.

Girod de l'Ain, Gabriel. *Bernadotte, chef de guerre et chef d'Etat*. Paris: Perrin, 1968.

Godechot, Jacques. *Les Commissaires aux armées sous le Directoire*. Paris, Presses universitaires de France, 1941.

———. *La Grande Nation, l'expansion révolutionnaire de la France dans le monde de 1789 à 1799*. 2d ed. Paris: Aubier-Montaigne, 1983.

———. *Les Institutions de la France sous la Révolution et l'Empire*. 4th ed. Paris: Presses universitaires de France, 1989.

Gopnik, Adam. "The Good Soldier." *New Yorker*, November 24, 1997, pp. 104–10.

Guillon, Edouard. *Napoléon et la Suisse, 1803–1815*. Paris: Plon; Lausanne: Payot, 1910.

Gutwirth, Madelyn. *The Twilight of the Goddesses: Women and Representation in the French Revolutionary Era*. New Brunswick: Ruters University Press, 1992.

Hauterive, Ernest d'. *Napoléon et sa police*. Paris: Flammarion, 1943.

Herriot, Edouard. *Madame Récamier et ses amis*, vol. 1. Paris: Hachette, 1904.

Histoire générale de la presse française: vol. 1, *Des origines à 1814*. Edited by Jacques Godechot. Paris: Presses universitaires de France, 1969.

Höjer, T. T. *Bernadotte, maréchal de France*. Translated by Lucien Maury. Paris: Plon, 1943.

Hofmann, Etienne. *Les Principes de politique de Benjamin Constant*. 2 vols. Genève: Droz, 1988.

Lefebvre, Georges. *Le Directoire*. Paris: A. Colin, 1958.

———. *The Directory*. Translated by Robert Baldick. New York: Vintage, 1967.

———. *La France sous le Directoire, 1795–1799*. Nouvelle ed. Preface by Albert Sorel, presentation of Jean-René Suratteau. Paris: Editions sociales, 1983.

———. *Napoléon*. 6th ed. Paris: Presses universitaires de France, 1969.

———. *Napoleon*. Translated by Robert Baldwin. London: Routledge & K. Paul, 1964–1965.

Ligne, Charles, prince de. "Lettres inédites du prince de Ligne à Madame de Staël." Edited by Simone Balayé. *Bulletin de l'Académie royale de langue et de littérature françaises de Belgique,* 1966.

———. *Lettres et pensées du prince de Ligne.* Edited by Madame de Staël. Paris, Genève: J. J. Paschoud, 1809.

Madelin, Louis. *Histoire du Consulat et de l'Empire.* 16 vols. Paris: Hachette, 1937–1954.

———. *The Consulate and the Empire.* 2 vols. Translated by Elsie Fennimore Bucklet. 1923–1938. Reprint, New York: AMS Press, 1967.

Marshall-Cornwall, James, Sir. *Napoléon as Military Commander.* Princeton, N.J.: Van Nostrand, 1967.

Périvier, André. *Napoléon journaliste.* Paris: 1918.

Rambaud, Patrick. *La Bataille.* Paris: B. Grasset, 1997.

Riegel, René. *Adalbert de Chamisso, sa vie et son oeuvre.* Paris: Editions internationales, 1934.

Rufer, A. *La Suisse et la Révolution française.* Paris: Société des études robespierrestes, 1974.

Savinel, Pierre. *Moreau, rival républicain de Bonaparte.* Rennes: Ouest-France, 1986.

Schom, Alan. *Napoléon Bonaparte.* New York: Harper-Collins, 1997.

Tuetey, Alexandre. "L'Emigration et le séquestre des biens de Necker." *La Révolution française* 69 (1916).

Tulard, Jean. *Napoléon et la noblesse d'Empire.* Nouvelle ed. Paris: Tallandier, 1986.

———. *Napoléon, ou le Mythe du sauveur.* Paris: Fayard, 1977.

——— and Louis Garros. *Itinéraire de Napoléon au jour le jour, 1769–1821.* 2d ed. Paris: Tallandier, 1992.

Vandal, Albert. *L'Avènement de Bonaparte.* 2 vols. Paris: Plon, 1903.

———. *Napoléon et Alexandre Ier, l'alliance russe sous le Premier Empire.* 3 vols. Paris: Plon, 1894–1897.

Wagener, Françoise. *Madame Récamier.* Paris: J. C. Lattès, 1986.

Welschinger, Henri. *Le duc d'Enghien.* Paris: Plon-Nourrit, 1913.

Index